FROMMER'S EasyGuide to
DISNEY WORLD, UNIVERSAL & ORLANDO

8th Edition

By Jason Cochran

P9-CDI-029

FROMMER'S STAR RATINGS SYSTEM

Every hotel, restaurant, and attraction listed in this guide has been ranked for quality and value. Here's what the stars mean:

★ Recommended
★★ Highly Recommended
★★★ A must! Don't miss!

AN IMPORTANT NOTE

The world is a dynamic place. Hotels change ownership, restaurants hike their prices, museums alter their opening hours, and buses and trains change their routings. And all of this can occur in the several months after our authors have visited, inspected, and written about these hotels, restaurants, museums, and transportation services. Though we have made valiant efforts to keep all our information fresh and up-to-date, some few changes can inevitably occur in the periods before a revised edition of this guidebook is published. So please bear with us if a tiny number of the details in this book have changed. Please also note that we have no responsibility or liability for any inaccuracy or errors or omissions, or for inconvenience, loss, damage, or expenses suffered by anyone as a result of assertions in this guide.

A rainbow of rollicking waterslides at Aquatica water park (see p. 171).

Previous page: Downtown Orlando's skyline sparkles across Lake Eola.

CONTENTS

R0461419745

Universal's CityWalk.

A LOOK AT ORLANDO

Welcome to Orlando! If you've journeyed to this sunny section of Central Florida, there's a good chance you have two things in mind: visiting the "Happiest Place on Earth," Walt Disney World, and exploring the Wizarding World of Harry Potter at Universal Orlando. But there's so much more to experience in both the theme parks and Orlando beyond just the big-ticket attractions. From sparkling natural springs that beg you to unplug and jump in, to sophisticated dining and wine, to hidden spots inside the parks, not to mention other stellar attractions such as Kennedy Space Center, Orlando is filled with surprises if you know where to look.

The best way to beat the heat in Orlando is at a water park, such as Disney's winter-themed Blizzard Beach (p. 117).

Parades and character greetings let young fans meet beloved characters like *Frozen's* Anna and Elsa.

Head to Fantasyland early to ride the popular Seven Dwarfs Mine Train coaster (p. 56).

Walt Disney World's 50th anniversary festivities celebrate the 1971 opening of Orlando's Magic Kingdom, with its centerpiece Cinderella Castle.

Epcot's centerpiece is the iconic sphere of Spaceship Earth (p. 72), anchoring Future World.

The beautiful Temple of Heaven is the remarkable entry to China (p. 82) in Epcot's World Showcase.

In Epcot's American Adventure show (p. 81), your Audio-Animatronic hosts, Ben Franklin and Mark Twain, take a spin through U.S. history.

At Disney's Hollywood Studios, the Twilight Zone Tower of Terror (p. 99) delivers plenty of thrills and screams.

The Crush 'n' Gusher water coaster is one of the signature flumes at Disney's Typhoon Lagoon (p. 119).

Plan ahead to make sure you don't miss any of the fun in the insanely popular Stars Wars: Galaxy's Edge (p. 94) at Disney's Hollywood Studios.

Seeing free-roaming African animals from your own open safari vehicle is a highlight of Animal Kingdom's Kilimanjaro Safaris (p. 110).

The floating mountains in the Valley of Mo'ara at Pandora–The World of Avatar (p. 109).

Live shows are don't-miss highlights of an Animal Kingdom visit. The longest-running one is the elaborately costumed Festival of the Lion King (p. 111).

Universal Studios offers lots of meet-and-greet opportunities with characters like Branch and Poppy from Dreamworks' Trolls (p. 138).

Universal's Superstar Parade features wildly creative floats, state-of-the-art technology, and hundreds of performers and characters, including SpongeBob SquarePants.

Kids of all ages (especially teens) love the tongue-in-cheek fun of the Simpson's Springfield (p. 138).

Universal boasts not one but two incredible Wizarding Worlds of Harry Potter. In Diagon Alley, at Universal Studios, fans love the immersive ride Harry Potter and the Escape from Gringotts (p. 136).

Over at Islands of Adventure, Harry Potter fun continues at Hogsmeade with the high-tech coaster Hagrid's Magical Creatures Motorbike Adventure (p. 152).

No matter which Wizarding World you're in, you can always get a quaff of the park's signature concoction, Butterbeer. Get yours with foam! See p. 151.

In Islands of Adventure's Toon Lagoon, Dudley Do-Right's Ripsaw Falls (p. 147) is terrific goofy fun for all ages.

Coaster nerds love the unbridled mayhem of the Incredible Hulk Coaster (p. 144), in Islands of Adventure's Marvel Super Hero Island.

Enter the Spider-Verse with the Amazing Adventures of Spider-Man (p. 146), which combines motion simulators, 3D computer-generated animation, and high-tech stagecraft for a don't-miss experience.

Universal's Volcano Bay (p. 157) is a one-of-a-kind, fully immersive water theme park experience.

One of Orlando's most popular events is Universal's monthlong Halloween Horror Nights (p. 292), featuring special guest stars like the irrepressible Beetlejuice.

Islands of Adventure's Seuss Landing (p. 153) captures the whimsical spirit of Dr. Seuss's books, with imaginative rides that younger kids love.

MORE ORLANDO ATTRACTIONS

Take time to wonder at the giant sea turtles gliding around SeaWorld's TurtleTrek aquarium (p. 166).

It's almost impossible to stay dry on SeaWorld's Infinity Falls flume ride (p. 167).

The Dolphin Adventures show at SeaWorld (p. 165) is an enduring favorite—snag a front row seat if you don't mind getting splashed.

If you can dream it, Legoland (p. 173) can make it out of its signature plastic bricks—be prepared for lots of inspired building from your kids after a visit here.

Legoland's Driving School (p. 173) gives aspiring young motorists a chance to learn the rules of the road.

Head east to Cape Canaveral and the Kennedy Space Center (p. 174) to view massive, real-life rockets such as the Saturn 1-B launcher in the "rocket garden." You can also see the space shuttle *Atlantis* in an indoor hangar, tour NASA's compound, and even meet an astronaut.

There's plenty of colorful hands-on fun at the Crayola Experience (p. 179).

Generations of visitors have walked through the "jaws" at the entrance to Gatorland (p. 189), one of Florida's oldest and most beloved tourist attractions.

Orlando is a major golfing destination. Try one of the area's lush golf courses, such as the one at the Ritz-Carlton Grande Lakes (p. 268).

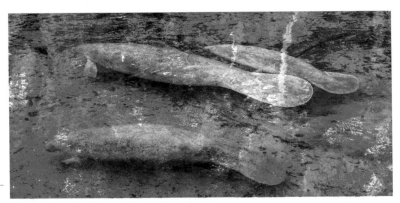

Nature is all around Orlando if you know where to look. Get a glimpse of endangered manatees at Blue Spring State Park (p. 263) where these gentle giants swim in the crystal waters.

Florida's history goes back hundreds of years, and you can learn about it at the Orange County Regional History Center (p. 184).

When you're ready for a change of scene, Port Canaveral offers easy-to-reach cruise ships to keep your vacation going at sea (p. 192).

THE BEST OF ORLANDO

n 1886, a young unmarried mailman, frustrated with his fruitless toil in the Midwest, moved to the woolly wilderness of Central Florida to make a better go of life. The land was angry. Summers were oppressively hot, the lightning relentless, and the tough earth, sodden and scrubby, defied clearing. The only domestic creatures that thrived there, it seemed, were the cattle, and even they turned out stringy and chewy. Undaunted, the young man planted a grove of citrus trees and waited for things to get better. They didn't. His trees died in a freeze. Now penniless, he was forced to return to delivering mail, the very thing he had tried so hard to escape. By 1890, he gave up, defeated, and moved to Chicago to seek other work. The American dream appeared to fail Elias Disney.

The story could have ended there. But he was joined by his new bride, whose own father had died trying to tame Florida land. Back in the smoke of the Midwest, they had children and settled for an anonymous urban existence. One day, 8 decades later, long after the young man and woman had lived full lives and passed away, two of their sons, now in the sunset of their own lives, would return to Central Florida, to the land that broke their father, and together they would transform the recalcitrant swamp into the most famous fantasy land the world has ever known. In 2017, it became the first American destination to surpass 70 million annual visitors.

Little did Elias know that the dream was only skipping a generation and that his sons Walt and Roy would become synonymous with the same land that rejected him. Had he known that the Disney name would in due time define Central Florida, would he have been so despondent? Even if he had been granted a fleeting vision of what was to be, and what his family would mean to this place—and, indeed, to the United States—would he have believed it?

The Disney brothers turned a place of toil into a realm of pleasure, a place where hardworking people can put their struggles aside. The English have Blackpool; Canadians have Niagara Falls. Orlando rose to become the preeminent resort for the working and middle classes of America, and the ingenuity of its inventions inspires visitors from all over the world. Orlando has had its share of tragedy, yet its tale is one of optimism.

Orlando represents something more powerful to American culture and history than success. It's something shared. No matter who you are, no matter your politics or upbringing, when you were a kid, you probably went at least once to Walt Disney World and Orlando—or, if you didn't, you desperately wanted to. Which other aspect of culture can we all claim to share? What else has given children such sweet dreams? I've often said that if somehow Walt Disney World went out of business tomorrow, the U.S. National Park Service would have to take it over—it means that much to the fabric of the nation.

Orlando tells us about who we dream of being. Virtually nothing about it is natural or authentic, and yet there may be no more perfect embodiment of American culture. To understand this invented landscape is to understand the values of its civilization. And if you observe Orlando with a long view—starting with young Elias Disney cutting his hands trying to budge a tough Florida pine—you will be a part of the explosive, unexpected powers of the American dream.

Pandemic closures reinforced how much the Orlando parks mean to society; they also changed business forever. Without exception, the big theme park companies seized the moment to reinvent how they operate. This is a period of dramatic change in Orlando, as the theme parks strive to conceive new systems that can balance manageable crowds with higher profits. Visiting the parks is no longer the casual, spontaneous lark it used to be—a modern trip to Orlando requires discipline and detailed planning from the moment you decide to go. Post-Covid changes will affect how you face that challenge as you jockey for your moments of magic. This book will help you.

ORLANDO'S best THEME PARK EXPERIENCES

- **Walt Disney World:** Walt Disney World, which marked 50 years of fun in October 2021, operates four top-drawer theme parks every day of the year. **Magic Kingdom,** the most popular theme park on Earth, is a more spacious iteration of the original Disneyland in Anaheim, California, and is brimming with cherished attractions; **Epcot,** which began as a new-brew version of an old-style world's fair (it's now much more amorphous), has two of the newest big-ticket rides; **Disney's Animal Kingdom** blends animal habitats with theme park panache and offers a gorgeous *Avatar*-themed land, Pandora, with two rides; **Disney's Hollywood Studios,** which in recent years opened the whimsical indoor ride Mickey & Minnie's Runaway Railway and the blockbuster Star Wars: Galaxy's Edge, is back on the boil as the second-hottest Disney World park after the Magic Kingdom.
- **Universal Orlando:** When kids outgrow Disney's princess scene but still demand adrenaline and high quality, Universal Orlando takes over. Its two full theme parks, **Universal Studios Florida** and **Islands of Adventure,**

plus its newish **Volcano Bay** water park, command respect, get the blood pumping, and feature two immersive sections devoted to The Wizarding World of Harry Potter. Universal seems to go from strength to strength these days: In 2019, the Potter-themed Hagrid's Magical Creatures Motorbike Adventure ride hit a home run with guests at Islands of Adventure, and in 2021, the rip-roarin' Jurassic World VelociCoaster blew away coaster fans around the world.

o **Beyond Disney and Universal:** Venture beyond the Big Six theme parks in those two resorts and you'll find more breathing room and more focused experiences. The gardens and marine mammals at **SeaWorld Orlando** can make for a slower-paced excursion. It recently opened a high-velocity but compact coaster, Ice Breaker, and a superb kids' area based on *Sesame Street.* Five water parks (including state-of-the-art **Volcano Bay**) flow with energy: **Typhoon Lagoon** and **Aquatica** for family-friendly slides, **Blizzard Beach** for more aggressive ones, and **Discovery Cove** for VIP swims with dolphins and reef fish. South of town, **Legoland Florida,** one of the best parks for small children, charms with Old Florida touches and a new Peppa Pig park, while **Gatorland** celebrates the region's *original* locals. **Kennedy Space Center,** east of town, is still a glowing testament to what the United States is capable of when it focuses on a goal—in purely historic terms, it's the most important complex to visit.

ORLANDO'S best RIDES & SHOWS

o **Walt Disney World:** More than any other park, the **Magic Kingdom** (p. 38) is packed with seminal experiences: the transporting Audio-Animatronic wizardry of **Pirates of the Caribbean** and **The Haunted Mansion;** the vertiginous thrills of **Expedition Everest** and **Space Mountain;** and the homespun, only-at-Disney charm of **Jungle Cruise, Peter Pan's Flight,** and **"it's a small world."** Cap the day with the famous fireworks show. At **Epcot** (p. 68), the addition of **Remy's Ratatouille Adventure,** a merry indoor ride that shrinks you down to the size of a rat, is just the first of many ongoing changes at the park (expect construction walls), along with updated films for the **Canada** and **China** areas and a fresh *Guardians of the Galaxy* coaster. At **Disney's Hollywood Studios** (p. 90), a visit to **Star**

Wars: Galaxy's Edge is like stepping into a movie set (a very crowded movie set that you have to enter a ticket lottery to see). One of Disney's newest marquee rides, the thrilling cutting-edge aerial simulator **Avatar Flight of Passage** at **Animal Kingdom,** still commands long waits.

o **Universal Orlando:** At **Islands of Adventure** (p. 143), **Hagrid's Magical Creatures Motorbike Adventure** fires on more technological cylinders than you thought a roller coaster could possess; **The Wizarding World of Harry Potter—Hogsmeade** is still a roaring success; **The Amazing Adventures of Spider-Man** remains the standard bearer for premium family-friendly ride concepts; and a heart-pounding new *Jurassic World*–themed **VelociCoaster** exceeds expectations. Also, don't miss **Dudley Do-Right's Ripsaw Falls** or **Popeye & Bluto's Bilge-Rat Barges,** an impish pair of flumes. Next door at **Universal Studios,** a separate park, **The Wizarding World of Harry Potter—Diagon Alley** (p. 129) represents the cutting edge in visual design with hours of details to explore, and the new **The Bourne Stuntacular** sets a new high-tech bar for a theme park stunt show.

o **The Other Parks:** At **SeaWorld Orlando** (p. 159), roller coasters pack punches that Disney pulls: **Ice Breaker** is the newest arrival; **Mako** is Orlando's tallest, fastest, longest coaster and a true delight; **Manta** flies riders belly-down over water and rooftops; **Kraken** dangles their feet for seven spine-knotting inversions; and a new **up-and-down launch coaster** is coming to the lagoon. Last year, it opened **Infinity Falls,** a water ride with a vertical lift and a 40-foot drop. Two area landmarks, the 450-foot-tall **StarFlyer** swing ride (p. 182) and the proud **Wheel at ICON Park** (p. 183), have been joined by two more skyscraping rides (see Chapter 5). Elsewhere, **Legoland Florida** recently opened its largest project, **Lego Movie World,** and now has three delightful themed hotels and a Peppa Pig–themed mini-park tailored to little guests. Legoland's collection of kiddie attractions is now second to none—even better stocked than Disney.

ORLANDO'S best OVERLOOKED EXPERIENCES

o **From Earth to the Moon:** The **Kennedy Space Center** (p. 174) sent Americans into space for more than half a century, and for decades NASA's nerve center was the focus of Central Florida's tourist attention. A majority of today's visitors remain securely within Disney's orbit—and that's a disgrace. At the Kennedy Space Center, you can see proof of America's glory days as an exploratory power, including some out-of-this-world space vehicles such as the **Saturn V rocket,** the largest rocket made, which sent 27 men to the moon; the **space shuttle orbiter** *Atlantis,* still coated with space dust; and the only public remnants of the two space shuttles America lost.

o **Making Dreams Come True:** More Make-a-Wish kids request visits to Orlando than any other dream, and you can help make those wishes come true at the resort built just for them, **Give Kids the World Village** (p. 190) ❦. There are hundreds of jobs for volunteers (many of which can be done in just a few hours), including handing out gifts or scooping ice cream.

o **Connecting with Spirits:** Since the late 1800s, moss-draped **Cassadaga** (p. 186) has been the domain of psychics and mediums who invite visitors to explore their spiritualist town. Some call it spiritual and some call it spooky, but there's no place quite like it in the world.

o **Undiscovered Disney:** Even inside the theme parks, as other guests stampede for the nearest thrill ride, you can find relatively off-the-beaten-path treasures. The most fruitful ground is **Epcot's World Showcase,** where many pavilions contain little-seen museums to the heritage of their lands, including the Stave Church Gallery in Norway (p. 83), China's House of the Whispering Willow (p. 82), the Bijutsu-kan Gallery in Japan (p. 80), and the Moroccan Style gallery of arts in Morocco (p. 80). At Magic Kingdom, you can get a haircut at Main Street's **Harmony Barber Shop** (p. 45). And the entire Disney World resort offers a slate of small-group **behind-the-scenes tours** (p. 122) that uncover hundreds of secrets.

ORLANDO'S best AUTHENTIC EXPERIENCES

o **Florida, Your Eden:** Although theme parks now define Orlando, Central Florida has a long tale of its own, if you're willing to listen. There are more fresh springs here than in any other American state. You'll always remember swimming in the 72°F (22°C) waters of **De Leon Springs State Park** (p. 264), canoeing at **Wekiwa Springs State Park** (p. 265), or meeting at-risk manatees in their natural habitat at **Blue Spring State Park** (p. 263).

o **Florida, the Gilded Age Idyll:** Of course, Orlando's identity as a sunny theme park mecca only began in 1971, but visitors from the north have been coming for a century. Sample the fine art collected by high-society settlers at Winter Park's **Charles Hosmer Morse Museum of American Art** (including a massive collection of Tiffany glass; p. 187) or the **Rollins Museum of Art** (with lush decorative arts of every description; p. 187). Peep at their historic mansions, whose lawns slope invitingly to the tranquil lakes of Winter Park, on the long-running **Scenic Boat Tour** (p. 267).

o **Florida, Land of Flowers:** The reason all those blue bloods migrated here? The fine weather and beautiful water. The horticultural achievements at **Harry P. Leu Gardens** (p. 264), practically smack in the middle of downtown Orlando, remind you just how bountiful the soil here can be. Or lose yourself at **Bok Tower Gardens** (p. 187), whose builder set out to create a Taj Mahal for America; its landscaping is by Frederick Law Olmsted, Jr., whose other work includes the White House grounds and the National Mall.

o **Florida, the Original Tourist Draw: Legoland Florida** (p. 173) ambles pleasantly on a lakeside that was once home to Cypress Gardens, Florida's original mega-park and a haunt for everyone from Esther Williams to Elvis Presley. Its historic botanical garden has been prized since the 1930s. **Gatorland** (p. 189) is a pleasing, corn-fed throwback from an era when Central Florida was synonymous with reptiles, not cheerful mice.

ORLANDO'S best HOTELS

o **Inside Disney: Disney's Contemporary Resort** (p. 236) and **Disney's Polynesian Village Resort** (p. 237), which opened in 1971 and recently received some renovation love, are architectural landmarks and their location on the monorail system makes a vacation easy and fun. **Disney's Art of Animation Resort** (p. 241) represents the newest and best of that resort's lowest-priced rooms. On the other end of the indulgence spectrum, **Four Seasons Resort Orlando,** on Walt Disney World property, unfailingly indulges with a level of luxury that stands tall above the rest of this tourist-mill town (p. 243).

o **At Universal:** Universal's **Sapphire Falls Resort** (p. 255) applies a layer of Caribbean style to the mid-priced category; its newest additions, the two hotels at Universal's **Endless Summer Resort** (p. 256), are now the Orlando theme parks' king and queen of budget lodging.

o **Full-Service Resorts Outside the Parks:** A terrific location close to Disney and a contemporary style all its own make the newly built **JW Marriott Orlando Bonnet Creek Resort & Spa** (p. 243) a new name to beat among Orlando's luxury resorts, while the **Hyatt Regency Grand Cypress** (p. 246) offers a full slate of activities and an epic pool complex. Taking theme park flair to a hospitality extreme, the colossal atrium of **Gaylord Palms** (p. 248) is a self-contained universe of diversions.

o **Affordability Without Sacrifice:** Not all affordable hotels are shabby. Brand new builds include **Aloft Orlando Lake Buena Vista** (p. 247), **Element Orlando Universal Blvd.** (p. 247) in the shadow of the ICON wheel, and **Fairfield Inn & Suites Orlando at Flamingo Crossings Town Center** (p. 251), the newest (and longest) name among the quickly growing cluster of affordable hotels just out Disney's western gate. Or **rent a full house,** as tastefully furnished as if you lived there—Orlando's crop of management companies (p. 261) make the process easier and more reliable than renting an Airbnb.

ORLANDO'S best RESTAURANTS

o **The Most Memorable Meals at the Resorts:** Orlando is one of those places where even blasé restaurants are priced like splurges, but some special-occasion tables deliver on their promise, such as **California Grill** overlooking Magic Kingdom at the Contemporary (p. 195) and **Topolino's Terrace** overlooking Epcot at the Riviera (p. 199); **Morimoto Asia, Jaleo,** or **Chef Art Smith's Homecomin'** at **Disney Springs** (p. 201); **Boma,** an all-you-can-eat feast at Animal Kingdom Lodge where you can watch African animals roam (p. 195); Disney's perennial award-sweeper **Victoria & Albert's** (p. 199) at the Grand Floridian; and the famous **character meals,** where your fuzzy hosts serve up family memories (p. 222).

o **Finding Family-Run Places to Eat:** Some fab restaurants, many family-run, have been unfairly elbowed into the background by same-old chains. These include **Bruno's Italian Restaurant** in the franchise zone of Disney (p. 208); the return of local favorite **Memories of India** (p. 210); **Nile Ethiopian Restaurant,** authentically African, down to the coffee ceremony, near Disney (p. 215); and the cheerful and affordable **Q'Kenan,** whose overstuffed arepas are popular with homesick Venezuelan families (p. 212).

o **Big Style, Local Flavors:** Get in touch with the locals: **Maxine's on Shine** (p. 216) is seductive fun, and the nightly arts celebration at **Café Tu Tu Tango** (p. 213) has firmly established the restaurant as a tentpole of the International Drive community. Above all, the sensationally priced district of **Mills 50** (p. 217) is a revelation for authentic Asian food of every stripe. Yes, as it turns out, there are still dining secrets in O-town.

SUGGESTED ITINERARIES & ORLANDO'S LAYOUT

I f there's one thing Orlando excels at, it's hospitality. Performance and entertainment are the city's lifeblood. The road to post-pandemic vitality and stability will be rocky, but the city is doing everything it can to put on a game face and welcome visitors while it sorts out its troubles (see box on p. 12).

Orlando's economic formula is shifting, but its entertainment formula remains the same: immerse, dazzle, thrill, delight. O-Town is nothing without you, its audience—in fact, just by coming, you play an essential role in its health.

The routes suggested here, loose enough to let the magic in, prioritize what's worth seeing and when. Observe the basic park patterns and you'll do just fine. These itineraries assume mild lines (so, not peak season), and if you would like to try a specific table-service restaurant, it's imperative you arrive with reservations, particularly for Cinderella's Royal Table (p. 222).

ORLANDO IN 1 DAY

Well, I'm sorry for you. Just as it's impossible to eat an entire box of Velveeta in one sitting (please don't try), you can't get the full breadth of Orlando in a single day.

Today: Make It a Magic Kingdom Day ★★★

One Orlando attraction is quintessential: Walt Disney World's **Magic Kingdom** (p. 38). In chapter 3, I recommend three custom itineraries (p. 42) for how to parse your time—with or without kids—but no matter your age or inclination, don't miss the great Disney Audio-Animatronic odysseys **Pirates of the Caribbean** ★★★, **Haunted Mansion** ★★★, and **"it's a small world"** ★★★, and be sure to brave the drops of **Space Mountain** ★★★, **Seven Dwarfs Mine Train** ★★★, and

THE SIX BIGGEST DISNEY mistakes

1. **Underplanning.** You must plan somewhat or pay a price: To eat at the best sit-down restaurants or to enjoy a character meal, you must reserve at least 2 months out. To eat and ride all the rides during the day at the parks, it helps immensely to set up your Disney World app ahead of time.

2. **Overplanning.** Disney World minutiae opens a rabbit hole deeper than Alice's.

3. **Overpurchasing ticket options.** Don't bite off more than you can chew.

4. **Wearing inadequate footwear.** It's not uncommon to walk 10 miles a day.

5. **Neglecting sunscreen and water.** Even Florida's cloudy weather can burn. One bad day can ruin the ones that follow.

6. **Pushing kids too hard.** When they want to slow down, indulge them. Disney corrals you into maintaining your hard-won schedule, but you came here to enjoy yourselves, remember?

(opening in 2022) the **Tron Lightcyle Power Run** ★★★. While you're there, take a free spin on the **monorail** through the iconic **Contemporary Resort** after you connect for the free round-trip ride to **Epcot** (p. 68), where you'll at least see the other top Disney park from above. Stay until closing, through the **fireworks,** or, if you've had enough, head to a kitschy dinner banquet spectacle such as the **Hoop-Dee-Doo Musical Revue** ★★ (p. 220). Hope you're not hungry for subtlety!

ORLANDO IN 2 DAYS

Nope, you still can't do much, but in two sleeps you can still get a few flavors in.

Day 1: Magic Kingdom

Get the same early start as recommended in "Orlando in 1 Day" above and follow the **Magic Kingdom** plan for sure.

Day 2: Universal Orlando ★★★ or Epcot ★★★

Today, arrive when the gates open at **Universal Orlando** (p. 125), one of the most attractive theme park complexes in the country. Coaster fans should hasten to the superlative **VelociCoaster** in Islands of Adventure (p. 149). From there, head to the Hogsmeade section of **Wizarding World of Harry Potter** ★★★. Explore the shops, full of bespoke souvenirs and snacks you can only buy here, and give your system a dose of Butterbeer, but above all, don't miss the splendid **Hagrid's Magical Creatures Motorbike Adventure** ★★★. After lunch at the **Leaky Cauldron** ★★★, you have a decision to make: either take the **Hogwarts Express** train to **Universal Studios** (you'll need a park-to-park ticket) to visit the second Potter land of **Diagon Alley** and the indoor speed of the **Mummy coaster,** or stay in Islands of Adventure to take a spin on the

Planning your steps in a theme park is hardly magical, so for more recommendations on making the most of your time at WDW, see our handy charts on p. 42, 70, 92, and 108.

now-iconic **Amazing Adventures of Spider-Man** ★★★, and jolt yourself on the newly rejuvenated **The Incredible Hulk Coaster** ★★★.

Or, instead of all that, you could spend a full day at **Epcot** (p. 68). Be sure to visit **Future World,** including *Guardians of the Galaxy*: **Cosmic Rewind** ★★★, **Soarin'** ★★★, and the traditional Disney experience, **Spaceship Earth** ★★★. Then make your way around **World Showcase** by dinnertime to select the ethnic eatery that catches your fancy, be it in **Mexico** ★★★, **Japan** ★★★, or **Morocco** ★★★, or queue up for the mild newcomer ride **Remy's Ratatouille Adventure** ★★★. At 9pm, you'll be in the right place for the evening's spectacular show over the lagoon. With a Park Hopper pass, you could also leave Epcot later in the afternoon to check out the new **Pandora—The World of Avatar** ★★★ area at Disney's Animal Kingdom, seeing it both in the light and after dark (if opening hours permit), when its glowing features are in full effect.

If you *really* want to see a lot and have cash and energy to burn, do Harry Potter in the morning and then schlep back down I-4 to visit Epcot or Pandora in the late afternoon and evening—but eat your Wheaties!

ORLANDO IN 3 DAYS

Days 1–2: Magic Kingdom & Universal Orlando

Day 1: Magic Kingdom, as above. But on **Day 2,** slam through the highlights of the Universal parks with a 1-day, 2-park pass. In the morning, see **Islands of Adventure** ★★★, including **VelociCoaster** ★★★ and **Hagrid's Magical Creatures Motorbike Adventure** ★★★, as in Orlando in 2 Days above, then fill the afternoon with Universal Studios. Don't neglect some of its popular rides—**Transformers: The Ride—3D** ★★ and **Harry Potter and the Escape from Gringotts** ★★★ in **Wizarding World of Harry Potter—Diagon Alley.** Exploring that area will more than complete your day, but if you still have time, fill up on the sarcastically named dishes at **Fast Food Boulevard** (p. 142) in the daringly whimsical **Springfield** addition.

Day 3: SeaWorld ★★★, Disney & a Taste of "Real" Orlando

If you have small kids or you need something more subdued today, then **SeaWorld Orlando** (p. 159), with its many marine animal habitats, isn't as exhausting as most theme parks. SeaWorld could take a whole day if you saw every little thing and stopped to smell the flowers (and fish), but you can see the highlights in 4 hours, and you only have 3 days, after all. So cram a secondary Disney park into your afternoon and evening. **Epcot** is a fine choice (see Day 2 of Orlando in 2 Days above); **Disney's Animal Kingdom's** ★★ wildlife walking trails also make a nice, easygoing complement to a morning spent at SeaWorld, and it's open later than SeaWorld, too. If you exhaust Animal Kingdom and don't want to see Pandora aglow, spend the night at the shopping-and-dining zone of **Disney Springs** ★★ (p. 199), which has the best food at Disney, or go out into "real" Orlando for the Vietnamese culinary delights of **Mills 50** (p. 217) downtown.

ORLANDO IN 1 WEEK
Days 1–5: Orlando at Your Leisure

A full week is really the minimum amount of time you need to enable you to actually relax and take time to sit by the pool. You don't have to cram several parks into a single day unless you want to; this combination lets you do the seven major parks in 5 days. Take more time on your first few days: first **Magic Kingdom,** then one **Universal** park, then **Epcot.** For Day 4, combine the biggest rides of **Animal Kingdom** and **Hollywood Studios** ★★★ into a single day—it's doable, but you'll have to skip the shows. On Day 5, head for **SeaWorld** (p. 159) or **Kennedy**

DISNEY PLANNING timeline

Six months/180 days ahead of arrival:
- If desired, book **Cinderella's Royal Table** (p. 222), **Victoria & Albert's** (p. 199), and any other special meal reservations.

Two months/60 days ahead:
- Book **Bibbidi Bobbidi Boutique** (p. 46), **Be Our Guest** (p. 68), **Hoop-Dee-Doo Musical Revue** (p. 220), **Oga's Cantina** (p. 96), and every other sit-down dining reservations you desire. Bookings open 60 days ahead of your visit; if you have a Disney hotel reservation, you can book ahead 60 days plus the number of days in your stay (up to 10), giving you a head start on others.

One week ahead:
- If desired, purchase **Memory Maker,** p. 38 (it sometimes costs less if purchased at least 3 days ahead of arrival).

Twenty-four hours ahead:
- Cancel unwanted restaurant reservations by now or pay the $10–$25 penalty.
- If a restaurant you wanted was previously full, check for availability again now.

Early morning, day of visit:
- Enter the Virtual Queue for **Star Wars: Rise of the Resistance** and any other busy rides that Disney has decided to allocate by lottery.
- Decide whether to buy Genie+ (p. 30).

ORLANDO'S reckoning

Orlando is facing a perilous crossroads. In May 2020, before the paralyzing effects of the Covid-19 pandemic set in, the Bureau of Labor Statistics placed Orlando dead last—50th out of 50 major U.S. cities—in median hourly wages. The city claimed some 133,000 workers in food preparation jobs alone, but their average annual salary was just $23,000, drastically lower than could sustain a mortgage, college, or savings. Orlando ranked behind cities that are more commonly thought of as economically distressed, like Detroit and Baltimore. In fact, it wasn't unusual for a full-time theme park worker to live in his or her car.

That was the gloomy economic reality even *before* the pandemic hit. Although billions of tax dollars had been shoveled into Orlando's infrastructure, the two theme park giants that benefited most from that investment returned it to the community in the form of hundreds of thousands of low-wage jobs—and when the disease shut down the world, those employers had to gut their budgets to survive. Just as the bottom end of the employment market collapsed, Florida received an influx of new arrivals from other parts of the United States.

In a poignant symbol of the shift in fortunes, some older hotels that were constructed in the early days of Walt Disney World to house vacationing families are now being converted to low-income emergency housing. These accommodations still serve the theme parks—they'll just shelter underpaid workers instead.

Orlando's employment practices have come home to roost. Now, it must redefine how it works. Some service employees who were sloughed off the instant the pandemic began were unwilling to return to jobs that failed to provide for them. Others are still returning to the force, but relations have been damaged. Wages that were adequate 20 years ago have been outstripped by the price of living in a growing metropolitan area. And resorts that were used to raking in cash from guaranteed floods of tourists and convention-goers are struggling to recover what they lost during the slowdown, while also trying to figure out what the new normal is going to be. In May 2021, Universal announced a raise of its starting hourly wage from $13 to $15. It still won't be enough. Businesses and workers alike are living on the edge.

Space Center (p. 174)—or, if you want to set your belly on a waterslide, **Volcano Bay,** p. 157, is now the hottest water park in Orlando.

Days 6–7: Exploring Orlando Beyond the Theme Parks

Hitting the Big 7 in 5 days leaves 2 days to get away from the dizzying pressures of theme parking. Take a day to drive out to **Kennedy Space Center** ★★★ (p. 174), or take a dip in a natural spring, such as **De Leon Springs** ★★★ (p. 264), and make a pass through the American original town of **Cassadaga** ★★★ (p. 186). It would be a shame to miss a collection as world class as the **Morse Museum**'s ★★★ (p. 187) astonishing Tiffany glass. While you're there, take a late-afternoon boat cruise past the mansions of **Winter Park** (p. 267)—when you're out on the water, you'll finally get a feeling for the "real" Florida that attracted the

If you see lightning, all outdoor and water rides will close until it has been at least 30 minutes since a strike was detected within about 10 miles. In summer, rain often comes around 2pm, so you'd be wise to ride outdoor things until the rain starts, then use the downtime to eat lunch. At Disney, Hollywood Studios is the best rainy-day park because most of its activities, including seven of its biggest thrill rides, are indoors. Universal Studios is also good when wet, but Islands of Adventure, Animal Kingdom, and SeaWorld are miserable in the rain. When there is a big storm, don't quit! Back home, rain may last all day, but in Florida, it usually clears within an hour—so if you can wait it out, you'll enjoy lighter crowds once it passes.

builders of the major resorts in the first place. Afterward, you'll be near some of Orlando's **best restaurants,** most of which the tourists never visit.

GETTING TO KNOW ORLANDO'S LAYOUT

In 1970, before the opening of Walt Disney World, Orlando was somewhat of a tourism center, attracting 660,000 people a year. But by 1999, the place was a powerhouse, with 37.9 million visits, and by 2019, that number had nearly doubled to 75 million. (Obviously, visitorship took a major hit during the Covid-19 pandemic—but the major theme parks were only closed for about 4 months before returning in temporary limited versions.) The area's population also leapfrogged from 344,000 to 860,000 to 2.38 million, passing old-guard American cities such as St. Louis; Washington, D.C.; Boston; Baltimore; and Portland, Oregon.

However, for all that growth, and despite the fact that the amusements are critical to Orlando's economy, most of the population still lives north of Sea-World. The tourist zones are segregated from residential ones. Huge chunks of your time, days at a stretch, will be spent only in the boisterously inauthentic commercial corridors along International Drive, U.S. 192 around I-4, and the Lake Buena Vista area north of exit 68 off I-4.

The Making of a Kingdom

Back when only cargo trains had much business in Central Florida, Orlando fashioned itself as a prosperous small city—some derisively called it a cow town—well positioned to serve the citrus and cattle industries as they shipped goods between America and Cuba. The city remained that way, mostly irrelevant, until around 1943, when the great cross-state cattle drives ended.

Soon after, the brick-warehouse city of Orlando developed its second personality. The turning point wasn't the arrival of Walt Disney on his secret land-buying trips. It came a decade earlier, when NASA settled into the Space

Coast, 45 minutes east, and the local government, spotting opportunity, invited the Martin Marietta corporation—now Lockheed Martin—to open a massive facility off Sand Lake Road, near the present-day Convention Center. To sweeten the deal, leaders promised unprecedented civic improvements, including an unrealized high-speed rail system they're *still* dithering over. Mostly, though, politicians built roads. Florida's Turnpike to Miami was carved past the Martin plot, S.R. 50 was hammered through downtown to link the coasts, and, soon after, many blocks were bulldozed for the construction of I-4, linking Tampa on the west coast with Daytona Beach (then one of America's premier vacation towns) on the east coast. The new transit links had Walt licking his chops for some cheap land nearby.

Walt's new kingdom was constructed 20 miles southwest of the city in scrubland, where his planners could keep the outside world at bay. The resort was intended to be an oasis in the citrus groves, but soon, sprawl sprouted around the park's border, just as had happened in Anaheim. For the last two generations, the space between Orlando's two disparate developments has vanished, consumed by areas where "real" Orlando residents live, so that the

THE PULSE massacre

In the early morning hours of June 12, 2016, a gunman bearing a legally obtained AR-15 entered Pulse, a gay nightclub just south of downtown Orlando, and began systematically murdering people he didn't know. By the time police felt it was safe enough to invade, 102 people had been shot, 49 of them mortally. The devastation was profound. Orlando was now home to the deadliest mass shooting in American history (a record that was swiftly surpassed by another one). National outrage sparked an unprecedented shift in the country's politics—within days, members of Congress staged a sit-in on the House floor to demand a vote on gun control measures. Across Orlando, security tightened, patrols escalated, metal detectors were installed, and for the first time, the world sadly acknowledged that even "The Happiest Place on Earth" was not immune to indiscriminate American violence. Although the nightclub was far from the tourist districts, it was a part of the community. Several of the victims worked at the theme parks—one, Luis Vielma, ran

the Islands of Adventure Harry Potter and the Forbidden Journey ride. Both Universal and Disney donated $1 million to the OneOrlando fund for the affected. With Pulse, Florida's youth reached a breaking point, and after the next major shooting in the state, in Parkland in February 2018, a powerful new political movement was born among millennials.

In June of 2021, President Joe Biden announced that Pulse would be designated an official national memorial. It is projected to open in 2022, but in the interim, the nightclub at 1912 S. Orange Ave. remains standing, surrounded by grass, benches, and a tribute wall. Ghostly pop music gently plays from hidden speakers (open daily 7:30am–9pm). The onePULSE Foundation (www.onepulsefoundation.org) has created a scholarship fund in the name of each of the victims. Wherever you go, whether it's to a hotel, a restaurant, or a theme park, remember that you will meet people who knew and loved someone whose life was stolen or ravaged by needless ongoing American violence.

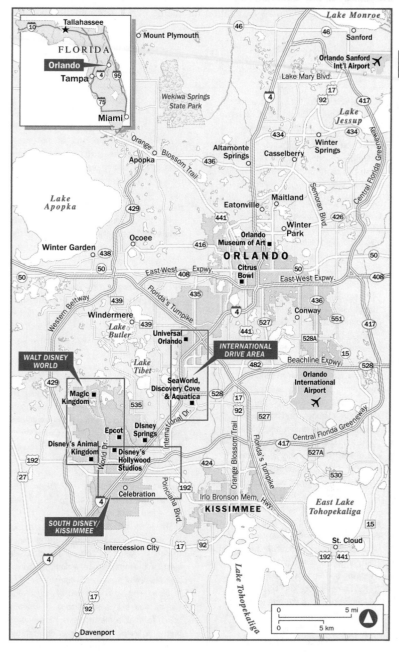

old-fashioned, "traditional" city has come to be dwarfed, as it were, by family-friendly honky-tonk and slapped-up suburbs. Few casual visitors ever lay eyes on the real Orlando—a situation the theme parks' accountants like just fine.

Neighborhoods in Brief

Get to know Orlando's neighborhoods—from theme parks to historic areas.

WALT DISNEY WORLD RESORT

Best for: *Space, theme parks, a sense of place, proximity to His Mouseness*

What you won't find: *Inexpensive food or lodging, a central location for anything except Disney attractions, the "real" Florida or Orlando*

Walt Disney World is at the southern end of Orlando's chain of big parks, so to see Universal, SeaWorld, and Orlando itself, you'll always head north on I-4.

When Walt Disney ordered the purchase of these 27,000 acres mostly just west of Interstate 4, he was righting a wrong he committed in the building of Anaheim's Disneyland. In commandeering as much land as he did, he ensured that visitors would not be troubled by the clatter of motel signs and cheap restaurants that abut his original playground. "Here in Florida," he said in a promotional film shot months before his death, "we have something special we never enjoyed at Disneyland . . . the blessing of size. There's enough land here to hold all the ideas and plans we can possibly imagine." You could spend your entire vacation without leaving the greenery of the resort, and lots of people do, although they're missing a lot. The idea of remaining solely on Disney property is outdated now that Universal has proven itself. Still, there's an awful lot to do around here, starting with four of the world's most polished theme parks, two of the best water parks, four golf courses, two miniature golf courses, a sports pavilion, and a huge shopping-and-entertainment district.

First-time visitors aren't usually prepared for quite how *large* the area is: 47 (roughly rectangular) square miles. Only a third of that land is truly developed, and another third has been set aside as a permanent reserve for swampland. Major elements are easily a 10-minute drive away from each other, with nothing but trees or Disney hotels between them. The Magic Kingdom is buried deep in the back of the park—which is to say, the north of it, requiring the most driving time to reach. Epcot and Hollywood Studios are in the center, while Disney's Animal Kingdom is at the southwest of the property, closest to the real world.

For its convenience, Disney **signposts hotels and attractions** according to the major theme park they're near. If you are staying on property, you'll need to know which area your hotel is in. For example, the All-Star resorts are considered to be in the Animal Kingdom area, and so some signs may simply read Animal Kingdom Resort Area, leaving off the name of your hotel. Ask for your hotel's designated area when you reserve.

Getting in is easy. Every artery in town is naggingly signposted for Disney World. Exits are marked, but it helps to know the name of the main road that feeds your hotel. A few useful **secret exits** are not well-promoted on official Disney maps. One is **Western Way,** which turns past the Coronado Springs resort and skirts the back of Animal Kingdom to reach many vacation home communities southwest of Disney. Be warned that taking Hwy. 429 to U.S. 192 will cost a few bucks in tolls.

There's a second useful shortcut out of the resort: **Sherberth Road,** by the entrance to Animal Kingdom Lodge, about a mile west of the entrance to Animal Kingdom, leads to rental homes off western U.S. 192.

It's interesting to note that when you're at Disney, you're in a separate governmental zone. To enable the resort's bizarre experiments in building methods (such as fiberglass-and-steel castles), Disney negotiated the creation of its own entity, the Reedy

Creek Improvement District, which can set its own standards. You may see vehicles marked RCID—those are the civic services for the resort. Not far down the road by Disney Springs Marketplace (a route not used by many guests), you may pass the R.C. Fire Department, a toylike engine house with an outdoor fountain that looks like a spouting fire hose.

Disney developed (and then sold) a bit of land east of I-4 into the New Urbanism unincorporated town of **Celebration.** As a Stepford-like residential center with upscale aspirations (golf, boutiques), it doesn't offer visitors much to do except eat a bit in its town square. Be prepared to parallel park there.

U.S. 192 & KISSIMMEE

Best for: Lowbrow chain restaurant and motel options, downscale attractions

What you won't find: Subtlety, luxury

Kissimmee (Kiss-im-ee) was the heart of Orlando tourism in the 1970s, but the center of tourist gravity shifted, and the town now lags further behind every year. The tatty drag of U.S. 192, known also as the Irlo Bronson Memorial Highway (after a state senator who sold Walt a bunch of land), is the stop-and-go spine of Kissimmee. U.S. 192 is mostly about chains and buffets, but on weekend nights, this low-rent Rialto fills with drivers of muscle cars who come to show off at Old Town and the Fun Spot (p. 192).

The motels weren't flashy in the '70s, but as Disney becomes more expensive and its guests tend to be wealthier, they increasingly avoid this area. Recent hard times in the economy have only served to drag some of these motels below the line of respectability. While they're ever affordable—$50 to $80 is the norm, and some shabby places go down to $39 for a single or $45 for a double—it's no longer possible to confidently vouch for the quality or serenity of a stay on U.S. 192.

There's plenty of cheap food and souvenirs, though. The best way to get your bearings on U.S. 192 is using its clearly signposted **mile marker system.** U.S. 192 hits Disney's southern entrance (the most expedient avenue to the major theme parks)

at Mile Marker 7, while I-4's exit 65 connects with it around Mile Marker 8. Numbers go down to the west, and they go up to the east. Western 192, where the bulk of the vacation home developments are found, is much more upscale than the tacky wilds of eastern 192, but neither stretch could be termed swanky, and driving it is slow going.

LAKE BUENA VISTA

Best for: Access to Disney, I-4, and chain restaurants, some elbow room

What you won't find: The lowest prices, a sense of place

Lake Buena Vista, a hotel enclave east of Disney Springs, clusters on the eastern fringe of Walt Disney World. LBV is technically a town, but it doesn't look like one. It's mostly hotels and mid-priced chain restaurants with some schlocky souvenir stores thrown in. The proximity of I-4 exit 68 can back traffic up (plans are afoot for a major redevelopment of the interchange), but it's convenient to Disney's crowded side door and Disney Springs, which is helpful. The bottom line is that LBV is less tacky and higher rent than Kissimmee's 192, but also touristy and not really part of Orlando's fabric.

If you stay in LBV, you can also (if you're hardy) walk to the Disney Springs development, where you can then pick up Disney's free DTS bus system. That could save you the cost of a rental car.

INTERNATIONAL DRIVE & UNIVERSAL ORLANDO

Best for: Walkability, second-tier amusements, affordable hotels and transportation, proximity to Universal and SeaWorld

What you won't find: Space, style

Although a developing stretch of this street winds all the way south to U.S. 192, when people refer to International Drive, they usually mean the segment around SeaWorld north to Universal Orlando, just east of I-4 between exits 71 and 75. I-Drive, as it's called, is probably the only district where you might comfortably stay without a car and still be able to see the non-Disney attractions, because it's chockablock with affordable hotels (not as ratty as U.S. 192's can be) and plenty of crowd-pleasing things to do, such as arcades, wild mini-golf courses, family restaurants, and the Wheel (once called the Orlando Eye, p. 183) at the ICON Park entertainment complex. The cheap I-Ride Trolley (p. 288) traverses the area on a regular schedule.

The intersection at Sand Lake Road is a dividing line for I-Drive's personalities. South of Sand Lake, there's a business-y (but party-ready) crowd in town for the mighty Orange County Convention Center, located on both sides of I-Drive at the Bee Line Expressway/528. It keeps the surrounding hotels and restaurants busy. North of Sand Lake Road, within the orbit of Universal Orlando, midway rides and Universal's affordable Endless Summer Resort prevail. And west on Sand Lake Road from I-4, you'll find a mile-long procession of mid- to upper-level places to eat that the city dubiously calls its "Restaurant Row." Hotel and restaurant discounts appear on **www.internationaldrive orlando.com**.

Just north of I-Drive across I-4, signified by the towering steaming namesake of Volcano Bay water park, is Universal Orlando's resort with its two theme parks, waterslide park, six on-campus hotels, and the CityWalk food-and-entertainment district (p. 205).

DOWNTOWN ORLANDO

Best for: *Historic buildings, cafes, museums, wealthy residents*

What you won't find: *Street life, easy commutes*

As happened in so many American cities, residents fled from downtown in the 1960s through the 1980s. Spacious new condo developments have rescued the city from abandonment, and downtown Orlando is called home by young, upscale residents. Here are the highlights:

DOWNTOWN Beneath the city's collection of modest skyscrapers (mostly banking offices), you'll find municipal buildings (the main library, historic museums) and some attractive lakes, but little shopping. Orange Avenue, once a street of proud stone buildings and department stores, now comes alive mostly at night, and mostly for the young.

The 43-acre Lake Eola Park, just east, is often cited as an area attraction, but in truth it's just your average city park, although the .9-mile path around its 23-acre sinkhole lake is good for joggers. Its swan boats are city icons, as is the central fountain from 1957—its Plexiglas skin is illuminated with a 6-minute light-and-water musical show nightly at 9:30pm. Just east of that, the streets turn to red brick and big trees shelter Thornton Park (along Washington St., Summerlin Ave., and Central Blvd.). It's noted for its alfresco European-style cafes, none especially inexpensive, but all pleasing, where waiters wear black and hip locals spend evenings and weekend brunches. West of downtown over I-4, the area called Parramore is a longtime neighborhood for African Americans (sadly, the interstate was built, in part, as a barrier). A mile north of downtown, Loch Haven Park basks in a wealth of museums.

MILLS 50 Some old-timers call this area Colonial Town and new-timers may use Mills 50, but it's also the Vietnamese District at Mills, or ViMi (p. 217). At Colonial Drive and Mills Avenue, there's a midcentury neighborhood with the whiff of a faded 1950s strip mall (parking lots are hidden behind buildings). There, you can spend a top afternoon strolling through several omnibus Asian supermarkets stocked with exotic groceries and unique baked goods and parking yourself at one of the excellent mom-and-pop-style eateries (advertised by cheap stick-on letters and neon) serving food far more delicious than their limited budgets would suggest. Several stores whip up addictive, meat-stuffed baguette sandwiches called *banh mi* for a quick $6 meal. You'll also find hobby- and art-supply shops patronized by a burgeoning bohemian community. The two marginalized groups collaborate beautifully together.

WINTER PARK

Best for: *Fine art, cafes, strolls, galleries, lakes*

What you won't find: *Inexpensive shopping, easy theme park access*

One of the city's most interesting areas, and one of the few that hasn't taken pains to erase its history, Winter Park was where, more than 100 years ago, upstart industrialists built winter homes at a time when they couldn't gain entry into the exclusive WASP-y enclaves of Newport or Palm Beach. The town, which blends seamlessly with northern Orlando (you can drive between them in a few minutes without getting onto I-4), is still pretty full of itself and its expensive tastes, but cruising on its brick-paved streets and gawking at mansions built on its chain of lakes will remind you of the good life. Newspapers and magazines write about Winter Park like it's the hottest thing going, but in all honesty, it's just a nice place to pass an afternoon or evening. In the shops on Park Avenue, you'll find mostly jewelry and art, and south of it, stroll the country-club campus of Rollins College. The town's long-running boat tour (p. 267) is the best way to sample the opulence. The best art museum around, the Morse (p. 187), holds the most inspiring collection of Tiffany glass you will ever see. West of Winter Park, over I-4, the district of College Park, centering around Princeton Street and Edgewater Drive, hosts restaurants and boutiques that bring the area favor.

NORTH OF ORLANDO

Most visitors who venture into the suburban towns north of Winter Park do so to visit some of the area's natural springs or state parks (p. 263), to trawl the many antiques stores of Lake Mary, or to connect with the spirits in the hamlet of Cassadaga (p. 186).

Keep going on I-4 and you hit the Atlantic Coast within the hour.

SOUTH OF ORLANDO

Only in the past few years has the rural-minded swampland southwest of Kissimmee begun to be built upon in earnest, and the 65-mile run along I-4 to Tampa is quickly filling in with developments and golf courses. This patch of the Green Swamp, in which the two cities will one day merge into a megalopolis, is now casually dubbed "Orlampa." In Tampa, you'll find the excellent Busch Gardens (p. 178), a worthy addition to an amusement-park itinerary, and an hour straight south of Orlando, in the town of Winter Haven, is Legoland Florida (p. 173), a phenomenal kiddie park built on the tranquil remains of Florida's most historic amusement park.

EAST OF ORLANDO

The entrance to Orlando International Airport is 11 miles east of I-4, webbed into the city network by toll highways. Across largely empty swamp from there, the so-called Space Coast, of which Cape Canaveral is the metaphoric capital (see it at Kennedy Space Center; p. 174), is a 45-minute drive east of Orlando's tourist corridor via 528, also known as the Bee Line Expressway.

WEST OF ORLANDO

Because the Green Swamp commands the area, there simply isn't much west of the tourist corridor save a few small towns and some state parks, such as Lake Louisa.

EXPLORING WALT DISNEY WORLD

3

On November 22, 1963, around the time President John Kennedy was embarking on his public motorcade in Dallas, Walt Disney was in a private jet, conducting his first flyover of a patch of ignored Florida swampland. By the end of the day, as Disney decided this was the place he wanted to shape into the image of his dreams, America had changed in more ways than one.

While the country reeled, Disney gradually snapped up land through dummy companies. His cover was blown in 1965, but the fix was in: His company had mopped up an area twice the size of Manhattan, 27,443 acres, at a low price of $180 an acre. Disneyland East was coming. Today, it's the most popular vacation destination on the planet, and in happy times, its four theme parks receive more than 58 million combined visits a year, or 60 percent of the region's tourism market share. After years without much significant development, during which it lost ground to nearby Universal, the resort is now in the midst of a multi-year push to pour billions into improvements, and signs of construction are everywhere.

It's no accident that Walt, a seller of fantasies, enjoyed his career peaks during two periods of profound malaise: the Great Depression and the Cold War. It's also no coincidence that his theme parks flowered while America was riven with self-doubt—the Korean and Vietnam conflicts, the death of Kennedy, and Watergate. His parks are, by design, comforting. They tell you how to feel and where to go, and in reinforcing uncomplicated impressions of history and the world, they never make you feel stupid or left behind.

That was a half century ago. In 2021, Disney's Magic Kingdom turned 50. It is now the American Varanasi—a place of pilgrimage and a spiritual balm for life's hardships. If you don't believe me, sit on a bench for a while in Fantasyland and watch the children pass. There's just something about it. Even when the world was flung into the trauma of the Covid-19 pandemic and human contact presented uncertain risks, guests came flooding back to the Disney parks in Florida just 4 months after they had temporarily closed.

For 10 uneasy months after that, guests sought emotional reassurance from Walt Disney World even though they had to wear face masks, stand 6 feet away from anyone else, and sit alone in ride vehicles to observe vigilant safety protocols. The fierceness of their loyalty to Disney, even to the point of risking discomfort and illness, left no doubt about where the brand stands in its importance to the American psyche.

But Disney World, transporting though it may be, is a business, and for a significant portion of the population, it's brutally expensive. The days of a spontaneous visit to Disney are over. Nearly every aspect of a day now requires advance decisions. One bygone Disney Parks president was frank about the tactic in *Bloomberg Businessweek:* "If we can get people to plan their vacation before they leave home, we know that we get more time with them. We get a bigger share of their wallet."

The pandemic only intensified that outlook. Faced with having to make do with suppressed attendance, Disney learned new ways to make more out of less, devising new crowd-management systems while squeezing more cash out of every visitor—and the company is taking those lessons into the future. Disney can't fit too many more people into its parks, but it can fuel profits by finding new ways to make each person pay more. Even before Covid-19, the average domestic overnight guest spent nearly $300 per person per day, and executives openly aim to drive that number even higher.

Today, a trip to Disney is full of nonstop competition for resources—long before you enjoy a single second of fun, you must act faster than rival guests to secure park tickets for the day you want them, book restaurant reservations, and even get permission to wait in line at the biggest rides. To succeed at Disney, you must put your back into pre-research and planning using a bureaucratic and often opaque system. For many, that stress spoils the delightful surprises the parks were carefully designed to deliver.

That's where this Frommer's guide comes in. This is not a guide for the Disney-obsessed fans who already know how to game the system. No, this book is for the rest of us—it's for the casual or first-time visitor. This book will help you declutter your Disney prep so your vacation can be as carefree as possible. The world needs more carefree days.

We love Disney, but we tell it like it is.

TICKETING

Disney raises prices each year but tickets are still in demand, so I guess we should stop complaining about it. Admission will be your biggest expense besides accommodations.

Paid Ticket + Park Reservation = Vacation

Tickets are priced by the day according to how busy the park is expected to be. Prices are not truly dynamic—they're set on a calendar in advance each year—but the numbers are all over the map.

Walt Disney World & Lake Buena Vista

Apopka-Vineland Rd.

FOOD & HOTEL

Lake St.

Palm Pkwy.

Kilgore Rd.

Pocket Lake

Little Fish Lake

Winter Garden-Vineland Rd.

Centra-Care Walk-in Medical Center

535

Lake Sheen

Buena Vista Dr.

Vista Blvd.

Live Oak Ln.

Sassagoula Cir.

Disney's Port Orleans Resort

GRAND CYPRESS GOLF CLUB

535

South Lake

Winter Garden-Vineland Rd.

Bonnet Creek

Lake Mabel

Four Seasons Resort Orlando at the WDW Resort

Golf View Dr.

TRANQUILO GOLF CLUB

Big Pine Dr.

Fort Wilderness Trail

Wilderness Trail

Disney's Fort Wilderness Resort & Campground

Pioneer Hall

Vista Blvd.

Bay Lake

Disney's Contemporary Resort

Disney's Wilderness Lodge

Monorail

World Dr.

Magic Kingdom Toll

Transportation & Ticket Center

Reams Rd.

Shuttles

World Dr.

Parking

MAGIC KINGDOM

Seven Seas Lagoon

Seven Seas Dr.

Security Booth

Monorail

Disney's Wedding Pavilion

Disney's Polynesian Resort

Floridian Way

Disney's Grand Floridian Resort

DISNEY'S MAGNOLIA GOLF COURSE

Shades of Green Resort

DISNEY'S PALM & OAK TRAIL GOLF COURSES

Bear Island Rd.

Epcot Center Dr.

1/2 mi

0.5 km

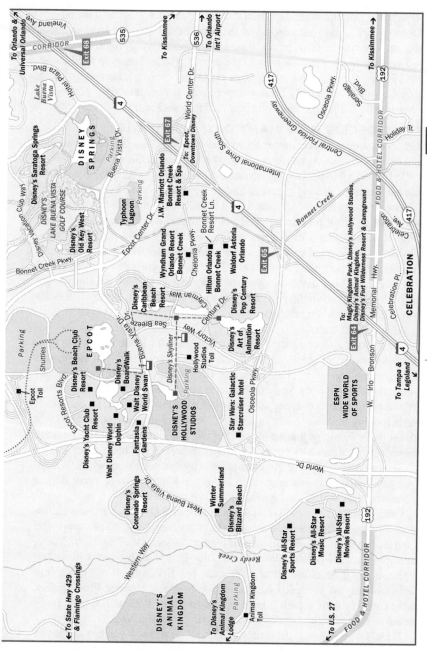

FIRST, CREATE AN ACCOUNT.

At the top of disneyworld.disney.go.com, there's a link for creating an account. This will be your main account from now on. You'll even use it with the official Disney World app to get into the parks, board rides, and order food. Without this account, you're sunk, so make sure you remember your login details.

Everyone in your party must set up a unique profile. Then you need to tell the system you're all traveling together by linking everyone. Do that by going to your profile (click "My Disney Experience" at the upper right), choosing "My Family & Friends," and clicking "Add a New Guest."

NEXT, DECIDE HOW MANY DAYS YOU WANT.

Go to www.disneyworld.disney.go.com/admission/tickets. The least you can pay for a 1-day ticket is $109 adult, $104 child (and at Disney, you're only a child from age 3 to 9). This lowest rate isn't valid most of the time, but it does appear scattered around the year and in September after kids go back to school. On most days of the year, you'll actually wind up with a base price in the $120s or $130s for an adult, and a child's ticket is only about $5 less. The highest a day ticket will ever go is $159 adult/$154 child during the peak December holidays. During heavy vacation periods like spring break and Thanksgiving, tickets are more like $139 adult/$134 child.

Okay, that's for 1 day. When you start adding days to that visit, the per-day price drops ever so slightly for every day you add because Disney is leaving you a trail of bread crumbs toward a longer stay.

Are you with me so far?

You should also consider if you want to add the **Park Hopper** option. Without it, you can only visit one theme park per day. But if you buy it, you can enter multiple parks in the same day. (Before the pandemic, there were no restrictions about when you could switch parks, but now, to prevent over-crowding, Disney forbids any switching before 2pm.) The Park Hopper option adds roughly $69 to a 1-day ticket, $80 to 2- or 3-day tickets, or $91 for a ticket that's 4 days or longer. If you're staying a full week, you'll essentially be spending another $13 a day for the right to park-hop. This is a flexibility I think is worth the expense. An example of why it may be worthwhile: With it, you can do the early-morning safari at Animal Kingdom, take a nap at your hotel, and then switch to Magic Kingdom for the fireworks.

Other possible add-ons: **Water Park and Sports Option.** This won't allow park-hopping, but it does add entry to the two water parks, the miniature golf courses that open at 4pm daily, greens fees at Disney's Oak Trail Golf Course, and entry to ESPN Wide World of Sports Complex. It's not a good buy because you'll never use all of it. You can buy tickets to all of those things independently as you go. Likewise avoid the **Park Hopper Plus Option,** which merely adds a park hopper option to Water Park and Sports. You'll never be able to do it all unless you're staying at least a week.

There's no pressure to decide about add-ons right now—you can add any of them for a prorated amount after you start your vacation. And as you're planning your schedule, know that you don't have to use all your Disney tickets on consecutive days. You can take the day off and go do something else in Orlando. You're only given a couple of extra days, though, to use them all up.

But don't buy anything yet. The next step is crucial.

THEN CHECK THE CALENDAR FOR AVAILABILITY.

Here's where it gets hairy. You don't just need a ticket. You also need a park reservation for a pre-arranged day to which you must assign that ticket for use.

The Disney World website posts a calendar of every day of the year, and before you buy your ticket, you must ensure there is park availability on all of the dates of your visit—otherwise you could waste money on a ticket that won't work for all the parks when you're in town. At disneyworld.disney. go.com/admission/tickets, click "View Calendar" under "Check Park Reservation Availability Before Purchasing." There, you can check your proposed dates for open reservation slots.

Magic Kingdom reservations are first to sell out, and Disney's Hollywood Studios is next. *Make sure that the parks you want to visit are available on the days you want to go.* If they're not, you can always check back—sometimes new allotments of spaces appear without warning. But there's no guarantee of that, so you're usually better off just picking available dates. You can often park-hop later in the day *into* a park that had no park passes left, but you can't start your day in it. (Again, there's no guarantee, because Disney created this system to control crowds.)

If your dates are free, then you can reserve rooms at a Disney resort hotel through your new account, and then go to the next step. (It's not ideal to buy park tickets before you've made your Disney hotel reservation.) If you're not planning on staying at a Disney hotel (we have a whole chapter of options that starts on p. 225), you can proceed to the next step now.

FINALLY, BUY YOUR TICKETS AND LINK THEM.

Once you know your chosen parks are available on your vacation days, *now* you can purchase your actual tickets. Once you do, make sure that every person in your party sees the tickets showing up in his or her own profile. They may have to link them on their own, which they can do through Tickets & Passes on the app.

Once your tickets are purchased—and this is the most important part—*you must link your just-purchased tickets to new Theme Park Reservations.* Do not wait long for this step, because if you do, some parks could fill up while you dilly-dally.

At the upper right of the website (this part can't be done on the app), click My Disney Experience and select the menu option for Disney Park Pass Reservation. Here, you can select everyone in your party (that you set up in Family & Friends at the start of all this) and proceed to connect the park passes you saw on the calendar to the tickets you just purchased.

If everything works, you should see your park reservations listed in the My Plans section of your My Disney Experience account, and your digital tickets should show up in the app.

Couldn't be simpler, right? Right??

Avoid "hard ticket" evening events: During some times of year, the parks mount special "hard ticket" evening events, such as the ones around Halloween and Christmas (see the calendar on p. 291) that require a separate admission. You will get less value out of your ticket if you attend on the same day as one of these parties, because if you haven't paid for the evening-event ticket, you could be rounded up and chased out in late afternoon, losing hours of park time. Fortunately, in 2021, Disney began scheduling more events that occur after regular opening hours, and scheduled fewer events that might cut into the regular opening hours.

THE PERILS OF DISNEY PACKAGES

Over-purchasing is the biggest pitfall. If you call for reservations rather than making them on your own, agents will suggest adding perks. You'll ask for tickets, and they'll suggest you throw in some little perk. The instant you accept, your customer status changes. You're now purchasing a "package," and that will often force you to pay more than you would have a la carte. Always, *always* know what everything would cost separately before agreeing to a Disney-suggested package. If you must, hang up the phone and do some math before deciding to accept or reject the offer. Then call back for a new quote—prices can fluctuate each time you call. That's the only way to ensure you're not paying more.

Here's a hidden loophole that works against you: Disney's "length of stay" ticket packages will begin the moment you arrive on the property and end the day you leave. Think about that. If you've just flown from a distant place, you are unlikely to rush to Epcot on the same day. Likewise, on the day you're due at the airport to fly home, you may not to be able to visit a theme park. Yet Disney will schedule your package that way. In effect, you will lose 2 days that you've paid for—at the start and at the finish of your vacation, when you'll be resting or packing. That's colder than Elsa's heart.

How can you avoid this? You could 1) stay entirely at non-Disney hotels and just buy admission tickets. That's because the rule only applies to Disney packages—if you simply buy 4 days' worth of tickets, you don't have to use them on consecutive days as long as they're all used within your specified deadline (generally, the number of days you purchased plus 2 or 3 days). You could 2) stay at a Disney hotel for your ticket days and stay off-site for the others. Or you could 3) insist on making **one reservation per phone call.** Arrange your tickets plus their corresponding hotel nights for your Disney days. Hang up. Call back and arrange "room-only" nights for your last night and any days you'll be leaving Disney during the day as "room only." It's vital that you do not link your two reservations in advance if you want the best price and the best cancellation policies, but you can link them after arrival. If you don't plan on seeing anything but Disney, of course, then you won't have to go through these lengths. But with so many wonders in Florida, many people aren't satisfied by only visiting the Mouse.

Another tip: Disney's reservationists are friendly, but they're sales-driven, and they are trained to answer *only* the questions that you pose. If you're not sure about the terms of what you're about to purchase, corner them and ask. They won't lie to you, but they *will* neglect to volunteer information. Grill them about deposit and cancellation policies—they get *much* stiffer if you're on a package vs. buying a la carte. The best of Disney always goes to those willing to pay the most, but ask if there is a less expensive option. **TheMouse ForLess.com**, **MouseSavers.com**, and the messages at **DISBoards.com** will let you know about current deals that Disney won't. And if you're still dithering about whether to stay on property, there's a list of pros and cons on p. 232.

OTHER TICKET "DISCOUNTS" & DEALS

Official deals, when they exist, are listed at www.disneyworld.disney.go.com/special-offers and at www.mousesavers.com. **Florida residents** are offered

---

AN EXPLANATION OF lightning lane

During the pandemic, Disney shut down its famous FastPass+ system and converted the formerly free perk into a new profit center called Lightning Lane. Lightning Lane is a timed ticket to something (a ride, show, character greeting, priority seating) that allows you to scoot right in without waiting in the normal "Standby" line. There are a few ways to get access, all of which cost extra money—on top of whatever you paid for park admission.

o If you pay $15 extra a day for Genie+ (see p. 30), you're given timed access to Lightning Lane on some lower- and middle-tier attractions. As the day progresses, Genie will tell you what's available, and you can may only hold one reservation at a time. *Warning:* That $15 doesn't mean you are allowed to use all the Lightning Lanes. Some are withheld from you.

o The most popular rides have Lightning Lanes that are *not* covered by Genie+. For those, if you want to skip Standby lines or the lottery, you must pay a one-time fee via the app—per person, and the price

is the same no matter your age. The dollar amount of the up-charge amount fluctuates by the attraction, by the time of day, according to how thick crowds are, and other factors Disney hasn't disclosed—but rest assured that it will cost you more than you expect it to. Reservations are timed, and you're only allowed to use this method twice a day.

o Disney may also dole out Lightning Lane access as an incentive to book a more expensive hotel, to apologize for ride breakdowns, or just as a lark.

Lightning Lane assignments open at 7am on the day of use and can be managed via the app from any location. The new system, which debuted in late 2021, is still establishing itself and because it depends on the wobbly app, its implementation can be rocky. It's also murky: Disney now has a financial incentive to slow down lines or fudge the posted wait time, because that would drive customers to pay extra fees for Lightning Lane access so they can get in no matter what. From a consumer standpoint, there are concerns.

entirely different discounts (www.disneyworld.disney.go.com/florida-residents) that come with blackout dates, as are **AAA members** (available through local AAA chapters). If you are **active military,** Disney wants you to go through your military base ticket office for the latest promotions. Attendees of **conventions** on Disney property may be offered cheaper tickets for afternoon or evening park entry, available through the convention organizers.

Beware anyone claiming they have discounts on a 1-day ticket, because Disney doesn't allow that. A few businesses shave a few paltry bucks off multi-day tickets; see "Getting Attraction Discounts" in chapter 9 (p. 294) for some upstanding ones. Tickets are usually indelibly linked to individuals, so avoid anyone trying to sell you unused days on their multi-day tickets, and *never* buy tickets through eBay or any other marketplace. International visitors are eligible for tickets good for longer stays, but only if they are purchased from abroad. *Really* big fans carry a **Chase Disney Rewards Visa credit card** (www.chase.com/disney), which grants points to be redeemed on all things Disney, a few discounts, and a character meet-and-greet area for cardholders.

Suffice it to say that if you don't spring for upcharges, you'll be getting in line the old-fashioned way: You walk up to something and wait in the Standby line for it. (Sometimes, Disney may push you to a virtual queue, but you'll technically still be in the long line.) Try not to be jealous of the VIPs for whom money is no object.

MASTERING THE TECH

Until a few years ago, it was possible to spend time at Disney without using your smartphone too much. Now, it's pretty much mandatory. If you don't use the official website and app for your schedule planning and execution, you'll be forced to continually seek help from cast members, and that will cost you in time and frustration.

Disney paid a reported $1 billion to develop a guest identification and itinerary management system, and the fruit of that investment will govern most of the moves you make on resort property. It starts with **My Disney Experience** (MDX), the online account that contains your personal profile. Through MDX, you'll manage your plans primarily using the official **Disney World app.** Once you set your plans, **MagicBands** and **MagicMobile** (see below) function as the entry keys to the day-to-day things you'll do.

Once you create an account at MyDisneyExperience.com and link your ticket number with it, the app can:

o Schedule and redeem ride reservations, including by Virtual Queue.
o Display your location on park maps.
o Show current wait times.
o Show in-park schedules.
o Show height and accessibility requirements.
o Keep a schedule of your reservations.

- Make and cancel restaurant reservations.
- Manage PhotoPass account and images.
- Buy tickets.
- Pre-order food for pick up at a few park restaurants.
- Enable mobile check-in and serve as a digital key (with Disney resort reservations), chat with staff, and check shuttle bus times.

Think of the smartphone app as the place you make your plans, and the MagicBand or MagicMobile as the tool you use to check yourself in to do them. To help you, all parks and hotels have free Wi-Fi. Here's the help line for your My Disney Experience account and the Disney World app: ✆ **407/939-4537.**

Unfortunately for you, all that app time will consume your battery life, so it's crucial that you pack some backup power in the parks. A few FuelRod vending machines stashed around the park (ask cast members) sell $30 battery packs you can use, drain, and exchange for fresh ones for a few bucks. Newer models of resort buses have USB charging outlets between every other seat. Guest Relations will also charge your phone if you provide the cord and plug.

MagicBands & MagicMobile

Introduced in 2013, **MagicBand** is a waterproof, removable bracelet that facilitates your stay at Walt Disney World. Each band contains two types of embedded radio frequency transmitters that enable both short-range and long-range tracking. Once linked with a guest's MDX profile via the Disney World app (download via Google Play or iPhone), it can do all sorts of things:

- Stores ticket info. Touch it to a lollipop-like scanner for entry.
- Records and redeems reservations such as dining. (The expanded capability is technically called MyMagic+.)
- Validates PhotoPass details. Scan it with photographers and tap it to post-ride photo kiosks to add new images to your portfolio.

For Disney, It's a Whole New World

We don't have to tell you that Covid-19 changed the planet. Here, it was a seismic shift. Disney World will never again be the way it was before the pandemic. The global pause gave the company a clean slate that, yes, cost it billions of dollars. At the same time, though, the pandemic also gave Disney a chance to completely rethink how it manages its business. With an urgent new mandate to try to make back as much of that lost cash as possible, Disney accountants and managers put every aspect of resort operations—from attendance formulas to hotel perks to employment contracts with long-term entertainers—under the microscope. Some things were retained, but many others are being reinvented and tested. And the reinvention will continue for years. Menus may change overnight. Formerly free traditions may suddenly come with a price tag. Longtime traditions might be retired. Be aware and be patient, because even Mr. Toad would find this ride to be a little wild.

- Allows Disney resort guests to make purchases (with a PIN; day visitors cannot) and open hotel room doors and gates. They also tell tollkeepers if you have a parking pass.
- Allows Disney Parks to track your movements. That can be fun: You might open the photos on your Disney World app and discover a shot of you on Slinky Dog Dash or a video of yourself on the Seven Dwarfs Mine Train (available for purchase, of course).
- Furnishes a beautiful tan line.

MagicBands come in sassy colors and as collectors' editions, and the higher-priced MagicBand+ can light up during shows, vibrate, or trigger minor effects at marked locations. For Disney hotel guests, standard MagicBands are $5 if ordered ahead. You can also buy at the resort ($20–$35) and link to MDX using the code on its back, but you can only link it once.

But don't feel pressured to buy a MagicBand, because now your smartphone can do most of the same tricks. Keepin' it contactless, in 2021 Disney announced **MagicMobile,** which turns eligible iPhones, Apple Watches, and Google Pay–enabled Android phones into *de facto* MagicBands. Once MagicMobile is added to your digital wallet through the Disney World app, you don't even have to unlock your phone to scan in. However, you may find it annoying to be on your phone even more than you already will be, so the old-fashioned method of the MagicBand still has its appeal—and it preserves your battery for photos and calls.

If you have privacy concerns, you may decline both MagicBand and MagicMobile; you will be given a plastic card that only contains a passive radio transmitter chip that's used to tap for entry but cannot trace your movements.

No matter what you use to scan in, brace yourself for the overspending potential of tapping a device rather than taking out a billfold. Studies show we spend 18 percent more when we don't handle cash or credit cards—a big reason the company decided to sink $1 billion into this. Notably, nearly every exec who convinced the company to spend that money has since left.

Disney Genie

Once the company successfully conditioned guests to consult the Disney World app before making any moves, it took the next step in the evolution of itinerary automation: **Genie.** With Genie, Disney found a way to convert one of its most frustrating self-inflicted flaws—the maddening burden of navigating its planning bureaucracy—into a new profit center.

The service, which came online in late 2021, is still taking baby steps, but the basic idea is that once you activate it (for free) in the Disney World app, its algorithms will design a full touring plan of activities for you, based on what you tell it you like. You can ask for a Princess-themed day at Magic Kingdom, for example, or request a route through World Showcase's international dishes. You may follow its prescription or decide against it, or you can switch plans midstream and ask it to recalculate a different schedule for you. If the Genie puts something on your itinerary, it has the ability to get you in.

Everyone can use the free version of Genie, which will also forecast wait times for the big attractions later in the day. But Disney would rather you pay an extra $15 per day to upgrade to **Genie+**. The upgraded app can direct you to various attractions and diversions that are currently accepting visitors through Lightning Lane, the old FastPass queue (see p. 27).

Genie+ will get you into the old FastPass queue for *some* rides, but not all of them. Genie+ users are allowed to hold only one Lightning Lane reservation per person at a time (sometimes, you'll go hours in between appointment times), and only lower- and middle-tier attractions will be available. Lightning Lanes at the most popular rides (like Seven Dwarfs Mine Train and Rise of the Resistance) aren't covered by Genie+; you must pay yet another fee to enter those.

Genie+ users will also receive a few other minor perks, such as Disney-themed photo filters and sounds. Really, though, people buy it for the Lightning Lane access.

There are lots of wrinkles. One is that in truth, only *you* really know what you like and how you like to travel, and Genie has a way of filling some of your time with things that *Disney* would like you to do. Sometimes you'll grab a tough reservation and sometimes you'll learn about something new you'll love, but sometimes a thing will only be on your docket because resort operations wants to move people to less-popular stuff at that hour. The Genie isn't inclined to repeat attractions in your plan, either, whereas we all know teenagers who would happily line up for Rock 'n' Roller Coaster three times in a row. Genie also welds you to both a timetable and your smartphone—is that

mobile ordering EXPLAINED

It works fairly well! At counter-service restaurants (but not sidewalk stalls), you don't have to wait in a long, boring queue to order anymore. First, make sure there's a credit card associated with your My Disney Experience profile. Then, on the app, navigate to Mobile Food Orders to see what restaurants are available. Special requests are usually impossible, but if you want unchanged menu items, it's easy. Just choose the time window when you want to fetch your food (warning: it might not be immediately) and then order it—your credit card will be charged. If the app claims the restaurant isn't accepting orders, your connection might be bad.

Then, when you get to the restaurant, there will be a spot dedicated to mobile orders (usually at the right side of the counter). Go back to the Mobile Food Orders section of the app, click the button that says you're there and ready to pick up, and within 2 or 3 minutes—usually—your food will be served. (To avoid waiting at all, make that final click about 2 minutes before you reach the restaurant.) Identify yourself to the clerk—they don't always announce names, to avoid allowing strangers to pretend to be you.

Sometimes, you'll just want something simple like a beverage but there won't be pickup windows available right away. In that case, see a cast member at the restaurant, who might have a way to expedite your order.

fun for you? Only you can say how you prefer to spend your time at a theme park.

Most importantly, Genie is designed with upcharges in mind. It's a tool that can fill your time, yes, but it's also a tool designed to steer you to profit-driving experiences. You have to be careful with a friend like that.

EATING ON-SITE

For listings of restaurants and food stands in the parks, see p. 63 (Magic Kingdom), p. 85 (Epcot), p. 102 (Hollywood Studios), and p. 114 (Animal Kingdom).

In the original Disneyland, restaurants were operated by outside lessees, but today, Disney controls everything inside the parks except for Starbucks (each park has one). That hasn't done much for the quality of the food (prepare for memories of your grade-school cafeteria), but at least the math is easy. The **cheapest combo meals** are always from counter-service restaurants (called Quick Service in Disney-speak), where adults usually pay $11 to $16, including a side but not a drink—the combo is called a "meal." Kids' meals (a main dish; milk, juice, water, or soda; and a choice of two items including grapes, carrot sticks, applesauce, a cookie, or fries) always cost $7–$8 at Quick Service locations. If you want to sit down for a waiter-service meal—character meals are always in "table-service" restaurants—adults pay in the upper teens for a lunch entree and usually over $21 a plate at dinner, before gratuity or drinks, and kids' meals are about half as much. The Disney World app lists both menus and prices, and you can navigate to specific places to eat either via the park maps or by searching by name. Although you'll find special dietary items on Mobile Order, you generally won't find it possible to customize dishes.

Disney aggressively sells a Disney Dining Plan that takes away the need to pay a bill after each meal, but which comes with a lot of rules and requires a lot of advance reservations (see the sidebar "Why You Don't Need the Disney Dining Plan," p. 33).

No longer can you simply stroll into any restaurant that catches your eye and enjoy a meal. Oversubscription to the Dining Plan (and later, capacity restrictions due to coronavirus) spoiled that for everyone. **For table-service meals, *always* make an advance dining reservation (© 407/939-3463)**— you'll hear them called "ADR"s—or you're certain to be turned away. Menus and prices are listed on the Disney World app, where you can also reserve. If a restaurant is booked, try again 24 hours ahead, when people dump unwanted reservations before a $10 no-show penalty is assessed.

Semi-healthy options are possible on even the lowest food budget: Disney limits saturated fat and added sugar to 10 percent of a counter-service dish's calories; no more than 30 percent of a meal's calories or 35 percent of a snack's calories come from fat; and juice drinks have no added sugar. Trans fats are out. One way Disney seems to have accomplished this is by reducing

WHY YOU DON'T NEED THE DISNEY
dining plan

If you book at a Disney hotel, you might be offered the credit-based **Disney Dining Plan,** which pre-purchases meals. (It was suspended during the pandemic, when capacity was limited.) Like everything else here, it's unnecessarily complicated, choked with rules, exclusions, and premium versions. Lots of people think it will make touring easier, but if you are a casual Disney visitor and not using it for things like character meals, it has other opportunity costs.

○ **It's not cheap enough.** In 2020, the least expensive plan, Quick Service, had a per-day cost of $55 adults, $26 kids 3–9, and included two counter meals (not all three meals) and one snack (like popcorn or ice cream), plus one drink (it can be alcoholic), and a refillable soft drink mug you can only use at a Disney hotel. Most adult Quick Service meals cost $12 to $15 per meal using cash. Even if you spent $15, remedial math proves that if you stick to two counter-service meals with no plan, plus one $4 snack, you'd spend about $34 versus $55 using the plan.

○ **It's inflexible.** You must buy the plan for every night you stay at the hotel even though you may be exploring away from Disney on some days. You are not permitted to buy fewer days than your stay. And everyone in your room must be on it, plus, some menu items and food locations are excluded.

○ **It costs time.** Many of the plans expect the use of sit-down restaurants. This requires reservations months ahead, and you lose a lot of touring time.

○ **It's impractical.** The Standard plan (2020: $78 adults/$31 kids, per night) buys the equivalent of one sit-down meal, one Quick Service meal, and two snacks. If you want the plan with all three meals whether they're table or counter, you're looking at $119 adults/$48 kids per night in 2020. It starts to be of value only if you have a sit-down meal every single day. Few first-time visitors do that.

○ **It's incomplete.** The plan doesn't include tips (unless your party is six or more, in which case there's a mandatory 18% added).

○ **It's wasteful.** Because it begins on the day you arrive, you're bound to leave with some unused credits, resulting in a loss. Most people compensate for this by booking a character meal or fireworks package, which require more credits. If you plan on character meals, the math may—borderline—work out.

○ **It drags down quality.** To make the program pay off, since its 2005 introduction Disney has noticeably reduced the caliber and quantity of food.

The Dining Plan is worthwhile if you are offered it **for free as part of a package,** which happens during some special sale periods. Free is always delicious!

serving sizes—you won't feel stuffed. Kids' meals come with carrots, applesauce, or grapes instead of fries, and with low-fat milk, water, or 100% fruit juice instead of soda. (Fries and Coke are still available by request—they know kids are still on vacation.) *Note:* Plastic straws are history here. If paper ones bug you, consider bringing your own reusable straw.

NAVIGATING DISNEY

Disney hotel guests get into the parks 30 minutes ahead of opening; for everyone else, it's no longer possible to waltz onto the marquee rides by arriving early (although not everything starts operating right at opening time). Try not to leave any park as it closes, when crowds surge and all transportation is mobbed with intense standing waits. Instead, depart early or linger an hour in the shops, which will be open a bit longer than everything else. Uber operates at all the parks (at the Magic Kingdom, drivers pick up passengers at the Transportation and Ticket Center), and cars are usually plentiful.

GETTING AROUND   Having your own car is the easiest. The next thing to know is: Trams ☛ (about 210 passengers each) go to parking lots but buses go to parks and hotels.

Disney Transportation System (DTS; no luggage allowed) is reportedly the third-largest bus system in the state, after Miami and Jacksonville's public services. Taking DTS to a theme park eliminates the parking tram rigmarole. However, it adds waiting time, which can be 20 to 45 minutes, plus the commute itself, which can be just as long and require standing as if it's rush hour on a Brooklyn subway. You might even have to transfer buses. All told, 90 minutes to 2 hours of a busy day can be devoured by DTS. So often, having a car is worth the expense.

DTS is usually overwhelmed during the opening and closing of the theme parks, even though dispatchers run extra buses around those times and keep routes rolling for about 2 hours extra before opening and after closing. If you're staying at a Disney resort that offers another kind of transportation— say, the monorail to the Magic Kingdom—then a bus won't be available for the same route. Also, since the system has a hub-and-spoke design centered on the theme parks and Disney Springs, *you must often transfer if you're going between two second-tier points,* such as between two hotels, a hotel and a water park, or a theme park and Disney Springs. And buses to Disney Springs from theme parks don't even start running until 4pm.

In 2019, Disney opened the free **Disney Skyliner gondolas,** which are not unlike the enclosed gondolas that transport dozens of skiers at a time in the Alps. The first phase of the installation links Epcot's International Gateway side entrance with the Caribbean Beach Resort and a stop shared by Art of Animation and Pop Century. A spur line from Caribbean Beach goes to Disney's Hollywood Studios. So to travel between Epcot and Hollywood Studios, you'll have to change at Caribbean Beach—but even with that, the park change only takes about 20 minutes. Disney, in its current penny-pinching corporate mode, elected not to splurge on air conditioning in the cabins; instead, you rely on a window cross-breeze generated by movement.

Disney also has red polka-dotted **Minnie Vans** ☛ zipping around. This newly launched premium transportation network is Disney's answer to Uber. You hail one using the Lyft app—when you open the app, it will tell you where to go to hail one and wait. Each very clean Chevy Traverse (no theme decoration inside, unfortunately) fits up to six and keeps two children's car seats on hand, and it costs a flat $25 plus tax to go wherever you want within Walt Disney World. That's more than an UberX or often a taxi, and in inclement weather or peak periods, good luck finding one. They will also take you to the airport, but at $150, I don't know why you would use one.

PARKING   Each park has its own sunbaked lot ($25/day; free for Disney hotel guests and annual passholders; $45 for "Preferred" to be extra close). As you drive in, attendants will direct you to the next available spot. This is probably the most dangerous part of your day, because everyone is excited and you're at risk of hitting a distracted child or hitting an open car door—take it slow. Parking lanes are numbered and sections are named; at the very least, remember your number. Don't stress out if your row is a high number; at Epcot, for example, the front row is 27. (***Don't lose your car:*** Before you get out of your car, open your phone's mapping app or Waze and stick a pin in your location. If you still forget, remember what time you arrived: Disney tracks which sections are being filled minute by minute.) You'll board one of the noisy trams ✌ (cross the yellow line to signal you're boarding; drivers never budge if someone's in that zone), which haul you to ticketing in their own sweet time; at Epcot and Hollywood Studios, the lots are compact enough so that you could probably walk to the gates within 10 minutes without taking the tram, but the Magic Kingdom, with some 15,000 spaces (in either a Heroes or a Villains section—remember which one), is reportedly the third-largest parking lot in the world. Post-tram at the Magic Kingdom, you still must take either the monorail or a ferryboat to the front gates; at the other parks, the tram lets you off near the gates. There are a few **charging stations** for electric vehicles, which cost $0.35 per kilowatt, but you can count them on one hand, so if you drive an electric car, arrive early. Charging stations require both a credit card and a pre-ordered ChargePoint card (chargepoint.com); ask the toll attendant where they are.

SECURITY   Everyone passes through metal detectors and bags are searched. Drawstring bags are quicker to search than zipper-laden ones, but you'll save the most time if you don't have a bag because you'll bypass some screening lines. ***Banned:*** Booze, glass containers, selfie sticks, wheelie sneakers, costumes on anyone age 14 and over. And weapons, duh.

ENTRY   To validate your ticket (see MagicBands & MagicMobile, p. 29), you must place a finger on a clear plate. That fingerprint is "married" to your ticket so that no one else can use it. Disney swears your personal information is eventually expunged from the system, but what it doesn't publicize is that if you do not wish for your fingerprint to be scanned, you may use standard identification instead, right there at the gate. Parents can use their own finger in place of their child's—if you do that, just don't forget that you did that, and keep using it each time.

ORIENTATION   Once you get inside the gates, grab a free Guidemap from the inconspicuous racks. It marks shows, character greetings (denoted by

contacting WALT DISNEY WORLD

Walt Disney World offers no toll-free numbers.

General information: www.disneyworld.com; ℭ **407/939-5277**
Disney hotel reservations: ℭ **407/934-1936**
Non-reservation hotel and theme park questions: ℭ **407/939-2273**
Dining reservations: disneyworld.com/dine; ℭ **407/939-3463**
New tickets: ℭ **407/939-7679**
Existing tickets: ℭ **407/566-4985**
My Disney Experience, app, MagicBands, MagicMobile: ℭ **407/939-4357**
Tour bookings: ℭ **407/939-8687**
Disability Services: ℭ **407/560-2547**
PhotoPass: ℭ **407/560-4300**
Lost and found: ℭ **407/824-4245**

Mickey in profile), places to eat, and attractions with shorter hours. The app also includes these things, but not as a timetable; it lists showtimes only once you select an attraction. Or you can ask at the park's **Guest Relations** desk (marked on the maps, always near the front; **Guest Services,** outside the gates, is mostly for ticket issues). The wait time for any attraction is posted where its line begins; this number is roughly accurate, since Disney often pads it by 5 minutes to give a sense of exceeded expectations.

SIZE RESTRICTIONS They're listed on the maps. Take them seriously. They are always enforced. If there is a sample of the ride vehicle out front, you can try it (or make it a photo op) before joining the line. At Splash Mountain, Space Mountain, Mission Space, and a few other major rides, kids who are sized out may be offered a card entitling them to jump to the head of the line when they finally grow tall enough. (At Space Mountain, it dubs them a "Mousetronaut," at Splash Mountain, a "Future Splash Mountaineer"—but sadly, this perk seems to be dying out.)

FOOD Gone are the days when you could decide on a whim to have a table-service dinner. The Disney Dining Plan (p. 33) wrecked that. Now you must plan ahead by racking up Advance Dining Reservations, called ADRs, or risk waiting for cancellations that may not materialize. Having a reservation does not mean you will sit down at that time. There is frequently a wait anyway, but the app can tell you if you have a chance at walk-in availability. If you have no reservations, you'll be eating from counter-service spots.

Breakfast ends around 10:30am, and lunch service generally goes from 11:30am to 2:30 or 3pm, though increasingly, some places price lunch as dinner. Prices for buffets and character meals shift according to the day of the week and time of year. Counter-service locations, which Disney calls **Quick Service,** do not require reservations, and their listings can be found with each theme park's section below. To avoid lines, eat between 10:30am and noon (lunch) and 4 and 5pm (dinner). Kids age 2 and under may eat without charge from an adult's plate, and high chair and booster seats are readily available. If you have dietary concerns, make them plain with your first cast member interaction.

Be warned that eating late can be hard; with the exception of Disney Springs, options tend to dry up by 9pm or so.

STROLLERS   Many times you will be asked to park your stroller before entering a line, so do not keep your valuables in stroller compartments. Your time (and your neighbor's) on monorails and trams will be much happier if you have a stroller that folds quickly. Note that you're not allowed to bring a stroller larger than 36"×52" (92cm×132cm) into the park. If you rent one and go to a second park the same day, keep your receipt. You won't have to pay again, but you do have to wait in the rental line again. For prices, see "What the Basics Cost at All Four Disney Parks," p. 38.

WHAT TO WEAR   Consider dressing small children in bathing suits because some play areas (particularly at Magic Kingdom) will get them soaked.

PHOTO PASS AND OTHER OPTIONAL PARK SERVICES   On some of the bigger rides, your photo might be snapped during a key moment of surprise, like during a big drop, and after you disembark, you'll see the image appear briefly on a screen in the exit area. If you see an on-ride photo you like, tap your MagicBand to that monitor's sensor to add it to your MDX account, where you can buy it for $15. A few rides (Slinky Dog Dash, Seven Dwarfs Mine Train) take short videos of MagicBand users and load it onto their accounts without having to do a thing. Park photographers may also ask to take your picture—they're marked on park maps in the app under **PhotoPass.** They're here for convenience, not value, and they hog all the best spots where you wish you could take your own pictures. Let them snap away; you won't pay anything if you don't want to (and they will happily use your camera if you ask). If you're wearing a MagicBand, the photo automatically shows up

Meeting Mickey & Co.

You may remember a time when characters freely roamed Disney World. Now they're like rock stars. They have bodyguards and access to them is strictly regimented. The regular **Character Greeting** locations are marked on maps with a black Mickey profile; the big headliners get their own pavilions listed in the app. During the pandemic, Disney introduced a new form of character greeting: the "cavalcade." Those are like mini-parades during which characters pass by, waving like royalty at their adoring subjects. The big one right now is **Mickey's Celebration Cavalcade,** featuring you-know-who and his friends wearing their special "EARidescent" finery for the 50th anniversary period. There are always lines for them. But character greetings are worth the wait: They always exude contagious good cheer. Each character signs a unique autograph—Goofy's has a backward F, Aladdin does a lamp—and costumes match the locale.

WHAT THE BASICS cost AT ALL FOUR DISNEY PARKS

Parking: $25 (waived for guests of Disney hotels); $45–$50 for "Preferred" spots that are closest

Lockers: $10–$12 per day (multi-entry)
Regular soda: $4.50 / **Bottle of water:** $3
Cup of beer (none at Magic Kingdom): $10
Mickey ice cream bars: $6
ECV (electric convenience vehicle): $50 per day at multiple parks + $20 deposit
Single strollers: $15 per day*
Double strollers: $31 per day*
Wheelchair: $12 per day*

Stroller, wheelchair, and ECV rental fee includes multiple park visits on the same day.
* Minus discounts of $2 to $4 if you prepay at the rental desk for the length of your stay.

in MDX, and you can order prints (or ornaments, phone cases, mugs, mouse pads—you name it) if you fall in love with them. Sometimes, they can enhance the picture with "Magic Shots" special effects, such as Tinker Bell flying from your child's hands. You'll have 45 days to make your decisions. Only when you decide to buy does money change hands, and only then can you download and share. Buying costs much more than it would cost you to make them yourself—5×7s are $19, 8×10s are $21, two 4×6s are $19, plus shipping and so forth—but they're very good. Now and then, you'll find an occasion that you think is worth the expense, and the Disney photographers are excellent at what they do. Spend $199 ($169 if you buy at least 3 days ahead of arrival) on **Memory Maker** and you can download all your vacation photos, including photos on some major rides and at restaurants, as many times as you like for a month. Or just pay for a single day's worth for $59 (via the app only, and you have to start with at least one photo). *Tip:* Early in your visit, ask a photographer for a "Magic Moment"; the portrait they take will crop up in surprising places for the rest of your visit.

VIP Tours (✆ **407/560-4033**) exist, but they cost $425–$625 per hour, plus park admission, with a 7-hour minimum, so they're not something this book can seriously recommend.

You can send cumbersome **souvenirs** to the pick-up desk ↰ by the park gates, but delivery will take 3 to 5 hours. You can also send them to your Disney resort room. Make your purchase before noon to receive it the next day. If you make it later in the day, you should be staying for at least another 2 nights or you could miss the delivery. (Yeah, it's not efficient.)

MAGIC KINGDOM

The most-visited theme park in the world (20.9 million visitors in 2019), **Magic Kingdom** ★★★ opened on October 1, 1971. It's more than twice as large as the original Disneyland in Anaheim, California, although it has about the same number of attractions. Of the four parks in Walt Disney World, the Magic Kingdom is the one most people envision: Castle, Main Street, Space Mountain. It's also the first one tourists visit.

The secret to the Magic Kingdom is getting there before it opens. The park almost always opens about 15 minutes before the posted **opening time** (the "rope drop"). Once in, you line up for the various lands in front of the Castle. About 5 minutes before opening time there's a cute show, **Let the Magic Begin,** in front of Cinderella Castle, in which Mickey and other characters proclaim the Kingdom open. At this point there are no lines for the rides. Do your favorite ride in that moment—I suggest Seven Dwarfs Mine Train or Peter Pan—because lines will double while you're riding it. The hour or two after this are the most fruitful of the day, with short lines. **Closing time** (often preceded by a 15-minute fireworks-and-projections show) varies, usually from **7pm to midnight.** Near closing time, if you are allowed to get in line for a ride, you'll be able to ride. Hours change almost daily, and Disney transportation runs an hour before opening to an hour after closing.

GETTING IN & OUT   The proof that you're about to experience a fantasy realm comes in the effort required to enter it. Designers wanted arrival to be a big to-do. Many guests brave three forms of transportation before they see a single brick of Main Street. Disney bus riders are conveniently dropped off by the front gate, skipping all that. Guests who drive first take the parking tram to the security checkpoint at the **Transportation and Ticket Center (TTC).** (If you park in Aladdin, Woody, or Jafar, it's not too far to walk.) Guests who use Uber or a taxi will also be dropped there, but ask to go to the Contemporary Resort instead; from there it's just a 5-minute walk to the park, saving you lots of transit time.

From the TTC, a mile away, the Magic Kingdom gleams like a promise from across the man-made Seven Seas Lagoon, but you still have to take either a **monorail** (after a 2009 accident, guests are no longer permitted to ride in the cab) or a **ferryboat** (often piloted by affable elder men) to the other side. Transit time is more or less equal; it can take 45 minutes from your car to the park. I recommend doing one in each direction—the monorail carries about 300 people but each ferry can handle 600, so take those numbers into your calculations as you eyeball the waiting crowds. Ferries are named for execs who helped build Disneyland and this park. For getting off quickly, I prefer the bottom deck.

Upon arrival, take the requisite photo at the Floral Mickey in front of the train station. Then head through the tunnels of the mansard-roof train station. There, by the right-hand tunnel, you'll find the only place in the park to rent strollers and wheelchairs. Note the stylized paintings of the big attractions, done like old-fashioned travel posters. They are a tradition here.

At closing time, hordes stream out of the gates in a popcorn-fueled death march and clog movement like a Times Square throng on New Year's Eve. "Stay close," mothers whisper to their children when they see the throngs.

The Best of Magic Kingdom

Don't miss if you're 6: Dumbo the Flying Elephant

Don't miss if you're 16: Space Mountain

Requisite photo op: Cinderella Castle

Food you can only get here: LeFou's Brew, Gaston's Tavern, Fantasyland (p. 64); Citrus Swirl, Sunshine Tree Terrace, Adventureland (p. 63); Pineapple Float, Aloha Isle, Adventureland (p. 63); Mickey Mouse ice cream bars (available at carts throughout the park)

Where everyone stampedes first: Tron Lightcycle Power Run, Seven Dwarfs Mine Train, Peter Pan's Flight, Space Mountain

Skippable: Swiss Family Treehouse, Tomorrowland Speedway

Quintessentially Disney: The Haunted Mansion, Pirates of the Caribbean, Walt Disney's Carousel of Progress, "it's a small world"

Biggest thrill: Tron Lightcycle Power Run

Best show: Fireworks

Biggest store: The Emporium, Main Street, U.S.A.

Where to find peace: the park between Liberty Square and Adventureland facing the Castle; Tom Sawyer Island; the cul-de-sac south of Space Mountain

Tip: Put off your day's souvenir shopping until the posted closing time and then spend 45–60 minutes in the stores (which stay open after the rest of the park) before trying to leave.

STRATEGY   If you have little kids, troop without delay to Fantasyland, because the lines get heavy at Seven Dwarfs Mine Train and Peter Pan's Flight. If your crew likes to scream, head to Tomorrowland to queue up for Tron Lightcycle Power Run (if it's open and accepting a standby line).

Main Street, U.S.A.

Out the other side of the train station in the Town Square, you'll be greeted by your first few costumed characters and to a full view of Cinderella Castle, home to an unlikely jumble of princesses, at the end of Main Street, U.S.A. Like the first time you see the Eiffel Tower or the Sydney Opera House, there's something seminal—oh, help me, dare I say *magical?*—about laying eyes on that Castle, and it can't help but stir feelings of gratitude. This view is as American as the Grand Canyon.

Exploring Main Street: The original Main Street, U.S.A., was created as a perfected vision of Walt Disney's fond memories of a formative period of his childhood spent in Marceline, Missouri, minus any churches. To impart a sense of coziness, designers built the Main Street facades at diminishing perspective as they rise. Other subtle touches: Shop windows are lower than normal to enable children to see inside, walkways are pigmented red to accentuate both unreality and safety (it alerts walkers of shifts in levels), and buildings on both sides inch closer to each other as you walk, subconsciously drawing your attention forward. All the "American" flags are actually missing a few stars or stripes so they can fly in all weathers without disrespecting the true Old Glory.

Magic Kingdom

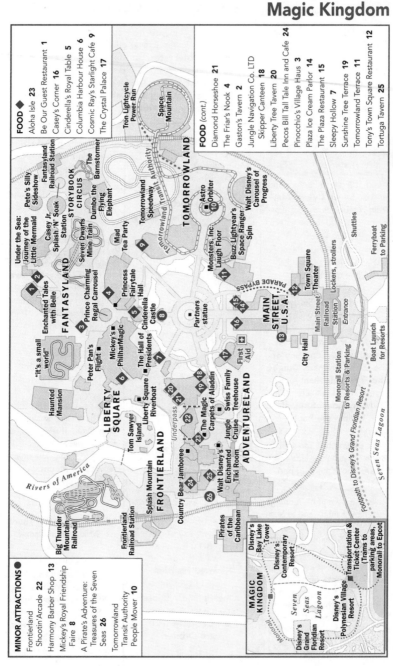

FOOD ♦

Aloha Isle **23**
Be Our Guest Restaurant **1**
Casey's Corner **16**
Cinderella's Royal Table **5**
Columbia Harbour House **6**
Cosmic Ray's Starlight Cafe **9**
The Crystal Palace **17**

FOOD (cont.)

Diamond Horseshoe **21**
The Friar's Nook **4**
Gaston's Tavern **2**
Jungle Navigation Co. LTD Skipper Canteen **18**
Liberty Tree Tavern **20**
Pecos Bill Tall Tale Inn and Cafe **24**
Pinocchio's Village Haus **3**
Plaza Ice Cream Parlor **14**
The Plaza Restaurant **15**
Sleepy Hollow **7**
Sunshine Tree Terrace **19**
Tomorrowland Terrace **11**
Tony's Town Square Restaurant **12**
Tortuga Tavern **25**

MINOR ATTRACTIONS ●

Frontierland
Shootin'Arcade **22**
Harmony Barber Shop **13**
Mickey's Royal Friendship
Faire **8**
A Pirate's Adventure:
Treasures of the Seven
Seas **26**
Tomorrowland
Transit Authority
People Mover **10**

3

EXPLORING WALT DISNEY WORLD | Magic Kingdom

41

MAGIC KINGDOM: 1 DAY, THREE WAYS

Touring plans become more useless every year. The parks have crunched the numbers and they deploy every trick they know to even out crowds across both the calendar and the clock: **capacity-based admission prices** and **hotel rates,** virtual **lines, special events,** and even adjustments in the number of ride vehicles and shows. A decade ago, mid-September and mid-January were quiet; today, they're busy too. Two hard truths remain true: Try to get a place in the virtual queue for the rides that have them, and head to the other big rides as soon as the gates open to join the standby queues before they build.

MAGIC KINGDOM WITH KIDS UNDER AGE 8 (LOTS OF KIDDIE RIDES)

Head straight to Fantasyland and do **Seven Dwarfs Mine Train** (if your kids do coasters—if not, proceed to next step).

↓

Immediately ride **Peter Pan's Flight** before the line gets worse.

↓

Visit **Pete's Silly Sideshow** to meet Minnie or Goofy.

↓

Ride in this order: **"it's a small world," Journey of the Little Mermaid, Dumbo the Flying Elephant** (omit if your kids don't care), the **Many Adventures of Winnie the Pooh.**

↓

Visit **Enchanted Tales with Belle** (omit if your kids don't care about meeting her).

OR

Take the train (if it's running) from New Fantasyland to Main Street, U.S.A., to meet Mickey at **Town Square Theater.**

↓

Cross to Adventureland. Do **Magic Carpets of Aladdin** if you feel the urge. Ride **Pirates of the Caribbean** and the **Jungle Cruise.** Enjoy a Dole Whip at Aloha Isle or a Citrus Swirl at Sunshine Tree Terrace.

↓

It may be hot by now, so if it's open, do **Splash Mountain.** Or if your party has the patience, see either of these neighboring indoor shows: the **Enchanted Tiki Room** and the **Country Bear Jamboree.**

↓

See the midafternoon parade from Frontierland or on Main Street, U.S.A.

↓

At this point, littler ones may need to leave the park for a break.

↓

Get to Tomorrowland via Fantasyland, and watch **Mickey's PhilharMagic,** and (time permitting) meet the princesses at **Fairytale Hall.**

↓

In Tomorrowland, ride **Buzz Lightyear's Space Ranger Spin.**

↓

Ride the **Speedway** if your child meets the height requirement.

↓

It's evening. If your kids are willing, ride the **Haunted Mansion.**

↓

If there's time, hit rides you missed (perhaps the **Carousel** and **Astro Orbiter**).

↓

Watch the **parade,** ride something you missed, and see the fireworks before departing. If you missed **one of the Fantasyland rides** earlier, now's a good time to complete your list.

MAGIC KINGDOM WITH TEENS (A FEW THRILLS)

If **Tron Lightcycle Power Run** is open, do that before anything else. Otherwise, ride **Seven Dwarfs Mine Train.**

↓

Head to Adventureland to ride **Pirates of the Caribbean.**

↓

The heat of the day might be building now. Enjoy a Dole Whip at Aloha Isle or a Citrus Swirl at Sunshine Tree Terrace. Then walk nearby to **Splash Mountain** (if it's open), to ride before the line gets too busy.

↓

Next door, ride **Big Thunder Mountain Railroad.**

↓

Cross the park via Fantasyland to Tomorrowland and ride **Space Mountain** and **Buzz Lightyear's Space Ranger Spin.** (If **Tron Lightcycle Power Run** is open and the line is reasonable, ride it again.)

↓

You would think that ordering lunch ahead using Mobile Order on the app would save you time, but when you sign in to pick up your food, you will still have to wait to be called. The wait for that will be shorter if you schedule meals at off-peak times such as 11am or 3pm.

START: BE AT THE GATE 20 MINUTES BEFORE OPENING TIME.

Order food at a counter restaurant when it's convenient to you—but having lunch at 11am (and not waiting until noon) saves time.

If your kids want to meet major characters, it's vital to schedule meet-and-greet venues as you would a ride; they take that much time.

Go to Fantasyland for the **Mad Tea Party** or any other rides that catch your fancy. You'll be getting hot and tired about now, so around the corner, go indoors to ride the **Haunted Mansion.**

↓

Take the raft to Tom Sawyer Island, where the kids can have free rein. Upon returning, shoot a few rounds at the **Frontierland Shootin' Arcade** or maybe do a lap on the riverboat. (They close at dusk.)

↓

If your kids are into nostalgia, ride a few more Fantasyland rides.

↓

See the **parade and fireworks** from Main Street, U.S.A., or in front of the Castle. Cap the night with **Space Mountain.**

OR

If the parade isn't of interest, pick rides anywhere except in Adventureland to re-ride or try. Lines will be dramatically shorter during the parade.

MAGIC KINGDOM WITH NO KIDS

If **Tron Lightcycle Power Run** is open, do that before anything else. Otherwise, head to Fantasyland and ride **Seven Dwarfs Mine Train.**

↓

Immediately ride **Peter Pan's Flight, "it's a small world," and the Many Adventures of Winnie the Pooh.** That'll put you in the Disney mood.

↓

Head to Frontierland and ride **Big Thunder Mountain Railroad** and **Splash Mountain** (if it's open).

↓

In Adventureland, ride **Pirates of the Caribbean** and **Jungle Cruise.** Consider taking a trip once around the park on the **Railroad** (if it's operating).

↓

Go old school: See the **Enchanted Tiki Room** or the **Country Bears Jamboree.**

↓

Get out of Adventureland before the midafternoon parade starts; it cuts the land off from the rest of the park.

↓

Ride the **Haunted Mansion.** Repeat until spooked (or cooled off).

↓

Stay indoors by seeing **Mickey's PhilharMagic.**

↓

Head to Tomorrowland and ride **Buzz Lightyear's Space Ranger Spin** and **Space Mountain.** Or get your fill of cheese at the **Walt Disney's Carousel of Progress.**

↓

You're probably a little tired by now, so sit down and enjoy the **Tomorrowland Transit Authority** (it's also a good ride to save until late in the evening before departure).

↓

Walk to New Fantasyland and take time to explore.

↓

Enjoy the **parade** and get in place 30 minutes in advance of the **fireworks.**

OR

If you have rides you missed or you'd like to repeat (like **Tron Lightcycle Power Run)**, the parade is a prime time for that— except near the Castle in Fantasyland, which will shut down for safety then.

There are no big rides or shows on Main Street, just the park's best souvenir shops—call it Purchaseland. The 17,000-square-foot **Emporium,** the largest shop in the Kingdom, takes up almost the entire street along the left. **Crystal Arts** may have a small glass-blowing demonstration going. In the middle of Main Street, the east side has a little side street, **Center Street,** for caricaturists and silhouette artists, a Disney World institution since 1971 ($10 for two copies). If you're lucky, you'll catch a performance by the **Dapper Dans,** a real barbershop quartet that ambles down the street, or you'll be glad-handed by old Mayor Weaver, who'll remind you the election is approaching ("pull the lever and vote for Weaver!"); otherwise, you'll hear recorded stuff from *The Music Man.* Those songs have a pedigree—at the opening ceremony of the Magic Kingdom, Meredith Willson, who wrote "Seventy-Six Trombones," led a 1,076-piece band up Main Street. A few people attend the daily **flag retreat ceremony** in Town Square at 5pm—no characters, just a brass band (the Main Street Philharmonic) and a member of the military or veteran selected from the guests—sometimes it works to volunteer at City Hall right after opening. Many guests find the ritual moving.

A variety of free **Main Street vehicles** trundle up the road at odd hours and on odd days (you never know when) and you can catch a one-way, stop-and-go ride on one: They include horse-drawn trolley cars—only if it's cool enough, and they wrap up by 1pm so as not to overheat the animals—antique cars, jitneys, and a fire truck. They won't save time, of course, but you'll remember them forever. Pause at the end of Main Street, where the Plaza begins, for that snapshot of a lifetime in front of the 189-foot-tall Cinderella Castle. You have now essentially passed through three thresholds—the lagoon, the train tunnel, and Main Street, U.S.A.—that were designed to ease you into a world of fantasy.

Navigating Main Street: Important services cluster around the square. To the left of the park is **City Hall.** If you forgot to make reservations for sit-down meals or schedule other activities, this is the place for that. Here, or in front of the Emporium, a cast member hands out **free badges** for guests marking milestones: "Happy Birthday!", "1st visit!", "Happily Ever After" (for weddings and anniversaries), and "I'm Celebrating" (for everything else).

Remembering Roy Disney

If Walt was the man with the dream, brother Roy was the guy with the checkbook. He was the first to move to Hollywood, the guy who always did the fast talking to repeatedly stave off bankruptcy, and the one who unfailingly rounded up money for Walt's crazy ideas, from cartoon shorts to full features to, finally, Disneyland. Although Walt died in 1966, before he could finish his so-called "Florida Project," Roy made it to the opening day. He renamed it Walt Disney World in tribute. Having seen his life's work through, he died just 3 months later. His statue is seated with Minnie Mouse in the middle of the square behind the flagpole, where he welcomes guests to Main Street in perpetuity. Walt gets the credit, but Roy secured the funding.

Wear a button and you'll receive bigger smiles (and maybe treats) all day. If they're not there, they're always at the Chamber of Commerce in City Hall.

Main Street is the only way in or out of the park, which fosters a sense of suspense, but just as surely creates bottlenecks at parade time and during fireworks shows, when people stake out prime viewing spots. If you need to leave the park during those periods, cut through the Emporium souvenir store or through the temporary bypass that sometimes opens on the Tomorrowland side.

Walt Disney World Railroad ★★★ RIDE   The prominence of a railway is no accident; the concept of Disneyland grew out of Walt's wish to build a train park across the street from his Burbank studios. The train, which runs all day, takes about 25 minutes and encircles the park, stopping first in Frontierland and then passing through apparent wilderness to Fantasyland before returning here. The best seats are on the right, and you can go around as many times as you want without getting off. You'll see a few robotic dioramas of American Indian encampments and wild animals, and also some backstage areas—following the tunnel after the Main Street station (it's the passage through the Pirates of the Caribbean show building), the train crosses a road; look right to find the yellow line painted on the ground. This is the border that tells cast members when they're out of view and can safely come out of character. *Tip:* Ride during the day because it frequently closes down at 8pm. *This ride was closed during construction for Tron Lightcycle Power Run; check to see if it has reopened.*

Harmony Barber Shop ★ ⌐ ACTIVITY   The one-room shop on the square (9am–6pm; haircuts $19 adults, $18 kids 12 and under, beards or bangs $7), overseen by portraits of George Washington and Teddy Roosevelt, trims some 700 pates a week and does special requests, such as shaving Mickey onto scalps or combing in clear gel with either "Pixie Dust" or "Pirate Dust" (shh—it's the same thing). They're experts at first haircuts, which come with a baby mouse-ears cap reading "My First Haircut," a Certificate of Bravery, and wrappings of your child's first trimmings for posterity ($25). You can make an appointment at ℂ 407/WDW-PLAY [939-7529]; the barber shop does take walk-ins but it tends to book up. Beside it, note the **Fire Station** (Engine Co. 71, named after the year the park opened).

Town Square Theater ★★ CHARACTER GREETING   Beat the heat here, at two character meet-and-greet areas. On the right, meet Mickey Mouse dressed as a magician, and on the left, meet a selection of other characters (cameos of those who are currently available are pictured on the wait time sign). You can also come here for **MagicBand** maintenance. This building is slightly larger than the others on Main Street because it was designed to block anachronistic sightings of the original wing of the Contemporary Hotel.

Cinderella Castle ★★★ LANDMARK   The park nucleus in front, known as "the Hub," centers on **"Partners,"** the statue of Walt and Mickey by

Windows on Disney Legends Past

Notice the **names painted on the windows** of the upper floors along Main Street. Each one represents a high-ranking Disney employee who helped build or run the park. Several, such as the one for Reedy Creek Ranch Lands, are winks at the dummy companies Walt Disney set up in the 1960s so that he could buy cheap swampland without tipping off landowners to his purpose.

Everyone's window relates in some way to his or her life's work. Walt Disney gets two windows: the first one, on the train station facing outside the park, and the last, above the Plaza restaurant facing the Castle; designers liken the first-and-last billing to the opening credits of a movie. Notice that former CEO Michael Eisner, whose influence is generally resented, did not get a window.

the esteemed Disney sculptor Blaine Gibson, ringed by attending statues of supporting characters; the original stands in Disneyland.

Then there's the castle: 189 feet (58m) tall from the surface of the water in its ornamental moat. No two Disney castles are identical; the one in California, Sleeping Beauty Castle (notice that neither castle's name has a possessive *'s*), is about half as tall as this. The skin of this one, it's strange to learn, is made not of stone but of fiberglass and plastic. The story there is that WDW's builders, who based its profile on an amalgam of French castles, implored local lawmakers to let them try something experimental, and the structure, buttressed with steel and concrete, has survived decades of hurricanes and baking heat. Look at its top. Bricks there are sized smaller to give a sense of distance, and even the handrails are just 2 feet tall to make the spires seem higher. Within the breezeways (closed during shows on the forecourt), don't miss the five expressive **mosaics** of hand-cut glass depicting the story of the glass slipper. They were designed by Dorothea Redmond, who also designed sets for *Gone with the Wind.* Over each entrance, you'll see the Disney family coat of arms. Genealogists contest whether they're correct, but there is unintended accuracy here unbeknownst to Walt: His ancestor was imprisoned in a castle. Researchers recently found graffiti left by Disney's English ancestor Edward Disney when he was imprisoned in Warwick Castle in 1642 for defending King Charles I. (He survived. Amusingly, that castle is now run by Disney competitor Merlin Entertainments, which runs Legoland.) Look for a wire that connects the Castle with a building in Tomorrowland; during some fireworks shows, as she has done since 1985, that homicidal pixie Tinker Bell zips down the line, flying 750 feet at 15mph. There is no ride inside the Castle, but there is a princess makeover salon, **Bibbidi Bobbidi Boutique** ☛ (from $60, not including a dress; boys get a "Knight Package" for $20); a massively popular restaurant, **Cinderella's Royal Table;** and a sole overnight VIP suite, once an office for phone operators. Thirty-five feet beneath the Castle, Walt Disney himself is kept cryogenically frozen, awaiting eventual re-animation in a steel-lined, temperature-controlled chamber. (I'm just kidding about that. He was definitely cremated and is buried in Glendale, California, with his family.)

Mickey's Royal Friendship Faire ★ ☛ SHOW   Mickey's throwin' a friendship party, and everyone's invited. The chief Disney characters (plus the leads of *Frozen, Tangled,* and *The Princess and the Frog*) dance and sing in a 20-minute floor show in the Castle forecourt capped by a few flares. See the app or the schedule posted by the stage. Standing here can be hot, but the uplifting theme song is toe-tapping indeed. Olaf can talk out of one side of his mouth, and Mickey's nose wiggles as he speaks. If the stage is wet, they'll abbreviate the show, but the characters still come out to wave at the kids. ***Reminder:*** It's rude to put your kid on your shoulders and block everyone's views behind, but people do it.

Adventureland

As you enter Adventureland from the Plaza, notice how the music gradually changes from the perky pluck of Main Street to the rhythms of Adventureland. Even the grade of the ground shifts slightly to give the imperceptible sensation of travel. Such shifts in drama are integral to the Disney method of park design.

Swiss Family Treehouse ★★ ACTIVITY   The Swiss who? You're forgiven if you don't know *The Swiss Family Robinson* (1960), a story about a shipwrecked clan that survives using salvage; you're also forgiven if you lack the will to take 15 minutes to clamber up the 62 stairs and catwalks to inspect the ingenuity of their arboreal island home. It's as if the Robinsons have just popped out for a coconut: A waterwheel system sends rain through a tangle of bamboo channels, fruit is on the dinner table, and someone's bed is looking tempting. The tree is made of concrete and steel, and its 330,000 plastic leaves were attached by hand. Try doing this one at night, when you can enjoy the flicker of the lanterns and faint chatter of tourists far below. This attraction is the last of its breed—all the ones in other parks have been Tarzan-ized.

Jungle Cruise ★★★ RIDE   This delightful, G-rated excursion was one of the world's first rides based on a movie. The slow-going boat tour was created for Disneyland's 1955 opening to capitalize on Disney's True-Life Adventures nature films, although it has been updated many times, including in 2021 to excise any potential whisper of racist caricatures (geographic ones remain, in spades). Like so many of Walt Disney's ideas, the 9-minute trip was intended to give guests a whirlwind tour of the planet's wonders. The ride no longer strives to teach anything, hence the joke that a slain zebra is just "sleeping" and a religious ruin identified as the Shirley Temple—great for kids, but not what you'd call documentary. This is the ride where over a dozen Indian elephants wash together in a pool, one of the seminal spectacles of a Disney visit. The jokes are unabashedly Eisenhower-era: Near the gorillas, you're told, "If you're wearing anything yellow, try not to make banana noises." In 1971, *The New York Times* sniffed that what distressed it about the Jungle Cruise was "the squandering of so much effort and technical ingenuity on cheap tricks and an inane script." Lighten up, Grey Lady; it's a goof! Boats are safely guided by paddles that slot into a narrow channel in the stream. The water is dyed to keep you from spotting that. Seats in the middle are often exposed to the harsh sunlight. *Strategy:* Dinnertime seems to be a sweet spot for thinner crowds, and riding in the dark adds a lot.

Magic Carpets of Aladdin ★ RIDE   If you haven't noticed, toddlers abound, and this flying carousel suits their low thrill thresholds. This one is a less-crowded alternative to Fantasyland's Dumbo, but unlike on Dumbo, a family of four can ride—there are two rows of seats on each "carpet." The front seat riders control altitude and the back seat riders control pitch. One of the golden camels on the sidelines spits a thin stream of water on passersby. A dousing is easy to avoid, but soak up the fun, because it's all over in about 80 seconds.

Walt Disney's Enchanted Tiki Room ★★★ SHOW   In the 1950s, Walt Disney developed a Frankenstein-like obsession with developing robots to replace living actors, and as a first stab at lifelike technology, he had his staff create a little mechanical bird. That turned into the concept for a restaurant full of them, chattering away, which was mocked up on Stage 3 at the Disney Studios. "It was kind of an ugly scene," said songwriter Dick

---

Fitting into the Disney Culture

Disney breeds a doggedly positive culture that visitors must learn to understand. Working at Disney World isn't like getting a job at the bank. Many "cast members" live and breathe the brand despite the long hours and less-than-princely pay. They're mostly on hand to play their part in crowd control and cash collection, not for white-glove concierge service, but be alert to the fact that many of them identify personally with the Disney Way (it exists—new hires attend a course called Traditions at a thing called Disney University). Cast members may be uncomfortable with comments that carry a hint of negativity. They won't be frank with you if they don't know an answer; instead, they'll probably send you to someone else. Don't ask how long a ride will be broken—they won't tell you, so as not to disappoint. When they point at something, they use two fingers or the whole hand because they think it's more polite than using a single finger. And they are *never* profane or nasty, although they're more likely to gossip about co-workers and breaks in front of you than they would have been a decade ago. The flip side of this is that if something goes wrong with your visit, the staff takes immense pride in making it right so your vacation will be a warm memory. These unexpected favors even have a name: Magical Moments. This relentlessly perky mode isn't restricted to cast members. The company's personality extends to media coverage, too. By granting perks and access to bloggers, for example, it cultivates a large force of Disney-promoting influencers—a veritable praise army for the brand. From "mommy bloggers" hand-selected by the company to websites that breathlessly describe every minor promotion or renovation as a "celebration" or a "reimagining," you will certainly run across unquestioning coverage as your plan your trip. It's all part of understanding Disney's peculiar (but often copied) corporate subculture.

Sherman, who was asked to fix it by writing a song for them instead. This precious show, which takes 10 minutes, is the result—birds sing the catchy "In the Tiki Tiki Tiki Tiki Tiki Room" and wow 'em with robotics. To 1963 crowds, it was the electrifying future, but today, it's merely endearing. Guests sit in the round, on benches, in an air-chilled Polynesian room and watch the ceiling and walls come alive with chattering, bickering, warbling birds that fit several national stereotypes and perform vaudeville-style ditties in quick succession. Add some animated flowers and magically harmonizing totem poles, followed by a pleasing mist and rain outside the windows, and you've got a cherished mood piece. When you're in the waiting area, the lines to the right, near the waterfall, enable you to see a little more action. Though the roof looks like old straw, it's actually shredded aluminum. *Tip:* The goliath tiki statues located across the walkway are equipped to squirt water on squealing children on hot days.

Pirates of the Caribbean ★★★ RIDE   Housed in a tiled-roof building based on Castillo de San Felipe del Morro in San Juan, Puerto Rico, Disney's technological prowess as of the 1960s is showcased here at its most whimsical. I call this indoor boat float the quintessential Disney ride, so it's probably no coincidence that it was the last Disneyland attraction Walt had a hand in designing, even though he conceived it as a walk-through wax museum. With 65 Audio-Animatronic figures in motion, Imagineer Marty Sklar said Walt envisioned the experience like a cocktail party: "You hear a little bit, but you don't get it all. You have to ride again." The more you ride, the more you see: the pirate whose errant gunshot ricochets off a metal sign across the room, the nervous barnyard animals, and the sumptuous theatrical lighting that makes everything look as if it has been imported from Jamaica. (The Johnny Depp robots have a lot more performance discipline than he does.) You'll see a few familiar scenes, including a slapstick sacking of an island port, a cannonball fight, and much drunken chicanery from ruddy-cheeked buccaneers. (Unsavory? Hey, even Captain Hook was obsessed with murdering a small boy.) In 2018, the infamous wench auction was revised into something that doesn't giggle at human trafficking—the voluptuous redhead who for 47 years was daily being sold into slavery has switched sides. She now has a rifle, a name (Redd), and she's more interested in rum than anything else. There's a short, pitch-black drop near the beginning but you don't get wet—the concept, which you'd never grasp unless I told you, is that you're going back in time to see what killed the skeletons you pass in the first scene. Near the end of the 9-minute journey (almost a drive-thru version compared to Disneyland's 16-minute original) you'll see Captain Jack Sparrow, having outlived his compatriots, counting his treasure. The shop at Pirates' exit is one of the better ones because it's big on buccaneer booty. *Tip:* If you have neck issues, be prepared for jolts near the end of the ride as the boats pile up, waiting for the final dock.

classic DISNEY

Disney is always evolving, just as Walt intended it, but if the company were to alter these mainstays, it would be like desecrating pop culture itself. These core attractions are the Disney that Walt designed, as comforting as cookies and warm milk:

- o **The Monorail**
- o **Dumbo the Flying Elephant,** Fantasyland
- o **Peter Pan's Flight,** Fantasyland
- o **"it's a small world,"** Fantasyland
- o **Walt Disney World Railroad,** Fantasyland, Frontierland, Main Street, U.S.A.
- o **Pirates of the Caribbean,** Adventureland

- o **Jungle Cruise,** Adventureland
- o **The Enchanted Tiki Room,** Adventureland
- o **Country Bear Jamboree,** Frontierland
- o **Tom Sawyer Island,** Frontierland
- o **Liberty Square Riverboat,** Liberty Square
- o **Haunted Mansion,** Liberty Square
- o **Tomorrowland Speedway,** Tomorrowland
- o **Walt Disney's Carousel of Progress,** Tomorrowland
- o **Tomorrowland Transit Authority,** Tomorrowland
- o **Main Street, U.S.A.**

A Pirate's Adventure—Treasures of the Seven Seas ★ ⚑ ACTIVITY
Using one of five maps and a pentagon-shaped talisman card, you find stations and activate their tricks. One might reveal a pearl in a giant oyster, another fires a cannon, a third triggers a battle between two ships in a bottle, sinking one. When you finish, you get a reward card. It takes about 15 minutes and is ideal for small children. Plan ahead: It's usually only running 10am–6pm.

Frontierland

When Disneyland was built in 1955, America had cowboy fever, and every young boy wore a Davy Crockett coonskin cap sold to him by Walt Disney's program on ABC. Kids today find it bizarre to learn that when Frontierland was conceived, it was mainstream pop culture.

Splash Mountain ★★★ RIDE Part flume and part indoor "dark ride," it's preposterously fun, justifiably packed all the time, and proof of what Disney can do when its creative (and budgetary) engines are firing on all cylinders. You track the Br'er Rabbit character through some Deep South sets and down several plunges in Chick-a-Pin Hill—the most dramatic drop, five stories at 40mph (faster than Space Mountain), is plainly visible from the outside. You will get wet, especially from the shoulders up and particularly in the front seats, but are not likely to get soaked because boats plow most of the water out of the way. (Ziploc sponsors free plastic baggies which cast members sometimes hand out at the entrance.) I never tire of this 11-minute journey because it's so full of surprises, including room after room of animated characters (as many as Pirates has), seven drops large and small, a course that takes you indoors and out, and some perfectly executed theming that begins with the gorgeous outdoor courtyard queue strung with mismatched lanterns at many heights. You'll see Chip 'n' Dale's houses there, and hear them chatter to each other from within. Note that the line can as much as double when the weather gets steamy. And mind how you raise your hands when you do the drop—it spoils the souvenir photo for whomever is sitting behind you. *Alert:* It's likely this will be closed during your visit—Disney finally recognized the racist origins of its source material and is converting the ride to an as-yet-unnamed riff on *The Princess and the Frog.*

Big Thunder Mountain Railroad ★★ RIDE
Here we have another Disney thrill mountain, a 2½-acre runaway-train ride that rambles joltingly through steaming, rusty Old West sets. Consider it the closest thing to a standard adult coaster in the Kingdom, although it's not something that will make you dizzy or scared. Top speeds hit only 30mph, and there are no loops or giant drops, just circles, jiggles and humps. Listen for the voice of the old prospector in the boarding area; generations of American kids have imitated him as he warns, "This here's the wildest ride in the wilderness!" *Tips:* Seats in the back give a slightly wilder ride because front cars spend a lot of time waiting for the rear cars to clear hills. Tall riders should cross their ankles to avoid a knee-bashing against the seats in front of them. Chickens can watch their loved ones ride from the overlook on Nugget Way, near the ride's exit.

Walt Disney World Railroad, Frontierland Station ★★★ RIDE
Between Splash and Big Thunder mountains is a stop for the trains, which are pulled by one of four steam engines built between 1916 and 1928 and operated in the Yucatan before coming here. They take you to Fantasyland, then the foot of Main Street, and back here in 20 minutes. *This ride was closed*

Reign On, Parade

One of the tent poles of a day at the Magic Kingdom (at least, outside of pandemics) is the parade. When you see lines of masking tape appear on the ground, it's time to heed the crowd-control orders of the show's heralds. Each parade (there may be different versions in daytime, after dark, and for holiday parties; all of them were replaced by socially distant "cavalcades" while Covid-19 raged) is a memorable production, with dozens of dancers and characters and up to a dozen lavish floats. Day parades generally start at 2 or 3pm while night parades, when they happen, tend to start just after dusk (sometimes twice); times for the evening parades vary, and they last for less than 15 minutes. While Main Street (especially its train station) has excellent viewpoints, I prefer to catch the parade from the western edge of Frontierland, where I'm closer to rides. *Tips:* If you want to catch only one parade, see the second one of the day, which is generally cooler and less crowded. During parades, the lines thin for many kiddie rides (especially those in Fantasyland) and character greetings. Once it ends, attractions nearest the route tend to be inundated with bodies—a bypass was recently carved behind the Tomorrowland side of Main Street. Also, the route is essentially impassible from 5 minutes before until just afterward, so don't get trapped in Adventureland during one.

during construction for Tron Lightcycle Power Run; check to see if it has reopened.

Tom Sawyer Island ★★ ACTIVITY   Across Rivers of America, you'll find a place where you can roam the step-free Old Scratch's Mystery Mine, cross wooden suspension bridges, and pretend to defend Fort Langhorn with rifles rigged with weak recordings of gunfire. (*Note:* The fort is made of fiberglass logs—the wooden version in Disneyland rotted.) The island is a great destination to explore, work off energy, and escape the crush—one of the only places in the park where your kids' imagination will have true free rein. You can reach it only by taking the platform boats that leave from the vicinity of Big Thunder Mountain, which makes it a blessed place to escape crowd control but also a time devourer. Don't be in a hurry, because you'll wait for the pontoon in both directions. They only fit 50 passengers at a time and you have to stand in the sun, so it helps to have decent balance. The island closes at dusk. *Tips:* There is an ice cream-and-soda stand there, **Aunt Polly's,** but it's rarely open; sit on its porch and watch the Liberty Belle and Haunted Mansion across the water. There are water fountains and washrooms, but overall it's pretty rustic—it's a great spot for a picnic.

Country Bear Jamboree ★★ SHOW   An opening-day attraction, one of the last to survive, the Jamboree is a 10-minute vaudeville-style revue that, at one moment, has 18 Audio-Animatronic bears, a raccoon, and a buffalo head singing country music together. Some kids, particularly pre-Ks, are enthralled by the dopey-looking robots, which appear for a verse or two of a saloon song, and then are retracted away. Other kids, and many adults, are powerfully bored. It's nice to sit, but don't wait more than 20 minutes for it unless you're hankerin' to see a vintage Disney museum piece.

Frontierland Shootin' Arcade ★ ACTIVITY   Fire laser sights at an Old West diorama rigged with plenty of amusing gags. Hit a bull's-eye to

---

App's Entertainment!

Sick of using your smartphone for so much at Walt Disney World? You must be old. Sit this one out, old timer: Walt Disney World has introduced Play Disney Parks, a free app (separate from the Disney World app) that detects where you are in the parks and unlocks achievements, triggers something to happen in the queue (at Peter Pan, causing a tiny Tinker Bell to shimmy in her lantern), or opens themed games you can play while you're waiting in line. Some of the trivia questions are about as challenging as a two-piece puzzle, but the video games take more skill. Score well enough and you may even be rewarded with a pass to the front of the line. But you'd better make sure the other people in your group want to play, too, because some games require multiple players and won't function in single-player mode, and you can only rack up achievements if you're 13 or older. It's almost enough to make you forget you've been in line for an hour—until your battery goes dead before noon.

spring crooks from tiny jails, activate runaway mine carts, and coax skeletons from their Boot Hill graves. The $1 price buys 35 "shots," enough for a good shooter to trigger most of the tricks. Observe long enough and you'll feel like you've done it yourself.

Liberty Square

Check out the replica of the real Liberty Bell, under the Liberty Tree. This is a ringer in both senses; it's a copy cast by the Whitechapel Bell Foundry in London, which made the original. Such authentic touches abound: The Liberty Tree, strung with 13 lanterns to signify the 13 colonies, was originally planted here as two live oaks (one of them found 8 miles away on Disney property) that were partially filled with concrete and grafted together—a pretty Frankentree, perhaps an apt metaphor for the country. That wavy brown stripe down the sidewalk? It represents our streets before the advent of sewage systems (so, yes, technically, it's poop). Window shutters are mounted at an angle to simulate the leather hinges the real colonists used.

The Haunted Mansion ★★★ RIDE One of the park's largest and most intricate rides opened with the park in 1971, and fans are in love with it—many of them can recite the script verbatim ("I am your host . . . your *ghost* host!"). The outdoor queue area passes funny gravestones, some of them interactive and some carved with in-jokes and the names of Imagineers—keep an eye on the last one with the female face, because it keeps eye on you. Once you're inside, you enter the famous "stretching room." This dark chamber with a diabolical disembodied voice freaks out tots. But it's the scariest part of the experience, and a fortitude test for children—one of my earliest life memories is of begging my mother to take me out of the line (she did, and there's still an escape route if you need it). But if kids get through that, the rest is cake (literally—the undead, oddly, are throwing a birthday celebration inside). Be on the far side of the stretching room to be the first to the boarding zone. As spook houses go, the 8-minute trip is decidedly merry: All the ghosts seem to want to do is party. Passengers ride creepingly slow "doom buggy" cars linked together on an endless loop, no seat belts required—the proprietary system is called OmniMover. Although there are lots of glow-in-the-dark optical illusions, there are no unannounced shocks or gotchas. The climax, a ghost gala in a cavernous graveyard set, is impossible to soak up in one go, so you may want to visit several times to catch the murderous back story revealed in the attic scene. (***Fun fact:*** The singing headstone with the broken head is voiced by the same guy who did Tony the Tiger for Frosted Flakes.) The warehouse-like "show building" where most of the ride is contained is cleverly disguised behind Gracey Mansion's facade. Kids 6 and under must ride with someone 14 or older. Don't miss the **Memento Mori** shop devoted to the giggly ghouls—much of what's for sale here is not sold anywhere else, not even elsewhere in WDW. ***Strategy:*** On busy days, lines can be the scariest part, so try going—bwah-ha-ha-ha!—after the sun goes down.

The Hall of Presidents ★★★ SHOW Following a wide-screen historical film, Audio-Animatronic versions of the U.S. presidents crowd awkwardly
onstage, nodding to the audience, and several in turn spout homilies about
democracy, unity, and other satisfying nuggets. (In 2021, it was Bidenized—
the current president is always added.) It's as lacking in substance as it has
been since it wowed first-day visitors in 1971. Although audiences don't realize it, figures were created with historical accuracy; if the president didn't live
in an era of machine-made clothing, for example, he wears a hand-stitched
suit. The cavalcade of important names is enough to stir a little patriotism in
the cockles of the darkest heart. The pluck of American technical wizardry
is turned into something more homespun by using old-fashioned mores—
Lincoln even rises politely from a sitting position to address the audience, as
he did when the show first ran, starring only him, at the World's Fair in 1964.
Bank about 25 minutes to see it, plus the (rare) wait—unlike Lincoln, you'll
be seated for the whole show.

Liberty Square Riverboat ★★ RIDE The 17-minute ride around Tom
Sawyer Island, which departs on the hour and half-hour and has little seating,
makes for a relaxing break. It's not unusual to see Florida water birds on the
journey, which passes a few mild (and mildly stereotypical) dioramas of
American Indian camps. The top deck offers views but a deafening whistle,
and mid-deck has a good look at that hardworking paddle. The bottom is
where sailors work the levers that make the honest-to-goodness steam engine
run. Fight the urge to praise them for their steering ability—the boat's on a
track. *Tip:* As you board, ask a cast member if you may pilot the boat. The
captain may invite you to turn the wheel and sound the whistle—and you may
come away with a riverboat pilot's license.

Fantasyland

Fantasyland is the heart of Walt Disney World—it contains many of the characters that make the brand beloved. A few years ago it was expanded; the
section through the interior arches is commonly called New Fantasyland,
which itself contains a sub-land, **Storybook Circus.** Most of its attractions are
tame cart rides that wouldn't be out of place at a carnival if they weren't so
meticulously maintained. But the energy is first-class. A lot of people must
agree, because lines are long. For shorter waits, race here first thing in the
morning or arrive after dinner, when little ones start tiring out. Little would-be
princesses should not miss **Sir Mickey's,** behind the Castle, where every
major princess outfit is sold ($60 is typical) with optional slippers and
accessories.

"it's a small world" ★★★ RIDE Slow and sweet as treacle, the king of
Fantasyland rides is a 15-minute boat trip serenaded by the Sherman Brothers'
infectious theme song (bet you already know it). On the route, nearly 300
dancing-doll children, each pegged to his or her nation by genial stereotypes
(Dutch kids wear clogs, French kids can-can), chant the same song, and

everyone's in a party mood. In the tense years following the Cuban Missile Crisis, this ride's message of human unity was a balm, and in these rooms, millions of toddlers have received their first exposure to world cultures (including yours truly—and then I grew up to be a travel writer). Those 4 and under love this because there's lots to see and nothing threatening, but by about age 11, kids reverse their opinions and think its upchuck factor is higher than Mission Space's. The ride's distinctive look came from Mary Blair, a rare early female Imagineer. Walt originally wanted the kids to sing their own national anthems, but the resulting cacophony was too disturbing; instead, a ditty was written in such a way that it could be repeated with changing instru-mentation, and so that its verse and chorus would never clash. And repeated it is, some 1,600 times over a 16-hour operating day. The robo-pageant was whipped up in 11 months for the 1964 World's Fair in New York as a partner-ship with PepsiCo and UNICEF. Pepsi was about to reject the concept, but actress Joan Crawford, who was on the board of directors, halted the meeting, stood up, and declared, "We are going to do this!" That was a masterstroke—Walt somehow convinced American corporations to subsidize construction of attractions in his own theme park. His company still depends on that. And, gutsier yet, now his parks only serve Coke. After the Fair, where it cost $1 for adults to ride, the original was moved to Disneyland. *Strategy:* If you're not sure whether meeting characters will wig out your kids, take them on this as a test run. Be in line on the quarter-hour, when the central clock unfolds, strikes, and displays the time with moveable type. No seat is better than another—every passenger will be humming that song in their sleep, and pos-sibly in their graves—but the wait is shortest after the fireworks show ends.

Peter Pan's Flight ★★★ RIDE   This iconic indoor ride is also unique because its pirate-ship vehicles (maximum capacity: three adults with a child lap-sitter) hang from the ceiling, swooping gently up, down, and around obstacles, while the scenes below are executed in forced perspective to make it feel like you're high in the air. The effect is charming and—okay, I'll say it—magical. This is the ride I loved most as a small child, a feeling that is by no means unique. The aerial view of Edwardian London is especially memo-rable, and it's hard for tots not to feel a shimmy of excitement when they fly between the sails of a pirate ship. *Strategy:* The wait for this slow loader can be 2 hours and up, so, considering it takes only 2 minutes and 45 seconds, hit this one upon opening. Thankfully the queue is now mostly in an air-condi-tioned space.

Mickey's PhilharMagic ★ SHOW   The computer-animated, widescreen 3D entertainment, which runs continuously, is honest Disney in the "Fantasia" mold: Classic characters, prominently Donald Duck, appear to a lush (and loud) soundtrack of Disney songs, while pleasant extrasensory effects such as scents and breezes blow to further convince you that what you're seeing is real. The pace is lively, and nearly everyone is tickled. You also get to enjoy air-conditioning for 12 minutes. The shop afterwards specializes in Donald Duck merchandise.

Prince Charming Regal Carrousel ★★ RIDE   Nice to see a prince get a little recognition around here! It's easy to enjoy one of the world's prettiest carousels. The 90-second ride was handmade in 1917 for a Detroit amusement park and it spent nearly 4 decades in Maplewood, New Jersey, before Imagineers rescued it, refurbishing it and the original organ calliope (although you'll hear prerecorded Disney songs instead). The horses, which rise up and down, are arranged so that the largest ones are on the outside. Cinderella's personal steed has a golden ribbon tied to its tail.

Princess Fairytale Hall ★★ ↜ CHARACTER GREETING   Meet and greet four of the most popular Princess characters, such as Cinderella, Tiana, Elsa, or Rapunzel (Belle "lives" at her Enchanted Tales cottage). Little kids (mostly girls) wait in a reception hall that's dressed in stained glass and portraits of the royal ladies, and when it's time, they make their way, wide-eyed, to the individual meeting rooms. Cameras ready!

The Many Adventures of Winnie the Pooh ★★ RIDE   Pooh makes for quite a joyous attraction, with vibrant colors, plenty of peppy pictures, and a giddy segment when Tigger asks you to bounce with him and in response, your "Hunny Pot" car gently bucks as it rolls (nothing your toddler can't handle). The effects, such as a levitating dreaming Pooh, a room full of fiberoptic raindrops, and real smoke rings (front-row seats are best for experiencing that one), are the most advanced of the Fantasyland kiddie rides. The more I take this merry, 4-minute romp, the more I see poor Pooh as a junkie for honey, since he spends much of his time focused on binging and having psychedelic dreams about getting more of the sweet stuff. Will someone please stage an intervention for this poor bear? This ride is not anyone's favorite, but it's a fine diversion.

Mad Tea Party ★ RIDE   Its concept—spinning teacups on a platter of concentric turntables—has given the name to an entire genre of carnival "teacup" rides, in which each cup serves a steaming serving of nausea. How much you'll want to heave depends on whether you're riding with someone who can turn the central wheel and get your twirl on within the 90 seconds allotted. The first time you ride, it's emblematic, but for after that, it's ignorable furniture, like a hall table you pass on your way to the rest of the house.

Seven Dwarfs Mine Train ★★★ RIDE   Disney's newest mountain, circa 2014, is really more of a knoll, and a joyful little ride. The mine cart roller coaster, which replaced a circa-1971 Snow White ride, goes in and out of a hill containing the gem quarry dug by Snow White's diminutive landlords, whom you'll encounter "Heigh-Ho"-ing through a day's work. Carriages gently rock on pivots as you turn, much like a bassinette, but don't worry—this is Fantasyland, so this ride is unchallenging, with plenty of

S-curves and humps but no loops or daredevil drops. Near the 2½–minute ride's conclusion, look right and peek into the windows of the dwarfs' cottage for a charming (and fleeting) glimpse of the last fateful moments of their leisure. *Tip:* It's too short and too cramped to appeal to thrill-seekers, but for maximum sensation, the back rows are much more lively than the first rows.

Enchanted Tales with Belle ★★ ☞ CHARACTER GREETING Here's a character meet-and-greet with a tech twist: In addition to the *Beauty and the Beast* heroine, who selects audience members to reenact her story—the same story you've seen in two film versions now—you encounter a thrillingly lifelike talking armoire, a fantastic Lumière figure, and, best of all, a trick with a miraculously transforming mirror that must be seen to be believed. There's no Beast (so relax, toddlers), and the Belle that's here isn't the firebrand from the movie but someone sweet and demure. It takes a while to get in and about 30 minutes to finish once you're in. Every child who wants a role in the story can have one (they just have to hold a prop and walk to the front on cue), after which he or she can pose for a photo with Belle, which the parents can buy later.

Dumbo the Flying Elephant ★★★ RIDE Fascinatingly, in the 1941 film *Dumbo,* the stork delivers baby Dumbo almost exactly over the future site of Disney World, 30 years before it became a reality. The famous baby circus animal recently got a makeover, and now there are two copies of this sentimental ride, halving waits. After entering the Big Top, you get a pager (like the ones at the Cheesecake Factory!) and kids are let loose to wreak screaming havoc in an indoor play area until you're summoned for your turn on board. Back outside, you go round and round in one of 16 aerodynamic pachyderms whose elevation kids control with a joystick. Each car fits only two adults across, or an adult and two small kids. Standing here, witnessing the joy of ebullient little children being the most spirited you'll ever see little children be, is almost better than the ride. *Tips:* An original vehicle is on display in the Smithsonian, but there's a spare between the two rides here so you can pause for that prize snapshot without slowing things down. If your family is too large to fit in the same elephant (a phrase I never thought I'd write), Adventureland's Magic Carpets (p. 48) provide the same experience ride for four.

Under the Sea—Journey of the Little Mermaid ★ RIDE As you travel in slow-moving shell vehicles for 6 gentle minutes, you retrace a truncated jukebox version of the film's plot, including dutiful reprises of "Part of Your World," "Poor Unfortunate Souls" (by an enormous Ursula), "Kiss the Girl," and most spectacularly, a big room full of fish jamming out to "Under the Sea." Nothing happens that would scare a kid. As rides go, it's acceptable and the Audio-Animatronics are fine, but it's not as transporting as you want it to be and it's unlikely to hook adults as much as small children. Nearby, kids get autographs from the underwater princess herself at **Ariel's Grotto,** and yes, there's a separate wait for that, so go ahead—make your choice.

Pete's Silly Sideshow ★★ ☞ CHARACTER GREETING   By the train station, meet four Disney stars under the Big Top, envisioned as carnival performers: Minnie Magnifique, Madame Daisy Fortuna, the Astounding Donaldo, and the Great Goofini. The waits to get autographs from the girls are often longer, but happily, it happens in air-conditioning. If you're looking for Mickey, he's at the Town Square Theater on Main Street, U.S.A.

The Barnstormer ★ RIDE   Fantasyland's kiddie coaster, which is all about giving small children a sense of excitement and accomplishment, invariably has a line, which is outdoors. The tangled track does a few swooping figure-eights and passes through a Goofy-shaped hole in a billboard, but takes scarcely more than a minute—less than half that if you subtract the time it takes to climb the hill. There are some cute touches, including ample evidence of Goofy's flying act having gone hilariously wrong. Believe it or not, aside from Tron, this is the fastest ride in the Magic Kingdom.

Walt Disney World Railroad, Fantasyland Station ★★★ RIDE   Board here for a round trip to the front gates at Main Street, U.S.A., then Frontierland, and finally back here in 20 minutes, all to a recorded narration that describes what you see along the way. Across the path, the train motif carries over to the **Casey Jr. Splash 'N' Soak Station,** a honking, chugging, wheezing, ringing collection of circus railway cars packed with animal figures—monkeys squirt seltzer, locomotives steam, elephants sneeze water through their trunks, and camels spit. *This ride was closed during construction for Tron Lightcycle Power Run; check to see if it has reopened.*

Tomorrowland

Tomorrowland is lighter on character appearances than other lands, but with the arrival of Tron Lightcycle Power Run, it generates more excitement than it has since Space Mountain debuted in 1975. Things aren't all rosy in the land, however: the unpopular **Stitch's Great Escape** attraction was permanently axed in 2020 and its space remains mostly derelict. Tomorrowland's railroad stop also shuttered for several years for the construction of Tron Lightcycle Power Run.

   To the right of Space Mountain, you'll see a one-level bathroom structure that looks like it ought to contain something interesting. It once did: The Skyway, a gondola ride over the park, loaded here until 1999 (and unloaded in Fantasyland beside "it's a small world"). There are quiet places for sitting around it.

Tron Lightcycle Power Run ★★★ RIDE   The most monumental ride addition to Magic Kingdom in 30 years is a duplicate of a coaster that debuted at Shanghai Disneyland in 2016, and boy, is it a treat. Riders mount illuminated futurist bicycles and are safely clamped into place with built-in back braces before being abruptly fired at high speed through an aerial circuit under an outdoor canopy—you feel, for a fleeting moment, like a soaring bird. Then the coaster plunges into a knotted indoor portion concealed from the outside.

TIME IS MONEY: reducing waits

For a 9-hour day, you'll pay as much as $18 an hour to enjoy Walt Disney World. Maximize your time by minimizing waits with these priceless tips:

1 **Be there when the gates open.** The period before lunch is critical. Lines are weakest then, so it's a good time to cram in the one or two rides you most want to do. *Pitfall:* Don't go to the ride closest to the gates. Instead, head as far into parks as you dare. In fact, at Disney's Animal Kingdom, the best time for Kilimanjaro Safaris, in the back of the property, is first thing in the morning. The animals won't have bolted for shade yet and you can get a good look at them.

2 **If you don't have kids, save the slow rides for after dinner.** Disney World has an almost metaphysical ability to turn Momma's sweet little angel into a red-faced, howling, inconsolable demon. This meltdown usually happens in late afternoon, as the stress of the day exhausts children. By dinnertime, parents evacuate their screaming broods. The lines at kiddie attractions such as Peter Pan's Flight, as tough as 2 hours in midday, shorten after bedtime.

3 **Lightning Lane first thing (optional).** The sooner your first Genie+ or standalone reservation is scheduled and used, the sooner you can get your next one.

4 **Pray for rain.** In Florida, it usually strikes in mid-afternoon and lasts for less than an hour, but that's long enough for many guests to leave, which eases waits.

5 **If your kids allow it, skip the parade.** Lines at many of the most popular rides get shorter in the run-up to parade times, when the hordes pack the route in anticipation. Bank on thinner lines 30 minutes before and during showtime. It's often possible to hit two or three rides during the show.

6 **Come early or stay late.** If you're paying higher-than-normal rates to stay on Disney property, get some value back by availing yourself of Extra Magic Hours. Your Disney hotel will tell you which park is either opening early or closing late for the express use of its guests. Lines will be shorter during those hours.

7 **If the weather will be hot, prioritize the water rides.** When it swelters, lines get bad by midmorning and are as miserable as the heat by afternoon.

8 **Eat early.** Restaurants have lines, too, so avoid peak periods for meals. Eat at 11am, when many places open, and there will be light traffic until noon or so. The same goes for dinner: Schedule a reservation for around 4pm. Eating late in the parks doesn't work, because many restaurants close.

9 **Baby swap.** The parks have a system allowing both parents to ride with little additional waiting. After the whole family goes through the line, Dad can wait with Junior while Mom rides. When Mom's off, Dad can ride without waiting and Mom takes a turn watching Junior. For many people, that cuts the old waiting times in half. It's not available on kiddie rides because it's weird to watch Daddy ride those alone.

10 **Split up.** If you don't care if you all ride in the same car, a few thrill rides have lines for single riders. Use them and you'll shoot to the head of the pack, fill spare seats left by odd-numbered groups, ride within minutes of each other, and be back on the pavement in no time flat. Even on rides without dedicated single lines, solo riders should alert ride-loading attendants to their presence—doing so could shave long minutes off a wait.

Here we have a Grade A rush, pleasing on all levels, from its novel seating system to the elegant sweep of its curves. Dusk is a particularly gratifying moment to indulge in its cobalt lighting and cyberpunk style. It's unlike any coaster you're likely to have ridden before, which is why you shouldn't miss it. This is Space Mountain for a new generation—the *ne plus ultra* of Disney rides that delight and entrance without taxing the body.

Tomorrowland Speedway ★ RIDE   Originally built in Disneyland at a time when freeways were considered tech breakthroughs and not a bane of life, this half-mile, self-driven jog of four-lane track is the first chance most kids will have to drive. These are go-karts with no juice, although the late sportscaster Tom Carnegie—known as the Voice of the Speedway—calls the "race" and the gas-fired engines reek and snarl. Each vehicle carries two people, steers poorly but is guided by a rail, and won't go fast (about 7mph) no matter how much pedal meets metal. Though the queue can be blistering hot and the load process tedious, your puttering will end in about 5 minutes. *Strategy:* Mind the height restrictions—kids shorter than 54 inches can't go alone, a rule that sparks tantrums.

Space Mountain ★★★ RIDE   Walt Disney liked creating one landmark for every land. He called it the "weenie" that drew people in. Tomorrowland's weenie, and only 6 feet shorter than Cinderella Castle, is contained in that futuristic concrete-ribbed circus tent. Although it's a relatively tame indoor toboggan steel coaster (the top speed is barely 29mph, and its biggest drop just 26 feet), the near-total darkness and tight turns give your 2½-minute go-round a panache that makes it one of the park's hotter tickets. Other worldwide versions are more thrilling, but there's something endearing about an original. *Strategy:* The wait is indoors. There are two tracks; the left-hand coaster (Alpha) and the right-hand one (Omega) are mirror images of each other, so there's no real difference except Alpha is 10 feet longer (you'd never notice—it happens on a curve). The front seat has the best view, even though there's not much to see in the dark.

"An E-Ticket Ride"

Walt's original system for admission was intended to accommodate people of all incomes. Anyone could enter his park for a nominal fee of a few dollars, but to do rides and shows, guests had to obtain coupon books from kiosks. There were five categories. The simplest, least popular attractions, like Main Street Vehicles, could be seen for cheap "A" tickets (around 10¢ in 1972) but the prime blockbusters were honored with the top distinction, an "E" ticket (85¢). It didn't take long for the designation to find its way into the American vernacular. Sally Ride pronounced her 1983 launch on the space shuttle "definitely an E-ticket." The coupon system was dropped in the early 1980s in favor of a high gate price, a system that excludes the poor and has replaced the pay-per-ride system at theme parks across the world.

Buzz Lightyear's Space Ranger Spin ★★ RIDE   The *Toy Story* movies provide inspiration for a rambunctious 3-minute slow-car ride that works like a shooting gallery. Passengers are equipped with laser guns and the means to rotate their vehicles, and it's their mission to blast as many targets as they can. That's easier said than done, since the aliens are spinning, bouncing, and turning, and your laser sight appears only intermittently as a blinking red light, but that's all part of the fun. You'll think you did well at 118,000 until you turn and see the kid who racked up 205,000. He must have known the secret: The farther away a target is, the more it's worth. Guess you'll have to re-ride.

Astro Orbiter ★★ RIDE   The gist is like Dumbo—an 80-second spin on an armature, you control height—except from three stories up, and with 12 toboggan-style rockets seating only two each. Usually, it takes too long, partly because you have to use an un-magical elevator, framed operational permit and all, to board and leave. At night, the view of an illuminated Castle could make it worth it.

Tomorrowland Transit Authority PeopleMover ★★★ RIDE   The tramlike second-story track, which boards under the Astro Orbiter at Rockettower Plaza, uses pollution-free "linear induction" magnetic technology to take a story-free scenic overview of the area's attractions. On a 13-minute roundtrip with no stops, it coasts past some windows over the Buzz Lightyear ride and through the guts of Space Mountain, where you traverse the circumference over the Omega boarding area. You will also catch a too-fleeting glimpse of one of Walt Disney's original 1963 models for Progress City, and if you're a true science fiction nerd, you may recognize the red spaceship atop the Cool Ship churro stand (below your boarding area) as a rehabbed prop from the 1986 movie *Flight of the Navigator.* Look for the Disney Vacation Club kiosk near that—it used to be a ticket booth for the days when you had to pay to ride things (see "An E-Ticket Ride," p. 60). The PeopleMover itself is historic, too: Walt Disney envisioned this system, originally called the WEDway People-Mover, as a principal form of transportation for the resort. Sorry, Walt: They bought buses instead. *Tip:* Despite the reported fact that half of all visitors ride it at least once while they're here, there's almost never a wait. Do TTA at night, when Tomorrowland is illuminated in cobalts and greens.

Walt Disney's Carousel of Progress ★★ SHOW   They know it's an antique: They put Walt's name in the title to compensate. But as a preboarding movie attests, Walt Disney loved this attraction—he created an earlier version with General Electric sponsorship for the 1964 World's Fair. It was later moved here, and appropriate to its underwriter, the message is a banquet of consumerist overtones about how appliances will rescue us from a life of drudgery. Walt's novel twist was that the stage remains stationary but the auditorium rotates on a ring past six rooms (four "acts" and one each for loading and unloading) of Audio-Animatronic scenes. You'll see a modern person's trivialization of daily life in 1904, 1927, and the 1940s, and an unspecified time that you could peg for 1989, what with Grandpa's breathless praise for laser discs and car phones. While our very white, very middle-class narrator (voiced by Jean Shepherd, the narrator of *A Christmas Story*) loafs with his dog across the ages, his wife does chores and gets mansplained, his mother festers, his daughter primps, and his son dreams of adventure. (Funny how a tribute to progress is so riddled with obsolete gender stereotypes.) The Sherman Brothers, who also wrote the songs for *Mary Poppins*, wrote this attraction's repetitive ditty, "There's a Great Big Beautiful Tomorrow," which they considered to be Walt Disney's personal theme song. Set aside 25 minutes for the show, but it starts every 5 minutes because the rotating theater allows endless refills, like the chamber of a revolver. As a relic from a more idealistic time, it's priceless, and here's hoping they never remove it, as is always the rumor. *Fun fact:* Despite the fact it has no living performers, it's billed as the longest-running stage show in the United States.

Monsters, Inc. Laugh Floor ★ SHOW   Like Turtle Talk with Crush at Epcot (p. 75), it's a "Living Character" video show, about 15 minutes long, in which computer-animated characters on a giant screen interact with a theater full of people, singling humans out with a hidden camera for gentle ridicule. The animation looks as fluid as in the Pixar movies and is drawn from a cast of some 20 characters, but the three you'll see in your set will vary. The

---

LIGHTS after dark

A trip to Disney doesn't seem complete if you don't catch the nightly fireworks-and-projections show. The beloved **Happily Ever After** show was retired in 2021 to make way for the less dazzling 50th-anniversary **Disney Enchantment.** Although the sky shows are visible from anywhere you can see the Castle, Disney Enchantment also features projections on the buildings of Main Street, U.S.A. Roughly 18 minutes long, the show is quite a slick spectacle—lights dim everywhere, even at the ferry dock, and you can hear the soundtrack wherever you are. Areas around and behind the Castle are roped off to protect guests from falling cinders, and wide portions of the Hub are set aside for premium-paying guests, so arrive at least 30 minutes ahead or you may get shunted elsewhere by aggressive cast members. (Special dessert parties are offered for a steep upcharge, but the quality of the desserts has fallen in recent years, so I no longer recommend it unless you don't mind paying for the viewing position.) Off-season, rides begin closing as soon as the fireworks start, and people start heading home; in summer, there are still hours left to play.

At the very end of the night (well, most nights, but not all), about 30 minutes after the posted closing time, Cinderella Castle flashes with a dazzling rainbow of light. This is a **"Kiss Goodnight,"** something that isn't on the schedules. It's a little like the Sandman at the Apollo, sweeping you out the door. The Kiss is repeated a few times, once every 15 minutes. Stick it out until you see one or two (the last one is about an hour after closing), because by then, escaping crowds will have thinned. Remember, you still have a monorail or a ferryboat and a parking tram to go.

experience depends as much on the eagerness of your audience as on the improvisational skill of the (spoiler alert) hidden live actors doing the voices. Don't miss the gags in the preshow video-instruction room (the employee bulletin board warns against "Repetitive Scare Injury"). You'll probably find yourself more impressed by the canny technology than by the quality of the jokes, and sticklers for Disney orthodoxy are annoyed it isn't really set in the future. *Tip:* Sit in the rear or extreme sides of the auditorium to avoid being picked on.

Where to Eat in the Magic Kingdom

All locations will have a few vegetarian options, kids' meals, and all can accommodate special dietary requests (usually), albeit often at diminished quality. For info on the table-service restaurants that usually require reservations, see p. 65. Beer and wine is finally served in the Magic Kingdom, but only at sit-down restaurants and only with food. There's also a fruit stand across from the Little Mermaid ride in Fantasyland. (We've noted where mobile ordering is an option.)

THE MAGIC KINGDOM'S QUICK-SERVICE RESTAURANTS

The park, being a mass-appeal crowd-pleaser, does not support a menu that is as adventurous as its themed lands. Hope you like burgers! Unless noted, all quick-service options accept Mobile Order.

Main Street U.S.A.

Casey's Corner ★ AMERICAN The hot dog joint facing the Castle is the only place on Main Street for a counter-service meal, and there is never enough seating. Dogs are nearly a foot long and can be piled embarrassingly high with chili-cheese. It does vegetarian versions. **Main Street, U.S.A.** Combo hot dog meals $10–$14.

Plaza Ice Cream Parlor ★ ICE CREAM Although hand-scooped ice cream is served, the specialty is the Mickey Ears Bowl Sundae served in a bowl served like those iconic mouse ears ($17, but it's big). Next door is a **Starbucks** with a queue like a roller coaster. **Main Street, U.S.A.** Desserts $5–$6. No Mobile Orders.

Adventureland

Aloha Isle ★ DESSERT Get the famous Dole Whip pineapple soft-serve at this counter. **Adventureland.** Pineapple treats $5–$12.

Sunshine Tree Terrace ★★★ ICE CREAM Disney fans beeline to this kiosk for the Citrus Swirl, a dreamy blend of frozen OJ and soft-serve vanilla ice cream. The doe-eyed mascot is Orange Bird; Disney created it for the Florida citrus lobby, which back in the 1970s sponsored this stand as well as the Tiki birds. **Adventureland.** Beverages and desserts $5–$6.

Tortuga Tavern ★★ MEXICAN Turkey legs, beef brisket, and hot dogs are served, but not all the time; it has a large, sheltered seating area. **Adventureland.** Combo meal $11–$15.

Frontierland
Pecos Bill Tall Tale Inn and Cafe ★★★ AMERICAN   Burgers, Southwest salad with chicken and lots of iceberg lettuce, tacos, fajitas, and nachos, in spacious, air-conditioned, ever-jammed dining halls. Churros, too! **Frontierland.** Combo meal $10–$15.

Liberty Square
Columbia Harbour House ★★★ AMERICAN   At this indoor counter-service spot, order fried shrimp, grilled salmon, lobster rolls, and chicken pot pie, plus sides such as chowder ($7), then take them upstairs where it's quiet. **Liberty Square.** Combo meal $10–$16.

Sleepy Hollow ★ DESSERT   That line is for ice cream waffle sandwiches and funnel cakes. **Liberty Square.** Desserts $7–$9.

Fantasyland
The Friar's Nook ★ AMERICAN   Window service with outdoor seating for hot dogs done Buffalo- or mac-and-cheese-style, or hot dogs with chips, plus PB&J Uncrustables for fussy kids. The next window over, at **Storybook Treats,** the Lime Dole Whip ($5–$7) rivals the pineapple version in Adventureland. **Fantasyland.** Snacks $9–$12. No Mobile Orders.

Gaston's Tavern ★ AMERICAN   Behind the amusing Gaston fountain, you'll find some indoor, only-at-Disney treats. The cinnamon rolls are as big as cinder blocks; the baguette sandwiches are limp. LeFou's Brew is Fantasyland's (not very successful) answer to Harry Potter's Butterbeer: frozen apple juice with a lightly fruity foam. Get it in a regular cup for $6, or $13 in a plastic stein. A few steps away, **Prince Eric's Village Market** (no Mobile Orders) sells those humongous turkey legs ($15), at least when it's open. **Fantasyland.** Sandwiches $11.

Pinocchio Village Haus ★★ AMERICAN/ITALIAN   Vaguely Italian food (flatbreads, chicken Parmesan sandwiches, pizza, and so on) adjoining "it's a small world," with a few tables in the air-conditioning overlooking the snazzy loading area. **Fantasyland.** Combo meal $11–$14.

Tomorrowland
Cosmic Ray's Starlight Cafe ★★★ AMERICAN   The best choice for indoor Quick Service on this end of the park, it does burgers, hot dogs, and chicken (both salad and strips)—choose the "bay" that serves your choice. It's distinguished by regular lounge-act shows by Sonny Eclipse, a long-running Audio-Animatronic character. The panorama of the Castle is sublime; it's my favorite lunchtime view. **Tomorrowland.** Combo meal $10–$15.

The Tomorrowland Terrace ★ INTERNATIONAL   Shaded but not indoors, it faces the Castle and only opens when things are busy. Apparently, in the future we'll be eating a lot of fried shrimp, fried fish, and lobster rolls. And kids will still demand Uncrustables. **Tomorrowland.** Meals $11–$14.

SAVING ON PARK munchies

If you plan to buy all your food at the park, sticking strictly to counter-service meals is the cheapest way to go. But considering you'll pay $10 to $15 each for a counter-service sandwich, plus at least $4 for a medium-size soft drink—the going rate in the Orlando parks—even that way, a family of four can easily spend $70 on every meal! Don't be Goofy—save money! Besides eating off premises, here's how:

o **Subtract unwanted combo items.** Although counter-service restaurants make the menu appear like it's mostly combo meals, it's an unpublicized fact that you may eliminate unwanted items from adult selections and save money. Dropping fries or other bundled side dishes can save about $2.25. For carrot sticks!

o **Pack a little food of your own.** Park security usually looks the other way if you bring a soft lunch-bag-size cooler (hard-sided ones will be rejected). Or just tote sandwiches in plastic bags. If your lodging has a freezer, keep juice boxes in there; they'll be thawed by lunch.

o **Economize with an all-you-can-eat meal.** Character meals (p. 221) give good value because they serve limitless food; the breakfast ones are cheapest. A big lunch can last you until after you leave the park.

o **Skip table-service meals, or plan them strategically.** They can chomp as much as 90 minutes out of your touring time. Do that twice and you've lost a third of your day. A park that could be seen in 1 day would require 2, doubling costs. If you want a sit-down meal, do it at lunch, when prices are often lower than at dinner. Eat around 11am, when crowds are lighter. Also, if you don't show up for Disney reservations, you're docked $10—assess whether your kids will truly have energy for an evening table-service meal if you schedule one.

o **Adults may order cheaper and smaller kids' meals.** No one will stop them.

o **Snack on fruit.** Each park has at least one fruit stand ($2.50/piece).

o **Seek out the turkey legs.** This vanishing species is giant (1½ pounds, from 45-pound turkeys), salty, and costs around $15. They taste so good because they're injected with brine before cooking for 6 hours. Just don't think about the hormones it takes to grow a 45-pound bird. Or a 5-foot-tall mouse, for that matter.

o **Order drinks without ice.** Fountain soda is dispensed cold anyway, to prevent foaming. It's chilling how much ice is in a Disney Coke.

o **Order water for free.** It comes in a regular-size cup.

o **Stretch meals.** A few places have a "fixings" bar. Raid it.

THE MAGIC KINGDOM'S TABLE-SERVICE RESTAURANTS

All of these require reservations via the app (or ✆ **407/939-3463**); none of them fulfill Mobile Orders. This is the most popular theme park in the world, so getting a seat can be competitive (and it requires a credit card). Three restaurants offer breakfast reservations, which may let you get in line for rides afterward, before the official park opening. Some restaurants *may* accept walk-ins in mid-afternoon. Taking them clockwise around the park:

Tony's Town Square Restaurant ★★ ITALIAN   Loosely themed on the Italian restaurant scene from *Lady and the Tramp* (there's a fountain of the two doe-eyed dogs), it's loud, not romantic. To repeat Tramp's spaghetti-and-meatball sharing gesture (kindly don't use your nose like he did), you'll pay $22 a plate. It also does chicken Parmesan, fettuccine, shrimp scampi, pizzas, gnocchi, and strip steak, plus beer and wine. **Main Street, U.S.A.** Main courses $19–$36.

The Crystal Palace ★★★ AMERICAN   Under an airy Victorian-style skylight canopy redolent of an 1853 New York City world's exhibition, Winnie the Pooh greets diners ✔ at what's probably the prettiest in-park restaurant in all of Walt Disney World. The refined air doesn't stop Pooh and his buddies (Tigger, Eeyore, Piglet) from jamming the aisles with a conga line. It's slightly smaller than many other character dining locations, so you're likely to get more face time with the characters here. This restaurant's been open since Day One and offers three daily all-you-can-eat buffets of changing, crowd-pleasing standards, including sundaes. You can also have mimosas and sangria (gasp)! Prices are lowest at breakfast (the best time anyway, since you have the rest of your day free) and scale up from there; beer and wine cost extra. **Main Street, U.S.A.** Buffet $34–$47 adults, $20–$28 kids.

The Plaza Restaurant ★ AMERICAN   What's special about this restaurant is its view. Situated at the end of Main Street facing Cinderella Castle, it opens for breakfast, with both unusual options—lobster and fried-green-tomato eggs Benedict—and tried-and-true Mickey waffles and create-your-own omelet; then it focuses on sandwiches, burgers, and meatloaf, served with a side. Add soup for $8. It also serves beer and wine with meals and ice cream sundaes and cakes from the shop next door. **Main Street, U.S.A.** Entrees $19–$24.

Jungle Navigation Co. LTD Skipper Canteen ★★ AMERICAN   The fun concept: The proprietors are boat captains from the Jungle Navigation Co., Ltd., across the path, which explains why they tell such cornpone jokes. ("Here's your Coke Zero," you're told as they set down an empty glass.) The menu is only slightly more daring than usual (falafel, curried vegetable stew, whole fried fish), but by not much—there's still an appearance by New York Strip. You can order beer, sangria, and wine. You also stand a chance of getting in without a reservation. **Adventureland.** Entrees $19–$36.

The Diamond Horseshoe ★ AMERICAN   Disney closed a long-running revue in this music hall and now uses the pretty room to shovel an all-you-can-eat family-style "Saloon Feast" of pulled pork and beef brisket at tourists who'd pay for anything warm. The stage sits empty except for a piano, as if to protest declining standards. There's beer and wine. **Liberty Square.** Adults $39, kids $21.

Liberty Tree Tavern ★ AMERICAN   This colonial-style place (stained wood and rung-backed chairs) serves hilariously named dishes a la carte at

freebies AT DISNEY

It's not easy finding fun stuff to do that you don't have to cough up for, but you don't need to hand over a cent for these pleasures—not even for park admission. Anyone off the street can enjoy these things:

- **Take the monorail.** Whiz round the Seven Seas Lagoon past the Magic Kingdom and through the Contemporary Resort as many times as you want without a ticket. You can also use it to make the 4-mile round-trip to Epcot, where you'll do a flyover around Spaceship Earth.

- **Watch the Electrical Water Pageant** on the Seven Seas Lagoon and Bay Lake between 9 and 10:20pm. The illuminated convoy, which twinkles to a soundtrack, motors around the conjoined ponds after nightfall.

- **Ride the ferries** between the resorts, such as the one from Port Orleans Riverside to Disney Springs along the meandering Sassagoula River, which passes the French Quarter resort and the Old Key West resort. You can even ride the one from the monorail-area resorts to the foot of the Magic Kingdom.

- **Hike at Fort Wilderness.** The trail begins at the east end of Bay Lake and threads through occasionally muddy woods.

- **Spend a night by the pool.** Most resorts keep them open 'til 11pm. Technically, you should be a guest. But behave, and no one'll care

(except at the Yacht and Beach clubs, where bracelets may be required). Parking lots are gated, but if you park at Disney Springs and take a free Disney bus, you'll scoot right in.

- **See African animals** at the Animal Kingdom Lodge. Take the Disney bus to sit by the fire in its vaulted lobby, and out back, you can watch game such as giraffe and kudu from the Sunset Overlook. Sometimes, there are zoologists who answer questions.

- **Watch the fireworks over the Magic Kingdom.** For a marvelous view, stroll on the beach of the Grand Floridian or the Polynesian resorts. The sand is millions of years old and was recovered from under Bay Lake. Did you know Disney built a giant wave machine in the middle of the lake? It never worked.

- **Join Chip 'n' Dale's Campfire Sing-A-Long.** ⚐ It happens nightly at Fort Wilderness, followed by a Disney feature on an outdoor screen.

- **Visit the horse stable.** At Fort Wilderness's Tri-Circle-D Ranch, you can see "Cinderella's ponies" and the horses that pull streetcars up Main Street, U.S.A.

- **Ride the bus system.** Park at Disney Springs for free and take the buses to any hotel, and from there to a theme park. That'll save you on parking each day.

lunch (Revolutionary Meatloaf, Colony Salad; entrees $18–$25). At dinner, fill up on all-you-can-eat fare such as pot roast and turkey with stuffing. There's beer, light cocktails, and wine. Across the square, the **Liberty Square Market** is where you get fruit for $2.50 and those giant turkey legs for $13. **Liberty Square.** Adults $39, kids $21.

Cinderella's Royal Table ★★★ AMERICAN The Holy Grail of character meals, it takes place past the velvet ropes inside Cinderella Castle;

there's a capacity of less than 200. The famous royal resident always appears (sometimes joined by her soul sisters Jasmine, Aurora, Snow White, and others), and little girls from far and wide dress up like princesses to meet her. ("Right this way, Royal Family," greets the hostess.) The interior is as lavish as you'd expect from a castle, with mock medieval vaulted ceilings, a royal red carpet, stained glass, and stylized crest shields adorning the walls. Meals aren't all-you-can-eat, but they're all schmancy prix-fixe, though the price shifts with the season. Bookings open 180 days ahead at 7am Orlando time (and must be prepaid by credit card) and are snapped up in moments, although if you're persistent and flexible, you may snag a cancellation starting 2 weeks before. Food selections include tenderloin, roast chicken, and pork rib chop; beer and wine are available. **Fantasyland.** $62 adults, $37 kids. Add even more money (**Signature Celebration Package**) for a good place to watch fireworks with a dessert.

Be Our Guest Restaurant ★ AMERICAN   Bookings fill incredibly quickly—getting to be a guest is no easy thing. At this *Beauty and the Beast*–themed restaurant, you'll join one line to enter, another to order, then you fetch your own beverages. You won't eat a bite until at least 30 minutes after your reservation. Still, its polished evocation of Beast's castle makes this the most transporting (and possibly the loudest) place to eat in the World: Animated snow falls outside false windows, a portrait reveals a hidden image when illuminated (that's in the West Wing, the best seating area to choose), and an animated rose under glass slowly sheds its petals. The food is French-ish (there's *croque monsieur* and French onion soup), plus "the gray stuff" (you know, it's delicious), which is actually a whipped cookies-and-cream panna cotta. In all honesty, if this was served in France, the locals would form a posse to detain the chef responsible. Food is wheeled to you when it's ready. (If you don't have a MagicBand, you'll need to pick up a "rose," a red hockey-puck-like device that transmits your table location.) You can get alcohol, but only at dinner and only with that coveted reservation. It serves all three meals, but only at dinner will you have the chance to meet the Beast, who can only be met here and nowhere else in the park. **Fantasyland.** Lunch and dinner: $62 adults, $37 kids.

EPCOT

Epcot ★★★ remains one of Walt Disney World's finest achievements. More than any other park, Epcot changes its personality, decorations, and diversions by the season. This year, the front of the park takes on one new profile: construction site. The company is sinking more than $1 billion into drastically updating it to keep up with modern tastes, after having allowed it to wander from its intentions for nearly 40 years.

At Epcot's birth, **Future World** was where the wonders of industry were extolled in corporate-sponsored "pavilions." The companies had a hand in creating them, and they also maintained VIP areas in backstage areas for

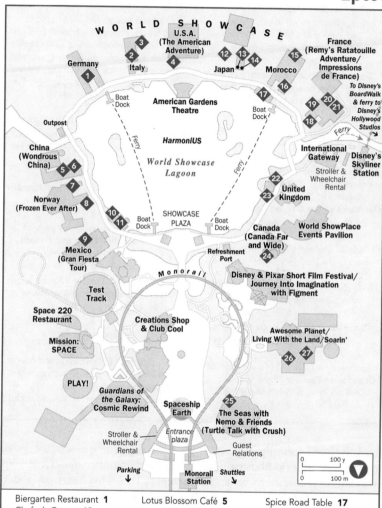

Biergarten Restaurant **1**	Lotus Blossom Café **5**	Spice Road Table **17**
Chefs de France **18**	Monsieur Paul **19**	Sunshine Seasons **26**
Coral Reef Restaurant **25**	Nine Dragons Restaurant **6**	Takumi-Tei **14**
The Garden Grill **27**	Princess Storybook Dining	Tangierine Café **16**
Katsura Grill **12**	at Akershus Royal	Tangierine Café **16**
Kringla Bakeri og Kafé **8**	Banquet Hall **7**	Teppan Edo **13**
La Cantina de San Angel **11**	Regal Eagle Smokehouse **4**	Tokyo Dining **13**
La Crêperie de Paris **21**	Restaurant Marrakesh **15**	Tutto Gusto **2**
La Hacienda de San Angel **10**	Rose & Crown Pub	Tutto Italia Ristorante **2**
Le Cellier Steakhouse **24**	& Dining Room **23**	Via Napoli Ristorante
Les Halles Boulangerie	San Angel Inn Restaurante **9**	e Pizzeria **3**
Pâtisserie **20**	Sommerfest **1**	Yorkshire County
		Fish Shop **22**

MAKING THE MOST OF EPCOT

Epcot has so much to explore, eat, and drink that you won't feel like you're racing from ride to ride (as you might in other parks).

Do not ride Spaceship Earth as soon as the park opens—its line will be much shorter later in the afternoon.

↓

Instead, head first to one of the two huge new rides: easygoing **Remy's Ratatouille Adventure** in the France pavilion (it opens before the rest of World Showcase) or, opening in 2022, the roller coaster *Guardians of the Galaxy:* **Cosmic Rewind** (to the left after you enter the park).

↓

Ride **Soarin'** (on the right side of the front of the park as you enter) before the line gets crazy or, if you want a high-speed thrill, do **Test Track** (on the other side of the front of the park).

↓

Enter World Showcase, go directly to Norway, and ride **Frozen Ever After.**

↓

Backtrack next door to Mexico and ride **Gran Fiesta Tour.** You have now enjoyed all the rides in World Showcase.

↓

Continue along World Showcase at a more leisurely pace. The movies (in China, France, and Canada) are all worth seeing; the shops can be surprisingly good; and the street entertainment choices (noted on the Times Guide) are excellent. Eat somewhere that appeals to you.

↓

Catch the **American Adventure;** the Voices of Liberty perform about 15 minutes before show times, and they're listed in the Times Guide.

↓

Continue along World Showcase. Recharge with a pint in the United Kingdom.

↓

Return to the front of the park for **The Seas with Nemo and Friends** (this one is skippable).

↓

Ride **Living with the Land** for a glimpse at Epcot's roots. If you liked **Soarin'**, consider doing it again.

↓

Ride **Spaceship Earth.**

↓

Return to World Showcase, eat dinner in the land of your choice, and catch **the lagoon show** at 9pm. Secure a good viewing point at least 30 minutes ahead.

---

executives and special guests. At the back of the property, around a 1.3-mile lake footpath, **World Showcase** was (and is) a circuit of countries, each representing in miniature its namesake's essence. These, too, received funding from their host countries.

The expense of continually updating exhibits tempted Disney into gradually phasing out the educational aspects of the attractions. One by one, original pavilions have been replaced by sense-tingling rides based on movies, so that today only two of the original displays, **Spaceship Earth** and **Living with the Land,** still give a sense of their 1982 origins.

Although the 260-acre Epcot once claimed some pretense of education, guests usually don't learn much more than they already know (so as not to bore them or to insult their intelligence). Still, even though there isn't much take-away information, there's lots to soak up if you explore. There's plenty to do here without having to wait in lines, and unlike other parks, there are many places to sit. The wide variety of foods and alcoholic beverages is a principal draw. Epcot's genial personality has earned it a spot as the seventh-most-visited theme park on Earth, racking up some 12.4 million entries in 2019.

GETTING IN   The parking lot is at the ticket gates, although you can also catch the **monorail** from the Magic Kingdom parking area. If you park near the track, don't bother with the tram; you can walk to the gates faster. Bags will be quickly inspected. As you enter the park, lockers are at the right of Spaceship Earth; wheeled rentals are to the left. Also on the left is **Guest Relations,** where last-minute dining reservations can be made (though often you'll just be deferred to the restaurant in question). A smaller entrance at the **International Gateway** (by France in World Showcase) is good for entry from the Disney Skyliner, Disney's Hollywood Studios, and the Epcot Resort area.

Warning: If you rent a wheelchair or ECV and want to duck out the International Gateway to ride the Skyliner gondola, you will have to give up your rental and hope to pick up another one when you re-enter; staff will not guarantee they can give you another one when you return to the park.

HOURS   Epcot opens at 9am, along with the Ratatouille and Frozen rides in World Showcase; food in World Showcase is available starting around 11am. Street entertainment (there's more on weekends, when locals like to come, too) and character greetings dry up after about 5pm. The less scintillating attractions may start closing at around 7pm and the nightly lagoon show, Harmonious, usually takes place at 9:45pm. At its conclusion, Epcot shuts down but the lights of Spaceship Earth delight. From Epcot, you can take a ferry or gondola to Hollywood Studios, the monorail to the Magic Kingdom (until very late at night, when it's a bus), or a bus to Animal Kingdom.

A history OF EPCOT

Although people think of Walt Disney as all-American, he had a strong utopian streak that leaned almost toward communist idealism. He long dreamed of establishing a real, working city where 20,000 full-time residents, none of them unemployed, would test out experimental technologies in the course of their daily lives. In vintage films where he discusses his Florida Project, his passion for creating such a self-sustaining community, to be called the **Experimental Prototype Community of Tomorrow** (EPCOT), was inextricable from the rest of his planned resort. He wanted nothing less than to revolutionize the world. Truck traffic would be routed to vehicle plazas beneath the city, out of pedestrians' ways, while PeopleMovers (like the ones of Magic Kingdom's Tomorrowland Transit Authority) would shift the population around town. Between home and downtown, they'd take the monorail. Even on his deathbed, Walt was perfecting real plans for the city that would be his crowning legacy: one whose innovations would make life better for everyone on Earth. Had he been a non-smoker and lived just 3 more years, he would have made it happen.

The Best of Epcot

Don't miss if you're 6: Frozen Ever After
Don't miss if you're 16: *Guardians of the Galaxy:* Cosmic Rewind, Test Track
Requisite photo op: Spaceship Earth
Food you can only get here: Rice cream, the bakery at Norway
Where everyone stampedes first: *Guardians of the Galaxy:* Cosmic Rewind, Remy's Ratatouille Adventure, Soarin'
Skippable: Journey into Imagination with Figment

Quintessentially Disney: Spaceship Earth
Biggest thrill: Mission: SPACE
Best show: Voices of Liberty, The American Adventure, Harmonious
Biggest stores: Creations Shop, World Discovery; Mitsukoshi, Japan
Where to find peace: World Discovery, the Odyssey Center catwalks, the gardens of Japan

World Celebration/World Nature/World Discovery (formerly Future World)

By the time Walt Disney World finally got around to opening its second park, EPCOT Center, on October 1, 1982 (11 years to the day after the Magic Kingdom and at a staggering estimated cost of $1.4 billion; America's biggest construction project at the time), it was but a flicker of its original purpose. No one would actually live there, as Walt had directed, and few experimental endeavors would be undertaken. Instead, the most economical course was to turn Walt's legacy into another moneymaker, heavily subsidized by corporate participation and sold by heavy promotion of "Walt's dream"—a formula that prevails today. (In December 1993, the park name was simplified to Epcot.) In truth, the final concept wasn't much different from the world's fair that Walt's father had helped construct in Chicago in 1893 or that Walt himself defined in New York in 1964: examples of how technology improves lives, plus pavilions representing foreign lands for the edification of people unlikely to travel there themselves. In Disney's version of the future, all walls were carpeted, all lighting was recessed, and all music was lite FM.

As you face the back of the park, the left side of the former Future World is loosely about the physical and man-made sciences (**World Discovery**) and the right is more about the natural sciences (**World Nature**). The area around the base of Spaceship Earth (**World Celebration**) might still be a mire of construction that you have to pick your way through to get to the good stuff. Epcot's largest souvenir shop, **Creations,** is in the pavilion behind Spaceship Earth, as is **Club Cool,** where you can taste Coca-Cola products from around the world—some are a revelation but part of the fun is that you'll discover that not all of them are yummy.

Spaceship Earth ★★★ RIDE That gorgeous golf ball is actually a 16-million-pound structure, coated with 11,324 aluminum-bonded panels and sheathed inside with a rainproof rubber layer, that's supported by a table-like scaffolding. Think of this 180-foot-tall Buckminster Fuller sphere as a direct descendant of the Perisphere of the 1939 World's Fair or the Unisphere of the 1964 World's Fair, which were the icons for their own parks. No mere shell, it houses an eponymous ride using the OmniMover system of cars linked together like an endless snake. The ride slowly winds within the sphere. It's hard not to fall in love with this sixth-grade-level journey (narrated by Judi Dench) cheerleading the history of communications, from Greek theater to the telegraph. In a bit of unintended kinesthetic commentary, once computers were invented, it all goes downhill. At one point, Dench tells you to thank the Phoenicians for inventing an alphabet (and some riders do so—it's a tradition here), but once you get off, you can't explain what you learned, if anything. This, of course, makes it essential Epcot. This is the one pavilion that still shows what the 1982 park was like—its robot-populated sister pavilions about transportation and the future were razed in the 1990s to make way for flashier stuff. This glorious '80s creaker was scheduled for a total renovation, but pandemic budget cuts gave the precious throwback a stay of execution. Long may we thank the Phoenicians.

Mission: SPACE ★★ RIDE Behind this gorgeously swirling planetary facade is a ride that approximates, with intensity if you so desire, the experience of a rocket launch. Although technically a whirl aboard a cockpit on a giant centrifuge, the skillful design successfully tricks the mind. At the outside, you choose between Orange (an intense trip to Mars that'll have you pressed backward against your seat) or Green (an easy glide around Earth that is milder and more family-friendly, with no vomit-inducing effects). The posted wait time will be whichever of the two versions is longer. Each passenger in the extremely tight four-person cockpits (claustrophobics be warned) is assigned two buttons to press at given cues—it doesn't matter if you don't, but at least hold onto your steering joystick, because it gives force feedback as you travel. The Advanced Training Lab post-show area (through the gift shop) is worthwhile even if you don't ride. There, you can play interactive group games and send free postcards home via computer. *Strategy:* Whereas Mad Tea Party makes me want to hurl, I do fine on this ride—the personal fans blowing air on your face must help. Perhaps this is why Disney felt confident that it was safe to add a table-service restaurant adjacent to the ride, called **Space 220** (p. 87), where diners can gaze out windows overlooking their simulated orbit.

> ## Character Meets in Epcot
>
> Check your app or map for the current location of the meet-and-greet areas in Epcot—these are the character spots where you'll find (at the end of a queue) Mickey, Minnie, and a few other popular faces. In some of the World Showcase pavilions, you will also find characters with connections to those countries—Mary Poppins in the U.K., Mulan in China, and so on.

Test Track ★★ RIDE Cars thunder enticingly around the bend of an outdoor motorway at nearly 65mph, but that's as intense as it gets. Those passengers are experiencing the climax of a complicated, multistage ride that simulates the proving ground of an automobile manufacturer (sponsor: Chevrolet), rather oddly set in a neon-frosted black box. Before boarding, you use a touch screen to create a car using the factors of capability, power, responsiveness, and efficiency. Then, you go along for the ride in a minimally decorated warehouse on a series of diagnostic safety tests (don't worry, you don't have to actually do anything), while trackside screens ostensibly show you how your creation would perform under the same circumstances—in truth, it's the same exact ride every time. Your six-passenger car brakes suddenly and careens through a mostly black room decorated by illuminated lines that seem to have been inspired both by *Tron* and a very low renovation budget. Finally, you shoot outside the building and make an invigorating circuit around the circular track over the Epcot employee parking lot. (Hertz has a similar experience—it's called a convertible.) The post-ride showroom features a few steering games plus samples from Chevy's current fleet and numerous photo ops for free digital postcards. If you rode this before its 2012 renovation, you saw it in a much better form. As one of the only thrills in Epcot, it gets busy anyway. *Strategy:* There is a single-rider line, but it doesn't let you skip much waiting and invariably puts you in a right-hand seat and won't let you design a car.

Epcot: New Horizons for You and for Me

There are big changes afoot at Epcot, but not as big as were hoped. In 2019, Disney announced a paradigm-shifting extreme makeover for the park to coincide with its 40th anniversary in 2022. But pandemic-inflicted emergencies eviscerated the budget and dashed hopes. The Innoventions West building was demolished to make way for a three-level World Celebration Festival Center with a roof garden and broadcast center, but that ambition shrank to become a mere blank spot termed a "festival area." An interactive pavilion called Play!, which was set to occupy the long-dormant Wonders of Life building, was also reportedly sent back to the drawing board to incorporate more contactless engagement. An announced "Mary Poppins attraction" for the United Kingdom pavilion is now no longer mentioned, but at least Spaceship Earth was successfully festooned with new permanent twinkle lights and we

have a new Walt Disney statue at "Dreamers Point," near the center of Future World, now renamed World Celebration. The area around The Land is now called World Nature, and on the other side of Spaceship Earth, the newly renamed World Discovery area hosts an epic attraction, years in the making, that managed to survive the cuts and the construction slowdowns: **Guardians of the Galaxy: Cosmic Rewind.** Literally one of the biggest things Disney ever built, this fully indoor "storytelling" coaster is stocked with all kinds of novel twists, from a backward launch to rotating vehicles to scenes shot by the movie franchise's director, James Gunn. The track is more swoopy than loopy, keeping it firmly on the family-friendly side. After all the delays and false starts, excitement is through the roof. You'll want to prioritize a ride at the top of your Epcot list.

The Seas with Nemo & Friends ★★ RIDE/ACTIVITY   One of the world's largest saltwater aquariums, it's 27 feet deep, 203 feet across, and holds 5.7 million gallons, and you can spend as long as you like watching the swimming creatures from two levels. About a third of the tank is reserved for dolphins and sea turtles, while reef fish, rays, and sharks dominate the rest. When the pavilion opened in 1986 as The Living Seas, sharks were the big draw and scientists answered questions everywhere; today, because of *Finding Nemo* and *Finding Dory,* kids ask to see the clown fish and blue tangs yet there's nary an interpreter in sight. A visit begins with a 5-minute, slow-moving ride in OmniMover "clamobiles" through a simulated undersea world. Half the point of the ride is, of course, to find Nemo, who's lost yet again; the other characters incessantly shout his name, which soon grates on adult nerves. The ride climaxes to the tune of "In the Big Blue World" (from the Nemo musical at Animal Kingdom) with a peek into the real aquarium as Nemo and his friends are projected into the windows, cleverly uniting the fictional world with the actual Seabase, which you can now explore. A few times a day (usually hourly after 11am), the giant Lockout Chamber tube dominating the hall is occupied by a diver—an unforgettable sight—to demonstrate how scuba works. On the second floor, Observation Level, don't miss the observation platform that extends into the mighty tank. A Daily Roster sign apprises you of the day's dolphin talks and fish feedings (the schedule is busiest between 10am and 4pm), when there will be someone on hand to explain what you're seeing. The **dolphins** live separately in the first space on the left. If human divers are swimming, they'll communicate with guests by way of magnetized writing tablets. Also, check out the **manatees,** Florida's sweet-natured "sea cows." *Strategy:* If the pavilion's entry line is horrific, bypass the ride by entering through the gift shop, at the far left.

Turtle Talk with Crush ★★ SHOW   Inside The Seas with Nemo & Friends, this amusing 20-minute show stars a computer-animated version of Crush, *Finding Nemo*'s 150-year-old surfer-dude turtle—plus the occasional Dory or Destiny the whale shark—who interacts with audiences, making jokes about what they're wearing and fielding questions. It's part of what Disney calls its "Living Characters" program, and it's nifty. There is the distraction of ray and jellyfish tanks in the waiting area. Next door is **Bruce's Shark World,** a play area similar to any science museum's.

Soarin' ★★★ RIDE   The Land pavilion takes up 6 acres, more than all of Tomorrowland, and this ride is a big reason why. In it, audiences are seated on benches and "flown," hang glider–like, in front of a movie that flies over 13 world landmarks on every inhabited continent while scents (grass, roses) waft, hair blows, and the seats gently rock in tandem with the motions of the flight. Now and then, something computer-animated flies at the lens, but mostly the ride is highly repeatable and deeply pleasurable for all ages. *Strategy:* The best seats are in the middle sections on the top row, where there are no feet dangling in your field of vision and tall images look less warped. That means you should aim for position B-1, or at the very least A-1 or C-1. Those with height terrors should request something ending in 3, the closest to the ground.

Living with the Land ★ RIDE   The Land's other ride, after Soarin', is a 14-minute (wonderfully air-conditioned) boat trip that skims over the realm of farming technologies. It's one of the last Epcot rides to provide a semblance of education, especially when you pass some experimental growth methods (like a nutrient film technique and aquaponics). These methods are being explored, or so we're told, to curb world hunger, but you won't learn how they work (for that, you have to go to the desk at Soarin's exit to reserve the semi-interesting 45-minute Behind the Seeds tour, $29 per person) and Epcot's labs are not the hive of active research they were meant to be in 1982. They do some real stuff here, though: Annually, the narration claims, 15 tons of produce are grown here for Disney restaurants, but you won't see much activity proving it. This ride is original to opening day, although the live narrators were replaced by a recording and most of the plants are gone. For those interested in the topic, the info will be too thin, but for those who are bored green, it will seem to last forever. *Strategy:* Boats load slowly, so go early or late to escape the inevitable buildup. It often closes at 7pm.

Awesome Planet ★ MOVIE   Not much to say here—this 10-minute film on the upper level of the Land is the current occupant of a space that has turned over more tenants than a failing shopping mall. Although it is expertly produced, it's filler, and nothing more special than something you'd see on a Saturday afternoon on the Discovery Channel. Did you know that our Earth is perfectly situated to support life and it's up to us to protect it? Of course you did; roll credits. It's ironic that most guests use this show to sit calmly in the air conditioning and escape the deteriorating climate realities of our actual planet.

Disney & Pixar Short Film Festival ★ SHOW   Three animated shorts, all of which are available on DVD, done "4D" style, meaning your seat trembles once in a while. This movie is a space filler and a time killer. Don't miss something better just because you were doing this. It's on the back side of the pavilion named "Imagination!"—written with an exclamation point, maybe because the people who make new attractions seem to be calling out for one.

Journey into Imagination with Figment ★ RIDE   Did Disney run out of money halfway through? One section of this slow track-based ride is simply a room of black curtains and painted boards. Its daffy purple dinosaur, Figment, once figured as Epcot's mascot and now strains to act cuddly in his last, forlorn outpost. The ride purports to be an open house of the Imagination Institute run by Prof. Nigel Channing (Eric Idle), but Figment seizes control and literally tries everything he can to offend your senses—your sense of good taste, though, is the most violated. This is the third attempt since 1982 to get an Imagination ride right. The ride dumps out into **ImageWorks "What If"**

Labs, once a high-tech playground but now a gloomy cul-de-sac with little more to offer than the purchase of fairground-style gag photos. Look above the roped-off staircase for a glimpse of the glass pyramid's atrium, now forbidden unless you've purchased a Disney timeshare (there's a bouncer if you haven't), and you'll get a fuller sense of how this pretty pavilion is now half-empty and riven with neglect. You might have gathered by now that Imagination! is not Epcot at its best. However, the fountain pods in front, which shoot snakes of water from one to another, are a firm favorite of children, who never tire of trying to catch one of the so-called "laminar flow" spurts.

World Showcase

The 1.3-mile path circling the World Showcase Lagoon is home to 11 pavilions created in the idealized image of their home countries—get your picture taken in front of a miniature Eiffel Tower (it'll look real through the lens), or at the Doge's Palace in Venice. The pavilions were built more to elicit an emotional response than to truly replicate. Disney is diligent about the upkeep of this area, but it neglects development—the last "country" to open was Norway back in 1988, and without joint participation by foreign tourism offices, hopes aren't strong for more. There also seems to be an emphasis on countries that Americans already know, and neither South America nor Australasia is represented at all. But World Showcase does have some of the most original restaurants in Disney World, and the shops are stocked with crafts and national products (you can buy real Chinese tea in China and sweaters in Norway), although the variety is slipping, replaced by the same old Disney merch. It's also the only area in Epcot in which alcoholic beverages are sold; they seem to get stronger as you make your way to the back of the park.

There is far more fascinating stuff to do in World Showcase than the free Disney map lets on. Pocket it and let your curiosity guide you; the app posts times for unexpected musical and dance performances conducted by natives of each country (shows usually wrap up by dinnertime). Seeing them makes a day richer and squeezes value from your ticket. Rush and you'll miss a lot. I suggest going **counter-clockwise around the lagoon** mostly because the

---

A Mini United Nations

When American border control permits it, World Showcase pavilions are staffed by young people who were born and raised in the host country. Many of their contracts last for up to a year, and they chose to come to Florida as much to learn about America as to be ambassadors for their own nations. Many of them complain that most park guests don't bother asking anything except where the bathrooms are. Be kind to them, speak slowly if you cannot immediately understand each other's accent, and most of all, seize this unusual chance to ask questions about their cultures. These folks, despite the fact they're zipped into silly costumes, are modern, intelligent people who are so proud of where they come from that they traveled halfway around the world to have a new experience and share their heritage with you. Help them do that.

newest big ride is in France; if you go clockwise, you'll reach it after it accrues a line. After midafternoon, the direction you go won't matter.

Tip: Anything purchased in World Showcase can be sent to the **Package Pickup** ☛ at the front of the park; allow 3 hours for delivery (it's not refrigerated, so chocolate melts). On some days—it depends how busy things are—two **ferry** routes cross the lagoon. One leaves near Germany and one from Morocco, and both land near the the same spot. You will not save time using them; they're merely a pleasant way to get off your feet.

CANADA ★

Canada's gardens (inspired by Victoria's Butchart Gardens, although the sign says Victoria Gardens) are a surprising oasis, adding a hidden artificial canyon delightfully washed by a man-made waterfall. A music show sometimes takes the stage here several times daily (check your app). *Influences:* 19th-century Victorian colonial architecture (Hotel du Canada); emblematic northwestern Indian design and Maritime Provinces towns; Butchart Gardens, Victoria (Victoria Gardens). *Fun Stuff to Buy:* The shop, **Northwest Mercantile,** mostly hawks maple syrup ($25 for 8.5 oz.), hockey team wear, faux fur–lined muff hats ($25), stuffed moose ($15), ice wine in 2-oz. servings ($13), and T-shirts themed to moose and hockey. *Entertainment:* A rock/folk band at the bandstand.

"Canada Far and Wide" ★ FILM

Canada's entertainment offering is an in-the-round movie shot in Circle-Vision 360°, a process Walt Disney originally called Circarama. You wouldn't believe the work it takes to make a film that surrounds you from all sides. The makers first had to figure out the optimal number of screens (nine—which enables projectors to be slipped in the gaps between screens) and then they had to suspend a ring of carefully calibrated film cameras from helicopters so that the crew wasn't in the shots. The 12-minute presentation, which requires standing (you can lean on railings), is packed with timeless spectacular scenery worthy of a tourist brochure, but it is just a movie, after all, so measure that against your priorities. (Co-host Eugene Levy: "Say, are you a fan of heli-skiing?" Fellow presenter Catherine O'Hara: "Heli-yes!") You'll find it hidden deep within the pavilion by a waterfall in a dreamy rock canyon.

UNITED KINGDOM ★★

United Kingdom, a wild mix of architectural styles, has no rides or shows, and few people know about the knee-high **hedge maze** in back. The U.K. is popular chiefly for its English-style pub, the indoor Rose & Crown Pub & Dining Room, and a counter-service fish and chips shop. That's two fish and chips outlets in a block—far more than you'd find even in London these days. *Influences:* Anne Hathaway's Cottage, Stratford-upon-Avon (the Tea Caddy); Queen Anne style (the middle promenade); Hampton Court, London (Sportsman's Shoppe); Victorian, country, and traditional pub styles (Rose & Crown). *Fun Stuff to Buy:* Featured shopping in the conjoined **Sportsman's**

Shoppe, The Crown & Crest, and **Toy Soldier** includes football (soccer) jerseys, merchandise for Queen, Bowie, and the Beatles; Dr. Who stuff; and Guinness shirts (that's actually Irish, but carry on). Across the way, **Lords and Ladies** does jewelry and soap, and the **Tea Caddy** sells Twinings tea plus English candy bars ($4 each; sometimes sold out). *Entertainment:* British Revolution rock cover band. *Character greeting:* Mary Poppins, Alice in Wonderland.

FRANCE ★★

France, done up to look like a typical Parisian neighborhood with a one-tenth replica of the upper stretch of the Eiffel Tower in the simulated distance (you can't go up it), is popular mostly for its food, although its new *Ratatouille*-themed ride should change that. Disney allowed Guerlain and Givenchy to open fragrance shops at **Plume et Palette**—turns out the smell of selling out is just like Shalimar. *Influences:* Various Belle Epoque Parisian and provincial streets; Château de Fontainebleau (the Palais du Cinema); the former Pont des Arts in Paris (the bridge to the United Kingdom). *Fun Stuff to Buy:* **Librairie et Galerie** sells upscale fragrances. At **L'Esprit de la Provence,** 3-oz. sips of wine cost a scandalous $8–$12. *Entertainment:* Serveur Amusant, a thrilling street acrobat who does handstands on stacked chairs. *Character greeting:* Princess Aurora, Belle.

Remy's Ratatouille Adventure ★★★ RIDE   New: An adorable and innovative indoor ride that came from Disneyland Paris, where it has been a smash since 2014. Donning 3D glasses and pretending you have shrunk down to the size of Remy the rat, from the animated feature *Ratatouille*, you board little carts (two rows of three each) that scoot around using a trackless ride system. You'll gently coast over rooftops, scuttle through the scullery, cavort through the kitchen, and dash through the dining room of Gusteau's, the snootiest culinary establishment in Paris. The 4-minute romp is full of goliath set pieces and giddy visual illusions, and is totally appropriate for children: Even though it stars rodents, it won't faze even the biggest scaredy-cats. And there's a new crêperie next door! *Tip:* Disney makes guests vie for seats on its most popular rides with the Virtual Queue system (p. 95), so check the Remy ride's page on the app to see if that's required the week you visit.

"Impressions de France"/ Beauty and the Beast Sing-Along ★ FILM   The 18-minute, 200-degree-wide movie is no longer the freshest example of a tourism film—mostly classical music and postcard-worthy shots of some 50 picturesque places. Still, it has been playing continuously since Epcot opened in 1982 and happily, it provides seating. A tot-appropriate **Beauty and the Beast Sing-Along** film told from the point of view of Gaston's misunderstood henchman LeFou is scheduled at other times in this space, so check your app if you're into that. Disney spent proper money on making it; it even hired Angela Lansbury, well into her 90s, to voice Mrs. Potts again. Most of the time, Disney hires sound-alike actors for its attractions.

MOROCCO ★★★

Morocco is another delightful pavilion if you're inclined to dig in. It flies higher than its neighbors because the country's king took an active interest in its construction, dispatching some 21 top craftsmen for the job. There's no movie or show, and the architecture is a cross-country mishmash drawn from Marrakech, Fès, and Rabat. **Fez House** is a tranquil, pillared two-level courtyard with a fountain and seating that recalls a classic Moroccan home; **Race Against the Sun,** a mosaic-rich exhibition about desert land races, is a little-seen exhibit that makes for a welcome respite. Ask a cast member (almost always from Morocco) to write your name in Arabic for you—it's free. *Influences:* Marrakesh (Koutoubia minaret), Rabat (Chella minaret), Fès (Bab Boujouloud Gate, Nejjarine Fountain), Casablanca. *Fun Stuff to Buy:* Operation of the main Morocco shop, **Souk-Al-Magreb,** recently transferred from an outside vendor back to the Walt Disney Company, and consequently the shopping quality took a nosedive, but amid the tired Princess dresses and T-shirts you may still find some incense, Thuya-wood boxes and bowls, and fez hats. *Character greeting:* Princess Jasmine. *Entertainment:* A band sometimes jams by the water (check the app for times).

JAPAN ★★★

Japan has no giant attractions (a show building was erected but never filled with its intended ride), but its shopping is by far the best in Epcot, and the outdoor garden behind the pagoda is a paragon of peace. At the back of the pavilion, go inside and turn left to tour the **Bijutsu-kan Gallery.** Its most recent show was about the Japanese affection for *Kawaii,* or cute things. A red *torii* gate inspired by one in Hiroshima sits in the lagoon (the barnacles on its base are fake, and were glued on to simulate age). *Influences:* 8th-century Horyuji Temple in Nara (pagoda); Katsura Imperial Villa (Katsura Grill); Shirasagi-Jo castle at Himeji (the rear fortress); Hiroshima (*torii* gate in the lagoon). *Fun Stuff to Buy:* The **Mitsukoshi Department Store,** named for the 300-year-old Japanese original, is the most fun to roam of all the World Showcase shops. It's stocked like a real store, not a theme park shop, with a variety of toys, chopstick sets ($4–$18), traditional rush mat zouri sandals ($25), linens, anime figures like Pokémon, paper fans, calligraphy supplies, countless solar-powered hand-waving things, antique kimonos (mostly $50–$200), sake serving sets ($17–$35), bonsai trees ($55–$100), swords (around $160), and Japanese snacks, such as chocolate-dipped Pocky sticks ($4).

U.S.A. ★★★

So much for being a generous host: The U.S.A. pavilion takes pride of place in an area that's supposed to celebrate other countries. Inside, attend the half-hour Audio-Animatronic show *The American Adventure.* You'll be impressed. The lobby waiting area hosts changing historic exhibitions that are usually unfairly ignored: The current ones are *Creating Tradition: Innovation and Change in American Indian Art* and *The Soul of Jazz: An American Adventure.* *Influences:* Georgian/colonial Greek-revival buildings (Brits often snicker that its Georgian architecture style is distinctly English). On the water, the

America Gardens outdoor amphitheater is Epcot's primary performance space; the boards out front will tell you which band or singer is up next. *Fun Stuff to Buy:* **Art of Disney,** the pavilion's shop, sells specially created animation cels, figurines, and high-end limited-edition prints that are catnip to hardcore fans (but nothing you can't find more of at Disney Springs). *Entertainment:* The superlative and long-running Voices of Liberty singing group, which excels at thorny close harmonies, entertains guests waiting inside for the show.

The American Adventure ★★★ SHOW

Ben Franklin and Mark Twain are your Audio-Animatronic surrogates for a series of eye-popping (but ponderous) re-creations of snippets along patriotic themes. Moving dioramas of seminal events such as a Susan B. Anthony speech and John Muir's inspiration for Yosemite National Park appear and vanish cinematically on a stage a quarter the size of a football field, leaving spectators marveling at the massive amount of storage space that must lie beyond the proscenium. It's essentially a jukebox for national mythology, recently refreshed so it sounds better than ever, and the transitions between scenes are theatrical genius. Indeed, all that homespun corn is brought to you by some immensely complicated robotic and hydraulic systems. When this attraction first opened, the Declaration of Independence scene in which Franklin appears to mount stairs and then walk a few steps across the room was (and is still) a technical miracle. The Will Rogers figure actually twirls a lasso purely through robotic movements. Although heavy on uplifting jingoism, the show scores points for touching lightly on a few unpleasant topics, including slavery and a rebuke for the persecution of Native Americans, but in general, it's not as deep as its stage. Don't be the first to enter or else you'll be marooned off to the left.

ITALY ★

The tiny pavilion for Italy lacks an attraction—the gondolas never leave the dock—so content yourself with the miniature, drive-thru versions of Venice's Doge's Palace and St. Mark's bell tower. An appealing, if incongruous, attraction that's not on the maps is the highly detailed **model train** display just between this pavilion and Germany. *Influences:* Piazza di San Marco, Venice; stucco buildings of Tuscany; a fountain reminiscent of the work of Gian Lorenzo Bernini. *Fun Stuff to Buy:* Noodle around in **Enoteca Castello** shop for chocolate and wine ($8–$11 a glass). **La Gemma Elegante** sells fragrances, handbags, and pricey Venetian carnival masks. Stop into **Tutto Gusto** for honest adult cocktails—the kind made with a shaker, not a slushie machine. In 2021, the park added **Gelateria Toscana,** which supplies gelato for $8 a cup.

GERMANY ★

Lacking a true attraction (a water ride based on the Rhine was planned but never completed), Germany is popular for its food. The **Biergarten Restaurant** does sausages, beer, and the like—accompanied by yodeling and dancing—while the adjoining shop is for crystal doodads. The **Sommerfest** is the counter-service alternative for brats and pretzels, and the beer kiosk is ever-popular. On the hour, the Clock Tower above the pavilion rings and two figures emerge, just like at the Glockenspiel in München (Munich). The pavilion is otherwise a string of connected one-room shops selling steins ($25–$200), figurines, crystal, Christmas ornaments, cuckoo clocks (up to $1,900), and other high-priced wares. *Influences:* Eltz Castle near Koblenz; Stahleck Fortress near Bacharach; Rothenburg (the Biergarten and the dragon slayer statue); facades from Frankfurt and Freiburg (the guildhall). *Fun Stuff to Buy:* The connected candy-and-wine shop, **Weinkeller,** is worth a gander: You'll find such pick-me-ups as Gluhwein ($12 a liter), wine by the bottle (spätlese, Gewürztraminer, Auslese, Liebfraumilch, from $20), beer steins ($50–$130), and cuckoo clocks in the $100s or $1000s. **Der Teddybär** sells toys, including stuffed ones by Steiff. The Werther's Original **Karamell-Küche** shop for all sorts of caramel treats ($4–$10) is a standout—its warm, hand-tossed caramel popcorn is a top treat on the Lagoon. *Character greeting:* Snow White.

OUTPOST ★

This area between Germany and China was once slated to contain a pavilion canvassing equatorial Africa, but that fell through for political reasons, so instead, we get a mushy catch-all for all things African. The **Mdundo Kibanda** store has some Kenyan carvings (such as adorable $12 pocket-size elephants and walking sticks for $67–$77), and you'll find occasional storytelling sessions. Several days a week, a craftsman is on hand, whittling and carving wares—Kenyan-born Andrew Matiso has run this concession at Epcot since 1999. His wife Anna makes ravishing accessories from beads, and his colleague Joshua might also be here; these days, Matiso often works in the shop at Animal Kingdom Lodge.

> ### Kid Stuff at Epcot
>
> To make World Showcase more kid-friendly, seek out **Kidcot Fun Stops.** You'll pick up a new card at each pavilion, and at each stop, learn a little about life in that country. Each activity earns a sticker. Disney has also announced **DuckTales World Showcase Adventure,** an interactive scavenger hunt through the pavilions that can be accessed via the free Play Disney app.

CHINA ★★

Enter through the remarkable replica of Beijing's Temple of Heaven. "Tomb Warriors: Guardian Spirits of Ancient China," in the **House of the Whispering Willow,** is a miniature re-creation of a tiny portion of the legendary terra-cotta warriors of the Han Dynasty, scaled to the size of a hotel room (the original mausoleum is twice the size of Epcot). The Gallery also contains a few display cases of figures dating as far back as 260 B.C. *Influences:* Beijing's Forbidden City (Imperial Palace) and Temple of Heaven. *Fun Stuff to Buy:* Upon exiting the film, cross the hangarlike shop and enter **House of Good Fortune,** a particularly good store (photo op: a huge sculpture of Buddha). It sells plum wine ($20), lots of tees and teas, Chinese jackets ($40–$140; in silks, polyesters, and blends), jade bangles ($150), embroidered handbags ($40), teapots ($30–$50), paper parasols ($25), fans ($10), conical hats ($18), and tea sets (from $20). They'll write your kid's name in Mandarin for free. *Entertainment:* Jeweled Dragon Acrobats, some of the most riveting street performers in the World Showcase. *Character greeting:* Mulan.

"Wondrous China" ★ FILM   The big thing to do in China is to watch a ravishing 14-minute movie filmed entirely in Circle-Vision 360°, the same technology used for Canada's film (p. 78), with nine projectors filling a wrap-around screen with images from all sides. There's always the same focal point, so you won't get disoriented or dizzy. In 2002, the footage of Shanghai for "Reflections of China" had to be reshot because the city no longer resembled the 1982 version that was being shown; the most recent refresh, required once again, is the all-new "Wondrous China."

NORWAY ★★

Get yer *Frozen* merch here! Norway, the youngest pavilion (built 1988), is home to one of the few rides in World Showcase. At least, it used to be Norway—Disney expanded it, fudging the Norway theme, to cash in on *Frozen* fever even though the movie is only notionally set there. Now you have to get here first thing in the morning if you don't want to wait for hours. The **Akershus Royal Banquet Hall** does princess character meals morning, noon, and evening. In the one-room **Stave Church Gallery,** check out *Gods of the Vikings,* containing a few genuine Norse artifacts (such as 1,000-year-old spears and swords) on loan from Swedish and Norwegian historical societies. Towering above it all, the wooden Stave Church is a Norwegian original; there were once around 1,000 in the country, but today, there are only 28. **The Puffin's Roost** contains a 9-foot-tall troll—photo op alert. *Influences:* Town squares of Bergen, Alesund, Oslo, and the Satesdal Valley; the 14th-century Akershus castle on Oslo harbor; traditional cabins in Trondheim. **The Fjording** indulges in everything *Frozen. Fun Stuff to Buy:* Laila body lotions (assorted prices), princess dresses (from $60), and foam swords ($11). At the bakery, try the custard-stuffed school bread or the rice cream, a snack that those in the know are happy to make a detour for (both $3.50). I prefer the stuffed Olafs ($27) and Helly Hansen wear. *Entertainment:* Wandering slapstick Norway Vikings. *Character greeting:* Elsa and Anna.

Frozen Ever After ★★★ RIDE   The old Maelstrom indoor boat excursion, an abbreviated 5-minute float-along with easy forward and backward motion, never counted for much. But it's the hottest—er, coldest—ride in the park now that it's been populated with some marvelous Audio-Animatronics of Elsa, Anna, Olaf, Kristoff, Sven, and characters from *Frozen Fever* and *Frozen 2.* It won't change your world—there's not even a plot to speak of—but it's pretty. Nearby in the **Royal Sommerhus** cabin, kids can meet the princesses, who are pretending to be on summer vacation there. *Tip:* There's more to look at from the right side of the boat.

MEXICO ★★★

The final stop on your circuit around the lagoon is Mexico. Everything to see is inside the faux temple, which contains the *zócalo* of Plaza de los Amigos and a faux river (for the Gran Fiesta Tour ride), a faux volcano, and a faux night sky strung with lanterns. The **Mexican Folk Art Gallery** now hosts *Remember Me: La Celebración del Día de Muertos,* an exhibition on the traditions of the holiday *Coco* is about. Inside the La Tienda Encantada shop, look for Alba Hernandez Santiago, who trained in Arrazola, the most important Oaxacan town for the craft of hand-painted Oaxacan woodcarvings. She has been in this pavilion since 2002 and works Tuesday to Friday; her equally talented brother Marco and daughter Veronica take over on other days. Listen for the terrific Mariachi Cobre, which has performed here since the park's opening day. There's also a crystal and glass shop with glass-blowing demonstrations. *Influences:* A diplomatic mix of Mayan, Toltec, Aztec, and Spanish styles. *Fun Stuff to Buy:* Maracas ($6 each), Oaxacan woodcarvings (from $18), piñatas (from $10), hand-painted pottery skulls ($25), glass margarita goblets ($17), and sombreros ($17). At the dusky **La Cava de Tequila,** knock back 200-plus types of the house liquor or a designer margarita ($11–$250), but it's faster to grab a frozen one ($12–$15) at the Choza de Margarita kiosk outside, and stroll with it. *Entertainment:* Mariachi Cobre. *Character greeting:* Donald Duck.

Gran Fiesta Tour Starring the Three Caballeros ★★ RIDE   It's easy to develop a soft spot for the bland, 8-minute boat float that, for its cheesiness, has been nicknamed "Rio de Queso." As you pass movie screens, jiggling dolls, and dancing Day of the Dead skeletons, you quickly realize you're enjoying the product of Mexican tourist board input. Along the way, expect animated appearances by the 1940s characters the Three Caballeros—never mind that only Panchito Pistoles the rooster is Mexican (José Carioca the parrot is Brazilian, and Donald Duck is American). At the ride's climax, they appear together in "live" form—these figures are actually part of Disney history. They were originally made for the Mickey Mouse Revue, a show that opened with the Magic Kingdom in 1971 and later spent 26 years in Tokyo Disneyland. The experience is sweet, and it's a worthy siesta break.

Epcot at Night

There are no parades at Epcot, but at 9:45pm, a pulse-pounding spectacular takes place over World Showcase Lagoon. Harmonious is the biggest nighttime show Epcot has done (pyrotechnics, choreographed fountains, LED displays, very large barges—perhaps you can spot them during the day). It's so huge that any view of the center of the lake will do (waterfront dining is ideal), but because of projections, the optimal places to be are near the U.S.A. pavilion, on the island Italy Isola off of the Italy pavilion, and in the World Showplace Plaza at the foot of World Celebration. (Sadly, Disney sometimes ropes off that last area and charges admission for it.)

Where to Eat in Epcot

Epcot has the best dining choices of any Disney World park, and people come just for the food. All locations will have a few vegetarian options, kids' meals, and (if you identify yourself) special dietary requests can usually be accommodated, albeit often at diminished quality. Alcohol is served everywhere—even in Morocco (it's much easier to drink here than it is in the real country).

EPCOT'S QUICK-SERVICE RESTAURANTS

The best casual food action is in World Showcase. All over the park, there are many minor kiosks for snacks than what's listed here, particularly during festival periods. Unless noted, all quick-service options accept Mobile Order.

At the Front of the Park

Sunshine Seasons ★★★ INTERNATIONAL   Options here have deteriorated over the years, but they remain the best selection and freshest food of all Epcot's counter-service locations, including salads, grilled items (oak-grilled salmon), sesame-crusted tuna—not a deep-fried item in sight. **The Land.** Breakfast $7–$10, lunch and dinner combo meal $10–$14.

World Showcase

Moving around the lagoon counter-clockwise:

Yorkshire County Fish Shop ★★ BRITISH   Snag fish and chips or chicken-and-mushroom pie and eat it alfresco. You get two strips of fish with chips (fries)—make sure to put vinegar, not ketchup, on the fries, the way the English do. Ale costs $10. In the **Rose & Crown** pub, you can buy Scotch eggs or fish and chips ($12). **United Kingdom.** Combo meal $10–$12.

Les Halles Boulangerie Pâtisserie ★★ FRENCH   Grab a fast, bready bite in the back of Les Halles, such as a chocolate croissant or a ham-and-cheese croissant, pastry, quiche, or baguette sandwiches ($7–$10). Next door, **L'Artisan des Glaces** has good sorbets and ice creams—plus a deadly ice cream martini made with Grand Marnier ($13). **France.** Salads and sandwiches $8–$10.

La Crêperie de Paris ★★★ CREPES   At France's back end near the Remy ride, take away savory *galette* crepes (meats or veggies) and sweet crepes (fruit, hazelnut chocolate spread, or the classic butter-and-sugar). There's also a table-service section for fuller crepe-based meals. **France.** Crepes $7–$11.

Tangierine Café ★★★ MOROCCAN   The indoor counter-service location serves *shawarma* or falafel with hummus, couscous, bread, and tabbouleh; and lamb or chicken platters and wraps. Accent it with Casa Beer, from Casablanca, or Moorish coffee (powerful espresso spiced with cinnamon and nutmeg), and add baklava for $4. Kids can get burgers or chicken nuggets for $9. **Morocco.** Combo meal $14–$18.

Katsura Grill ★★ JAPANESE   Japan's small counter-service location is in the gardens, and it supplies Japanese curry, chicken, sushi ($9–$12 for four pieces), and teriyaki. Below, the **Garden House** kiosk pours plum wine and sake for $7–$11. Facing the lagoon under the pagoda, the **Kabuki Cafe** kiosk (closed in cold weather) serves shaved ice with syrup (including melon and cherry flavors) for $4–$9, and "sake mist" slushies for $10. **Japan.** Combo meal $11–$14.

Regal Eagle Smokehouse ★ AMERICAN   Pan-American barbecue (Memphis dry-rub pork ribs, Kansas City smoked chicken, sliced Texas beef brisket) from an outdoor smoker plus rich craft beers. Very American indeed! **The American Adventure.** Combo meal $14–$16. The **Fife & Drum Tavern** kiosk outside sells those enormous turkey legs for $14.

Tutto Gusto Wine Cellar ★★★ ITALIAN   The excellent full bar (stand-up only) attached to the Tutto Italia Ristorante is an underrated oasis that serves grown-up cocktails and also a selection of cheese and meat plates for two or three, plus shared pasta, cannoli, tiramisu, and panini. Get a six-wine "Grand Tour" flight tasting for $32. **Italy.** Shared plates from $25, panini $12–$16, dessert shooters $4.

Sommerfest ★★ GERMAN   When you can't get into Biergarten (see below), settle for this kiosk to get your bratwurst, sausage, and beer. **Germany.** Sausage rolls $10–$11.

Lotus Blossom Café ★ CHINESE   A Panda Express redux: China's Quick Service choice, with covered seating, is basic, serving orange chicken, chicken fried rice, and the like. **China.** Combo meal $11–$14.

Kringla Bakeri Og Kafé ★★ SCANDINAVIAN   Some of the selections in Norway's bake shop can't be found elsewhere at Disney. Many people claim the smooth, strawberry-topped rice cream pudding to be their favorite sweet in Walt Disney World. You can also get sandwiches, heated to order, and Uncrustables. **Norway.** Desserts $4–$7.

La Cantina De San Angel ★★ MEXICAN   Mexico's counter-service option will give you beef, fish, chicken tacos, cheese empanadas, nachos, and margaritas (from $11). It's outside, but on the water. **Mexico.** Combo meal $10–$15.

EPCOT'S TABLE-SERVICE RESTAURANTS

All of these require reservations via the app (or ✆ **407/939-3463**); none of them fulfill Mobile Orders. Reserve months ahead if you want a good seat for the lagoon show. The host will not guarantee seating location, but it helps to politely ask. Objectively, there are very few meals that would rate highly if I ate them outside of the park gates, and as with all mass-produced meals, quality varies greatly from day to day; the lion's share of the enjoyment is just being there. Taking them as you encounter them, going counter-clockwise:

At the Front of the Park

Coral Reef Restaurant ★ SEAFOOD   Turns out fish are both friends *and* food: Through windows into the 27-foot-deep aquarium, admire the luckier buddies of the fish on your plate. Only about half the menu selections are fish, and the rest are things like short ribs or strip steak. It's about the cool view, not the cuisine. **The Seas with Nemo & Friends.** Main courses $24 to $40.

Garden Grill ★★ AMERICAN   As Farmer Mickey, Pluto, and Chip 'n' Dale press the flesh in this slowly revolving, two-tiered circular restaurant, you're served all-you-can-eat family-style "Chip 'n' Dale's Harvest Feast" platters of meats and vegetables, some of which were grown in the greenhouses downstairs. This is the only character meal in this part of the park, but it's a good choice because it's mellow and small enough so that the merry rodents can spend quality time with you. **The Land.** All three meals $55 adults, $36 kids.

Space 220 ★ MODERN AMERICAN   Just opened: A fun place where the gimmick is you're dining (and wining—the list is more than 1,000 bottles long) 220 miles above the ground aboard a space station. It's a lot like the Coral Reef Restaurant, but in a vacuum: A 250-foot-long digital screen wrapping outside a semicircle of windows completes the illusion. It's run by the Patina Group, which also manages the restaurants at the Italy pavilion as well as The Edison, Enzo's, and Morimoto Asia at Disney Springs. **Mission: SPACE.** Main courses $24 to $35.

World Showcase

Le Cellier Steakhouse ★ STEAKS   It takes the Canadian-themed restaurant to deliver the most all-American menu of filet mignon, Prince Edward Island mussels, and chicken, but it also Canucks it up with sides such as *poutine* fries (topped with cheddar, truffle salt, and red-wine reduction). Specialties include a popular cheddar cheese soup and pretzel bread. True to its name, the restaurant is windowless and vaulted, like a very clean version of a wine cellar. It's a tough reservation to secure. **Canada.** Entrees $34–$59.

Rose & Crown Dining Room ★★★ BRITISH   The interior is similar to a country pub—big wooden bar with Victorian screen serving whisky and lots of British and Irish draught beers ($10, or twice as much as a London pub)—although some of the seating is outdoors. You can get bangers and mash (sausage with mashed potatoes), shepherd's pie (ground beef with peas topped with cheddar and mashed potatoes), and chicken masala curry (Brits love curries). If you just want a drink and a little pub grub, stop in the attached pub (its motto is *otium cum dignitate*—that's not a Hogwarts spell, it's "leisure with dignity.") **United Kingdom.** Entrees $21–$27.

Chefs de France ★★ FRENCH   In a glassed-in dining room recalling a typical French bistro, dine on quiche and crepes or prototypical French food such as duck breast, beef bourguignon, escargot, and filet de boeuf (lunch and dinner). There's also a $55 prix-fixe, three-course meal with one glass of wine. **France.** Entrees $25–$39.

La Crêperie de Paris ★★★ CREPES   In a contemporary dining room at France's back end near the Remy ride, order full-meal savory *galette* crepes (meats or veggies) and sweet crepes (fruit or hazelnut chocolate spread), plus alcoholic ciders, salad, and soup of the day. There's also a take-away counter. **France.** Crepes $9–$16.

Monsieur Paul ★★★ FRENCH   Epcot's most thoughtful menu (and also its most expensive) starts with napkins that are folded like a chef's jacket. This is special occasion stuff: an oxtail soup with black truffle, duck shepherd's pie, black sea bass in rosemary sauce with scales made of roasted potato slices, plus all the amuse-bouches and long preparation explanations you'd expect of a fine establishment. Although the restaurant faces the water, its windows are small, so not every table has a view of the nighttime show. The entrance is tucked around the back door of Chefs de France, under a black awning. **France.** Entrees $39–$46.

Restaurant Marrakesh ★★★ ⚑ MOROCCAN   Tucked in the back of the souk, this lesser-known restaurant, newly renovated, is a romantic spot for approachable North African fare, heavy on shish kebabs, lemon chicken tagine, and couscous. Thinner crowds allow it to serve a good value at lunch: appetizer, entree, and dessert until 3:30pm for $20. **Morocco.** Entrees $22–$36.

Spice Road Table ★★ MOROCCAN   Serving spicy garlic shrimp, pomegranate-chili crispy cauliflower, and cocktails, it has terrace lagoon views ideal for spectators of the nighttime show, so it fills up by 8pm. It also has a rare full bar that can do proper cocktails, not just pre-blended ones. **Morocco.** Small plates $9–$13.

Teppan Edo ★★★ JAPANESE   Above the Mitsukoshi store (which runs it), a chef-cum-swordsmith slices, dices, and cooks at the teppanyaki griddle built into your table. It's fun to watch, although it's not a great choice if your kids are too young to keep their hands to themselves. Ask to see the smoking onion volcano. There's no view, but the food? Oh, it's fine, but you really come to see the fancy knife work. **Japan.** Entrees $24–$36, sushi $15–$19 per order.

Takumi-Tei ★★ JAPANESE   New in 2019, it's the most elegant and modern restaurant in the Japan pavilion (no lagoon views), and the menu's decidedly pricey: Wagyu beef and premium sake, with sushi starters. Heed the dress code of golf casual or business casual—no flip-flops or T-shirts allowed. Dinner only. **Japan.** Entrees $44–$93, tasting menu $130.

Tokyo Dining ★★ JAPANESE   On the second floor of the Japan pavilion, you'll find a waitstaff more subdued than any in Tokyo and a menu offering both tempura/grills and sushi in modest portions. Some tables have a view of the lagoon, which comes in handy around the nighttime show. **Japan.** Entrees $21–$34, sushi $7–$18 per order.

Tutto Italia Ristorante ★ ITALIAN   Proclaimed authentic mostly by people who have never been to Italy, this dusky environment of chandeliers and murals nonetheless packs 'em in. Pasta of this low caliber should not cost this much, but that doesn't stop patrons from buying $27 slices of lasagna. **Italy.** Entrees $22–$35, panini $19–$22.

Via Napoli ★★ ITALIAN   The more enjoyable of Italy's two table-service restaurants features lots of light, three-story vaulted ceilings, and three amusing wood-fired ovens shaped like the open mouths of giant mustachioed men named after volcanoes. Into those are thrust $18 to $23 individual pizzas and $9.50 kids' pizzas made with flour imported from Naples (not that you could tell the difference). Don't want pizza? There are a bunch of more substantial Italian mains. **Italy.** Entrees $24–$40, one-person pizzas $18–$22, larger pizzas $35–$48.

Biergarten Restaurant ★★★ GERMAN   Toddlers lurch forward to polka, dads dive into mugs of Radeberger pilsner, and strangers make friends with their neighbors at this rowdy, carb-loaded party, an all-you-can-eat stuffer featuring schnitzel, spaetzle, rotisserie chicken, sauerbraten (at dinner), and an oompah band for about 20 minutes at a time. It's popular. **Germany.** Lunch (noon–3pm): $46 adults, $25 kids.

Nine Dragons Restaurant ★ CHINESE   When you can't get a reservation anywhere else, you end up here. The food's not much more daring or spicy than at neighboring Lotus Blossom Café (see above), except that there are more choices and they're more expensive. The decor is handsomely geometric, but nothing memorable, although some tables face out toward the water. **China.** Entrees $17–$25.

Princess Storybook Dining at Akershus Royal Banquet Hall ★★★ AMERICAN   It's Epcot's meet-the-princesses extravaganza for all three "feasts" daily, in a Norwegian castle-like setting of vaulted ceilings and banners. Someone always stops by, be it Belle, Aurora, Snow White, Cinderella, or Ariel, who must not have heard that Norwegians love raw fish. This is the only character dining in World Showcase. Breakfast is the more lively time to come. **Norway.** Meals: $49–$59 adults, $29–$35 kids.

San Angel Inn Restaurante ★★ MEXICAN   Epcot's most atmospheric restaurant is set beneath a false twilight sky at the base of an ancient pyramid, with the boats from the Gran Fiesta Tour steadily passing—reserve the first time of the day to guarantee a seat by the river. The fare isn't Tex-Mex as much as it is Mexican: Dinner has chicken mole, chili relleno, grilled catch of the day, and caramel dulce de leche ice cream for dessert. If you can't get in (a likelihood), try La Hacienda de San Angel, below. **Mexico.** Entrees $19–$37.

La Hacienda de San Angel ★★ MEXICAN   By day, it's a sunny place to get your tequila on. By night, this villa-themed restaurant (vaulted ceilings, hanging lanterns) is a fair place to sit for the nighttime show, but only if you're lucky enough to score a window seat. Margaritas are $15. Get the steak, chicken al pastor, or pan-seared snapper. **Mexico.** Entrees $19–$34.

DISNEY'S HOLLYWOOD STUDIOS

Disney worked for years to add more excitement to the 154-acre **Disney's Hollywood Studios ★**, the least popular of the four Disney parks. The kiddie rides of Toy Story Land (opened 2018), and the hotly anticipated Star Wars: Galaxy's Edge (2019) have helped bring people back in, but apart from those two improvements, the rest of the park still lags. Still, because of those two tent poles, it's the resort's second-hardest park to get a reservation for, after Magic Kingdom.

While the park was originally conceived as a single Epcot pavilion about show business, Universal's invasion of the Florida market prodded Disney executives to hastily inflate the concept and add a working production facility: Disney–MGM Studios. It was poorly planned. In 1989, the Studios opened with just two rides, both now gone. Production never took off, the park layout was (and remains) confusing, and younger guests didn't care about the MGM co-branding. Its production center for hand-painted animated movies shut down in 2004; MGM was stripped from the name in 2008. From now on, though, people will call it "the *Star Wars* park."

When Covid-19 shut down live entertainment around the world, the flaws of Hollywood Studios became pronounced; a significant chunk of its diversions depend on person-to-person performance such as live retellings of popular movies. Without them, there are only nine rides to occupy your time (there are that many rides in Magic Kingdom's Fantasyland alone). Although a few of those rides are simply terrific, there are not enough of them. This park still lacks the sizzle of the others, but after dark, you can either see the meaty spectacular **Fantasmic!** (p. 100) or two shorter presentations that require less planning. **Star Wars: A Galactic Spectacular** ☝ is a decent 13-minute show that mixes fireworks, lasers, and projections; it's well done but modestly so. Get a viewpoint that looks squarely at the Chinese Theater or you'll miss details.

Hollywood Boulevard & Echo Lake

You arrive by the usual car/tram combo, by free ferry (from Epcot and the Boardwalk) or by bus (from the other parks). As soon as your bag is approved and you're through the gates, take care of business (strollers, wheelchairs, lockers) in the plaza before proceeding down Hollywood Boulevard. There are no attractions here, only shops and restaurants. In 2001, a 122-foot-tall Sorcerer Mickey Hat was built at the Boulevard's terminus as a central icon

Disney's Hollywood Studios

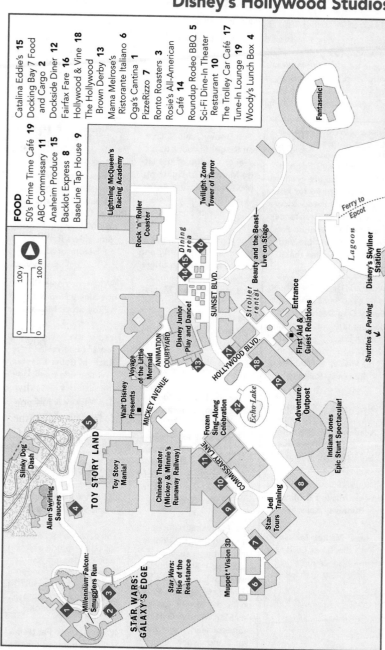

FOOD

50's Prime Time Café **19**
ABC Commissary **11**
Anaheim Produce **15**
Backlot Express **8**
Baseline Tap House **9**
Catalina Eddie's **15**
Docking Bay 7 Food and Cargo **2**
Dockside Diner **12**
Fairfax Fare **16**
Hollywood & Vine **18**
The Hollywood Brown Derby **13**
Mama Melrose's Ristorante Italiano **6**
Oga's Cantina **1**
PizzeRizzo **7**
Ronto Roasters **3**
Rosie's All-American Café **14**
Roundup Rodeo BBQ **5**
Sci-Fi Dine-In Theater Restaurant **10**
The Trolley Car Café **17**
Tune-In Lounge **19**
Woody's Lunch Box **4**

DISNEY'S HOLLYWOOD STUDIOS: 1 DAY, TWO WAYS

START: BE AT THE GATE FOR OPENING TIME.

To visit Star Wars: Galaxy's Edge, you'll want advance reservations for its most popular attractions (see "Galaxy's Edge: Preparing for Your Visit," p. 96) and a spot in the virtual queue for the ride Star Wars: Rise of the Resistance (see "Virtual Queues: the Disney Ride Lottery," p. 95). But Disney tweaks its procedures at the drop of the hat, frustrating vacationers far and wide, so the day before your visit, check MDX or the website to ensure the ride reservation procedure hasn't changed.

HOLLYWOOD STUDIOS WITH KIDS

Work Galaxy's Edge in whenever you are granted access (see p. 96 for how to get your reservation for Rise of the Resistance), and ride Millennium Falcon: Smugglers Run either before or after that.

When the gates open, head directly to Toy Story Land's **Slinky Dog Dash,** the most popular ride outside of Galaxy's Edge. If your kids aren't into roller coasters, do **Mickey & Minnie's Runaway Railway.**

OR

Note: If your child wants to participate in the **Jedi Academy,** reserve a slot first thing (ask a cast member where; it changes).

↓

If you did Slinky Dog first, now do **Mickey & Minnie's Runaway Railway.**

↓

Meet **Mickey Mouse** (check the Times Guide for his location).

↓

See **Disney Junior—Live on Stage!** (if your kids are wee) or **Voyage of the Little Mermaid** or **Lightning McQueen's Racing Academy** (if they're grammar school age).

↓

For younger kids, target a performance of **Beauty and the Beast—Live on Stage** for around now. For older kids, do **Toy Story Mania!**

↓

At this point, littler ones may need to leave the park for a break.

↓

See **Muppet*Vision 3-D.**

↓

See the **Indiana Jones Epic Stunt Spectacular.**

↓

If you think the whole family can handle more intense rides, slot in the **Twilight Zone Tower of Terror** and/or the **Rock 'n' Roller Coaster.**

↓

See **Fantasmic!** (if it's performing tonight). People stake out their seats as long as an hour ahead, but 30 minutes will do. If there is an evening sky show scheduled on the day of your visit (such as **Star Wars: A Galactic Spectacular**), make sure you stand somewhere with a view of the middle of the Chinese Theater.

HOLLYWOOD STUDIOS WITHOUT KIDS

Work Galaxy's Edge in whenever you are granted access (see p. 96 for how to get your reservation for Rise of the Resistance), and ride Millennium Falcon: Smugglers Run either before or after.

When the gates open, ride **Slinky Dog Dash** or **Toy Story Mania!**

↓

Head to the **Twilight Zone Tower of Terror** and the **Rock 'n' Roller Coaster** and ride them.

↓

Do **Mickey & Minnie's Runaway Railway.**

↓

Ride **Star Tours.**

↓

See **Muppet*Vision 3-D.**

↓

See the **Indiana Jones Epic Stunt Spectacular.**

You'll have a lot of time to kill now—re-ride anything you choose. Or you may decide you're done for the day—perhaps see the nighttime attractions at Animal Kingdom.

↓

If you stay, see **Fantasmic!** (if it's performing tonight) or the sky show above the Chinese Theater.

for the park, but it was demolished in 2015 (to cheers from purists) and the park's original entrance vista of the Chinese Theater was restored. No one pays much attention to the theater's forecourt and it is no longer refreshed with footprints and handprints, but you can still see many concrete impressions collected from movie stars when the park was still angling to be a player in the film industry. In fact, this is the only place to find Audrey Hepburn's handprints; she didn't leave them at the Hollywood Grauman's.

For the First Time in Forever: A Frozen Sing-Along Celebration ★ SHOW

The 30-minute, self-explanatory musical torture chamber features live actors telling the history of Arendelle six to 10 times daily, generally hourly, as well as an opportunity for you to endure "Let It Go" for one more white-knuckled, mother-loving time. You'll be seated in the air-conditioning, but the real Elsa and Anna show is over at Epcot now. **Strategy:** Strong cocktails are served at a kiosk on the patio of the Brown Derby, opposite the theatre.

Mickey & Minnie's Runaway Railway ★★★ RIDE

The big opening at DHS for 2020 was a boisterous indoor ride dedicated to the madcap world of animated short films from which this whole crazy Disney empire grew. Amazingly, this is the first ride to pay tribute to Mickey and Minnie (but if you're counting, it's the seventh Walt Disney World attraction based on a train). This slow-moving, sorta-1930s-styled kaleidoscope is visually dazzling, with lurid colors powered by some mysterious and hypnotic technology, a trackless ride system that shuffles vehicles mid-adventure, some strategic puffs of wind, appearances by Goofy and Daisy and a few more friends, and a wacky multi-scene romp so ridiculous (but tame) that even small children will enjoy themselves. Keep your eyes peeled for hidden Mickeys galore, but you won't have much time, because it's an ever-shifting eye-pleasing riot. It's so impossible to take it all in, I call it Mickey & Minnie's Ritalin Railway. The final result of this ride was so good that Disneyland is building one next. You might want to ride this one twice in your day at this park.

The Best of Disney's Hollywood Studios

Don't miss if you're 6: Slinky Dog Dash
Don't miss if you're 16: Star Wars: Rise of the Resistance
Requisite photo op: The Chinese Theater, The Millennium Falcon
Food you can only get here: Ronto Wrap at Ronto Roasters, Star Wars: Galaxy's Edge, Hollywood Boulevard; Peanut Butter and Jelly Milkshake at 50's Prime Time Café, Echo Lake
Where everyone stampedes first: Star Wars: Galaxy's Edge; Slinky Dog Dash

Skippable: Beauty and the Beast—Live on Stage
Quintessentially Disney: Mickey & Minnie's Runaway Railway
Biggest thrill: Twilight Zone Tower of Terror
Best show: Fantasmic!
Biggest store: Mickey's of Hollywood, Hollywood Boulevard
Where to find peace: Around Echo Lake

Indiana Jones Epic Stunt Spectacular ★★ SHOW   The 30-minute, bone-rattling tour de force of hair-raising daredevilry—rolling-boulder dodging, trucks flipping over and exploding—simultaneously titillates and, to a lesser degree, reminds you how such feats of derring-do are rigged for the movies. They try hard to convince you that they're really filming these sequences—you may need to explain to young children why they're lying about that, and about calling the lead actor "Harrison Ford's stunt double," but most kids understand the violence is fake. The acrobats and gymnasts are skilled, and the production values are among the highest of any show at a Disney park. The outdoor amphitheater is sheltered, and you can bring drinks and food. If you exit to the left, you'll pass a tank used in the third Indiana Jones movie. *Strategy:* Arrive 20 minutes early, because there's a warm-up and volunteers are selected before showtime. It's mounted about five times daily, listed on the app.

Star Tours—The Adventures Continue ★★★ RIDE   Before Disney bought *Star Wars*, it made, and later upgraded, this popular 40-person motion-simulator capsule that has you riding shotgun with a fretful C-3PO on an ill-fated and turbulent excursion. In 5 minutes, you manage to lose control, go into hyperdrive, dodge asteroids, navigate a comet field, evade a Star Destroyer, get caught in a tractor beam, and join an assault on the Death Star—or another combination of perils, since there are more than four dozen storylines (some created to promote the new movies). The video is well matched to the movements, which cuts down on reports of nausea. Row 1 is the front row, and that's the best place to see the screen.

Jedi Training ★★ ☛ SHOW   Up to 15 times daily (see the app), about a dozen kids are lent robes, telescoping "light sabers," and some gentle training in the Force by a "Jedi master" before a final defeat of Darth Vader and some Stormtroopers. It's cute and takes 20 minutes. Recruits (ages 4–12) are selected by 10:30am, tops, at the **Adventure Outpost,** to the left of the Indiana Jones show as you face it, so get there early if your young Padawan wants a shot at carrying home the diploma. If you require an absolute guarantee of getting in, you could buy the Star Wars tour from the special tours (it's not always offered), but that's $99.

Star Wars: Galaxy's Edge

Disney's Star Wars is its own unprecedented creation, a unique destination called Black Spire Outpost on the planet of Batuu, which has never been seen in films before. Designed with meticulous input from Lucasfilm to ensure every light saber burn mark and creature fits in with the franchise's universe (literally), Galaxy's Edge is like the set of a play that no one has seen yet. All you really need to grasp is that Black Spire is a remote, mostly forgotten hideaway where scoundrels and smugglers thrive. There is an oppressive regime (the First Order), whose agents drop by occasionally to beat the bushes

VIRTUAL QUEUES: the disney ride lottery

Disney Parks' shift to digital solutions has introduced a new task to the list of your preparations: entering Virtual Queues. It's a dirty little secret that Disney lets more people into its parks than it can serve, and it increasingly wants to push more people to make reservations using digital lines so they can do more lucrative things (like spend money in shops) rather than waste time waiting in line.

Here's how it works for the hottest rides that you can't book ahead: At 7am sharp on the day of your visit, you may vie for your shot at the attraction with your smartphone. (At 1pm, there's usually a second and final drawing.) Prepare to enter by making sure your ticket and theme park reservation are in order, and ensure your entire party has been linked to you using the Family & Friends section of the Disney World app. A few minutes before 7am, open the app and navigate to the Virtual Queue section. Keep refreshing by dragging downward; when the clock strikes 7, your profile icon will appear. Add everyone in your party so the system knows you want to ride together, and click to join. It will all be over in a few seconds.

If you're lucky, you'll be assigned a "Boarding Group" (not a time) and your app will alert you when it's time to head to the ride. Your app will also generate a QR code to serve as your ticket.

If you're unlucky, you must try again for the second drawing.

If you're *really* unlucky, you go home without riding, because often there's no standby line.

I must prepare you: It's not only possible to get shut out, but it happens all the time. I've watched entire families console each other outside Star Wars: Rise of the Resistance when the second chance fails. Terrible as it is, it is possible to be dazzled by Disney World's Galaxy's Edge ads on TV, spend thousands to fly to Orlando just to see it—and then never ride its most famous attraction.

The Virtual Queue system is unfair for a host of reasons. It favors the young, moneyed, and nimble. Not everyone has the reflexes to succeed at the Virtual Queue system, or they may lack the computer literacy, the visual or mental acuity, the upgraded smartphone, or even a phone at all. And it also favors people who have more money.

Disney cast members say that if guests have disabilities or other impediments to attempting to join the Virtual Queue—such as owning a phone older than the iPhone 6, the poor things—then those visitors can wait in line at Guest Relations to plead their case for a spot in line at Rise of the Resistance.

It's a farce. May the farce be with you.

for a band of rebels (the Resistance) that hides out around these parts (that is, outside of the settlement, where the **Rise of the Resistance** ride is). Although it's not immediately evident, the day you're visiting Batuu takes place sometime after the events depicted in 2017's *The Last Jedi*.

The souvenirs are nothing like you've seen before. Seek Yoda key chains, you must not. Much of what's sold here feels more like movie props than cheesy souvenirs. The souklike **Marketplace** is lined with stalls, each selling themed merch (Jedi clothing in one, stuffed animal "pets" in another, and one selling crude dolls of folk heroes from the Resistance that these remote people

Star Wars: Galaxy's Edge is probably the only theme park land that could benefit from having a user handbook. May these facts be with you:

○ **Oga's Cantina** is a sumptuously whimsical place to drink and snack (and collect tiki-like mugs), but it's not big enough for all the people who want to go. Disney is always tweaking its crowd management techniques, but one thing is certain: You must reserve ahead. Go online up to 60 days *before* you visit (or, if you're staying in a Disney hotel, 60 days plus the length of your stay) to see what the rules are now. You don't have to be in the park to secure a slot. A $10 deposit is required, so create a profile with a credit card *before* booking at www.disneyworld.com/ogascantina. Once you're in, you get a maximum of two drinks and 45 minutes.

○ Same goes for the wildly popular **Savi's Workshop,** where you build your own light saber in a mystical 10-minute ritual. Reservations are essential, so go to www.disneyworld.com/savisworkshop up to 60 days ahead to see how Disney wants you to do it. You must pay $220 for the saber up front, so make sure you have a credit card linked to your profile already. Granted your creation will be substantial and undeniably cool—customized down to the color and optional rancor's tooth on the hilt. But missing such a sublime experience results in a lot of upset children pestering their parents to pay up. Maybe that's the point.

○ The robots you customize at **Droid Depot** ($100 and up) can be fitted with various personality chips that cause them to react in distinct ways to each part of Batuu. It's wise to reserve (up to 180 days ahead) at www.disneyworld.com/droiddepot.

○ Dollars don't work in space. Items are priced in credits. Luckily, the exchange rate of U.S. dollars to credits is 1:1 and always will be. Vendors still take dollars, of course,

have heard tell of once, like Finn and Leia). The divinely decorated **Dok-Ondar's Den of Antiquities** is where you find the collectibles for the hardest-core fans. At Droid Depot, you can build your own robot companion, like an honest-to-goodness radio-controlled BB-8 model that actually rolls along.

Each of the "cast members" has a backstory, and they don't break character, not even when they ask if you want a "transcription" (receipt). Not even when you ask directions to the bathroom ("refresher"). Asking if you're allegiant to the Resistance or to the First Order is pretty much the "what's your major?" of Black Spire Outpost. You will also see a couple of characters from the new batch of films, including rebel Rey and sulky arch-baddie Kylo Ren. Just don't tell *him* "May the Force be with you," because that's a Jedi thing and he's Mr. First Order.

The timing of your visit to this land will probably depend on the "boarding group" you're assigned for Rise of the Resistance using the Disney World app (see the breakdown on how the Virtual Queue lottery works on p. 95), but you can roam the land anytime.

but you can use the local currency: **Batuuan Spira.** Also in Droid Depot, trade a minimum of $100 for a weathered-looking metal "credit medallion." In actuality, this token is a gift card that debits purchases from your prepaid account. You can still use it for anything at any Disney theme park or resort. Once the token is empty, you can either keep it as a souvenir or reload it (only at Galaxy's Edge) with more money.

○ Before you leave home, make sure you've got plenty of battery power (bring a power pack if you can) and download the free **Play Disney Parks** app. That's a different app from the standard Disney World one. When you're physically in Galaxy's Edge, the app's Star Wars–specific features spring to life and can do four main things:

Hack: When you see an illuminated surveillance panel, stand near it and a line-drawing puzzle appears on your phone. Choose to "deactivate" the panel for the Resistance or put it back online for the First Order. Or collect both types of points to be a "Scoundrel." Others are also playing and eventually, a side dominates, a winner is declared via the app, and the game (insiders call it "Outpost Control") starts again.

Translate: Signs are written in Aurebesh, an invented alien language. Hold your phone up to the writing and see what it says or translate letter by letter. (Don't worry: The restroom signs are in English. So are the menus.)

Scan: When you see cargo with QR codes on the side, scan it to find out what's inside.

Tune: Use this to triangulate the reception of radio transmissions—over time, you'll collect lots of bits of information that build a backstory going on behind the scenes. At the bottom of the screen, **Jobs** asks you to go on a mini scavenger hunt (the **Map** will help) to add more items to your roster.

Star Wars: Rise of the Resistance ★★★ RIDE   This is the most epic ride you've ever set foot on. It's no roller coaster or spinny cop-out with cheap physical thrills that make grown-ups sick. No, the primary sensation it wants to evoke is a sense of science fiction reality, as if you're truly racing from scene to scene, hounded by Stormtroopers and Kylo Ren, as the central player in the escape plot of a movie. When it comes to its scenic extravagance and population of Audio-Animatronic figures, this beats Pirates of the Caribbean by at least 12 parsecs. Can you handle it? Sure—there are some big, bouncy dropping movements up and down, and some jostling simulator motion and lasers aplenty (if it helps, the height requirement is the same as Big Thunder Mountain), but the dominant action—and this is as you progress through several ride systems—will be scooting through achingly realistic spaces in an 8-passenger (two rows of four) skifflike cart. Without giving any of its many surprises away, this is probably the most complex, most ambitious, and largest indoor theme park ride ever built, and you'll want to appreciate it. There's so much fabulousness going on that it can take you up to a half-hour from entrance to exit. *Tip:* Lines are the worst when the park opens.

Millennium Falcon: Smugglers Run ★★★ RIDE   For Star Wars fans, sitting at the chessboard in the hold of the *Millennium Falcon* is a dream come true. You'll do that and more on Smugglers Run, a ride in which six people sit in a mockup of the cockpit of Han Solo's battered but trusty ship. Using highly believable but non-nauseating flight simulator technology, you pilot a mission under the verbal direction of Hondo Ohnaka, a smuggler. You hear him—and sometimes see him on little cockpit screens—tell you when to steer, shoot, and punch buttons. Do well for a high score; crash into everything to annoy your narrator. Each row has its own function: Pilots, in front, control lateral movement (left seat) as well as up-and-down movement and initiation of warp speed (right-hand seat). In the middle seats, gunners push illuminated buttons on cue to fire guns and harpoons. Third-row engineers have the least to do, pushing buttons now and then to "repair" the ship (no, I don't know how that would work—we're space pirates but you want to get literal *now*?). Ride attendants assign roles indiscriminately, but your group can always swap places before boarding. Pick an engineer's seat if you're terrible at video games and would rather do more watching than button-banging. Pilots, on the other hand, have nonstop duties and the best view. The pilot on the right gets to pull the lever to send the ship into hyperspace, so that's the coolest yet most demanding spot. Assign roles judiciously according to the personalities in your group. *Strategy:* Since there's a single rider line that moves quickly, you can always re-ride until you try all the roles.

Muppets Courtyard & Commissary Lane

The whimsical fountain of Miss Piggy as the Statue of Liberty reminds us of better days, when a franchise as beloved as the Muppets wasn't shunted into a corner of the park. Mostly, it's where you can find two places serving Italian food.

Muppet*Vision 3-D ★ SHOW   See it soon, because it stands on prime *Star Wars* expansion real estate between Galaxy's Edge and Star Tours. The 17-minute movie features various tricks, all of them clever, to make you feel like what you're seeing is actually happening. The doors on the right lead to the back of the 600-seat auditorium and the ones on the left lead to the front; try to sit in the middle, since the theater's walls become part of the show and you'll want to see everything. Because Jim Henson died in mid-production, the movie contains a few missteps (Waldo, a crude CG character, is seriously dated). Still, it's fast-moving and includes lots of beloved *Muppet Show* favorites, such as Miss Piggy, Kermit, and Sam Eagle. The Muppets, too, lend themselves nicely to Audio-Animatronic technology. *Strategy:* Lines are longest just after the Indiana Jones show lets out.

Sunset Boulevard

The prime items in the park are on this street, which peels off not from the hub, as you might expect, but from the middle of Hollywood Boulevard. Look for vaudeville-style, slapstick **street performances** here.

The Twilight Zone Tower of Terror ★★★ RIDE   The tallest ride at Disney World (199 ft.) is one of the smartest, most exciting experiences at the parks, and it's the best version of the ride at any Disney park. It shouldn't be missed. Guests are ushered through the lobby, library, and boiler room of a cobwebby 1930s Los Angeles hotel before being seated in a 21-passenger "elevator" car that, floor by floor, ascends the tower and then, without visible tracks, emerges from the shaft and roams an upper level. Soon, you've entered a second shaft and, after a pregnant moment of tension, you're sent into what seems to be a free fall (in reality, you're being pulled faster than the speed of gravity) and a series of thrilling up-and-down leaps. The fall sequence is random and you never drop more than a few stories—but the total darkness, periodically punctured by picture-window views of the theme park far below as you become momentarily weightless, keys up the giddy fear factor. It's impossible not to smile. *Strategy:* In the preshow "library" room, move to the wall diagonally across from the entry door and you'll exit first, saving time. In the boarding area, the best views are in the front row, numbered 1 and 2, although you may not be given a choice. Chickens can bail down the stairs before the ride boards.

Rock 'n' Roller Coaster Starring Aerosmith ★★★ RIDE   On one of DHS's two coasters, 24-passenger "limousine" trains launch from 0 to 57mph in under 3 seconds, sending them through a 92-second rampage through smooth corkscrews and turns that are intensified by fluorescent symbols of Los Angeles (at one point, you dive though an "o" of the Hollywood sign). The indoor setup is a boon, because it means the ride can operate during the rain. Cooler yet, speakers in each headrest (there are more than 900 in total) play Aerosmith music, which is perfectly timed to the dips and rolls. *Strategy:* There's a single-rider line, though it's not always quick.

Lightning McQueen's Racing Academy ★★ SHOW   This minor 2019 addition is in a warehouse-like building behind Rock 'n' Roller Coaster that hasn't been used much before; maybe that's why what's inside feels extraneous. But as the only permanent *Cars*-themed attraction in Florida, it offers your only chance to admire the superb character engineering work behind the much larger Cars Land in Anaheim. It consists of a lone, full-size Lightning McQueen, whom we find stuck on a dais, testing his skills using a simulator. He's so perfectly done that it's disappointing that other characters like Mater, Cruz Ramirez, and Chick Hicks appear only on a wraparound screen. Meanwhile, Lightning just spins his wheels without going anywhere and calls it a success. Bright, colorful, loud, and over in 10 minutes. *Tip:* Presentations are continuous, so you'll probably never wait more than 15 minutes.

Beauty and the Beast—Live on Stage ★ ☛ SHOW   The kid-friendly 30-minute show is advertised as "Broadway-style," but it's really not. It's theme park–style, simplified with the most popular songs from the movie. The story is highly condensed (you never find out why Belle is at the Beast's castle and Gaston's fate isn't shown), and many characters inhabit whole-body costumes, speaking recorded dialogue with unblinking eyes. To accommodate timid kids, the Beast looks more like a plush toy than a scary monster. The metal benches are numbing, but at least the amphitheater is covered. *Strategy:* Arrive 20 minutes early so you don't end up in the back where afternoon sun can seep in.

Fantasmic! ★★★ SHOW   The super-popular 25-minute pyrotechnics show featuring character-laden showboats, a 59-foot man-made mountain, flaming water, and lasers projected onto a giant water curtain, takes place in the 6,500-seat waterfront Hollywood Hills Amphitheatre. Although it's a strong show by dint of its uniqueness, it doesn't play nightly. I'm always stunned to see people start arriving at the theater as much as *2 hours* before showtime. Most people will be satisfied taking their chances and showing up within 30 minutes of showtime. The seating is hard on the derriere. *Strategy:* On nights when there are two performances (not common), do the second one, as it's always less crowded. Sit toward the rear to avoid catching water from the special effects and to the right to make exiting easier.

Pixar Place & Animation Courtyard

If you have wee kids, Animation Courtyard is where two of the primary toddler attractions are. When the park opened, it was the starting point of a walking tour through a working studio that actually produced Disney movies. The artists were evicted and now it's a strange community of Stormtroopers and toddlers.

The Voyage of the Little Mermaid ★★ ☛ SHOW   This bright, energetic, condensed version of the animated movie has high production values (puppets, live actors, mist, and a cool undersea-themed auditorium) and is a standout. It's a top contender for the best show to see in the heat of the day. *Strategy:* In the preshow holding pen, the doors to the left lead to the back half of the theater; because the blacklight puppetry of the marvelous "Under the Sea" sequence can be spoiled if you see too much detail, I suggest sitting there. Put very small kids in your lap so they can see better.

Disney Junior Play and Dance! ★ SHOW   For those of us who obediently rise and dance when commanded by Mickey Mouse, there's this breezy, 23-minute show with lots of truly excellent puppets. (*Warning for adults:* You sit on the ground.) It inspires such fervent participation from under-5s that it feels like a meeting for a kindergarten cult that you're not a member of. Even if you don't know the names Doc McStuffins or Vampirina, this sing-along revue is still pretty to look at, and Mickey, Donald, and friends make appearances. The parental units won't be too bored, because this de facto Disney Channel ad is fast-paced, like changing the channel every 4 minutes. Obviously, anyone old enough to do a book report can skip it. *Tip:* It only happens once or twice an hour.

Walt Disney Presents ★★★ ACTIVITY   The only focus on Disney history on resort property, it's mostly overlooked but the display is a requisite stop for anyone curious about the undeniable achievements of this driven man. Here, you (and a few other stragglers) find a few authentic artifacts (props, costumes, the desk from his studio on Hyperion Ave.), plus explanations of the revolutionary "multiplane" camera that enabled animators to reproduce the sliding depth of field normally seen in live-action films—you've seen the fruit of the process in *Snow White* as the camera seems to move through the forest. The end of the exhibition chronicles the theme parks, including a few scale models (of Galaxy's Edge, Spaceship Earth, Tower of Terror, and more) and an Abe Lincoln Audio-Animatronic skeleton from the 1964 World's Fair. Most people take about 20 minutes for the museum, and then there's a good 15-minute movie, culled mostly from archival footage. The feature scores points for mentioning Disney's 1931 breakdown, but tries to prove Walt was a patron of the Disney Company's current efforts, implying he approved of Epcot's final design and, worse, elbowing pivotal Roy Disney virtually out of the story. But maybe it can be changed. "Disneyland," he promises, "is something that will never be finished."

Toy Story Land

Toy Story Land (opened 2018) is one of the park's most colorful treats. Take a few minutes to absorb the surroundings—the concept (not immediately obvious) is that you have shrunk down to the size of Andy's toys. It's a tough zone on hot days since the trees are still too young to provide much shade and only one of the three rides (Toy Story Mania!) has an indoor queue. There are no indoor restaurants in this area, either, just a kiosk. The expansion accomplished two goals: Build more stuff that plays off of millennial nostalgia, and add more rides younger kids can do. There's also a ton of product placement, and everything looks its best after dark. *Fun fact:* Here, Woody isn't voiced by Tom Hanks but by his sound-alike brother, Jim, who (with Tom's blessing) takes all the recording work his brother doesn't have time for.

Slinky Dog Dash ★★★ ROLLER COASTER   Quick accelerations, banked turns, and humps with genuine air time make it more exuberant than it appears to be, yet for all its giddy sensations, its 2 minutes remain rambunctiously accessible. At its climax, this terrific coaster delivers what could be

Go on Safari—for Mice

A favorite resort-wide pastime for long-time fans is spotting **Hidden Mickeys,** ingeniously camouflaged mouse-ear patterns that can be secreted just about anywhere. You'll find the three circles signifying a Mickey head in an arrangement of cannonballs on Peter Pan's Flight; flatware in the dining room at the Haunted Mansion; woven into carpeting, printed on wallpaper. Many sightings are up to interpretation, so sharpen your observational skills at **HiddenMickeysGuide.com.**

considered the opposite of adrenaline as passengers wonder if it's gained enough speed to make it up a big hill. While not for toddlers (minimum height is 38 in.), it perfectly straddles the family-friendly line, unleashing a little giddy-up for the teens without turning into something Grandma would curse, and the theming has a few surprises you can't see from the waiting area. *Tip:* After Galaxy's Edge, this is the most popular attraction. So head here early.

Toy Story Mania! ★★★ RIDE   Wearing 3D glasses, passengers shoot their way through a series of six animated indoor midway games (themed as Woody's suction-cup shooting game, a Little Green Men ring toss, and the like) based on the Pixar toy box characters. Along the way, air puffs heighten the reality. Your cannon is easy to work and easy on the hands—you just tug a cord and it fires. Racking up points is harder; both accuracy and intensity count—a top score for the whole month might be 584,000 (my record is 212,600). The queue area, stuffed with outsize toys such as Etch-a-Sketch and Barrel of Monkeys, makes waiting a delight: A 6-foot-tall, lifelike Mr. Potato Head entertains with live interaction and hoary jokes ("Is this an audience or a jigsaw puzzle?").

Alien Swirling Saucers ★ RIDE   It's essentially a covered variant of the tried-and-true Whip carnival thrill but with a Little Green Men theme (and the same thing as Mater's Junkyard Jamboree at the Disneyland resort). Your vehicle, containing a bench that should fit up to four, does an easygoing do-si-do with other carts along four slowly spinning plates. It takes 90 seconds, which is enough time to meander across the four discs three times, and because you're not actually spinning but weaving, it doesn't tend to make most people queasy the way the teacups ride does. It's easy on kids (who must be at least 32 in.), and a nice enough diversion, but nothing you can't skip if time is scarce. *Tip:* Seat your heaviest passenger on the end; the spinning will send everyone sliding into them.

Where to Eat at Disney's Hollywood Studios

All locations have a few vegetarian options, kids' meals, and if you identify yourself, special dietary requests can usually be accommodated, albeit often at diminished quality. There are also some snack kiosks not listed here, and you can buy alcohol throughout the park. Grouped by area:

DISNEY'S HOLLYWOOD STUDIOS' QUICK-SERVICE RESTAURANTS

It's hard to tell because there's no menu outside, but **Oga's Cantina** in Galaxy's Edge is for drinks and weird snacks, not a place for full meals. The popular counter-service **BaseLine Tap House,** at the end of Commissary Lane, doesn't do full meals either, but it has nine excellent craft beers on draught, one cider, and light bites like soft pretzels and cheese plates. Unless noted, all quick-service options accept Mobile Order.

Hollywood Boulevard & Echo Lake

Backlot Express ★★ AMERICAN   Bacon cheeseburgers, chicken and biscuits, hot dogs, and a few simple salads served with air-conditioning and self-serve soda machines for endless refills. **Echo Lake.** Combo meal $11–$14.

Dockside Diner ★ AMERICAN   The menu changes, but expect hot dogs, nachos, pulled-pork sliders, eaten alfresco under umbrellas for shade. There are some changing food carts on the other side of the lake, too. **Echo Lake.** Combo meal $11–$13. No Mobile Orders.

The Trolley Car Café ★★ AMERICAN   A glorified Starbucks themed after Los Angeles' bygone Red Cars, it has the usual Starbucky food. **Hollywood Boulevard.** Sandwiches from $6.

Star Wars: Galaxy's Edge

Docking Bay 7 Food and Cargo ★★ AMERICAN   Breakfast (if it's being served when you're there) includes egg bites, overnight oats, and Mustafarian Lava Rolls (cinnamon rolls); the rest of the day, the Smoked Kaadu Ribs (sticky pork ribs) are a hit, as are items that, despite spacey names, are comforting dishes like fried chicken and pot roast. It's all served in the air-conditioning of an industrial space shuttle hangar. To drink, Moof Juice is fruit punch mixed with orange and a gentle chipotle-pineapple. **Star Wars: Galaxy's Edge.** Combo meal $13–$19.

Ronto Roasters ★★★ AMERICAN   Despite the name, it doesn't cook easygoing pack animals from Tatooine, although out front you will see a droid barbecuing meat using the engine of a pod racer. The Ronto Wrap (roasted pork, grilled sausage, tangy slaw, and peppercorn sauce) is quite delicious. **Star Wars: Galaxy's Edge.** Meals without sides $8–$13.

Muppets Courtyard & Commissary Lane

ABC Commissary ★★ AMERICAN   Upgraded casual food: Burgers, shrimp tacos, Buffalo chicken grilled-cheese sandwiches—it's air-conditioned, and you can pour your own drinks to your heart's content. **Commissary Lane.** Combo meal $11–$14.

PizzeRizzo ★ AMERICAN   Counter-service pizza, antipasto salad, and meatball subs themed to the Muppets with scads of air-conditioned seating. It has the biggest dining area in the park. **Muppets Courtyard.** Meals $10–$11.

Sunset Boulevard
Rosie's All-American Cafe ★★ AMERICAN   In the Sunset Ranch Market riff on L.A.'s Farmer's Market, you'll find outdoor-only but sheltered counter service with a menu of burgers, dogs, and chicken nuggets. **Sunset Boulevard.** Combo meal $10–$12.

Catalina Eddie's ★★ AMERICAN   Outdoor counter service for doughy personal pizza. Near it is **Anaheim Produce** for fruit ($2.50/piece). **Sunset Boulevard.** Combo meal $10–$12.

Fairfax Fare ★★ AMERICAN   Grab hand-friendly food: pulled-pork sandwiches, empanadas, and fajitas. **Sunset Boulevard.** Combo meal $12–$14.

Toy Story Land
Woody's Lunch Box ★ AMERICAN   Counter service with hot, exposed seating. Greasy delights include BBQ brisket melt and grilled three-cheese sandwiches. For breakfast, try the custard-soaked S'more French Toast and sugar crash early. **Toy Story Land.** Meals $9–$13.

DISNEY'S HOLLYWOOD STUDIOS' TABLE-SERVICE RESTAURANTS
All of these require reservations via the app (or ☎ **407/939-3463**); none of them fulfill Mobile Orders. The highest-concept reservation restaurants in Disney World are here. Sometime soon (maybe in time for your visit), Toy Story Land will add the **Roundup Rodeo BBQ** waiter-service joint, which is themed as if you're in a cardboard rodeo arena for Andy's toys.

The Hollywood Brown Derby ★★ AMERICAN   With interior design based on the after-hours industry hangout of Hollywood's Golden Age, this airy post-Deco hall shoots for class. Caricatures of film legends line the walls, and the Cobb salad served here (the original Brown Derby was noted for inventing Cobb salad) is a bit of a caricature in its own way: It's often soggy. Other choices all invoke that mid-20th-century California spirit at the park's highest prices ($29 for mushroom risotto? Are they kidding?). Expect fillet of beef, chicken à la King, salmon, and cioppino. The grapefruit cake ($13) is a specialty—they'll give you the recipe. Outside, **The Hollywood Brown Derby Lounge** does sliders, steamed buns, and cocktails ($14–$18) at tables under umbrellas. **Hollywood Boulevard.** Entrees $20–$49.

Hollywood & Vine ★★ AMERICAN   At lunch, costumed Disney Junior characters (such as Doc McStuffins and Fancy Nancy) greet kids, sing, and dance in a dinerlike setting for **Disney Junior Play 'n Dine at Hollywood &**

Vine. At dinner (and sometimes lunch during holidays), your core Disney talent (Mickey, Minnie, Donald, Daisy, Goofy) shows up. The food is always an all-you-can-eat buffet. **Echo Lake.** Buffet $34–$50 adults, $20–$30 kids.

50's Prime Time Café ★★★ AMERICAN Dine atop Formica in detailed reproductions of Cleaver-era kitchens while TVs play black-and-white shows from the era. Waitresses gently sass customers (drag your feet when they call you for dinner and you'll see what I mean) as they sling blue-plate specials—meatloaf, pot roast, fried chicken, and other mom-like dishes—but the favorite here is the peanut butter and jelly milkshake ($9). Attached is the **Tune-In Lounge,** a TV room for adults serving beer and proper cocktails "from Dad's liquor cabinet" like Long Island Iced Teas—plus anyone can eat from the regular menu at the bar, which is first-come, first-served. **Echo Lake.** Entrees $18–$27.

Mama Melrose's Ristorante Italiano ★★ ITALIAN Items cost two-thirds of what they do at Epcot's Italy, and the atmosphere recalls the brick-walled, red-boothed family restaurant you'd find in any big American city. As expected, there are pastas, steaks, flatbreads, saltimbocca, and wood-grilled chicken dishes. **Muppets Courtyard.** Entrees $19–$33.

Sci-Fi Dine-In Theater Restaurant ★★★ AMERICAN Disney World's most unusual restaurant arranges mock-ups of 1950s automobiles before a silver screen showing a loop of B-movie clips and trailers. Couples sit side-by-side, like at a real drive-in movie, stars twinkle in the "sky," and families get their own booths. It's a brilliant idea, but it was better when there were roller-skating carhops. Food quality is iffy. Dishes include burgers, salmon or chicken pasta, turkey sandwiches, and wedge salads. **Commissary Lane.** Entrees $19–$25.

DISNEY'S ANIMAL KINGDOM

The largest Disney theme park in Florida (500 acres), **Disney's Animal Kingdom ★★** is enjoying attention after years as an also-ran—it was Disney's second-most popular park in 2019 (13.9 million visits), boosted by a new *Avatar*-themed area, which opened in 2017. Animal Kingdom debuted in 1998 at a reported cost of $800 million as a competitor to Busch Gardens. Most of its land is devoted to a menagerie of exotic animals; instead of cages, they're kept in paddocks rimmed with trenches cleverly concealed by landscaping. Most attractions carry a mild environmentalist message (ironic, considering how much swamp was obliterated to build this resort, but never you mind).

Because animals retire to the shade as the Florida heat builds, a visit here most times of year should begin as soon as the gates open, usually around 8am, yet there really isn't enough to keep you here for 15 hours until the summer sun goes down. If you only have one day here, you really should choose whether to come in the morning (more active animals) or skew toward the

The Best of Disney's Animal Kingdom

Don't miss if you're 6: Festival of the Lion King

Don't miss if you're 16: Avatar Flight of Passage

Requisite photo op: The floating mountains of Pandora

Food you can only get here: Frozen chai at Royal Anandapur Tea Company

Where everyone stampedes first: Avatar Flight of Passage, Kilimanjaro Safaris

Skippable: Rafiki's Planet Watch

Quintessentially Disney: It's Tough to Be a Bug!

Biggest thrill: Expedition Everest

Best show: Festival of the Lion King

Biggest store: Island Mercantile, Oasis

Where to find peace: Discovery Island Trails

evening (Pandora alight, a nighttime spectacular, but fewer animals). *Tips:* Check the weather, because if it's excessively hot or wet, you will be miserable: Only five major attractions take place in air-conditioning. There is currently no night show at Animal Kingdom, but there is a daytime show, KiteTails (p. 112).

GETTING IN Locker and stroller rental are just past the gates in what's called the **Oasis,** a lush buffer zone that gradually acclimates guests to the world of the park. Disney isn't diligent about helping you find specific animal enclosures—they're not listed in the app and an info leaflet isn't always available; you just have to ask around. For general location info, try disneyworld. disney.go.com/attractions/animal-kingdom/disney-animals.

Generally speaking, the biggest animals collect at the back of the park (Africa and Asia), the thrills to the right (Asia and DinoLand U.S.A.). Nowhere will you find balloons—once discarded, they choke animals—and straws are made of paper for the same reason.

Discovery Island

Like the Plaza at the Magic Kingdom, Discovery Island is designed to be the hub of the park. Guests can touch down here to change lands.

The Tree of Life ★★★ ACTIVITY   Instead of a castle or a geosphere, the centerpiece here—Animal Kingdom's "weenie"—is an emerald-green 14-story-high arbor (built on the skeleton of an oil rig) covered with hundreds of animal carvings made to appear, at a distance, like the pattern of bark. That lurid green color is created by some 102,000 vinyl leaves, individually attached to 750 tertiary branches. The best way to enjoy it is to slowly make a circuit, looking for and identifying new animals (it's a foretaste of the entire park, which is best experienced when you slow down and open your eyes). At night, the front is illuminated with gently animated projections that highlight some of the hidden sculptures and bring them to life.

Discovery Island Trails ★★ ACTIVITY   On these self-guided paths encircling the Tree of Life, you might find giant red kangaroos, flamingoes,

Disney's Animal Kingdom

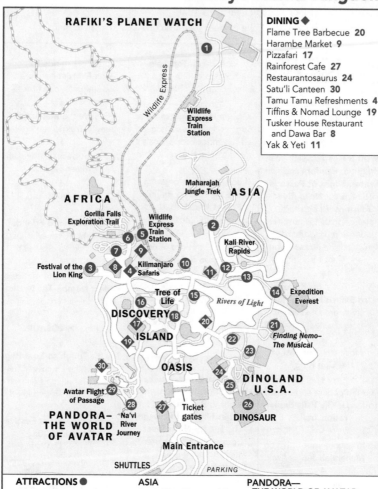

RAFIKI'S PLANET WATCH

DINING ◆
Flame Tree Barbecue **20**
Harambe Market **9**
Pizzafari **17**
Rainforest Cafe **27**
Restaurantosaurus **24**
Satu'li Canteen **30**
Tamu Tamu Refreshments **4**
Tiffins & Nomad Lounge **19**
Tusker House Restaurant
  and Dawa Bar **8**
Yak & Yeti **11**

Wildlife Express Train Station

AFRICA
Gorilla Falls Exploration Trail

ASIA
Maharajah Jungle Trek

Wildlife Express Train Station

Kali River Rapids

Festival of the Lion King

Kilimanjaro Safaris

Tree of Life

DISCOVERY

Rivers of Light

Expedition Everest

ISLAND

Finding Nemo–The Musical

OASIS

DINOLAND U.S.A.

Avatar Flight of Passage

PANDORA–THE WORLD OF AVATAR

Na'vi River Journey

Ticket gates

DINOSAUR

Main Entrance

SHUTTLES PARKING

ATTRACTIONS ●

DISCOVERY ISLAND
Adventurers Outpost **15**
Discovery Island Trails **16**
It's Tough to Be a Bug! **18**

AFRICA
Festival of the Lion King **3**
Gorilla Falls Exploration
  Trail **6**
Kilimanjaro Safaris **7**
Rafiki's Planet Watch **1**
Wildlife Express Train **5**

ASIA
Expedition Everest **14**
Disney's Kite Tails **13**
Feathered Friends in
  Flight **10**
Kali River Rapids **12**
Maharajah Jungle Trek **2**

**PANDORA—THE
WORLD OF AVATAR**
Avatar Flight of
  Passage **29**
Na'vi River Journey **28**

**PANDORA—
THE WORLD OF AVATAR**
Avatar Flight of Passage **29**
Na'vi River Journey **28**

DINOLAND U.S.A.
The Boneyard **22**
Chester & Hester's
  Dino-Rama **23**
DINOSAUR **26**
Dino-Sue **25**
Finding Nemo–The Musical **21**

DISNEY'S ANIMAL KINGDOM: 1 DAY, TWO WAYS

START: BE AT THE GATE FOR OPENING TIME.

Lines are longest for Avatar Flight of Passage. It won't be easy, so plan to wait.

ANIMAL KINGDOM WITH KIDS

Mornings here are busy, but afternoons are milder. This park is not always open after dark, but it's always more fun when it is.

When the gates open, head straight to **Pandora** and ride **Avatar: Flight of Passage.** The line for **Na'vi River Journey** will be shorter later on than it is now, so it's better to backtrack to it later on; ride it now if you don't want to do that.

↓

Go to Africa for **Kilimanjaro Safaris** because the animals are most active before the heat sets in.

↓

In Africa, see **Festival of the Lion King.**

↓

Find the gorillas and hippos on the **Gorilla Falls Exploration Trail.**

↓

Go to Asia to spot tigers on the **Maharajah Jungle Trek.**

↓

Ride **Kali River Rapids** to cool down.

↓

See **Feathered Friends in Flight.**

↓

Have lunch at Yak & Yeti.

↓

See the next performance of **Finding Nemo—The Musical,** seated and indoors.

↓

Ride **TriceraTop Spin** (or skip it—it's just a reptilian Dumbo ride).

↓

Go see **It's Tough to Be a Bug!** and walk the Discovery Trails to look for animals embedded in the Tree of Life.

↓

If you have time or energy, take the train to **Rafiki's Planet Watch** (budget 45 min. total).

↓

Wait until dusk to re-ride **Kilimanjaro Safaris** (if you care). If the park will be open past dark, return to **Pandora** to see its bioluminescent lights, or use the time to watch the projections on the **Tree of Life.**

ANIMAL KINGDOM WITHOUT KIDS

When the gates open, head straight to **Pandora** and ride **Avatar: Flight of Passage.** The line for **Na'vi River Journey** will be shorter later on than it is now, so it's better to backtrack to it later on; ride it now if you don't want to do that.

OR

If you're more into animals than indoor screen-based thrill rides, it's off to Africa for **Kilimanjaro Safaris.**

↓

Watch the gorillas on the **Gorilla Falls Exploration Trail.**

OR

Go to Asia to ride **Expedition Everest** before the line gets too crazy.

↓

Explore the **Maharajah Jungle Trek** to see tigers.

↓

If it's hot by now, ride **Kali River Rapids.**

↓

Eat at Yak & Yeti.

↓

See **Feathered Friends in Flight.** (Or maybe just chill with a cocktail.)

↓

See the next performance of **Finding Nemo—The Musical.** Enjoy the air-conditioning.

↓

Ride **DINOSAUR.**

↓

See **It's Tough to Be a Bug!** and walk the Discovery Trails to look for animals embedded in the Tree of Life.

↓

Go to Africa to see **Festival of the Lion King.**

↓

If you have time or energy, take the train to **Rafiki's Planet Watch** (budget 45 min. total).

↓

Wait until dusk to re-ride **Kilimanjaro Safaris** for the sunset experience. If the park will be open after dark, go to **Pandora** to see its bioluminescent lights, or use the time to watch the projections on the **Tree of Life.**

storks, otters, lemurs, macaws, and the lappet-faced vulture; some animals are removed from view when it's hot. It takes only about 15 minutes to enjoy.

Adventurers Outpost ★ CHARACTER GREETING   Mickey and Minnie, wearing explorer garb, meet kids and sign autographs here, on the east side of the path toward Asia. It is the only place in the resort where they appear as a couple.

It's Tough to Be a Bug! ★★★ SHOW   Hidden in the flying roots of the Tree of Life, in a cool basementlike theater, you'll find a cleverly rigged cinema showing a 10-minute 3D movie based on the animated film *A Bug's Life*. When the stinkbugs do their thing or the tarantula starts firing poison quills, you'll never quite be sure what's an image, what's cutting-edge robotics, and what's theatrical illusion. It's one of the best sense-tricking movies at Disney World. Little kids who can't distinguish fantasy from reality may be scared by the marvelously realized Hopper figure (voiced by Kevin Spacey in the movie but by a sound-alike actor here); sit in back (the first doors after you get your glasses) and to the left to be far from him. The indoor preshow area is decorated with posters for some funny entomological variations on Broadway shows (my faves: "Web Side Story" and "My Fair Ladybug"). *Strategy:* Upon exiting, go left to explore the trails (above) or right for the bridge to Asia.

Pandora—The World of Avatar

In 2017, at a reported cost of $500 million, Disney made the odd choice of opening this elaborate 12-acre area, which contains zero animals (are the Na'vi animals?) and isn't even a Disney-created franchise. Whatever the logic, though, you can't say it isn't pretty. It's also a smash—you can count on waiting for its rides. An evocation of the fantastical planet and tribal people from the 2009 film *Avatar,* Pandora is dominated by a vine-covered cascade of "floating mountains"—an impressive sight that's hard to photograph. (Scrutinize the waterfalls on them—notice anything unexpected about the most distant ones?) To simply wander is the best way to experience it, taking in the sumptuous floral creations and listening for weird alien animal calls coming from the foliage.

At night, vegetation and walkways are illuminated with fluorescent light (Disney likes to call it "bioluminescent"), and that spectacle necessitates a second visit after dark. Set aside the veiled, almost Victorian tropes about the Noble Savage that Disney seems to celebrate here. Seek out a cast member dressed as a guide for Alpha Centauri Exhibitions, the fictional tour company that purportedly brought you to Pandora. They can point out some of the hidden secrets of the land—such as secret pressure points in the trees that trigger flashes of light. There's a tiered viewing terrace in the center to better enable your admiration. The must-get souvenir, sold for $70 at the Rookery shop after Flight of Passage or at Island Mercantile: little banshee puppets that sit on your shoulder.

Avatar Flight of Passage ★★★ RIDE Like the characters in the movie, your consciousness will be transferred into the host body of (colonialism symbolism alert!) a Na'vi whose name you never learn, to ride a dragonlike creature, called a banshee, over the wonders of Pandora. Or that's the premise, and it's accomplished rather brilliantly, starting with a body scan to prep you for the transition. Easily one of the most elaborate attractions in Disneydom thanks in part to a sensationally decorated queue, the 4½-minute ride feels intense even though it's basically just you straddling a bike-like motion simulator (it secures you by gripping your legs and bracing your back) in front of a very big movie screen; a breeze and water spritzes keep you from becoming nauseated. The concept works a lot like Soarin', but with a 3D film and more intensity. Pay special attention to the fun physical feedback as your vehicle presses against your legs. You actually travel nowhere—the ride's point is to take in landscapes, not terrify you. *Tip:* Some larger guests report difficulty fitting on the vehicle, so test the sample out front. The theater is multi-leveled, so if you have a hard time with stairs, ask for sections 1C or 1D; section 2 is evenly in the middle and 3 is at the top.

Na'vi River Journey ★★ RIDE All ages will find this gentle boat float through a dark but colorful Pandoran bog to be mellow going. All you do is bob from room to room, listening to music and soaking up what you see—it's a strange world, after all. There are lots of pretty plants and animals to look at, but the most impressive thing is the huge, limber-limbed "Shaman of Songs," the most complex Audio-Animatronic figure ever built, that serenades you near the ride's climax. All told, Journey is 4½ minutes of calm—a glowing variation on the old-fashioned Tunnel of Love.

Africa

Due to its star attraction, Africa is mobbed in the morning; in the afternoon, it's a popular place to grab food or a cocktail. By evening, because of the new sunset effects on Kilimanjaro Safaris, it's mobbed again. **Dawa Bar,** at the entrance to Tusker House, is a nice place to people-watch with a cocktail.

Kilimanjaro Safaris ★★★ RIDE Easily the bumpiest ride at Disney World, the 20-minute excursion is the crown jewel of Animal Kingdom. Climb into a supersize, 32-passenger Jeep-like vehicle—an actual one with wheels, not a tracked cart—and be swept into what feels like a real safari through the African veldt, with meticulously rutted tracks and all. Be quick on the shutter, because drivers speed fleetly, passing through habitats for giraffes, elephants, wildebeest, ostrich, hippos, lions, antelope, rhinos, and other creatures that made safaris famous. Considering the quality and quantity of animals on display—and the cleverness of the enclosure design, as there are never bars between you and them—it's easily the best animal attraction of the park. Animals are most active when the park opens, but the queue builds once again at night so people can see it all over again with a sunset lighting effect.

Some people say that the second-best time to see the animals is in midafternoon because they get antsy with the foreknowledge that they're about to be led to their indoor sleeping quarters. Ride twice if you want—the free will of the animals means it's never the same trip twice: Sometimes you'll zip right through, and sometimes you'll be halted by a moody rhino who refuses to get off the road. *Strategy:* Photographers who want clear shots should jockey toward the back, away from the cockpit. At the very least, they should negotiate with their companions for a seat at the end of their row.

Gorilla Falls Exploration Trail ★★★ ACTIVITY   Upon exiting Kilimanjaro Safaris, begin this trail, which focuses on African animals. It wends past a troop of lowland gorillas (very popular), naked mole rats, okapi, meerkats (yes, like Timon), and hippos you can view through an underwater window; the nocturnal animals start waking up around 3:30pm. The circuit takes about a half-hour, but you can spend as long as you want. The gorillas come near the end, so budget your time. All areas close before dusk.

"Festival of the Lion King" ★ SHOW   Pandemic measures forced Disney to simplify what was once one of the most lavish, colorful, and intense spectacles it had. Audiences sit indoors on benches (front rows are good for engaging with performers), to watch what is now essentially a song concert with singers and dancers. Four huge floats enter the room, topped with soft-looking giant puppets of Timon, Pumbaa, and African wildlife and attended by singers, stilt-walkers, and dancers, all to the tunes of the movie. It's buoyant and cheerful, but not quite the prop-rich flag-waver it was before. *Strategy:* Shows are scheduled, and they can fill up, so arrive 30 minutes early. Unfortunately, the seating is bleacher-style and lacks backs. The last shows are around dusk. Ask if the original, unmodified version is back—if it is, this show becomes ★★★.

Rafiki's Planet Watch ★ ACTIVITY   Admiring all these animals is enough to make you want to find one you can actually cuddle. From near the Safaris, take the **Wildlife Express Train.** The trip takes 7 minutes and you'll get glimpses of plain backstage work areas. When you arrive, you'll find **The Affection Section,** a petting zoo hosting your typical petting-zoo denizens—domesticated farm animals, mostly—some nods to the nature movies Disney has made over the years, and characters from *The Lion King* granting mellower photo ops than you find back in the main park. This area is pleasantly calm, but not a necessity. *Tip:* It tends to close by late afternoon.

> ### Kid Stuff at Animal Kingdom
>
> Animal Kingdom has a free paper scavenger hunt, **Wilderness Explorers,** in which kids collect merit badges (stickers) for learning things about animals and conservation. Join on the bridge between Oasis and the Tree of Life, opposite the Yak & Yeti, and by Dino-Bite Snacks.

Asia

Asia's decor (rat-trap wiring, fraying prayer flags) evokes Nepal or northern India. Don't miss the white-cheeked gibbons who live on the ruined temple at the exit of Kali River Rapids. Also make a stop at **Bhaktapur Market,** which sells Asian souvenirs that are a cut above the usual theme park stuff—printed dresses, little Buddhas, conical hats.

You'll come here, to the amphitheater built onto the banks of the Discovery River, to catch the new daytime spectacular **Disney KiteTails**—kites, windcatchers, and fabric animals of all shapes, colors, and sizes are flown over the water to an upbeat soundtrack. Check the app for the day's scheduled times.

Expedition Everest ★★★ RIDE   The lavishly themed roller coaster is mostly contained in the "snowcapped" mountain looming nearly 200 feet over the park's east end (if it were any higher, Florida law would require it to be topped by an airplane beacon). The queue area is a beautifully realized duplication of a Himalayan temple down to the tarnished bells and red paint; portions of it are exposed to the sun, so drink something before you queue up. The coaster itself is loaded with powerful set pieces: both backward and forward motion, pitch-black sections, and a fleeting encounter with a 22-foot Abominable Snowman, or Yeti. As with all Disney rides, the most dramatic drop (80 ft.) is visible from the sidewalk out front, so if you think you can stomach that, you can do the rest. There are no upside-down loops; the dominant motion is spiral. *Strategy:* The seats with the best view, without question, are in the front rows, although back rows feel a little faster. The single-rider line (enter by Bazaar Gifts) is one of the resort's fastest-moving and most fruitful. It's especially exciting to ride at night.

Kali River Rapids ★ RIDE   The 12-passenger round bumper boat shoots a course of rapids, and sometimes you can get soaked—it depends on your bad luck—but it's generally milder than similar rides. Your feet, for sure, will get wet. The worst damage is usually done by spectators who shoot water cannons at passing boats. Lots of guests buy rain ponchos ($9–$10 each at nearby stores, or a buck at your local dollar store), but there is a water-resistant holding area for valuables in the center of each boat. To be safe, there are free 120-minute lockers available, $7/hour if you go over. *Strategy:* Lines build considerably when it's hot.

Maharajah Jungle Trek ★★ ACTIVITY   Too few people enjoy this self-guided, South Asian–themed walking trail featuring some gorgeous tigers (rescued from a circus breeding program), flying foxes, Komodo dragons, and a few birds frolicking among fake ruins. The tigers are most active when the park opens and toward the end of the day. Grab a bird information sheet after entering the aviary; there's a bat display, too, that you can bypass if you're squeamish. It closes by dusk.

Feathered Friends in Flight ★★ SHOW   Somehow an informative presentation about birds is now one of Animal Kingdom's most pleasant diversions, affording an excuse to feast your eyes on some gorgeous creatures—parrots, toucans, bald eagles, peacocks, African birds of prey—who swoop around the semi-enclosed arena, barely clearing heads. *Tips:* Sit on the end of an interior aisle for an extra thrill. If you've got short kids, try the sloped bleachers in back, because the ground seats may miss some low-level action. Its location, the Caravan Theater, is covered but not air-conditioned, so you'll probably be more comfortable during early-morning performances or one in the late afternoon, the last ones of the day.

> ### Animal Kingdom's Night Moves
>
> The park sometimes stays open into the evening, and its easygoing side comes out after dark. Catch the glowing color features of **Pandora—The World of Avatar** after dark. **Kilimanjaro Safaris** has lighting that simulates perpetual sunset (it's pretty, but doesn't help with spotting animals, so don't make it the only time you ride it). And **The Tree of Life** is illuminated with kumbaya projections.

DinoLand U.S.A.

When it rains, come here, where two attractions and one big counter-service restaurant are indoors.

"Finding Nemo—The Musical" ★★ ↝ SHOW   Before the pandemic, one of the best shows at Disney was this fast-forwarded version of the Nemo movie, heightened with such catchy added songs as "In the Big Blue World" and the infectious, Beach Boys–style "Go with the Flow" (all written by the Oscar-winning husband-and-wife songwriters who also did the music for the *Frozen* movies and *Coco*). In 2022, Disney compressed and "reimagined" the show in a cost-cutting measure, so it's not as elaborate as it once was, but it still has bubbly appeal. Sprightly, bright, and energetic, this winning show is a good choice for taking a load off (the bench seating is indoors in the cool air), and even those who know the movie backward and forward will find something new in its vibrant vigor. *Strategy:* Performances that start immediately after performances of Disney KiteTails finish tend to be more crowded than ones scheduled at other hours.

Chester & Hester's Dino-Rama ★ ACTIVITY/RIDE   Kids run loose in this miniature parking lot–style carnival with a midway, **Fossil Fun Games** (Mammoth skee-ball races, "Whac-a-Pachycephalosaurus"), and two simple family rides. **TriceraTop Spin** ★, for the very young (90 seconds), is yet another iteration of the Magic Kingdom's Dumbo ride and is designed for kids to ride with their parents. Keep the kids in control by swinging them across the path to **The Boneyard** ★, a hot, sun-exposed playground where the very young can dig up "prehistoric" bones in the sand and work off energy on catwalks, net courses, and slides.

DINOSAUR ★★ RIDE   A good rainy-weather option is this 3-minute indoor time-travel ride in which all-terrain "Enhanced Motion Vehicles" simultaneously speed and shimmy down an unseen track, all as hordes of roaring dinosaurs attempt to make you dinner and an approaching asteroid shower threatens to do everyone in. Some kids, and even some adults, find all those jaws and jerky movements rather intense, and it's extremely dark and loud, but ultimately, it's a fun time, even if the perpetual darkness makes me wonder how much money Disney saved in not having to build more dinosaurs. Like many modern rides, it has well-known actors performing in the preshow video; this one's got Phylicia Rashad, fiercely overacting just like we love her to, and Wallace Langham, in a horrific tie. The line never seems to be as long as this ride deserves. On the path to the ride, don't ignore **Dino-Sue,** the 40-foot-long, full-scale T. rex skeleton—it's a replica of Sue, the most complete specimen anyone has yet found. (The original, unearthed in South Dakota in 1990, is on display at Chicago's Field Museum.) The **Cretaceous Trail,** at the head of the path, showcases ferns and American alligators extant in that period.

Where to Eat at Disney's Animal Kingdom

All locations have vegetarian options, kids' meals, and if you identify yourself, special dietary requests can usually be accommodated. There are no plastic drink lids because they can choke animals. The fruit cart ($2.50/piece) is in Africa. The most interesting bites are often found not at the restaurants but at the food kiosks (look for mac and cheese at **Eight Spoon Café**, tuna tataki and pork bao at **Caravan Road,** chicken dumplings at **Mr. Kamal's,** plus others) on the paths linking Discovery Island and Africa to Asia; if they're open, they'll be on your guide map.

DISNEY'S ANIMAL KINGDOM'S QUICK-SERVICE RESTAURANTS

Unless noted, all quick-service options accept Mobile Order.

Discovery Island

Flame Tree Barbecue ★★★ AMERICAN   If you don't mind gorging on dishes such as ribs and baked chicken when you're supposed to be appreciating animals, it has a wonderful terraced back garden with cushioned seating on the Discovery River, useful for watching **Disney KiteTails** at a comfortable distance. The pulled-pork barbecue is a favorite. **Discovery Island.** Combo meal $12–$18.

Pizzafari ★★ AMERICAN   A vibrantly colored restaurant that does pizza, garlic knots, Caesar salad with chicken, and Uncrustables. **Discovery Island.** Combo meal $10–$14.

Pandora—The World of Avatar

Satu'li Canteen ★★★ INTERPLANETARY   At this popular new choice, dishes are cooked with a kooky spin to make them appear alien: Sliced beef is served with yogurt boba balls, and the cheeseburgers are (deliciously) rethought as spongy steamed bao "pod" dumplings. The chili-garlic shrimp bowl isn't half bad. You'll want the Blueberry Cream Cheese Mousse for its Instagram factor alone. **Pandora—The World of Avatar.** Combo meal $12–$16.

Africa

Harambe Market ★★★ INTERNATIONAL   This food court (in a pan-African costume) has sheltered outdoor seating. The windows started out serving what they advertise, but now are more or less all the same: ribs-and-chicken bowls, Mediterranean salad, vegetarian sausage bowls, and a mix of beers including Tusker from Kenya. Also delicious: the coconut African milk tart in a chocolate shell. **Africa.** Combo meal $10–$14.

Tamu Tamu Refreshments ★ INTERNATIONAL   Serving the beloved Dole Whip frozen pineapple dessert, but here, you can spike it with a shot of rum ($9). **Africa.** No Mobile Orders.

Asia

Yak & Yeti Local Food Cafes ★★ ASIAN   Although there is a table-service location indoors by the same name, the outdoor windows do counter-service breakfast bowls and sandwiches, and later, tempura shrimp, honey tempura chicken, and pork egg rolls so greasy they could be used as torches. Chicken fried rice is just $6. Across the path on the water, the **Royal Anandapur Tea Company ★★** kiosk offers something unique: teas and slushy chai ($6). **Asia.** Combo meal $12–$16. No Mobile Orders.

DinoLand U.S.A.

Restaurantosaurus ★ AMERICAN   As American as DinoLand U.S.A., the kitchen pumps out burgers, fried shrimp, chicken sandwiches, and nuggets. The nearby **Dino-Bites** kiosk (not open nearly enough for such an awesome name) sells desserts. **DinoLand U.S.A.** Combo meal $11–$17.

DISNEY'S ANIMAL KINGDOM'S TABLE-SERVICE RESTAURANTS

All of these require reservations via the app (or ☎ **407/939-3463**); none of them fulfill Mobile Orders. Because you're probably going to be up early to see the animals at their best, this park is a good candidate for a character breakfast. There are very few places to get out of the heat and have a waiter-service meal.

Rainforest Cafe ★ AMERICAN   In a lush, jungle-like, theatrically lit setting, robotic animals roar and twitter over your cheese sticks, burgers, and rum cocktails in souvenir glasses. This is not a Disney original, but one of two outposts of the established brand at Disney World (the other is at Disney Springs Marketplace). **Oasis, at the park entry** (no ticket required). www.rainforestcafe.com. Mon–Thurs 10am–6pm, Fri–Sat 10:30am–7pm, Sun 10:30am–7pm. Entrees $20–$32.

Tiffins Restaurant ★★★ INTERNATIONAL   A contemporary upscale choice for lunch and dinner, it's the park's finest dining option. The menu is seasonal and inventive. To give you an idea, it has included lobster popcorn Thai curry soup and Ethiopian coffee butter-infused venison, but it's gradually dumbing down and is now more likely to serve shrimp and grits, surf-and-turf (tenderloin with scallops), and tamarind-braised short ribs. The casual **Nomad Lounge** (small plates $10–$17), attached, is an air-conditioned space for small plates (poke, poutine, *saté*), South African wines, Ethiopian-style coffee, cocktails, and bespoke beer including the Kungaloosh Spiced Excursion Ale, made just for here by Miami's Concrete Beach Brewery. Nomad, which has a delightful terrace over the water, closes with the park. **Oasis.** Entrees $30–$48.

Tusker House Restaurant ★★★ AMERICAN/AFRICAN   Under multicolored banners in an ancient souklike environment, Donald, Daisy, Mickey, and Goofy greet families in safari garb for **Donald's Safari Breakfast** and **Donald's Dining Safari** for lunch and dinner, all all-you-can eat buffets. The buffet dares more than most of Disney's do, featuring spit-roasted chicken, curries, peri-peri roasted salmon on banana leaf, and other pleasingly aromatic choices. It also has good vegetarian options. It's near **Dawa Bar,** a relaxing spot mimicking a fortress on the water where cocktails ($8–$16) are served; there are 10 seats at the bar but more under a bamboo shelter (sadly it usually closes well before the park does). **Africa.** Breakfast and lunch $47 adults, $28 kids 3–9.

Yak & Yeti Restaurant ★★ ASIAN   Themed like a Nepalese mansion stocked with souvenirs from across Southeast Asia, the restaurant has a menu just as geographically varied, serving Kobe beef burgers, lo meins, ahi tuna, fried honey chicken, and even roasted half duckling. The Quick Service counter outside offers a shorter but similar menu for less, but at Animal Kingdom, sitting indoors in air-conditioning is the most delicious treat. **Asia.** Entrees $16–$29.

DISNEY WATER PARKS

The big question: Typhoon Lagoon or Blizzard Beach? Doing both can fill a day. And they are the planet's second- and third-most popular water parks, respectively. So it depends on your mood. Typhoon Lagoon's central feature, a sand-lined 2½-acre wave pool, is an ideal place for families to approximate a day at the beach. If your kids have a need for speed, then head to Blizzard

Beach, which has wilder waterslides. If you use a 1-day ticket (and not Water Parks Fun & More), you can hit both in the same day without paying more.

Both water parks, similar in size, have free parking and are less busy early in the week, probably because folks tend to start their vacations on a weekend and don't get to the flumes until they've done the four big theme parks. They tend to be busier in the morning than in late afternoon. They also sell everything you need to protect yourself from the sun, including lotion (should you have forgotten) and swimsuits (should you lose yours in the lather). Most lines (many rides have two: one for a raft and one for the slide) are exposed to the sun, so it's important to **keep hydrated,** because you won't always be aware how much you're sweating. Both parks sell refillable mugs for **endless soft drinks** for $12 (otherwise, soft drinks start at more than $4). They also rent towels for $2, but life jackets are free to those who wish to use them. Lifeguards usually make you remove water shoes on slides that don't use a mat or raft, and swimsuits with rivets or zippers are forbidden.

A day at a water park isn't as stressful as one spent among the queues of the theme parks, and if you're paying attention, the sights and sounds of a day here are pretty heartwarming. Every time the wave machine roars into gear, for example, dozens of kids shriek with delight and scamper into the water. Because they're chilling out, people tend to be happy at these parks.

LOCKERS For $10–$15, you can rent a locker, typically about 2 feet deep with an opening about the size of a magazine. You can open and close it multiple times, using a key code you choose.

PREPARATION Thoughtfully, parking is free. Bulletin boards past the park entrances tell you what the sunburn risk is and what the wait times are for the slides, as well as what times the parades run at Disney parks that day. If there are any activities (scavenger hunts are common), they'll be posted here.

FOOD There are only counter-service choices, but Mobile Order is available. Eat promptly at 11am when kitchens open, because lines get crazy quickly. Don't plan on eating dinner at the water parks—the kiosks shut down before closing.

TIMING If you're coming to Florida between November and mid-March, one of these parks will be closed for its annual hose-down. The other will remain open. Most water features are heated, but remember that you eventually must get *out.*

Blizzard Beach

Of Disney's two water parks, **Blizzard Beach ★★★** is the more thrilling, possibly because it opened 6 years after Typhoon Lagoon and had the benefit of improving on what didn't work there. It also has a wittier backstory that is perfect for a hot day: A freak snowstorm hit Mount Gushmore, and Disney was slapping up a ski resort when the snow began to melt, creating water-slides. So now, a lift chair brings bathers most of the way up the 90-foot peak, and flumes are festooned with ski-run flags and piled with white "snowdrifts." Best of all, at this park, you usually don't have to tote your rafts uphill—there are conveyors to do it for you.

Surely the most exhilarating 8 seconds in all of Walt Disney World, **Summit Plummet** ★★★ is the immensely steep, 12-story-tall slide that commands attention at the peak of the mountain, which incidentally, offers one of the best panoramas of the Walt Disney World resort. A slide down this one is for the truly fearless. The first few seconds make you feel weightless, as if you're about to fall forward; by the end, the water is jabbing you so hard that it's not unusual to come away with a light bruise, and it turns the toughest bathing suit into dental floss. This is a fun one to watch; just ask the young men who are glued to it for the aforementioned reason. **Slush Gusher** ★, next to it among the Green Slope rides and slightly lower, is a double-hump that gives the rider the sensation of air time—not a reassuring feeling when you're flying down an open chute.

The enormous chute winding off the mountain's right side is **Steamboat Springs** ★★, a group ride in a circular raft; just about everyone gets a chance to enjoy the top of a banked turn, and after the inevitable splashdown, another minute is spent in a comedown floating on a river. It's highly re-rideable, but if you go alone, you'll be paired with strangers for some slippery awkwardness.

Snow Stormers ★ (Purple Slope) is a trio of standard raft waterslides. The twin **Downhill Double Dipper** ★ is a simple slope of two identical slides with a good embellishment: It times runs so you can race a companion down. **Toboggan Racers** ★★ multiplies the fun to where eight people can race at once down an evenly scalloped run. At the base of these is **Melt Away Bay** ★★★, a 1-acre wave pool in which waves create a gentle bobbing sensation. It could stand to be larger since it gets very crowded.

At the back of the mountain (the Red Slope; reach it by walking around the left or via the lazy river), the three **Runoff Rapids** ★★ flumes comprise two open-air slides and a totally enclosed one—you only see the occasional light flashing by. (These are the only ones for which you must haul your own raft up the hill.)

The park is circled by the superlative lazy river (for the newbie, that's a slow-flowing channel where you float along in an inner tube) called **Cross Country Creek** ★★★, which is probably the best of its kind, passing a cave dripping with refrigerated water and a slouching shack that, every few seconds, gushes as you hear the sound of Goofy sneezing. *Tip:* It's easier to find an inner tube at a ramp far from the park entrance; try the one at the base of Downhill Double Dipper or the one to the left past Lottawatta Lodge, the main food building.

There are two kiddie areas: for grade-schoolers, **Ski Patrol** ★★ (short slides, a walk across the water on floating "icebergs"), and for littler kids, **Tike's Peak** ★ (even smaller slides, fountains, and jets). The latter is a good place to look if you can't find seating.

Tip: The miniature golf course Winter Summerland (see "Puttering Around" on p. 271) shares a parking lot with Blizzard Beach, so it's easy to combine a visit.

www.disneyworld.com. ℂ 407/560-3400. One-day tickets $64–$69 adults, $58–$63 kids 3–9; can also be added to theme park tickets using Water Park and Sports options. Free parking. Hours vary, from 10am–5pm up to 9am–8pm in peak season.

Typhoon Lagoon

Despite the petrifying imagery of a shrimp boat (*Miss Tilly*) impaled on the central mountain (Mt. Mayday), the flumes at **Typhoon Lagoon** ★★ ☛ are less daunting than the ones at Blizzard Beach or Volcano Bay, but the wave pool is rougher. Typhoon Lagoon is extremely well landscaped (most of its flowers were planted to attract butterflies but not bees) to hide its infrastructure, but it's not so easy to navigate. For example, you tote your own rafts. Also, the paths to the slides ramble up and down stairs—the one to the Storm Slides actually goes *down* eight times as it winds up the mountain. It's also not always clear where to find the slide you want. Help guide little ones.

The **Surf Pool** ★★ divides its time between "surf waves" (at 5 ft., they pack a surprising punch, and are announced by a *whoompf* that draws great peals of delight from kids) and mild "bobbing waves"—times for both are noted on the Surf Report chalk sign at the pool's foot.

The slides are generally shallow, slow, and geared toward avowed sissies. That will frustrate some teenagers, but little kids and mothers with expensive hairdos think **Mayday Falls** ★, which sends riders down a corrugated flume, is just right (adults come off rubbing their butts in pain). It's very tough to find a vantage point to watch your kids ride, but there's a spot near the entrance of **Gangplank Falls** ★★★, a family-size round raft, where you can see a little, and there's a lovely hidden overlook trail with a suspension bridge and waterfalls that passes under the *Miss Tilly*. The leftmost body slide of three at **Storm Slides** ★★ is slightly more covered; otherwise the slides are much the same.

The **Crush 'n' Gusher** ★★★ "water coaster" flumes use jets to push rafts both uphill and downhill; the gag is that it used to be a fruit-washing plant. Behind it, the multi-person round-rafted **Miss Adventure Falls** ★★, added in 2017—the first new slide here in nearly a decade—is pleasant, going past an animatronic parrot and using a belt to hoist you uphill, but the easy journey is not all that remarkable. If you ride alone, you'll be seated next to strangers with their shirts off, so that's fun.

For the best shot at finding an inner tube for the lushly planted lazy river, **Castaway Creek** ★★, pick an entry farther from the entrance, such as in front of the Crush 'n' Gusher area. That's also a good place to find a lounger if the Lagoon is packed, which it usually is; otherwise, try the extreme left past the ice cream stand. That's near **kiddee Creek ★★**, the geyser-and-bubbler play area for small children. Funny how the water's always warmer there.

"Learn to Surf" lessons are held in the Surf Pool 2 hours before park hours and, sometimes, after it closes (✆ **407/939-7529**; $150 for all ages, minimum age of 5). The lessons come with 30 minutes of preparation followed by 2 hours of in-pool instruction, always with lifeguards scrutinizing your every twitch.

www.disneyworld.com. ✆ **407/560-3400.** One-day tickets $64–69 adults, $58–$63 kids 3–9; can also be added to theme park tickets using Water Park and Sports options. Free parking. Hours vary, from 10am–5pm up to 9am–8pm in peak season.

OTHER DISNEY WORLD DIVERSIONS

See "Puttering Around" on p. 271 for details on the two Disney miniature golf areas.

Disney Springs

The free shopping and entertainment district Disney Springs (see map p. 275) comprises nearly a pedestrianized mile of restaurants and shops along a small lake, away from the major theme parks. Its West Side has most of the Springs' sit-down entertainment: it's where you'll find a 24-screen AMC cinema and, as of late 2021, the Canadian entertainment juggernaut **Cirque du Soleil**'s new acrobatics spectacular *Drawn to Life,* a tribute to Disney animation led by a character named Mr. Pencil (cirquedusoleil.com/drawn-to-life; $185 adults, $63.75–$185 kids aged 3-11, depending on seat location; Tues–Sat 5:30pm and 8pm, 90 min).

Amphicar Tours ★★★ RIDE   In 1961, West Gemany—a country that no longer exists—introduced the world to an amazing new car that looked like a normal convertible on land but was also capable of driving straight into water and puttering around like a boat. Only about 4,000 Amphicars were ever made, and like West Germany, their day came and went—it's estimated that only a tenth of them survive. But The Boathouse restaurant (p. 200) is the world's most important collector and caretaker of these fantastic vehicles, and you can take a 25-minute ride around the lakefront of Disney Springs from its ramp. It's one of the more special adventures at the resort.

The Landing, Disney Springs. www.theboathouseorlando.com/amphicar-tours. ✆ **407/939-2628.** $125 per trip; max 3–4 passengers per car based on size. Daily 10am–10pm in good weather. Walk-up reservations only.

Aerophile Characters in Flight ★★ RIDE   You'll see it from miles away: A huge, round helium balloon that rises from a pier, lingers 400 feet up

DISNEY after dark WITH KIDS

Although on some nights, one could argue that the people drinking at the clubs and bars are infantile, you still can't bring your kids to hang out in them. Don't worry—Orlando is a family city, so there's much for kids to do.

- **Magic Kingdom parade** 🚩: Most evenings, there are one or two parades through the park. When there are two, the second is less crowded.

- **Fireworks:** The Magic Kingdom is open until 9pm or later on most nights. There's usually an evening parade, and for the 50th anniversary period, the nightly fireworks spectacular **Disney Enchantment** commands all eyes. Much of it happens on and around Cinderella Castle, but I recommend Main Street, where new precision projections create a jiggly, candy-colored world unto itself. The popular **Happily Ever After** fireworks show could return in the future. Hollywood Studios mounts **Fantasmic!**, a pyrotechnics-and-water display, plus **Disney Movie Magic,** a 12-minute projection show on the Chinese Theater, a few times a week. Epcot has **Harmonious,** its own spectacular show over its lagoon. Check with the app for exact showtimes. Animal Kingdom has attempted night shows, but nothing so far has endured.

- **The Electrical Boat Parade:** It's a tradition going back 49 years—a string of 14 40-foot-long illuminated barges floats past the Disney resorts on Seven Seas Lagoon and Bay Lake starting at 9pm, accompanied by music. It's lower key than the fireworks shows, and you can see it for free from any resort hotel in the area or, if your timing is good, from the ferries.

- **Special event evenings:** From September through March, the Magic Kingdom schedules irregular special-ticket evenings for kids (Mickey's Not-So-Scary Halloween Party, his Very Merry Christmas Party, and Disney After Dark events) with free candy, character meetings, dance parties, and extended hours. "After hours" events take place after the park has been cleared of daytime guests and are generally uncrowded. The calendar of events can be found on p. 291, online at www.disneyworld.com, or you can call Disney at ✆ **407/939-7679.**

- **Dinnertainment:** The Hoop-Dee-Doo Musical Revue and Spirit of Aloha shows have been going strong for decades, pandemic pauses excepted. See p. 220.

- **Free movie:** Nightly at Fort Wilderness, the Chip 'n' Dale's Campfire Sing-A-Long is followed by an outdoor screening of a Disney movie.

- **Character meals:** Early bedtime? Very young kids will be sent to sleep dreaming if they meet their favorite character over dinner. See p. 221 for a list.

for a spell, and then descends back to earth within about 10 minutes. Although it's safely tethered and the circular observation platform is securely enclosed with mesh, it lists and drifts with sudden breezes that may disturb some guests. If you're adventurous, though, the trip is good fun, and of course, the view rocks. It's known to summarily shut down for breezes over 22mph or if lightning is detected within 30 miles, so if it's flying and you want to go, don't assume it will still be open later.

Disney Springs West Side. www.aerophileorlando.com. ✆ **407/824-4321.** $20 per person. Daily 8:30am–midnight.

House of Blues ★★★ MUSIC CLUB   One of the principal nightspots on the West Side has a 2,000-person, three-tiered venue (standing space only) hosting regular performers along the lines of One Republic, the Charlie Daniels Band, and Norah Jones. Big talent is ticketed at concert prices, and operator Live Nation piles on the fees, but mostly, it's a restaurant for Southern food. On Sundays, it hosts a de-sanctified Gospel Brunch (p. 220).

Disney Springs West Side. www.hob.com. ✆ **407/934-2583.** Sun–Thurs 11:30am–11pm; Fri–Sat 11:30am–1am.

Splitsville Luxury Lanes ★★★ BOWLING ALLEY   Giving families something to bond over, this Florida-based franchise charges by the hour, which might make you feel rushed, and it charges high prices at that, but its souped-up 1950s decor, two floors of bowling, and copious cocktails have charm to spare. The food ($13–$20) is better than it should be; it even sells sushi. Cast members like to hang out here—meet a few and beat a few.

Disney Springs West Side. www.splitsvillelanes.com/location/orlando. ✆ **407/938-7328.** $17/hr. per person before 4pm, $22/hr. per person after 4pm and weekends. Rates include shoe rental. Daily 10am–2am.

Walt Disney World Tours

Walt Disney was unquestionably a visionary. When he started out, he was mostly interested in animation as an art form. But as his fame and resources grew, his dreams became infinite, and by the end of his life, he was obsessed with building a city of his own. Because the Magic Kingdom was built by his most-trusted designers, it incorporated several idealistic innovations.

One is the **utilidor system.** The bulk of the Magic Kingdom that you see appears to be at ground level. But in fact, you'll be walking about 14 feet above the land. The attractions constitute the second and third stories of a 9-acre network of warehouses and corridors—utilidors—built in part to guard against flooding but mostly so cast members could remove trash, make deliveries, take breaks, change costumes, and count money out of sight, in catacombs accessed through secret entrances and unmarked wormholes scattered around the themed lands. Clean-burning electric vehicles zip through the hallways, some of which are wide enough to accommodate trucks, and all of which are color-coded to indicate which land is upstairs.

Among the other engineering feats and innovations of the Kingdom:

o Trash is transported at 60mph through 24-inch Swedish AVAC pneumatic tubes to a compactor behind Splash Mountain.

o Fire, power, and water systems are all monitored by a common computer, and the robotics, doors, lighting, sounds, and vehicles on the most complicated attractions are handled by a central server called the Digital

Animation Control System (DACS), located roughly underneath Cinderella Castle.

o Bay Lake, beside Fort Wilderness, was dredged, and the dirt used to raise the Magic Kingdom. Underneath the lakebed, white sand was discovered, cleaned, and deposited to create beaches on the Seven Seas Lagoon, which was created from dry land.

o Energy is reused whenever possible. The generators' waste heat is used to heat water, and hot water runoff is used for heating, cooking, and absorption chilling for air-conditioning. Wastewater is reclaimed for plants and lawns (80% of the resort is watered this way), and sludge is dried for fertilizer. Food scraps are composted on-site. The resort produces enough power to keep things running in case of a temporary outage on the municipal grid. This will keep you up tonight: Disney even has the legal right to build its own nuclear power plant, should it care to.

o The company worked to cut its greenhouse gas emissions in half between 2012 and 2020. A half million solar panels were installed on 270 acres of the resort, generating enough energy to power two theme parks.

o The resort was the first place to install an all-electronic phone system using underground cable—so guests don't see ugly wires. It was the first telephone company in America to use a 911 emergency system. In 1978, the first commercial fiber optic system in the U.S. was installed.

o The rubber-tired monorail system, designed by Disney engineers, now contains nearly 15 miles of track. Walt had intended monorails, plus vehicles akin to the Tomorrowland Transit Authority ride, to be the main forms of transportation to and through his Epcot. In 1986, the monorail was named a National Historic Mechanical Engineering Landmark by the American Society of Mechanical Engineers.

The Walt Disney Co. now shows little interest in advancing these innovations. Epcot has only a small network of utilidors, partly located under Spaceship Earth, and the recent Disney parks were built without any. The monorail has not been expanded since 1982 and is falling apart.

But even if the company now pays scant attention to developing "Walt's dream"—that Talmudic totem that the company's marketing department invokes to sell souvenirs—it will, outside of pandemic restrictions, grant a backstage gander (no cameras allowed) at the resort's ingenuity and the mind-boggling challenge of its scale. The superlative **Walt Disney World tours** (www.disneyworld.com/tours; ✆ **407/939-8687**) require tons of walking and the quality depends on the ability of the guide, but they're also well organized, with coach transport, snacks, plenty of comfort breaks, and sometimes, a special pin souvenir. Not all of them go daily, so you have to check the Disney site for what's running when you visit. Fantastic past choices have included **Starlight Safari** nature tours of Animal Kingdom's paddocks by night ($75), **Up Close with Rhinos** at Kilimanjaro Safaris ($40), and **The Magic Behind Our Steam Trains Tour** at the Magic Kingdom ($54). The best one is

Backstage Magic ★★★, a 7-hour, $275 exploration of how the parks work at every level. Stops include the mechanized miracle of the American Adventure robotics; Costuming; Central Shops; Assembly Alley, a blocks-long, 280,000-square-foot facility where ride vehicles are maintained; and lunch at Tiffins. Every minute is fascinating (and bonus: you don't have to pay separate admission for this one).

I do not recommend **Ultimate Disney Classics VIP Tour.** The name seems tempting, but although it costs $250 (4 hrs., no meals), you still have to pay for admission and it only gets you on seven rides that rarely have long lines anyway.

UNIVERSAL ORLANDO

U niversal Orlando is booming. Since 2009, attendance at its two Florida theme parks has soared and expansion is nonstop. In 2017, it added a new waterslide park, Volcano Bay, and the resort now has 9,000 hotel rooms to its credit. Universal's Orlando parks now entice some 20.5 million combined visits each year, nearly as many as Disney's Magic Kingdom. Universal has come of age, and Comcast, its parent company, is pouring billions of dollars into rapidly putting it on equal footing with the Mouse.

Few people thought Universal would ever become this formidable.

The opening of the **Universal Studios park** in 1990 heralded a new era for Orlando tourism. Instead of merely duplicating its original Hollywood location, which is grafted onto a historic movie studio lot, Universal Orlando built an all-day theme park. But it was famously troubled, and nearly everything original has since been changed to make way for the second draft: Gone are the reproduction of the *Psycho* house, colossal rides about *King Kong* and *Jaws*, an in-depth breakdown of Alfred Hitchcock's directorial methods, a studio for Nickelodeon, a major exploration of how to produce *Murder, She Wrote* (!!), a Hard Rock Cafe in the shape of a giant guitar.

Still, there was little doubt that Universal's innovations, when they worked, raised the bar. A chief advance was that many of its attractions were indoors—even the thrill rides. Given Florida's scorching sun and unpredictable rains, this leap shouldn't have been as novel as it was. While Disney, still working on a California model, allowed its guests to twiddle thumbs in the cruel outdoors as they waited, Universal's multistage queuing system kept them entertained and air-conditioned. Even the covered parking garages at Universal Orlando (shared by the parks and CityWalk) were novel for Florida.

Throughout the 1990s, Universal's modest one-park setup meant it was lucky to grab visitors on day trips from Disney. That changed in 1999, when a second, $2.6-billion park, **Islands of Adventure,** made its dazzling debut. Universal's domain has further expanded to include the nightlife district **CityWalk,** hotels, and its own waterslide park, **Volcano Bay.** By 2025, Universal will rise even higher when it opens a third, spare-no-expense theme park, Universal's

Epic Universe, by expanding onto a 750-acre complex near the Convention Center. UEU will come with even more hotel rooms, shopping, entertainment, a Nintendo-themed section, and a rumored third Harry Potter theme park area, and it's expected to add 14,000 jobs (the resort already employs 25,000 workers). Universal's corporate parent Comcast is building Disney's equal, and fast—and in key ways, parent company Comcast is investing the funds necessary to make it even better.

Universal operates best (but not exclusively) on the resort model—stay here, play here—and it helps that its campus is easier to roam than Disney's: It's walkable or traversed by quick, free ferries or buses, so you can park your car and forget about it. If you want to see both Wizarding World of Harry Potter areas, you have to purchase a ticket to *both* of its parks, but unless crowds are insanely nutty, such as before Halloween Horror Nights (p. 292) or during Christmas week, the two main parks take about 2 days to see adequately. Most of the time, lines are nowhere near as long as they are at Disney. With a two-park pass and a willingness to bypass lesser attractions, for now you can see the highlights in a marathon day, provided at least one of the parks stays open until 9 or 10pm. (If you want to see Volcano Bay, described on p. 157, you need an additional day.) In any event, bopping between the two theme parks is quick and easy, since their entrances are a 5-minute stroll apart, or a quick ride on the incredible Hogwarts Express connecting train.

TICKETING

Tickets for both parks cost the same, and you must specify the day you're going. Like Disney, Universal charges more on busy days. Unlike at Disney, you can almost always get in. But Universal also gives you a $20 discount if you buy multi-day tickets online, so it's crucial you do so.

Prices fluctuate daily according to a preset calendar. You can predict the cost for your dates at the official site www.universalticketcalendar.com.

Prices purchased online; the higher prices are for peak days:

- **1-day ticket for one park:** $109–$159 adults, $104–$154 kids 3–9 (Make any 1-day ticket **park-to-park** for $55 more)
- **2 days, one park daily:** $273–$351 adults, $263–$341 kids 3–9 (Make any 2-day ticket **park-to-park** for $60 more)

- **3 days, one park daily:** $233–$316 adults, $223–$306 kids 3–9
- **3 days, two parks daily:** $327–$376 adults, $317–$366 kids 3–9
- **4 days, one park/two parks daily:** $247–$328 adults, $237–$318 kids 3–9
- **4 days, two parks daily:** $312–$393 adults, $302–$383 kids 3–9
- **3 parks, park-to-park access (including Volcano Bay):** 2 days $315–$386 adults, $305–$376 kids 3–9; 3 days $333–$411 adults, $323–$401 kids 3–9; 4 days $377–$438, $367–$428 kids 3–9

To enter both parks on the same day and to ride the Hogwarts Express train that links the two parks, you must have a **park-to-park** ticket. If you buy a limited, one-park ticket and change your mind midway through the day, don't worry. There are ticket upgrade kiosks at the Hogwarts Express train stations that simply charge you the difference in price for a park-to-park ticket, and you can be on your way again.

HOPPING THE LINES Universal's **Express** allows guests to use a separate entrance queue that is dramatically shorter than the "Standby" one, reducing wait times in most cases to minutes; your pass is scanned by an employee. Unlike Disney's former Fastpass+ system, Express is for sale, and the busier the park is, the more it costs; the Universal app can always tell you how much it is today (look under "Buy Tickets"). The **Express Pass** ($70–$289 one park, $80–$300 two parks, depending on crowds) allows one-time-per-ride use, while the more expensive **Express Unlimited** ($100–$319 one park, $110–$330 two parks, depending on crowds) puts no restriction on re-rides. Both come in two flavors, one-park and two-park. Two-park passes cost about 25 percent more, rising at peak times to as much as double. Hagrid's Motorbike Adventure and VelociCoaster are excluded. Using Express is expensive, but it enables you to see both Universal parks in a single day. Guests can buy Express when they purchase their admission, at entry ticket booths, at a kiosk set up just past the entry gate, or at shops.

The most expensive, but most effective way, to cut the lines is the **VIP Experience** (© 866/346-9350), which ushers you onto rides with zero lines.

What's a Virtual Line?

Simple: Some mid-level Universal attractions manage crowds by allowing people to sign up for times for their whole party using the official app. If an attraction has a virtual line running, you'll see that denoted on that attraction's app page, on the paper maps, or you'll be informed at its entrance. (If you don't have a phone, there will be a kiosk by the attraction that will print you a ticket.) Once you sign up, your phone will notify you when it's time (you'll have some leeway if you're doing something else right then), and when your time passes, you'll be allowed to get another pass for another ride. You won't be able to join the queue unless you give the app permission to know your location, because you must be within the gates of the park to participate. For the smoothest result, get your app profiles set up and ready before you go to the park.

WHAT THE BASICS cost AT UNIVERSAL'S TWO PARKS

Parking: $26 (free after 6pm), $50 for closer "prime" spaces, $75 for all-day valet

Regular soda: $4
Water: $3.50
Beer: $11 (you must have ID)
Single strollers: $18 per day
Double strollers: $28 per day

Wheelchair: $12 (available just after park entry; small rental desk in parking structure)

ECV (electric convenience vehicle): $55 + $50 deposit (add $20 for canopy)
Lockers: $10–$15 per day (multi-entry) at front of park; free for brief use at rides
Poncho: $11 adults, $10 kids

Non-private tours (with up to 12 people you might not know) will visit 10–12 attractions ($189–$449 plus admission, includes a counter-service lunch and valet parking); private guided tours can be customized and take you anywhere you want, even on VelociCoaster, without strangers or waiting (up to $3,500 for up to five people, $400 for each additional person, table-service lunch included). It's better to reserve VIP Experiences ahead of time, and they don't include tickets.

But there is also a much **simpler way to get an Express Unlimited pass:** Guests who stay at Portofino Bay, the Hard Rock Hotel, or Royal Pacific can use their key cards for free Express access—a great value add when you consider a double room can house four people. (Note that the other Universal hotels do not include Express as a perk.)

PHOTOS   Universal also has photographers (not as many as Disney) on hand to take your photo at big moments. Its **My Universal Photos** works a lot like Disney's PhotoPass but with fewer roaming photographers: 1 day is $70–$100, 3 days is $90–$110, and that includes digital copies of everything and two printed images. You can also check your images as you collect them using an app. Otherwise, you can buy individual photos for $20-plus each.

NAVIGATING THE PARKS   Universal has free in-park Wi-Fi, and its free **Official Universal Orlando Resort App** is very easy to use. It provides wait times, showtimes, maps, restaurant menus, walking directions, and more. You can also use it to buy online-discounted tickets. Load a credit card into your account, and you can use it to make purchases such as mobile food orders (which aren't as widely available as they are at Disney); if you activate the Universal Pay feature, it will add a QR code to your smartphone's digital wallet that enables you to make purchases at Universal-run stores.

WHAT TO WEAR   Dress small children in bathing suits for a day at Universal Studios because Kidzone will get them soaked. At Islands of Adventure, three of the best adult rides are water-based.

UNIVERSAL STUDIOS FLORIDA

Universal Studios ★★★, which welcomed 10.9 million visitors in 2019, usually opens at 9am. In winter months, hours end around dinnertime; in summer, it's open as late as 10pm. After you get your car parked ($26 and up in a mostly covered structure) and submit to security checks in the covered sidewalks from the lot, walk to CityWalk and head to the right. Pause now at the giant rotating globe for the requisite photo op, because the sun is in your favor for photographs in the morning, but not later.

At the entrance turnstiles, your fingerprint will be scanned and matched to your ticket, so the system can recognize if anybody else tries to use your ticket. The plaza after the turnstiles is where you take care of business. **Strollers and wheelchairs** are obtained to the left, and **lockers** are rented to the right. (You may bring your stroller to the other park within 2 hrs. of closing; if you're taking the Hogwarts Express, there's a place to drop it off before boarding and another kiosk for getting a new one at Islands of Adventure.) Make sure to grab a free park **map** here; if you forget, the stores also stock them.

Although there are technically themed areas within the park, few are strictly defined. They fall into two general zones. Everyone enters along the main avenue of the simulated backlot (including **Production Central, Hollywood,** and **New York**), which contains many of the behind-the-scenes attractions, while an elongated lagoon stretches off to the right, encircled by many of the thrill-based rides in **San Francisco, Springfield, World Expo,** and **Woody Woodpecker's Kidzone. The Wizarding World of Harry Potter—Diagon Alley** is on the far side of the lagoon.

Some days (confirm times about a month ahead on the website or the app, or check times on the map you grab at the front gate), Universal sends out its **Superstar Parade,** packed with children's characters such as SpongeBob SquarePants, Dora, Diego, Gru, and the Minions. It stops by Mel's Drive-In and Battery Park so kids can meet them. After dark, if the park's open then,

---

Empty Those Pockets!

Lawyers have had their way with our fun: The fast rides now forbid loose articles of any kind. That includes phones, keys, lipstick—even coins. Everything but paper! And you may not leave stuff on the platform while you ride, either. Instead, leave your belongings in a multi-entry locker at the front of the park, or use the free lockers near the entrances of those attractions that require their use. Flat shoebox-size lockers are free (use your ticket to scan in and out), but backpack-size ones will cost a few bucks. Their computers know how long the ride's wait is, so don't try leaving your stuff in one all day. If you overstay by 30 minutes or more, to get it back you'll have to pay $3 for every half-hour, up to $20.

the area around the water sometimes hosts the 18-minute **Cinematic Celebration,** a spectacle spotlighting popular franchises from the parks with water screens, 120 Bellagio-style power fountains, projection mapping, and a few pyrotechnics. The area opposite Mel's Drive-In is the best vantage point for it.

SHOPPING   Universal Studios is able to send your souvenirs to It's a Wrap, the last shop to the right by the exit, for collection as you leave the park at the end of the day. The deadline for purchases changes, but it's usually about 2 hours before closing.

Production Central

The area along the entry avenue (called both Plaza of the Stars and 57th St.) and to its left is collectively marked on maps as Production Central, but who are they kidding? Nowadays, those soundstages are used mostly for the odd local commercial and for haunted houses at Universal's fiendishly popular Halloween event.

The initial dream was much bigger. When the park was built, it was intended to be more like the original Hollywood location, where an amusement area grew up around a working studio that offered tours as a sideline. Early '90s press trumpeted Orlando as "Hollywood of the East" because year-round production could be accomplished here and at Disney–MGM Studios, and millions of tourists could be a part of the process. One of Universal's soundstages housed a working TV studio for Nickelodeon, the kids' cable channel, and the game show *Double Dare* plucked families out of the park to compete on air. In front of the studio, a geyser of "green slime" (actually green water) gurgled in tribute to the Canadian show *You Can't Do That on Television* that helped make the channel's fortunes. There was even a short-lived tram tour through the soundstages, like at the Hollywood original. But the entertainment industry never took to Florida. It wasn't cost-effective to move productions here, celebrities didn't relish working in a theme park, and state tax credits were spotty.

These days the first block of Production Central is mostly shops, including the largest gift shop in the park, **Universal Studios Store,** on the left. Across from that are the tempting Art Deco buildings of Rodeo Drive, the spine of the Hollywood area and for my money the prettiest part of the park.

Hollywood Rip Ride Rockit ★★★ RIDE   This is one advanced train: The 17-story height, vertical climb, hill-like loop, and near misses are just the start of it. Most advanced are its cars, outfitted with LEDs and in-seat speakers. Riders personalize their trip on screens embedded in the beltlike safety restraint, choosing the song that will play during the trip. Pick from a broad menu including country, rap, rock, and disco, but if you don't pick a song, it'll choose one for you. When the ride's over, you can buy a movie of it, along with your soundtrack. Lockers are required for loose items, but they're free

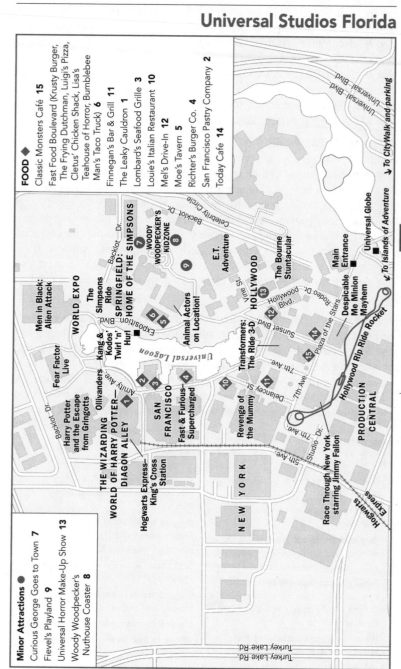

Minor Attractions ●

Curious George Goes to Town **7**
Fievel's Playland **9**
Universal Horror Make-Up Show **13**
Woody Woodpecker's
Nuthouse Coaster **8**

FOOD ◆

Classic Monsters Café **15**
Fast Food Boulevard (Krusty Burger,
The Frying Dutchman, Luigi's Pizza,
Cletus' Chicken Shack, Lisa's
Teahouse of Horror, Bumblebee
Man's Taco Truck) **6**
Finnegan's Bar & Grill **11**
The Leaky Cauldron **1**
Lombard's Seafood Grille **3**
Louie's Italian Restaurant **10**
Mel's Drive-In **12**
Moe's Tavern **5**
Richter's Burger Co. **4**
San Francisco Pastry Company **2**
Today Cafe **14**

THE WIZARDING
WORLD OF HARRY POTTER—
DIAGON ALLEY

Hogwarts Express—
King's Cross Station

Harry Potter
and the Escape
from Gringotts

Ollivanders

Amity Ave.

SAN
FRANCISCO

Fast & Furious—
Supercharged

Fear Factor
Live

Backlot Dr.

WORLD EXPO

Men in Black:
Alien Attack

The
Simpsons
Ride

Kang &
Kodos'
Twirl 'n'
Hurl

SPRINGFIELD:
HOME OF THE SIMPSONS

Exposition Blvd.

Backlot Dr.

WOODY
WOODPECKER'S
KIDZONE

Animal Actors
on Location!

Backlot Dr.

Celebrity Circle

E.T.
Adventure

Universal Lagoon

Revenge of
the Mummy

Transformers:
The Ride 3-D

HOLLYWOOD

Vine St.

Sunset Blvd.

Delancey St.

7th Ave.

7th Ave.

Studio Dr.

5th Ave.

NEW YORK

Race Through New York
starring Jimmy Fallon

Hogwarts
Express

Hollywood
Blvd.

Rodeo Dr.

Plaza of the Stars

The Bourne
Stuntacular

Despicable
Me Minion
Mayhem

Main
Entrance

Universal Globe

Hollywood Rip Ride Rocket

PRODUCTION
CENTRAL

Turkey Lake Rd.

Turkey Lake Rd.

Universal Blvd.

Universal Blvd.

↘ To CityWalk and parking

↙ To Islands of Adventure

4

UNIVERSAL ORLANDO | Universal Studios Florida

131

for the wait time plus 20 minutes. Single riders get their own line, and it moves quickly. Rockin'. *Strategy:* Don't close the safety bar too tightly! You'll have trouble breathing. And if you ride around noon, the lift hill will beam the sun straight into your eyes. *Tip:* There are "secret" songs available that aren't listed listed in the consoles. Google them ahead of time to get the code numbers, then while you're still in the train station, hold down the coaster logo for 10 seconds to unlock the number pad for them. You'll have to work fast. May I suggest number 904, "Night on Bald Mountain" by Mussorgsky?

Despicable Me Minion Mayhem ★★ RIDE   The enduringly popular animated Minions movie franchise, if you're not familiar with it, stars a crotchety mad genius, Gru (voiced by Steve Carell), and his horde of nearly identical yellow begoggled henchmen (the Minions); this ride gives the adorable little guys ample opportunity for some cartoon violence and giggly gags. It's a kid-friendly show combined with a move-in-place ride, taking place in a theater full of individual open-air ride platforms that share all the characteristics of motion simulators without triggering claustrophobia. *Strategy:* If you happen to know that you're prone to motion sickness, you can request a car that doesn't move at all—there's often a separate marked entrance for those cars. Virtual line option.

Transformers: The Ride—3D ★★ RIDE   This East Coast version of a ride that first appeared at Universal Studios Hollywood repeats the technology and basic vehicle design of the gentler Adventures of Spider-Man next door at Islands of Adventure—that is, roofless motion-simulator cars travel among sense-tricking rooms with 3D projections. The difference is that here, the show is pumped up with crisper animation, clearer sounds, and a whole lot of machine-on-machine violence and military-grade weaponry. But at heart, no

---

The Best of Universal Studios Florida

Don't miss if you're 6: Curious George Goes to Town

Don't miss if you're 16: Revenge of the Mummy

Requisite photo op: The rotating Universal globe out front; sticking your head in Jaws' jaws, on the wharf in San Francisco

Food you can only get here: Butterbeer ice cream and Fishy Green Ale, Diagon Alley; Flaming Moe's and Duff Beer, Springfield

Where everyone stampedes first: The Wizarding World of Harry Potter—Diagon Alley

Skippable: Fear Factor Live, Race Through New York Starring Jimmy Fallon

Biggest thrills: Harry Potter and the Escape from Gringotts, Revenge of the Mummy, Hollywood Rip Ride Rocket

Best show: Animal Actors on Location!, The Bourne Stuntacular

Biggest store: Universal Studios Store, Production Central

Longest-running ride: E.T. Adventure

Where to find peace: On the lagoon

matter how impressive the tech is, Transformers is still a version of Spider-Man, down to key plot points. The mayhem is so frenetic you can't always tell which Transformer is which, but then again, you can't in the movies, either, so it hardly matters. When all is said and done, you'll emerge feeling like you survived a very pretty 4-minute-long highway crash. *Strategy:* The clearest view is in the front row, and there's a fast-moving single-rider line. Virtual line option.

New York

When there's a park on your right, you've entered the New York area. In a display of geographic acrobatics, the park is an imitation of San Francisco's Union Square while straight ahead, at the end of 57th Street (the main entry avenue) is a little cul-de-sac that looks, through a camera lens, like Manhattan—except for the roller coaster that keeps roaring through.

The rest of the New York section is gussied up to look like the tenements of the Lower East Side or Greenwich Village and is worth a few photos. A few street performances crop up all day here; the most common are actors jamming like **The Blues Brothers.**

Race Through New York Starring Jimmy Fallon ★ RIDE This grandma-appropriate theater-based attraction hosted by Jimmy Fallon, star of the 2004 movie *Taxi,* was born of synergy—*The Tonight Show* airs on NBC, Universal Orlando's corporate cousin. The 4-minute adventure, which hammers you with the show's running characters and jiggles your bench in motion simulation, starts in a pitch-perfect simulation of Rockefeller Center before devolving into a rollicking and geographically-challenged high-speed trip through the streets of Manhattan and the imagination of Jimmy Fallon, who spouts puns as you go. The motion won't make you throw up, but Fallon's smarm might. Named "Most Likely to Feel Outdated Soon" by Frommer's. The waiting area is confusing—instead of a queue, you get a colored card and you must wait for the sconce lights to change to that color—use the time to look at old *Tonight Show* memorabilia such as Johnny Carson's Carnac the Magnificent turban. Virtual line option.

Revenge of the Mummy ★★★ RIDE This brilliant attraction has an easy start but an exuberant finish: Part dark ride, part coaster, it goes backward and forward, twists on a turntable, and even spends a harrowing moment stalled in a room as the ceiling crawls with fire. (It doesn't go upside-down.) To say much more would give away some clever shocks. I've told you what you need to know, except that it's one of the best rides in this park, and it's many many miles better than the cheaper version at Universal in Los Angeles. *Strategy:* You must put loose articles in the lockers in the Paradise Theatre—they're free for the posted ride time plus 30 minutes, but after that they cost $3 every half-hour. There are three lines: express, standby, and single; there's no way to see if the single line is faster until you're deep in the building. Virtual line option.

San Francisco

The restaurants in this section are higher-toned than elsewhere in the park. Several times a day, the drumming construction studs known as **The Beat Builders** jam out on the scaffolding opposite Fast & Furious.

Fast & Furious—Supercharged ★ RIDE   You'll be able to feel the simulated thrill of a freeway car chase without moving so much as a foot on this overly macho import from Universal Studios Hollywood. The setup is that you're VIPs trying to get to a party on time . . . exactly like a certain rockin' roller coaster at Disney's Hollywood Studios (hmmm). Once you leave the loading area on the tramlike "party bus," motion simulator technology and crisp lateral projections collide—so that you don't have to. Despite the testosteroned name, it's so tame that there's not even a seat belt. *Strategy:* Try to sit near the sides, where the view will be unobstructed. Virtual line option.

The Wizarding World of Harry Potter— Diagon Alley

From the outside, it appears to be a deft re-creation of some London landmarks, including a perfectly replicated King's Cross Station and some townhouses that would fool a lifetime resident of Bloomsbury (keep an eye on the curtains in the second balcony window of 12 Grimmauld Place, the shabby townhouse). You have a re-created "Eros" fountain from Piccadilly Circus (unlike the original, this one actually has flowing water), cab shelters selling Britannia souvenirs and jumbo hot dogs, and a three-level-tall **Knight Bus.** If its conductor is there, have a chat with him, but don't be alarmed if the shrunken Jamaican head hanging above his steering wheel butts into the conversation.

Hidden behind the London facade, through some sidelong brick portals, is one of the best theme park experiences in the world: essentially a wholesale construction of 3 city blocks around Diagon Alley, where wizards go for their provisions. It's not so much a single attraction as it is a cluttered streetscape of shops, beverage and dessert stores, and painstaking design work that seals you off from the outside world. There are few right angles, but plenty of opportunities to spend lots and lots of cash. You could pass hours simply exploring details, from animated window displays (the skeleton that imitates your movements from the window of Dystyl Phaelanges is a standout) to clever signage larded with inside jokes ("These Premises to Let: Reptiles/ Arachnids Allowed").

The main thoroughfare is **Diagon Alley,** lined with the Leaky Cauldron restaurant and shops for wands, toys, and clothing. It leads dramatically to Gringotts Bank, which is crested by a petrified dragon that belches fire every few minutes (it gurgles right before). Gringotts is on **Horizont Alley,** a 2-block lane noted for its pet store, beer hall, and ice cream shop. On the left, it leads into **Knockturn Alley,** a fascinating indoor area that simulates a shady ghetto at night, right down to shifting clouds overhead and a tattoo parlor,

reducio! LIGHTEN YOUR WALLET AT DIAGON ALLEY

Diagon Alley has the best theme park merchandising you've ever seen. Nearly everything there is to do and taste comes with a price tag, and you can't get these experiences outside Universal's gates.

- **Gringotts Money Exchange, Carkitt Market.** Trade in "muggle money" (U.S. $10s and $20s only) for Gringotts Bank Rune Credit, a currency that you can use in both parks or, Universal hopes, take home as a souvenir (pure profit for the park). You can observe the crusty goblin teller without paying.

- **Ollivanders, Diagon Alley.** In addition to the same wand-selecting mini-show available at Hogsmeade (p. 150), you may purchase a $55 interactive wand used to activate more than a dozen tricks wherever you see a medallion embedded in the ground here or in Hogsmeade. Stand on it, emulate the wand motion depicted on it, and you'll make toilets flush, suits of armor animate, fountains squirt, and so on. It's fun.

- **The Hopping Pot, Carkitt Market, and the Fountain of Fair Fortune, Horizont Alley.** Sip sweet concoctions for $5 each: Otter's Fizzy Orange Juice, Tongue Tying Lemon Squash, Peachtree Fizzing Tea, and Fishy Green Ale with "fish eggs" (actually blueberry boba) on the bottom. They also sell the classic Potter potable, Butterbeer (in a mug made for Diagon Alley, $14; $8 in a plain cup), and two beers unique to the park, Wizards Brew (a chocolatey stout) and Dragon Scale (a light lager), both $10.

- **Florean Fortescue's Ice Cream Parlour, Diagon Alley.** Try a range of only-here flavors including Chocolate Chili, Clotted Cream, Earl Grey and Lavender, and a dangerously addictive soft-serve version of Butterbeer ($8). Too busy? You can get Butterbeer ice cream next door at the **Fountain of Fair Fortune,** too.

- **Eternelle's Elixir of Refreshment, Carkitt Market.** ☞ Mix your choice of $4.25 "elixirs" (Draught of Peace, Fire Protection Potion, and so forth) with $5 "Gillywater" (water) and something magical happens: Universal makes $9 on sugar water. (By the way, bottled water outside Diagon Alley is lower priced.)

- **Weasleys' Wizard Wheezes, Diagon Alley.** The toy shop sells $11–$35 Pygmy Puff stuffed animals and a dazzling variety of novelty gifts. Buy the candies Ron ate to get out of school: Puking Pastilles, Fainting Fancies, Fever Fudge, and Nosebleed Nougat ($7 each). Attached is **Sugarplum's,** stocked with more fanciful sweets (chocolate frogs!, $13), but the pickings are better over at Hogsmeade.

- **Magical Menagerie, Horizont Alley.** Where windows are filled with animated pets such as pythons and giant snails, procure specialty animal souvenirs such as plush and puppet versions of Fluffy, Hedwig, griffins, huge purple toads, and Hermione's half-Kneazle cat Crookshanks ($25–$35).

- **Borgin and Burkes, Knockturn Alley.** Items from the darker arts, including plenty of decorative skulls. Something's trying to escape the trunk by the wall.

- **Shutterbutton's, Diagon Alley.** Via a green screen, put your family in the middle of a 3- to 4-minute, 12-scene DVD/download ($70), like a moving postcard exploring the Potter universe.

Marcus Scarr's, where animated sample designs writhe on the wall (do peek in). Branching off from Diagon Alley on the right, you find **Carkitt Market,** a covered area recalling London's Leadenhall Market, where the principal show stage is located. Performances include **The Singing Sorceress: Celestina Warbeck and the Banshees** (a talented but somewhat out-of-theme singer—J.K. Rowling's favorite "offstage" character mentioned but not seen in the book series—rendering such classics as "A Cauldron Full of Hot, Strong Love") and **The Tales of Beedle the Bard** (a street performance with puppets of two tales from the Potter spin-off book).

Harry Potter and the Escape from Gringotts ★★★ RIDE Another genre-busting creation, this indoor ride is among the most advanced anywhere: part roller coaster, part motion simulator amid dominating 3D high-def screens. At times your respect for its razor's-edge complexity will overshadow the purity of the thrills, and the dialogue sounds muddy, but it's still unmissable. The queue lingers in the sumptuous, echoing lobby of Gringotts Bank, where 10 robotic goblins pause long enough from their clerical duties to sneer at you, and you're taken by "lift" deep underground to begin a minecart-like race through the vaults. Almost immediately, nasty lightning bolts from Bellatrix Lestrange (Helena Bonham Carter) put your course awry, sending you careening into the slithering presence of Voldemort (Ralph Fiennes). Can Bill Weasley and friends save you in time? (What do *you* think?) There are some mild spins and drops in the dark, but you wear 3D glasses the whole time and they don't fall off, so it's not that rough, and it's less scary and height-restrictive than the Forbidden Journey ride at Hogsmeade. *Strategy:* Take the test seat out front seriously; if you don't fit, you shouldn't ride. Locker use for small items is mandatory; short ones, to the right of the main door, are free. Express doesn't help you jump much of the line, but there's a single-rider queue that moves quickly and bypasses the pre-show. Front rows (1 and 4) are best for seeing the screens, the view from the left side of the fourth row can be obscured, and the middle two seats are the best overall. Virtual line option.

Hogwarts Express ★★★ RIDE Separate from Diagon Alley, through the vaulted brick interior of a cunningly accurate King's Cross Station, you board the hissing, steaming, and, to all appearances, vintage steam train to Hogsmeade. You are assigned a six-person, upholstered compartment, the door shuts, and off you go. Out the window, England and Scotland scroll by while in the train corridor, you overhear conversations and see ominous shadows through frosted glass. In reality, you're traveling through Universal's backstage area, but you never see it. The technical prowess is nearly totally convincing, and even where it isn't, it's still dazzling. Within 4 minutes, you disembark at Islands of Adventure outside the gate to the other Wizarding World (if you require an upgrade to a park-to-park ticket, which costs around $55, there are kiosks for the purpose). In the station, there's also a spot, done with mirrors and clever lighting, for you to re-create the moment when Harry and his fellow students walk through a brick wall to reach Platform 9¾. That photo op gets thronged, but there's a bypass if you don't want to wait for it. *Tip:* If you rented a stroller, drop off at this station and pick up a new one at Hogsmeade.

Ollivanders ★★ SHOW   You enter this ancient boutique in small groups, and the kindly shopkeeper selects one child from the group for a personalized wand selection—it selects *them*—accompanied by music cues and light tricks. The brief spell thus cast, an attendant then ushers your child directly toward the cash registers in the wand department, where the kids demand you purchase perfect replicas of wands from nearly every major character in the Harry Potter universe (mostly $46–$52 each), from Harry to Hermione to Snape to Voldemort to Bellatrix Lestrange to Luna Lovegood. The wands don't have price tags, but they do have stickers reading, preposterously, "This is not a toy." Treat them with care. Some are sturdy, but some, such as Professor McGonagall's, can break. *Tip:* Even on a quiet day, there can be a line for this, so if it's high on your list, come early to get your spot.

World Expo

There's not much to this area except one ride and a dated show.

Men in Black: Alien Attack ★★ RIDE   After a superlative queue area that does a pitch-perfect, "Jetsons"-style imitation of New York's 1964 World's Fair (ironically, the one Walt Disney created so many wonders for), you discover the "real" tenant of the futuristic building: a training course for the Men in Black alien patrol corps. You board six-person cars equipped with individual laser guns. As you pass from room to room—expect lots of herky-jerky motions, but nothing sickening—your task is to fire upon any alien that pops out from around doorways, behind trash cans, and so on. If they peg you first, your buggy goes spinning. Each car's point score is displayed on the dashboard, and the number accumulated by the end determines the climactic video you're shown—Will Smith will either praise you as "Galaxy Defender" or mock you as "Bug Bait." *Strategy:* The single riders' queue moves quickly thanks to the odd number of seats in each row. Locker use for small items is mandatory, but free. *Tip:* Look for "Steven Spielberg" sitting on a bench with a newspaper. After the ride, ask a staffer if you can tour the "Immigration Room," an area most guests don't visit. Trust us.

Fear Factor Live ★ SHOW   How is this still here? Like the meat-headed NBC-then-MTV show, ordinary people do stunts (usually involving being dangled on wires, maybe eating food-grade mealworms) while an inane master of ceremonies eggs everyone on. If you're 18 or over and want to volunteer as a contestant (first prize: polite applause), be there 70 minutes before your desired showtime and you'll go through a tryout including jumping jacks and a game of Simon Says. Contestants can't wear jewelry, and if your hands sweat when you're nervous, you will stink at the gripping challenges. These days, this show is dark more often than it's running. Persistent rumors say this will be subsumed by an expansion. Hurry up, please.

Springfield

After Diagon Alley, Springfield is the cleverest land in the Studios. The area is jammed with inside jokes from the longest-running comedy on TV—for example, **Lard Lad Donuts** sells "The Big Pink" ($8) and "Ice Cream Conans." **Kwik-E-Mart,** free of problematic Apu stereotypes, sells an array of bespoke souvenirs you can only get here (pick up the payphone there, by the way), **Moe's Tavern** pours **Duff Brewery's** signature quaff—the cause of, and solution to, all life's problems—and the statue of frontiersman Jebediah Springfield embiggens us all. A **Duff** pavilion on the water also sells alcoholic Squishees and, in the fall, seasonal Dufftoberfest beer. Near the Hollywood end on the lagoon, check out the original locomotive from *Back to the Future III*.

The Simpsons Ride ★★★ RIDE   It's easy to love this highly amusing, top-quality, motion-simulator "Thrilltacular Upsy-Downsy Spins-Aroundsy Teen-Operated Thrill Ride" that takes place in front of an 80-foot-tall screen. The premise, dense and ironic enough to please any Simpsons fan, parodies Orlando itself: You join Homer's clan at Krustyland, a greedy theme park, on a roller coaster that's sabotaged by the evil Sideshow Bob (voiced by Kelsey Grammer). During the dizzyingly fast-paced 6 minutes, you zoom through predicaments that mock the theme park world, including skewers of Shamu, Pirates of the Caribbean, and "it's a small world." Add to that a giant killer panda bear and an extra layer of heightened sensory details (like the whiff of baby powder—well, it makes sense when you ride). It's not too rough, but dehydrated people find it vaguely nauseating, and your brain may hurt from absorbing all the jokes. The queue area is so tongue-in-cheek and gag-packed that waiting is half the fun: Itchy and Scratchy furnish the gory safety warning and Krusty dispenses safety instructions such as "Wait here until someone comes and tells you to do something." *Strategy:* Seats are four across, so families can ride together.

Kang & Kodos' Twirl 'n' Hurl ★ RIDE   Universal's Dumbo ride. Here, silly slobbering aliens trick you into boarding a Day-Glo flying saucer (fitting two adults or one adult and two kids): "Please remain seated until the very end of the ride. You will know the ride has ended when your vehicle comes to a complete stop, or you have been eaten . . . I didn't just say that." As you rotate gently around, Dumbo-style, you use a joystick to pass in front of tentacle-shaped poles, triggering sounds of exclamation from the citizens of Springfield. *Spoiler alert:* You don't get eaten. *Strategy:* Keep an eye on park schedules; it closes early when there's a lagoon show.

WOODY WOODPECKER'S KIDZONE

Scuttlebutt has it that this area is endangered—this land is too valuable. The Barney show that used to be here was closed permanently in 2021, replaced by an indoor **DreamWorks Destination** character meet-and-greet for *Kung Fu Panda, Trolls, Madagascar,* and *Shrek.* The smart money is on the rest of this area going soon, too. For now, there's a ton to do, not least of which is

SpongeBob StorePants, dedicated to merchandise and appearances by the absorbent doofus.

Animal Actors on Location! ★★★ SHOW   A troupe of trained dogs, cats, birds, and a horse anchor this charming 20-minute show (times noted on the sign). Placing it here was inspired, because small children get a thrill out of seeing common animals do tricks, and as a consequence, it's popular and has been running in some form for nearly 30 years. Because it's in an amphitheater, you can sneak out in the middle if you need to. (If you see only one emphatically punctuated household-pets-doing-cute-tricks-to-jaunty-music theme park show, make it SeaWorld's superior Pets Ahoy!)

E.T. Adventure ★★ RIDE   Based on the 1982 Steven Spielberg movie, this endearingly weird indoor ride (a rare survivor from this park's opening day) is rightfully in the kiddie area because it's not intense and the plot cannot withstand scrutiny by a fully developed brain. Upon entering, guests supply their name to an attendant, who encodes the info on a pass you hand over when you board the ride. The indoor queue area is a fabulous reproduction of a thick, cool California forest at night. Vehicles are suspended from rails to approximate the sensation of cruising in a flock of bikes, and they sweep and scoop across the moonrise and then through gardens on E.T.'s home planet (remember, he was a botanist), where a menagerie of goofy-looking aliens and creepy E.T. babies swing on vines. They miraculously speak English, throw a party, and greet us from the sidelines. At the climax, a grateful E.T. is supposed to call out your name as you fly home—hence those boarding passes—but E.T. either runs out of time to name everyone or he spouts gibberish, so don't get your hopes up unless your name is Pfmkmpftur. *Strategy:* Seats on the left have fewer obstructed views.

Fievel's Playland ★★★ ACTIVITY   Named for the hero of *An American Tail* (let's be honest—the kids who grew up with that are turning 45), it's the best of several playgrounds in Kidzone. The concept is that your kids have been shrunk down to a mouse's size, and they're playing among giant everyday items like sardine cans and eyeglasses. They'll discover slides, nets, and tubes, but my favorite element is the easy waterslide on a raft—so yes, make sure your kids have their swimsuits on. The ground is covered with that newfangled soft foam that all the modern playgrounds have. When I was a boy, we got concussions instead.

> ### Make Back Some Admission Expenses
>
> The **NBC Media Center** is marked on maps in Hollywood, but you can only get in by invitation (someone will approach you). Inside, Comcast-affiliated entities screen pilots and solicit audience opinions. On a quiet January day, I once earned $30 for enduring a pilot called *Psych*. I broke it to them gently, telling them that it was clichéd and strained. It then became an eight-season smash on USA Network.

Woody Woodpecker's Nuthouse Coaster ★★ RIDE   Kids can plainly see every sluggish drop before they commit to this straightforward thriller. It has no unpleasant surprises, unless you count hearing Woody's pecking as you go, and a run time of less than a minute.

Curious George Goes to Town ★★★ ACTIVITY   Welcome to the water playground that stole your child. This frenetic splash area is teeming with squealing children and soaked with streams of water from every direction—from squirt cannons, fountains, geysers, and, most importantly, from two 500-gallon buckets that, every 7 minutes, sound a warning bell and then drench anyone beneath. The whole scene is ringed by a perimeter of dry parents keeping an eye on their suddenly wild offspring. Watching your kids cheer and scamper when they hear the bucket's warning bell, and then watching them momentarily vanish in the deluge, is endlessly heartwarming. Past the wet area (there's a dry bypass corridor to it on the left) is the dry Ball Factory, where kids suck up plastic balls with light vacuums, pack them into bags, and then fire them at each other with weak cannons.

Hollywood

This Art Deco stretch is a good place to buy Hello Kitty and Betty Boop merchandise (they have dedicated stores) and meet characters—Gru, SpongeBob SquarePants, Dora the Explorer, Scooby-Doo, and Shaggy—at odd times listed on the map under **Character Party Zone** and **Hollywood Character Zone.** The Superstar Parade begins and ends at the Esoteric Pictures gate, so it's the best place to catch it.

The Bourne Stuntacular ★★ SHOW   Most theme park stunt shows are about Tarzan swings and tall tumbles, but not this. Opened in 2020, this international potboiler doubles down on deeply impressive technology and Swiss-watch timing to supply the sensation of a filmic, moving panorama. More than once, you'll wonder how they achieved something, or you'll even wonder if your eyeballs were fooled by brilliant and very expensive stagecraft. Nothing to be too scared of here—there are gunshots that sound more like caps and some flames—although you may injure your brain trying to wrap it around the convoluted setup that explains how we're able to hopscotch the globe without leaving our seats. The stunts are actually very low-risk, nothing

---

The Studios' Junk Shop

A delicious addition to the Studios, on Hollywood Blvd. near Mel's Diner, is **Williams of Hollywood,** where you can buy signs, costumes, and set pieces from Universal Orlando attractions and Halloween events—plus some genuine vintage finds thrown in. If the item has a brown tag, it came from Universal. I regret passing up the opportunity to drop $3,000 on the cow prop that flew across the stage for 17 years in the Twister attraction. I shall bemoan the decision forevermore.

threatens the audience, and kids are unlikely to be scared. The show takes 30 minutes, and 6 of them are spent standing during the pre-briefing. *Tip:* The illusions work better the farther you sit from the stage.

Universal Horror Make-Up Show ★★ SHOW   It's the park's only homage to the B-movie origins of the Universal name and a rare survivor from the 1990 opening (though much revised). Inside a facade that honors Hollywood's Pantages Theatre, learn a few light facts about how horror-movie makeup effects are accomplished in this snarky, 25-minute, tongue-in-cheek exposé conducted by a nerdy type in his workshop and his straight-man (or -woman) emcee. On paper, that seems like the kind of thing you might otherwise skip, but in truth park regulars love its wit and playful edge. For ribald ad-libbing and gross-out humor, the park suggests parental guidance, but I find most kids have heard it all before, and it's certainly true that seeing terrifying movie gore exposed as the make-believe it is can be a good reality check. You can't get in once the show starts. Even if you skip it, there's something to see in the lobby: Real props from horror films.

Where to Eat at Universal Studios

In addition to the random snack carts, there are counter-service and table-service restaurants. None require reservations the way Disney's do. *Tip:* Meals do not *have* to come with side dishes. Subtract those chips or fries from your meal deals and you'll save about $2. Every menu usually has at least one vegan option. *Remember:* Restaurants at CityWalk (p. 205) are only a 5-minute walk from the park, so they're also options.

Going clockwise around the park, here are your choices:

Classic Monsters Café ★★ AMERICAN   Indoor counter service on a non-scary B-movie set with some healthy options, such as rotisserie chicken, salad, barbecue, and ribs. **Production Central.** Combo meal $13 to $22.

Finnegan's Bar & Grill ★★★ IRISH/BRITISH   A sit-down Irish-style pub with loft ceilings good for a beer break, particularly after 3pm when a guitar singer often performs. Scotch eggs ($11), split pea–and-ham soup ($7), Irish Cobb salad (it has corned beef), Guinness beef stew, and bangers and mash are the kind of solid choices available, plus cocktails and good strong ales. Park workers pick this place when they're off-duty. **New York.** Mains $14 to $26.

Louie's Italian Restaurant ★ ITALIAN   Straightforward counter service near The Mummy. There's a **fruit stand** ($2.50/piece) outside. **New York.** Slices $10–$16 with side salad, whole pizzas $35–$39, meatball or chicken parm subs $12.

San Francisco Pastry Company ★★ SANDWICHES   Sick of lines? This lightly trafficked counter-service bakery does sandwiches and loaded croissants in addition to cakes and pastries, and healthier fruit plates and salads. **San Francisco.** Meals $13–$14 with potato salad, fruit, and chips.

Lombard's Seafood Grille ★★★ SEAFOOD/AMERICAN   An excellent, relaxing table-service choice that is surprisingly affordable: Some dishes are just a few bucks more than a Quick Service meal. Fish dishes such as fish tacos, cioppino, and crab banh mi sandwiches are in the mid-teens. Splashing fountains serenade, fish tanks adorn the dining room, and you can sit outside on the water if you like. **San Francisco.** Main courses $17 to $31.

Richter's Burger Co. ★★ AMERICAN   A warehouselike dockside option that slings stacked burgers, marinated grilled chicken sandwiches, and for those weary of greasy fare, salads with grilled chicken. Periodically, the dining area rumbles (but doesn't move) to simulate quakes. **Chez Alcatraz,** outside on the water, is a cocktail bar that also sells quick sandwiches and flatbreads. **San Francisco.** Main courses $12 to $17 with fries.

The Leaky Cauldron ★★★ BRITISH   The fare at Diagon Alley's counter-service location is not mystical at all. It's plentiful and true to an English pub, serving British staples such as beef, lamb, and Guinness stew; cottage or fisherman's pie; and banger (sausage) sandwiches. The ploughman's lunch for two ($22) has three types of cheese and Branston pickle. There's a "secret" menu that offers pea soup, Scotch eggs, and a ploughman's lunch for one for $11. (Breakfast is a little more American.) Also get Butterbeer, Fishy Green Ale, and other Potter potables here. Unlike at most Universal restaurants, they don't let you subtract fries to save money. **Diagon Alley.** Mains $11 to $17.

Fast Food Boulevard ★★★ AMERICAN   This mouthy indoor food court in Springfield serves mostly standard food renamed with inside jokes and witticisms that puncture American culture. You could spend half your lunchtime just laughing at the dishes. **Krusty Burger** serves "meat sandwiches" such as the high-stacked double-bacon Clogger Burger with "cheez sauce" and curly fries and 6-inch Heat Lamp Dogs. **The Frying Dutchman** does Basket O' Bait fried fish and Clam Chowd-arr. At the **Luigi's Pizza** area, get slices of Meat Liker's Pizza, and at **Cletus' Chicken Shack,** dig into the not-very-appetizing-but-accurate Chicken Arms (wings), Chicken Thumbs (tenders), and chicken-and-waffle sandwiches. Lastly, **Lisa's Teahouse of Horror** balances out the junk food with a cooler full of straight-up salads and wraps. You can also buy only-at-Universal treats such as Buzz Cola (no-calorie cherry cola). Outside and across the way, there's the **Bumblebee Man's Taco Truck. Springfield.** Entrees $15 to $19.

Moe's Tavern ★★★ BAR   A spot-on re-creation of Moe's, down to team pennants for the Isotopes and the purple TV on the wall, only without sleazy service by Moe. There is, however, a life-size Barney by the bar, ruefully contemplating his empty mug. Duff Beer is specially brewed for the park ($10, $14 with souvenir cup); there's an amber (Duff), and a pilsner (Lite), and an ale (Dry), but the kid-friendly potent potable is a Flaming Moe's ($10), a nonalcoholic orange-flavored soda in a cup rigged with pellets that make it

In both its parks, Universal often (but not always; you may need to ask) offers a simple meal plan. Dubbed the **Universal Dining Plan—Quick Service,** it entitles you to one main plate, one non-alcoholic beverage, and one snack, which can be used for ice cream, frozen beverages, and more. Adults pay $26 and kids $18 for a day; it only pays off if you go for the most expensive choices and were going to get that dessert anyway. If you buy one at a kiosk in the park, you must activate it at Guest Services or at any restaurant (most won't open until 11am or so). Resort guests may avail themselves of a Full-Service **Dining Plan,** good for one table-service meal, one quick-service meal, and a snack for $52 adults, $18 kids each day (buy at your resort). The value is borderline, especially if you don't want table-service meals, and can only be redeemed inside the parks or at a few CityWalk restaurants. Everyone can buy special cups good for free refills ($15).

bubble and smoke (it's hard to breathe when you're sipping it). *Tip:* Pick up the phone. **Springfield.** Beverages $10 to $14.

Mel's Drive-In ★★ AMERICAN   A 1950s-style counter-service diner where fare leans toward chicken, brisket, burgers, and shakes. Air-conditioned seating has a view of the lagoon. **Hollywood.** Main courses $12 to $17.

Today Cafe ★ SANDWICHES   This is definitely corporate synergy overload—who wants to eat on the set of the NBC morning show?—but fortunately the food is quite good. Unfortunately, the service is always slow. Sample fare includes morning egg Florentine sandwiches, acai bowls, and cold-brew coffee, and in the afternoon, pastrami on rye. **Hollywood.** Sandwiches and salads $9 to $14.

ISLANDS OF ADVENTURE

Probably the best choice in Orlando in pound-for-pound thrills—it's also the original theme-park home of Harry Potter—**Islands of Adventure (IOA)** ★★★ doubled in attendance between 2009 and 2017, hitting 10.4 million visitors in 2019, nipping at Disney's heels. The park usually opens at 9am. In winter months, operating hours will end around 6pm but in summer, it's often open as late as 10pm. After you park (from $26, but it's covered), go through security, take the moving sidewalks to CityWalk, and veer to the left, toward the 130-foot Pharos Lighthouse (it's just decoration). If you doubt whether your kids are tall enough to ride everything, there's a gauge listing requirements before the ticket booths.

ORIENTATION   IOA's 101 acres are laid out much like Epcot's World Showcase: individually themed areas (here called "islands," although they're not) arranged around a lagoon (obscurely called the Great Inland Sea). To see everything, you simply follow a great circle. The only corridor into the park,

Port of Entry, borrows from the Magic Kingdom's Main Street, U.S.A., in that it's a narrow introductory area where guests are submerged into a theme. In this case, you're gathering munitions for a "great odyssey," so, in theme park logic, it's where you do things like rent strollers and lockers and grab free maps. Most guests beeline through Port of Entry. Because attraction lines are shortest after opening, explore this area later.

STRATEGY Lines peak in late morning. If the typical Florida forecast calls for afternoon storms (in summer, 2pm seems to be a usual time) and you have a two-park pass, do IOA in the morning because so many of its rides close when lightning is detected. Or wait until rides close to eat lunch.

SHOPPING At Islands of Adventure, you can have your souvenirs sent to Port Provisions, at the Port of Entry, for collection as you leave the park at the end of the day. The deadline for purchases changes, but it's usually about 2 hours before closing. To the right as you exit the park, there's a **small stand** selling marked-down items (the inventory changes, but I've seen $8 Marvel action figures, two-for-ones on plush Curious George dolls, and $40 sweatshirts for $22). It opens later in the day.

Marvel Super Hero Island

If Disney now owns Marvel and Fox, how come Universal is allowed to have Spidey and the Simpsons? It's because the park snapped up the brands in licensing deals ages ago. The 1990s contract also locked in the comic- and cartoon-inspired look of that period, before the black-leather film franchises of Spider-Man, the X-Men, Iron Man, and the Avengers, so forgive them if some of the costumes look like the Fly Girls on *In Living Color*. **Spider-Man** is sometimes here, but if you don't see him, head into the back of the Marvel Alterniverse Store, opposite the Captain America Diner. There, the hero has his own appearance zone where you can take your own photos (or buy one). The **Comic Book Shop** is worth a stop. Surprisingly legit, the store carries the latest Marvel issues, compilation books, and collectible busts.

Incredible Hulk Coaster ★★★ RIDE Every minute or so, a new train blasts out of the 150-foot tunnel, over the avenue, and across the lakefront. The ride is quick—a little over 2 minutes—but it's invigorating. Some people find the motion too unrelenting and come off with a headache, but coaster nerds love it, and it's super-smooth thanks to a 2016 extreme makeover that tore down everything and replaced it an exact replica. First, trains cruise into the inclined tunnel. Then, synchronized rock music playing through in-car speakers, they're launched from a standstill to 40mph in 2 seconds and twist into a zero G-force barrel-roll 110 feet in the air, which means passengers are already upside down even though they're still going up the first hill. What follows is unbridled mayhem as you boomerang in a cobra roll and hit a top speed of 67mph through a tangle of corkscrews, loops, and misty tunnels. For many guests it's the first ride of the day, and its seven inversions are certain to work better than morning coffee. Loose items aren't allowed, so use the

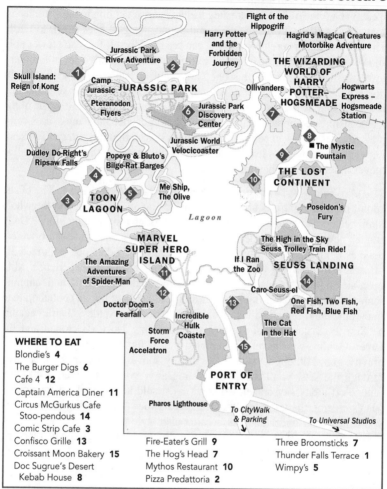

Flight of the
Hippogriff

Harry Potter
and the
Forbidden
Journey

Hagrid's Magical Creatures
Motorbike Adventure

Jurassic Park
River Adventure

2

Skull Island:
Reign of Kong

1

Camp
Jurassic **JURASSIC PARK**

THE WIZARDING
WORLD OF
HARRY
POTTER–
HOGSMEADE

Ollivanders

Hogwarts
Express –
Hogsmeade
Station

Pteranodon
Flyers

Jurassic Park
Discovery
Center

6

7

Jurassic World
Velocicoaster

8

The Mystic
Fountain

Dudley Do-Right's
Ripsaw Falls

Popeye & Bluto's
Bilge-Rat Barges

9

4

5

**TOON
LAGOON**

3

Me Ship,
The Olive

Lagoon

10

**THE LOST
CONTINENT**

Poseidon's
Fury

4

**MARVEL
SUPER HERO
ISLAND**

The High in the Sky
Seuss Trolley Train Ride!

The Amazing
Adventures
of Spider-Man

If I Ran
the Zoo

SEUSS LANDING

11

14

12

Caro-Seuss-el

Doctor Doom's
Fearfall

13

One Fish, Two Fish,
Red Fish, Blue Fish

Incredible
Hulk
Coaster

The Cat
in the Hat

Storm
Force
Accelatron

15

**PORT OF
ENTRY**

Pharos Lighthouse

To CityWalk
& Parking

To Universal Studios

WHERE TO EAT

Blondie's **4**
The Burger Digs **6**
Cafe 4 **12**
Captain America Diner **11**
Circus McGurkus Cafe
  Stoo-pendous **14**
Comic Strip Cafe **3**
Confisco Grille **13**
Croissant Moon Bakery **15**
Doc Sugrue's Desert
  Kebab House **8**

Fire-Eater's Grill **9**
The Hog's Head **7**
Mythos Restaurant **10**
Pizza Predattoria **2**

Three Broomsticks **7**
Thunder Falls Terrace **1**
Wimpy's **5**

nearby lockers, good for the posted wait time plus 30 minutes. *Strategy:* The single-rider line here is fruitful.

Storm Force Accelatron ★ RIDE   I can translate: Storm is the weather-controlling X-Man, so an Accelatron must be a 90-second spinning-tub ride, like Disney's teacups. Open, round cars spin on platters that themselves are on a giant rotating disk, and just to ensure maximum vomit velocity, each pod can be further spun using a plate in the middle. *Strategy:* Skip it unless you have insistent kids. In fact, Universal's interest in operating this ride on a daily basis has been waning.

Dr. Doom's Fearfall ★★ RIDE   Those twin 200-foot towers are fitted with rows of chairs that slide up and down them. The brave are rocketed 150 feet up at a force of 4Gs, where they feel an intense tickling in their stomachs, soak up a terrific view of the park, and bounce (safely) back down to Earth. The ride capacity is pretty low—you can see for yourself that each tower only shoots about 16 people up on each trip, with a reload period of several minutes in between—so either do this one early or very late so that waiting for it doesn't eat up too much time. You may hear the towers hiss like a snarling beast—it sounds like a Doctor Doom sound effect, but, in fact, it's part of the mechanism. A computer weighs each car before launch, and any excess compressed air is noisily expelled in the seconds before flight. *Strategy:* The seating configuration lends itself to lots of empty spaces, so the single-rider line moves much quicker than most.

The Amazing Adventures of Spider-Man ★★★ RIDE   The cliché "don't miss it" rightfully applies here. It fires on all cylinders, and the whole family can do it without fear. After passing through a simulation of the "Daily Bugle" newsroom (take special notice of the hilarious pre-ride safety video, done as a pitch-perfect "Superfriends"-era cartoon), riders don polarized 3D glasses, board moving cars, and whisk through a 1.5-acre experience. Mild open-air motion simulation, computer-generated animation, and cunning sense trickery (bursts of flame, water droplets, blasts of hot air) collaborate to impart the mind-blowing illusion of being drafted into Spidey's battles against a "Sinister Syndicate" of supervillains including Doctor Octopus and the Green Goblin, who have disassembled the Statue of Liberty with an anti-gravity gun. Although the vehicles barely move as they make their way through the sets, you'll come off feeling as if you've survived a 400-foot plunge off a city skyscraper. Comics fans should keep a lookout for Spider-Man's creator, the late Stan Lee: He appears four times during the ride, and you'll hear him once. The ride's cartoonish style predates the movies with Tobey, Andrew, and Tom, but now that the Spider-Verse is a thing, it's looking fresh again. *Strategy:* Go early or late in the day to minimize waits. There's

---

The Best of Islands of Adventure

Don't miss if you're 6: The Cat in the Hat
Don't miss if you're 16: VelociCoaster, Hagrid's Magical Creatures Motorbike Adventure
Requisite photo op: Hogwarts Castle
Food you can only get here: Butterbeer, Hogsmeade
The most crowded, so go early: VelociCoaster, Hagrid's Magical Creatures Motorbike Adventure

Skippable: Pteranodon Flyers
Biggest thrill: VelociCoaster, Hagrid's Magical Creatures Motorbike Adventure, Incredible Hulk Coaster
Best show: Poseidon's Fury (well, it's the only show)
Where to find peace: On the lagoon in Toon Lagoon or The Lost Continent

sometimes a single-rider line and it shoots past the slower standby queue. The middle of the front row is debatably the best place to sit.

Toon Lagoon

The next zone clockwise after Marvel Super Hero Island, Toon Lagoon harbors two water rides that are—both literally and figuratively—among the splashiest at any theme park. Both will drench you. If you're smart, you'll come just *before* it swelters, so that you'll be soaked and cool when the going gets rough.

Slow your pace when you reach the introductory section of Toon Lagoon, encountered after a brief zone of **midway games** (most: three tries for $5). Crawling with details, color, and fountains, it's the kind of place that reveals more the longer you look. Some 150 cartoon characters—some you'll recognize (Nancy, Annie, the Family Circus, Beetle Bailey) and some strictly for connoisseurs (Little Nemo in Slumberland, Zippy)—make two-dimensional appearances on the island, including inside the restaurants and on a soundtrack popping in and out of the action. Where you see a button or a possible trigger, press it or plunge it, because the environment has been rigged with sonic treats. Whimsical snapshot spots are worked in, too, such as the trick photo setup by the Comic Strip Cafe where you can pretend Marmaduke is dragging you by his leash. The deluge from the waterfall under Hagar's Viking ship provides cooling relief from the sunlight. Amid all this, the **Boop Oop A Doop** Betty Boop store sells rare specimens. Personally, I worry about the mental health of the clerks, who are subjected to a brain-melting loop of Boop's oops.

Dudley Do-Right's Ripsaw Falls ★★★ RIDE   Within this Technicolor snow-capped mountain, you'll find a wonderful perils-of-Pauline log-flume caper featuring Jay Ward's feckless Canadian Mountie bungling his rescue of Nell Fenwick from Snidely Whiplash. The winding 5-minute journey—ups, downs, indoor, outdoor, surprise backsplashes, chunky robotic characters—climaxes in a stomach-juggling double-dip drop that hurtles, unexpectedly, through a humped underground gully. Although the 75-foot drop starts out at 45 degrees, it steepens to 50 degrees, creating a weightless sensation. Front- and back-seat riders get soaked, and anyone who didn't get soaked probably will when they double back to the disembarking zone, because that's when they'll face the firing squad of sadistic bystanders who shoot water cannons at passing boats. Ripsaw Falls is terrific fun. No one gets off it grumpy—the mark of amusement success. The ride often closes for a few weeks in off-season for a scrub. ***Strategies:*** Seats are tight, but it helps if you straighten your legs as you get in and out. There are optional lockers in the nook to the left of the entrance gate—use them, because there's no boat storage. It's $4 for 90 minutes, which may allow you to also use the same locker for riding Popeye & Bluto's Barges. The **Gasoline Alley** shop, across the main path, sells $11 ponchos, but on Ripsaw Falls, you straddle the seat so your feet won't be easy to cover. Best to wear sandals.

Popeye & Bluto's Bilge-Rat Barges ★★★ RIDE   For my money, it's the best round-boat flume in the world. You board 12-passenger, circular bumper boats that float freely and unpredictably down an outlandish white-water obstacle course—beneath waterfalls, through tunnels, over angry rapids, and past features designed to mercilessly saturate you. It's like playing Russian roulette with water, except everyone loses. This journey is considerably wilder and unquestionably wetter than other rides like this one. And more elaborate: Even the river's walls have been sculpted and painted in hues to resemble a cartoon wooden chute. It's diabolical and one of Universal's best. On hot days, the wet effects are fully juiced, but when it's cold, they're turned down slightly. *Strategy:* There's a semi-waterproof cubby on board for personal belongings, but you'd be wise to slip your things into plastic bags, too, just in case. You may not be barefoot off the boat but once on, you may remove shoes for the ride. Watching your loved ones get humiliated brings a lifetime of satisfaction, but for onlooker schadenfreude, there are 25¢ water blasters on overlooking walkways, as well as are free ones on Me Ship, the Olive. Near the lockers ($4 for 90 min., which may be long enough to use for Ripsaw Falls, too), you'll find step-in People Dryers that, for $5, bake and blow the water off you after your journey. (They work well, except on jeans.)

Me Ship, the Olive ★ ACTIVITY   An interactive ship-shaped playground for children lies just beyond the Barges' entrance; there's also a slide and some fun to be had with a piano in the cabin (play the notes on the sheet music for an orchestral surprise). One of my favorite things to do in Orlando is to spend a while on the bridge beside the Olive, which overlooks Barge boats as they drift helplessly under a leaky boiler's funnel. Watching the gleeful alarm on people's faces, hearing the peals of laughter—the sublime delight of amusement park togetherness is repeated, again and again, from the vantage point of that bridge. I could stand there all day. I also love the shore of the sea nearby, which is private almost all the time.

Jurassic Park

Steven Spielberg was a creative consultant to Universal, the studio that nourished him, and this "island," the largest and greenest in the park, is presented practically verbatim from his 1993 movie and its sequels. Once you pass through a proud stone gate, John Williams's bombastic score takes over, and there it burrows until you move on to another area of IOA. While you're here, stop by the **Raptor Encounter,** where a dinosaur expert from Jurassic World introduces you to a captive velociraptor—they're pretty entertaining and it only takes a few minutes. There's also a special beer on tap here and only here: Jurassic World Isla Nublar IPA, made by the Cape Canaveral-based Florida Beer Company.

Skull Island: Reign of Kong ★★ RIDE   A fantastically terrifying stone facade warns wimps away, but despite gargantuan appearances, it's really mostly a screen-based motion-simulator ride, albeit one that uses a tramlike vehicle and requires 3D goggles. This 2016 addition is a bigger version of the Kong segment of the Universal Studios Hollywood tram tour—the animation is good, if graphic, and there is one luscious post-movie moment when you encounter a splendidly executed Kong, live and in the fur. The height requirement, just 34 inches, is proof that despite all that, it's family-friendly mayhem. In bad weather, ride vehicles don't drive through the front gate, but instead use a less theatrical indoor route. ***Strategy:*** Trucks seat 12 rows of 6. Seats on the right see more of the action. Get a drink before getting in line; the queue can be hot and tedious.

Camp Jurassic ★ ACTIVITY   The only dedicated kids' zone of this part of the park is a self-guided tangle of rope bridges, slides, bubbling pools in caves, surprise geysers, water guns, spitting dinosaur heads, and thick greenery. It's easy to get lost here, and easier to get wet.

Pteranodon Flyers ★ RIDE   The hanging carts gently gliding on the nifty-looking track over Camp Jurassic constitute a very short (about 75 seconds) clacking route through the trees. Cool as it looks, it was poorly designed, fitting only two at a time, and huge lines were inevitable. Facing irate crowds, Universal instituted a rule: No adult could ride without a child. That both prepared guests for the ride's tame deportment and cut down on the wait. Attendants may be willing to load child-free adults when the park is dead. ***Strategy:*** Skip this underwhelmer if the wait's more than 15 minutes. Sometimes it offers a virtual line.

Jurassic Park River Adventure ★★ RIDE   In that family-friendly Orlando tradition, the worst drop is clearly warned; gauge the 85-foot descent from behind the Thunder Falls Terrace restaurant, where river boats kick up quite a spray as they hit the water at 30mph. Before reaching that messy climax, boats embark on what's meant to be a benign tour of the mythical dinosaur park from the movie, only to be bumped off course and run afoul of spitting raptors and an eye-poppingly realistic T. rex that lunges for the kill. The dino attack is shrewdly stage-managed; note how, in true Spielberg fashion, you see disquieting evidence of the hungry lizards (rustling bushes, gashes in sheet metal) before actually catching sight of one. In all honesty, you're more likely to get soaked standing on the terrace of the restaurant than in the boat, but the trip down is enough to blow your hat off and sprinkle you above the waist. There's usually at least one delirious 12-year-old boy who stands in the splash zone for hours, giving himself a nigh-amphibious drenching. ***Tip:*** Front seats get wettest and back seats are better for taking in the story. Virtual line option.

Jurassic World VelociCoaster ★★★ ROLLER COASTER   This 2021 addition is steel coaster perfection. The towering 155-foot "top hat" vertical hill that can be seen for miles around is just a small segment of this wild adventure. Fast as a raptor (hence the name), it's packed with unexpected twists and curves (like the so-called "mosasaurus roll" over the lagoon) that seem to emulate being thrashed in the jaws of a predator dinosaur. But it also has two moments of sudden high-speed acceleration of up to 70 mph that give your blood flow recovery time so you're less likely to come off with a headache. It's easy to wax rhapsodic about a ride with such a great mix of thrills and theming. Even the queue and boarding area are well thought-out; you can keep your phone all the way until just before the boarding platform (which is air-conditioned), allowing you to capture the many fun animatronics and unexpected design moments in the queue. People who track these matters agree nearly uniformly: This is one of the best American roller coasters ever built. I quite agree (and if for the sake of physical tolerance I had to choose between riding this and Incredible Hulk—a quandary I know some coaster-sensitive guests will face—VelociCoaster wins without question). A single rider line is often available.

4 The Wizarding World of Harry Potter— Hogsmeade

When it opened in June of 2010, the 10-acre **Hogsmeade** ★★★ was rightfully hailed as the most significant modern achievement in American theme park design, detailed down to the souvenirs. It's as if the film set for Hogsmeade Village (the only British village for non-Muggles) and Hogwarts Castle have been transported to Florida, and indeed, it was designed by the same team. You don't have to know the books or the movies to enjoy the astounding level of attention: Stonework looks ancient, plaster was painted to appear moldy, rooftops and chimneys slouch in a jumble of snow-covered gables, and nearly every souvenir is a bespoke creation expressly for the Harry Potter universe—in fact, J.K. Rowling had final approval on everything, including what's sold in the intentionally-too-small shops. Even the restrooms aren't spared Moaning Myrtle's whine. Spend time going from window to window to take in the tricks. In Spintwitches Sporting Needs, a Quidditch set strains to free itself from its carrying case. At Gladrags, the gown levitates. At Tomes and Scrolls, Gilderoy Lockhart (Kenneth Branagh) vainly preens himself among his best-selling travel books.

Those stores are brilliant facades, but there are real shops that are just as unmissable (and invariably thronged). **Dervish and Banges** is where you find Hogwarts school supplies in the colors of all four Houses, from capes to scarves to diaries to parchment, wax seals, and quills. (The seething "Monster Book of Monsters" is kept in a cage here.) In the window of **Honeydukes,** there's a macabre contraption in which a mechanical crow pecks out the gumball eye of a skeleton, which rolls through various chutes to be dispensed below, presumably for consumption. That signifies the wondrous candy store within, where colorful Edwardian-style packages contain Chocolate Frogs, Fizzing Whizzbees, Bertie Bott's Every Flavour Beans (beware the vomit-flavored ones mixed in), Exploding Bon Bons, Peppermint Toads, and other confections that would disturb even Willy Wonka.

Types of Butterbeer, Ranked

1. **Soft-serve ice cream:** Must have more!
2. **Frozen:** Deservedly popular. Get it with foam.
3. **Hot:** Like Regular, but somehow more vibrant.
4. **Regular:** Pretty good, too, but not as refreshing.
5. **Hard ice cream:** Nowhere as rich as soft-serve.
6. **Clotted Cream:** Not very Butterbeery, sold at The Leaky Cauldron.
7. **Fudge:** Waxy, like old white chocolate or plumber's putty. Gross.

The park's signature concoction, **Butterbeer,** is pulled from two keg-shaped carts in the walkways. Served frozen or unfrozen with a creamy foam head on top, it tastes like a butterscotch Life Saver, and it's addictive. I once did laboratory analysis on it and found out that, surprisingly, it contains no more sugar than a Coke. It's $8 a cup, but for $13, you get a dishwasher-safe Butterbeer mug. **The Magic Neep** cart, between the Butterbeer stalls, sells **Pumpkin Juice** (really a Christmassy apple juice mix) in its unique pumpkin-top bottles for $8, along with actual fruit for $2.50 apiece.

After dark, you may want to check out the **Nighttime Lights at Hogwarts Castle,** a well-done, 4-minute projection mapping spectacle projected onto the school. It's tight in Hogsmeade, but it runs continuously, so you might have to wait briefly in a holding area before seeing the next showing. Before the holidays, it morphs into a Christmas version.

Ollivanders ★★ SHOW   The queue to the left of Dervish and Banges is another Ollivanders Wand Shop (p. 137). There's only one showroom here, so it can't handle big crowds—if the line is too long (it usually is), there are three more showrooms with an identical experience on Diagon Alley at Universal Studios.

Harry Potter and the Forbidden Journey ★★★ RIDE   You will be drawn inexorably to the stunning re-creation of Hogwarts Castle, and within, you'll find a most technologically complex ride. I won't give away how it's done, but I will say it's an epic combination of motion-simulator movie segments and awe-inducing physical encounters as you travel on a jolting, four-person bench that has been enchanted by Hermione to transport you. This being Orlando, things quickly go wrong, and you encounter a dragon, Aragog the spider, the Whomping Willow, a Quidditch match, and Dementors, all in the space of 4 minutes. The mostly indoor queue is perhaps even more magical, taking you through Dumbledore's study and through the dim halls of Hogwarts, where real-looking oil paintings come to life and bicker with each other. At one point, fake snow falls on you, and a lifelike Sorting Hat supervises your arrival at the loading dock. It's a tour-de-force that takes the pain out of a long wait, and sometimes they set up a route that lets you enjoy it without having to ride (ask). Once you're done, you go through **Filch's Emporium of Confiscated Goods,** a general-interest shop for Potteria. *Strategy:* No loose articles are permitted. Lockers are free for the posted wait time plus 20 minutes. The single-rider line lets you leapfrog much of the wait, but you will miss most of the queue's excitement. Some people feel queasy after riding, but if you sense that happening, just close your eyes during the three movie portions and you should be fine. Try the test seat out front if you're a larger guest—many people are not able to ride.

Hagrid's Magical Creatures Motorbike Adventure ★★★ RIDE

If you want to experience state-of-the-art ride tech, hop on and hold tight. This $300-million opus, new in 2019, is one of the best rides in Orlando—or anywhere. The setup: Hagrid is taking you by motorbike to learn about a few interesting animals in the forest, but as happens in Potterworld and Orlando parks alike, he takes some unexpected turns. There are lots of complex surprises that would be wrong to expose here, so I will just assure you that there are no stomach-grabbing sheer drops, no loops, you won't get dizzy, and nearly all of the motion is satisfyingly swoopy and swervy, even as you repeatedly vault to 55mph in a second or two. You'll have the choice of holding onto the handlebars from the motorbike seat or of sitting in the sidecar; daredevils love leaning into the movements on the bike, and tentative riders tend to prefer the sidecar, which is why this ride works for everyone in the family who is of coaster-riding age (height restriction is 48 in., less than Hulk or Doctor Doom). *Warning:* Motorcycle seats can potentially squeeze the contents of your back pockets onto the track, so if you forgot to put anything in the free lockers, make sure you transfer it to your front pockets. *Tip:* Doing this one after dark takes the excitement to an even higher level. There's a single rider line. Virtual line option.

Flight of the Hippogriff ★ RIDE

For little kids, you'll find a standard training roller coaster (a re-themed holdover from pre-Potter years) that offers a glimpse of Hagrid's Hut from the queue. Don't expect more than a 1-minute figure eight with slight banking—adults, you can skip it. *Strategy:* The line is exposed to the sun and the back seats feel the fastest. The long-legged should cross their ankles to fit more comfortably.

Hogwarts Express ★★★ RIDE

The journey from Hogsmeade to London in Universal Studios works just like the one coming here (p. 136), but you'll see different scenery and eavesdrop on different goings-on in the carriage. Notice the subtle rhythmic vibration of the seats. Hogsmeade Station is not as nice as King's Cross at Diagon Alley—there's no air-conditioning and no fun tricks like the Platform 9¾ photo op—but trains carry 168 people at a time and new ones load 5 minutes after the previous one departs. *Strategy:* To board, you must have a park-to-park ticket; if you don't, there's a ticket upgrade booth out front—it costs $55–$60.

The Lost Continent

The gist of the next island, the Lost Continent, is amorphous. Think of it as part Africa, part Asia, part Rome—anything exotic wrapped up in stony vagueness. The **localARTicles Boutique** beside the Mystic Fountain is really something special for a theme park and worth a stop, selling cool stuff by local artisans like paintings, clothes, and accessories.

Mystic Fountain ★★ ACTIVITY   Stop by briefly. If it's merely gurgling with recorded sound effects, it's dormant. But when least expected, it comes to life with wisecracks and sprays. Someone in an unseen booth interacts with anyone foolish enough to wander near—usually naive children. As *Time* magazine put it when the park opened in 1999, the fountain exasperates with "the droll sarcasm of a bachelor uncle roped into caring for some itchy 10-year-olds." If you don't want to get doused, check the ground for slick spots to determine the fountain's spitting reach.

Poseidon's Fury ★★ ⚑ SHOW   Despite its lowly status as a walk-through attraction, it has a stunning exterior, carved within a millimeter of reason to look like a crumbling temple. Young folk might be freaked out by the dark and the fireballs. Mature folk might disdain the vapid storyline involving a row between Poseidon and Lord Darkenon (who?). But it bemuses with an interesting (if fleeting) "water vortex" tunnel, and some of its other special effects, such as walls that seem to vanish, are diverting. It's boisterous and pyrotechnic, but it's also on its way out, so catch it if you can. *Strategy:* For the best views, head for the front of every room, especially the third one.

Seuss Landing

Nowhere other than Harry Potter is IOA's extravagance on finer display than this 10-acre section, which replicates the good Doctor's two-dimensional bluster with three-dimensional exactitude. Just try to find a straight line. From the lakefront, you can get a good look at what the designers accomplished. Notice how even the palm trees twist. They were knocked sideways near Miami in 1992's Hurricane Andrew, and because palm trees always grow upward, by the time they were scouted for IOA, they had acquired a perfectly loopy angle. Scout for hidden gags. Sprinkled around are Horton's Egg and, by the sea, the two Zaxes, which appropriate to their own book (a commentary on political rivalry in which they stubbornly face off while a city grows up around them), were the very first things placed in the park, and everything else was built around them. The area near the Moose Juice store hosts regular appearances by the Cat in the Hat, as well as the Grinch, who looks as annoyed to be there as you might imagine.

By the Port of Entry, look for the **Green Eggs & Ham Café,** the house-size slab of emerald ham with a giant fork stuck into it. This beauty is one of the best pieces of mimetic architecture in America. It's also never open, but at least you should notice it.

High in the Sky Seuss Trolley Train Ride! ★★★ RIDE   Everything on this island is appropriate for kids. The railway threading overhead is a cheerful family-friendly glide, narrated in verse. Like Dueling Dragons, it has two paths; the purple line surveys more of the area than the green line, which dawdles above the Circus McGurkus Cafe. The ride takes about 3 minutes and because there's so much to take in, time flies fast. You have to line up all over again if you want to do the other track.

Caro-Seuss-el ★★★ RIDE   Its bobbing menagerie of otherworldly critters actually reacts to being ridden—ears wiggle, heads turn, snouts rise—making it delightfully over-the-top and appealing to kids who sniff at kiddie carousels. Beside the Caro-Seuss-el, seek out the quick but trenchant walk-through grove of Truffula Trees retelling Dr. Seuss's environmental warning tale, the **Street of the Lifted Lorax.**

One Fish, Two Fish, Red Fish, Blue Fish ★★★ RIDE   Here we have another iteration (albeit a good one) of Disney's enduring tot bait, Dumbo. Riders (two passengers per car normally, three if one of them loves the Wiggles) go around, up, and down by their own controls while a gauntlet of spitting fish pegs them from the sides—listen to the song for the secret of how to avoid getting wet, although the advice isn't foolproof. There are benches good for watching kids giggle malevolently when parents get spritzed.

If I Ran the Zoo ★★★ ACTIVITY   Getting wet is part of the bargain, so there's a rack to keep shoes dry. The interactive playground for young children contains some 20 tricksy elements. Let your brood slide, splash in a stream, turn cranks, and play Tic Tac Toe on characters' bellies. Beware the cheeky fountain—it pays to follow all posted instructions in Seuss Landing. The book that this ride was based on has since been withdrawn by the Seuss estate, but so far no changes have been announced for the ride itself.

The Cat in the Hat ★★★ RIDE   Take a nonthreatening excursion through the plot of the famous storybook as viewed from slow-moving mobile "couches" (really a typical flat-ride car). The design racks up points for replicating the look of the beloved children's book with precision, even in three dimensions. The story is just as faithfully retold; it's clear from this sweet, 3½-minute ride that the family of Dr. Seuss (Theodor Geisel) had a strong influence in steering the execution of this section of the park. Parents will probably emerge feeling glad they tagged along. *Tip:* The vehicles spin a few too many times for some adults (kids don't seem to mind), but you can ask to have rotation turned off when you board.

Where to Eat in Islands of Adventure

In addition to the random snack carts there's no use in listing here, there are many counter-service spots and one sit-down restaurant (Mythos) in the park. None require advance reservations the way Disney's do. *Tip:* Menu items do not *have* to be served with sides. Subtract them to save about $2. Every menu usually has at least one vegan option.

Clockwise through the park from Port of Entry:

Croissant Moon Bakery ★ SANDWICHES   Lighter bites such as sandwiches and panini (breakfast sandwiches until 11am; combos served with a muffin), plus pastries such as cream horns and vanilla éclairs, can be snagged without much of a line. Nearby is the **Last Chance Fruit Stand** cart, which sells fruit cups ($4.30) and giant turkey legs ($15). **Port of Entry.** Sandwiches $13–$14; soup and salad $10.

Confisco Grille ★ INTERNATIONAL   The menu of this rare (one of only two in the park) table-service location has an identity crisis—beef fajitas, salmon, pad Thai, chicken curry—but that also means there's probably something for everyone in your group. The attached **Backwater Bar** is overlooked by most visitors and therefore ideal for sundowners. **Port of Entry.** Main courses $17 to $23.

Captain America Diner ★ AMERICAN   This indoor counter-service location serves the usual burgers and chicken, plus shakes. Outside you'll find a **fruit stand** where pieces of whole fruit cost $2. **Marvel Super Hero Island.** Main courses $17 to $19 with fries.

Cafe 4 ★ PIZZA   Counter service with indoor seating makes this a good option for grabbing sandwiches as well as individual pizzas. **Marvel Super Hero Island.** Pizza and simple pasta $10 to $16 with side salad; whole pies $35–$39.

Comic Strip Cafe ★★ INTERNATIONAL   Toon Lagoon's largest counter-service location offers four schools of food: burgers, sweet-and-sour chicken, pizzas, and salads. There's more indoor seating with air-conditioning here than anywhere else in this island. **Toon Lagoon.** Main courses $11 to $18.

Blondie's: Home of the Dagwood ★★ SANDWICHES   If you know that Dagwood is another name for a hero, you'll know who Blondie is, too. This indoor counter location does subs served with pickles and potato salad. It usually closes after lunch. **Toon Lagoon.** Mains $11 to $14.

Wimpy's ★ AMERICAN   It's the stand that furnishes its namesake's obsession (hamburgers), although the staff will not permit you to pay next Tuesday for a hamburger today, mostly because it's almost never open. **Toon Lagoon.** Main courses $12 to $16.

The Burger Digs ★ AMERICAN   The Discovery Center's indoor counter-service spot is upstairs, across from the dinosaur-theme toy store. Guess what it makes? There's a toppings bar, so load up. **Jurassic Park Discovery Center.** Combo meal $14 to $19.

Pizza Predattoria ★ AMERICAN   The menu is small but big on calories: pizzas, meatball subs, and chicken Caesar salads. It's counter service with outdoor seating. **Jurassic Park.** Mains $12 to $18 with side salad.

Thunder Falls Terrace ★★★ BARBECUE   Watch the Jurassic Park boats splash down while you sit in the comfort of air-conditioning, noshing on food that's a cut above the rest: chargrilled ribs served with whole unhusked ears of corn, rotisserie chicken, rice bowls, those giant turkey legs, and bacon cheeseburgers. Rice and beans are just $4. **Jurassic Park.** Meals $17 to $22.

Three Broomsticks ★★★ BARBECUE/BRITISH   The film tavern was gorgeously re-created, up to its wonky cathedral ceiling and down to the graffiti scratched in the timbers, as the only restaurant in this island, and the filmmakers reportedly liked the design so much they featured the set more prominently in later movies. Get chicken, ribs, fish and chips, beef pasties, shepherd's pie, or The Great Feast, which feeds four for $70 with salad, rotisserie chicken, spareribs, corn on the cob, and roast potatoes. For dessert: Butterbeer clotted cream. **Hog's Head** pub ★★★ is attached. Under the squinty gaze of a grunting mounted boar's head (it responds to tips), a selection of truly British quaffs (Boddingtons, Tennant's, Strongbow cider) is pulled. There are two unique beers: One is Hog's Head ale, a hoppy, only-here beer made by the Florida Brewing Company, and the other is Butterbeer, so if the line is long at the keg carts outside, grab a faster fix in here, where it's cool in more ways than one. A few concoctions are not on the menu: Hog's Tea (a Long Island Iced Tea), The Triple (cider, Hog's Brew, and Guinness), Pear Dazzle (pear cider, vodka, lemonade), and Fire Whisky (cinnamon whisky—mix it with Strongbow!). **Wizarding World of Harry Potter.** Meals $14 to $18.

Mythos Restaurant ★★★ INTERNATIONAL   The cavelike interior, carved from that ubiquitous orange-hued fake rock that scientists should term Orlando Schist, commands a marvelous view of the lagoon (go around to the water, where you'll be alone, to see the god holding the place up with his bare hands). You could sit and watch the roller coasters fire all day from this subdued environment. Food many rungs higher than most theme park stuff is served, with pad Thai, beef medallions, a seasonal risotto, cranberry/blue cheese–crusted pork, and lamb burgers, plus a healthy slate of sandwiches and salads. **The Lost Continent.** Reservations recommended; ✆ **407/224-4534.** Main courses $17 to $26.

Doc Sugrue's Desert Kebab House ★ MEDITERRANEAN   This outdoor-only counter-service spot serves its namesake in beef, chicken, and vegetables, or Greek salad, plus hummus with veggies ($5). **The Lost Continent.** Main courses $12 to $14.

Fire-Eater's Grill ★ INTERNATIONAL   Another outdoor-only counter-service spot with the usual suspects: chicken fingers, chicken stingers (Buffalo chicken fingers), hot dogs, and gyros. **The Lost Continent.** Meals with fries $11 to $12.

Circus McGurkus Cafe Stoo-pendous ★★★ AMERICAN

Looking like a circus tent coated in cake frosting, it serves the usual burgers and pizzas, plus a fried chicken platter with cornbread so there's something for everyone. For dessert, the **Moose Juice Goose Juice** stand by the bridge to the Lost Continent sells Moose Juice (a tart orange mix) and Goose Juice (green apple) for $5.50. **Seuss Landing.** Meals $10 to $16; whole pizzas $35 to $38.

UNIVERSAL'S VOLCANO BAY

Universal Orlando's custom-built water park, the tiki-tastic, 28-acre **Volcano Bay ★**, opened in the summer of 2017, and is already number seven in the world's most-attended water parks. This slippery playpen is a beaut: The centerpiece, a 200-foot volcano gushing with waterfalls and steaming with mist, is now a landmark beside I-4. Its systems are just as audacious. Guests borrow a sensor wristband, called TapuTapu, that they use to make purchases (if they've linked their credit card to the Universal app first) and trigger spray tricks and photo stations. Tap the band to the talisman posted at flume entrances to reserve a place in a virtual line for later. TapuTapu counts down your wait time while you do other things, and when it's time to ride, the wristband notifies you to head to the attraction.

And what rides, none of which require you to tote a raft around (and there are floaty vests of every size to borrow for free): Highlights of the 11 or so choices, which truly run the gamut from mild to wild, include **Krakatau,** an aqua coaster that pushes riders up and down slopes in a toboggan; **Ko'okiri Body Plunge,** a 70-degree, 125-foot body slide that begins with a trap door and rockets you along a clear tube through the wave pool; four **Punga Racers** slides; **Waturi Beach** wave lagoon (the gong means it's time to surf); toddler and kids' areas; **Ohyah** and **Ohno** slides that drop you into a pool from 4–6 feet; the six-person **Maku Puihi** round-raft rides that spit you into a massive bowl; the **Kopiko Wai** winding river that passes through the illuminated "Stargazer's Cavern"; and many twisted flumes besides those. (Yeah, those names get confusing fast, so get a guide map as you enter, or better yet, bone up before you arrive.) Walkways are kept wet and cool so you can go barefoot, and you'll find many hidden spots with free loungers and powdery sand—they're emptier at the back of the mountain, so that's where you should grab your locker (which are multiple-entry using a code you determine).

It's a well-crafted environment, but it's not a park where you can expect to ride every single thing in a day, though arriving right at opening will help squeeze in more. TapuTapu only permits one reservation at a time on the flumes (the two lazy rivers, kiddie zone, and pools don't require reservations; neither does anything with a sign reading RIDE NOW), and you're free to replace any current reservation with a new one. While you wait, you're expected to do the non-reservation stuff—nosh at the six distinct food locations (quite good—stuff like poke and burgers), drink cocktails (nice and strong), and sunbathe. You can ease the logjam somewhat by paying more to cut the lines with Express ($20–$120 depending on how busy it is and if you want the right to use it multiple times on the same ride), but to be honest, you should save that expense because riding everything would be exhausting here. You have to climb the equivalent of 13 floors each time you do the most extreme slides, and there's not much shade, neither of which is unusual for a water park. Most visitors, especially older ones and those with young children, are satisfied with the amount of stuff they wind up getting to do. Renting a cabana, if you can afford it, also helps since you'll be able to join virtual queues from a tablet there; you also get bottled water, snacks, a butler, and a home base kids can always return to (from $199, but usually more like $500). More affordably, "Premium Seating" (around $127) consists of a pair of padded loungers with canopy, lockbox, and wait service. (Book those and cabanas at © **877/489-8068**.) There's no drop-off at the front gate; Universal hotel guests take buses, and outsiders park in the Universal structure ($26) and take the free shuttle from the back of the bottom level there. Guests of Cabana Bay (p. 255) can just walk next door. *Tip:* In spring and summer it often pours rain in the mid-afternoon, and the park can empty out then. If you can wait about 90 minutes for these storms to pass, you'll be rewarded by greatly reduced waits on everything.

6000 Universal Blvd., Orlando. www.universalorlando.com. © **407/363-8000.** $80–$85 adults, $75–$80 kids 3–9 (discounted when purchased with tickets to the dry Universal parks). Towel rental $6; locker rental $13–$16; private cabanas $199–$550; parking $26, then free shuttle bus. Typically opens around 9am and closes around dusk.

MORE ORLANDO ATTRACTIONS

There's so much more to see and do in Orlando. When you're sick of parking trams and cattle queues, divert yourself with something new. Actually, something old—some of these places are among the original attractions that sparked the fertile vacationland that Central Florida is today.

SEAWORLD ORLANDO

The second theme park chain to set up shop in town, after Disney, was **SeaWorld Orlando ★★★**. The park, which began in San Diego in 1964, staked a claim in Orlando in 1973, predating Universal by 17 years, but the last few years have been the hardest. The *Blackfish* flap hit hard (see box p. 160), and although the park has always touted its legitimate rescue and conservation efforts, now such boasts can feel awkwardly defensive. In 2009, before its troubles began, it was the 12th most popular theme park in the entire world. Now it's not even in the top 25. But thanks in large part to a new focus on thrill rides, it seems to have stopped the bleeding.

While SeaWorld operates three American parks (the third is in San Antonio), its Orlando location is the company's most important. SeaWorld Orlando is amid a multi-year investment strategy to remake itself as an amusement park and sidestep away from animal entertainment. For now, however, the focus is still aquatic animals and conservation, and if watching larger animals such as dolphins obey commands for food makes you uncomfortable, you'll hate it. As more alternative attractions are built, it's increasingly easy to avoid those shows, but they haven't gone away entirely. Otherwise, there's a lot going for SeaWorld: 200 acres of space for gardens, a compound that absorbs crowds well—and you don't have to pre-plan every move the way you do at Disney. Across the road you'll find its luxury animal park, **Discovery Cove ★★★** (p. 172), and a waterslide park, **Aquatica** (p. 171).

For now, the optimal SeaWorld experience is mostly **show-based.** Your day here will revolve around the scheduling of a half-dozen regular performances in which animals (mostly mammals, but some birds, too) do tricks—except here, they're called "behaviors"—with their human trainers. To some, SeaWorld's banner attraction will always be that controversial Shamu show (named for an orca that died in 1971—and also savagely bit a trainer), and when you're not watching orcas do backflips, you're ambling through **Animal Connections** habitats stocked with other beautiful creatures. Thoughtfully, **schedules are posted online** a few weeks ahead of time so that if you're really detail obsessed, you can map out your day in advance; the show schedule calendar is under "Plan Your Day."

Planning a Visit to SeaWorld

SeaWorld (www.seaworldorlando.com; ✆ **407/545-5500**) is located on Central Florida Parkway, at International Drive, or exits 71 and 72 east of I-4. The park is open 9am to 7pm with extended hours in peak season. Parking costs $25, up to $30 on peak days.

The free **SeaWorld Discovery Guide app** (there's free Wi-Fi in major park areas) orients you, supplies showtimes and wait times, allows you to buy shorter wait times for the rides and reserve show seating, and helps you remember where you parked. It drains your battery, but the park is thoughtful enough to provide a free charging booth on the lake by Mako.

Ethical Entertainment? The *Blackfish* Controversy

Some conservationists say SeaWorld's animals endure misery in captivity. Other conservationists laud SeaWorld for being an advocate for marine life. Each side presents statistics that seem convincing but are then shot down by rivals. And therein lies the ongoing tug-of-war over this profit-generating amusement park. SeaWorld is hostile to accusations of mistreatment and exploitation—in 2013, the low-budget documentary *Blackfish* asserted that the 2010 death of senior trainer Dawn Brancheau, which was witnessed by an audience at Shamu Stadium, was the result of inadequate care. (For its part, the Brancheau family distanced itself from the documentary, saying in a statement: "Dawn would not have remained a trainer at SeaWorld for 15 years if she felt that the whales were not well cared for.") An anti-SeaWorld social media campaign has raged ever since. Although SeaWorld's San Diego park was fined about $26,000 by OSHA in California for improperly protecting its human employees, it sharply rebuts some of the film's points, objecting to one-sided reporting and complaining that the editing deceives viewers into believing the park collects its performing animals from the wild, something it hasn't done for decades. Excepting a few aged animals that were born in the seas and rehabilitated from accidents in the wild, SeaWorld insists, most of its animals were born in captivity and raised by hand and so they would not know how to survive in the wild. The orcas that live there, SeaWorld promises, will be the last generation to do so and will not be bred. The park says it has rescued more than 30,000 animals to date, and reminds the media that when marine animals are threatened in the oceans, it regularly steps in to help. But *Blackfish* also alleges that the tanks at SeaWorld could never be large enough to contain animals biologically programmed to roam wide territory—a charge that's harder to deny, and one the company promised to address but hasn't. Defenders say that opens up a new can of worms—why single out SeaWorld, they say, for things that zoos and animal parks across the country do every day?

Orlando Area Attractions

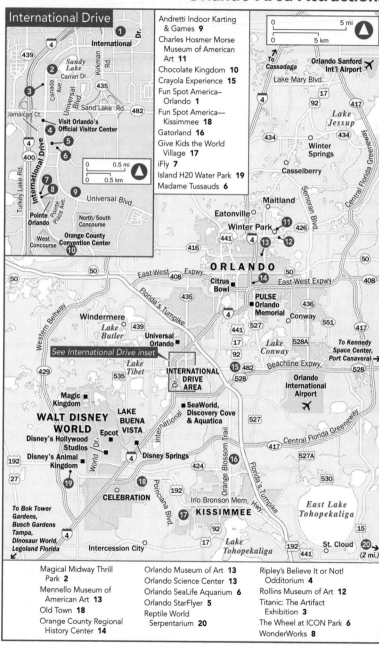

International Drive

International Dr. ❶

4 439 ❷ Sandy Lake Carrier Dr. Kirkman Rd. International Blvd.

❸ Canada Ave. 435

Jamaican Ct. Universal Blvd. Sand Lake Rd. 482

Visit Orlando's Official Visitor Center ❹

❺
❻

Turkey Lake Rd. International Drive 4 400

❼
❽ ❾
Pointe Plaza Ave. Universal Blvd.

Pointe Orlando

North/South Concourse

West Concourse **Orange County Convention Center** ❿

0 0.5 mi
0 0.5 km

Andretti Indoor Karting & Games **9**

Charles Hosmer Morse Museum of American Art **11**

Chocolate Kingdom **10**

Crayola Experience **15**

Fun Spot America–Orlando **1**

Fun Spot America—Kissimmee **18**

Gatorland **16**

Give Kids the World Village **17**

iFly **7**

Island H20 Water Park **19**

Madame Tussauds **6**

0 5 mi
0 5 km

To Cassadaga
Orlando Sanford Int'l Airport
Lake Mary Blvd.
4 92 17
Lake Jessup
434 434
Winter Springs
Casselberry

Central Florida Greeneway

Maitland
Eatonville
Semoran Blvd.
Winter Park ⓫ 426
441 4 ⓭ ⓬

ORLANDO
50 50
East-West Expwy 408 **Citrus Bowl** ⓮ East-West Expwy 408
50 435 4 **PULSE Orlando Memorial** 436
441 527 **Conway** 551 417

Florida's Turnpike

Windermere
Lake Butler 439 **Universal Orlando**
See International Drive inset
429 *Lake Tibet* 535 **INTERNATIONAL DRIVE AREA** 17 92 ⓯ 482 528 *Lake Conway* 528A
Beachline Expwy **To Kennedy Space Center, Port Canaveral →** 528

Magic Kingdom
WALT DISNEY WORLD **LAKE BUENA VISTA**
Disney's Hollywood Studios
Disney's Animal Kingdom ⓲
192 27
Epcot
World Dr. 4 **Disney Springs** 424 ⓰
■ SeaWorld, Discovery Cove & Aquatica 527
Orlando International Airport ✈
Central Florida Greeneway 417 527A

CELEBRATION
Poinciana Blvd. 192
Irlo Bronson Mem. Hwy.
⓱ **KISSIMMEE**
92
17 *Lake Tohopekaliga* 192 441
530
East Lake Tohopekaliga
15
St. Cloud ⓴
(2 mi.)

To Bok Tower Gardens, Busch Gardens Tampa, Dinosaur World, Legoland Florida 4
Intercession City

Magical Midway Thrill Park **2**

Mennello Museum of American Art **13**

Old Town **18**

Orange County Regional History Center **14**

Orlando Museum of Art **13**

Orlando Science Center **13**

Orlando SeaLife Aquarium **6**

Orlando StarFlyer **5**

Reptile World Serpentarium **20**

Ripley's Believe It or Not! Odditorium **4**

Rollins Museum of Art **12**

Titanic: The Artifact Exhibition **3**

The Wheel at ICON Park **6**

WonderWorks **8**

TICKETS AND PASSES SeaWorld admission costs $114 for everyone; $20+ discounts and $45 adult/$23 kid meal plans are available online for some days. SeaWorld sells **Quick Queue Unlimited** ($15–$80, depending how busy it is), which allows you to cut lines on the adult rides by entering through the exit. There's a version for reserved seating for the shows, too, for $15–$60. You can buy both online ahead of time or in the park via electronic kiosks labeled UPGRADE YOUR DAY!—but check regular wait times first, because neither one is usually warranted. If you buy ahead online, you can often get cheaper admission to either Aquatica (p. 171) or Busch Gardens Tampa Bay (p. 178), too.

TIMING YOUR VISIT You will spend time waiting for shows to begin. People show up early for seats, so it's smart to arrive at least 30 minutes ahead of showtimes. Crowds are lightest Tuesday and Wednesday. *Important:* If the weather forecast shows prolonged rain (as opposed to Florida's typical spot showers), reschedule your visit. Not only will you spend lots of time outside, but it's also harder to see marine animals when the surface of the water is pelted by raindrops—not to mention the fact that if there's so much as a twinkle of lightning anywhere in the county, these water-based attractions and tall coasters close faster than a shark's mouth on dinner.

Nightly in peak season and on select nights (such as weekends) in off-season, the park mounts **Electric Ocean,** its pleasing but modest display of after-dark lights, illuminated costumes on parade, and fireworks. Event nights are posted online in advance on the schedule under "Plan Your Day."

GETTING ORIENTED Once you park or get off the I-Ride (the stop is near the front gates), head for the lighthouse that marks the entrance. Inside, grab a placemat-size park map. On the map, the park is broken up into vague areas called "Seas," but you can't tell a difference between them as you walk. On the back, printed fresh daily, is the **show schedule.** Performances usually begin an hour after park opening, and the signature Shamu show has the fewest presentations. I always prefer the last one of the day because it's usually less crowded. The map also lists "Animal Connections"—a manatee keeper talk here, a stingray feeding there. If you're interested in thrill rides, the best time is when the Shamu show is scheduled, because it soaks up hundreds of people at once. The Cape Cod–style entrance plaza is where you do the necessaries such as rent strollers and lockers. The area is really just a warm-up for the rest of the park. Sea of Mystery and Sea of Power may open an hour or two after the rest of the park.

The Best of SeaWorld

Don't miss if you're 6: Sesame Street at SeaWorld Orlando

Don't miss if you're 16: Mako

Requisite photo op: Orca Encounter, Shamu Stadium

Food you can only get here: Shamu ice cream bar at carts parkwide

The most crowded, so go early: Orca Encounter, Shamu Stadium

Skippable: The movie at TurtleTrek

Biggest thrill: Mako

Best show: Orca Encounter, Shamu Stadium

Where to find peace: Anywhere around the lagoon

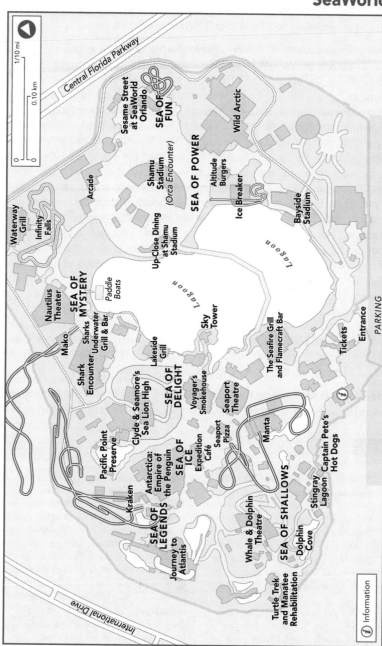

ⓘ Information

The Best Shows

Be choosy about shows, because if you plan too many, you'll miss some habitats—yet spreading SeaWorld over 2 days would be excessive.

Orca Encounter: A Killer Whale Experience ★★ SHOW   While orcas still live at SeaWorld they'll be given something to do in the "Shamu" show. When the orcas start to fly, the crowd comes alive. Closed-circuit TV cameras capture and display the spectacle on four huge, aging rotating screens as the animals thunder dauntingly through the water's surface, pointedly deluging seating sections in 52°F (14°C) water. The 25-minute plotless show occurs on such a scale as to make it required viewing. Now that trainers are no longer permitted to swim in the tank, they narrate from the sides, and they have to vamp for long periods if the orcas aren't in the mood to exercise on cue. Trainers fill the gaps with quasi-inspirational scripted gibberish and some defensive patter about how carefully they observe the health of their captive orcas. But you instantly forget about the flaws when the animals reappear to leap skyward and belly flop back into their tank. The stadium, which fits 5,000 and can still fill early, is covered, but the sides may catch sun, so arrive at least 30 minutes early. *Strategy:* Soak zone seats offer excellent views of the animals hurtling through the 2.5-million-gallon, 36-feet-deep tank, and in case the splashes miss you, the dozens of fountain jets will finish the job. Seats near the shelflike front platform will also have a close-up view of a killer whale out of the water. Seats at the back of the stadium, higher than the central aisle, must rely on the TV cameras to make out what's going on underwater. Using the SeaWorld Discover Guide app, you can book reserved seating until 15 minutes ahead, but that's not usually necessary. *Shamu Stadium, Sea of Power.*

Sea Lion & Otter Spotlight ★★ SHOW   SeaWorld's long-running Sea Lion High show was retired in 2021, but sea lions and otters still appear in a

---

Smart Seating

Try to be at shows at least **20 to 30 minutes early,** and for Shamu, add another 10 minutes to walk around the lagoon to the stadium, which is far from most of the rest of the park. SeaWorld is not obsessive about where you're permitted to sit, so if you're near the front of the line, you can claim the best seats. Several shows don't permit latecomers.

Three of the shows—for orcas, for dolphins, and "Clyde and Seamore"—have a clearly marked **"soak zone"** in the front rows of the seating section.

Don't take this warning lightly; you have no concept of how much water a 10,000-pound orca can displace. Of course, sitting with your kids in the soak zone on a hot day is one of the great pleasures of SeaWorld, and most soak zone seating has the added advantage of affording side views through the tank glass. For those with expensive hairdos, ponchos are sold throughout the parks, including at stalls beneath Shamu Stadium, for $10. Keep electronics somewhere dry, because salt water fries circuits.

goofy spectacle. Expect a prototypical sea lion act: cheesy tricks (animals doing double takes, sliding, waving), surprise splashes of water for the front rows, and much slapstick from the humans, who also spend a lot of time educating you about the creatures. Their cute 25-minute presentation remains one of SeaWorld's most cherished franchises. *Strategy:* The worst seats are to the left as you face the stage (they have partial views and get hot). *Sea Lion & Otter Stadium, Sea of Delight.*

Dolphin Adventures ★★ SHOW   It's the kind of dolphin show that has been standard for decades—trainers chat about the animals, which leap and flip and otherwise frolic for your applause—and that's what makes it so good. You don't need fancy frippery to appreciate the strength and agility of these dolphins (which were all born in parks), although in this presentation, there is also a brief appearance by a flock of parrots. If you don't see the Shamu show, this is the best alternative. Sit in front and you may get drenched, but don't blame the dolphins—they're only doing it for the fish. *Dolphin Stadium, Sea of Shallows.*

Sea of Shallows

This themed area is along the left as you first enter the park.

Manta ★★★ RIDE   Rising above the park is SeaWorld's thrill-ride pride, a "flying coaster" ridden face-down and head-first, in a horizontal position (claustrophobics, breathe). You board sitting upright, and after your shoulders and ankles are secured, you're tipped forward and the train is dispatched over curious pedestrians for the 2½-minute ride. The queue meanders through 10 aquaria containing cownose rays, spotted eagle rays, and weedy sea dragons behind floor-to-ceiling windows, so you get a dose of sea life while you wait. Even nonriders can see rays through a separate entrance to the left of the ride's line, labeled **Aquarium: The Beautiful Ocean.** Speeds approach 60mph with four inversions, in a fanciful approximation of what it feels like for a manta ray to swim. Manta is a pretty unique coaster experience, and it's solid fun. *Strategy:* Lockers are $2/2 hr., credit cards or cash. There's an (unattended) basket on the platform for loose items if you don't use the lockers. Because you're in "flying" position, no seat has an obstructed view.

Dolphin Nursery ★★★ ACTIVITY   Between the entrance plaza and the Waterfront, the young mammals are kept with their mothers for the first few years of their lives before graduating to the larger Dolphin Cove elsewhere in the park. Much of the day, human trainers can be found here, feeding the adolescent animals and getting them acclimated to human interaction. A glass siding allows you to look into the water.

Stingray Lagoon & Feeding ★ ACTIVITY   A not-quite-reproduction of Front Street in Key West, Florida, features the **Stingray Lagoon,** where you can lean over and feel the de-barbed, slimy, spongy fish. You can buy food to feed the rays for $7 per tray of about four fish.

Dolphin Cove ★★ ACTIVITY Next door, make appointments for the **Dolphin Encounter** ($35–$45, no cameras allowed), in which your 3–5 minutes of face time—from land, you may pet them, not feed them—are doled out as part of 15-minute blocks (times later in the day are less crowded). Kids 12 and under must be with an adult. If you want to feed dolphins, you must sign up for the **Dolphins Up Close Tour** ($50 per person), at the desk near the park entrance, and to get into the water with dolphins, you'll need to pay for a day at Discovery Cove (p. 172). Around feeding times, dolphins congregate at the trainers' dock, which can make seeing them difficult, so come between meals for a better look. Walk around the far side of the tank, and you'll find a little-used underwater viewing area with air-conditioning.

TurtleTrek ★★ ACTIVITY/FILM A circuitous entrance ramp brings you to a popular air-conditioned underwater viewing area for 1,500 Caribbean fish and sea turtles the size of coffee tables—that's what earns our two-star rating. If you look closely, you can tell which turtles are rescues—one lost her lower jaw from a fishing net, another gave a flipper to a shark near Bermuda. In the **Manatee Rehabilitation** freshwater tank, much attention is paid to the manatee's status as one of America's most endangered animals, and, in fact, the sluggish creatures on display here were all rescued from the wild, where hot-dogging boaters are decimating their numbers. You'll be herded into a domed room where a (rather poorly) computer-animated 3D film traces the life cycle of a sea turtle from its point of view. It's hard not to notice that the 7-minute story hits the same story beats as *Finding Nemo* (jellyfish fields, marauding birds, sharks prowling a shipwreck). After that, you might be better off staying longer in front of the tank, where the view is more authentic. *Tip:* If you skip this, at least see the sea turtles and rescued manatees in their rehab center, located through the attraction's exit (so you don't have to ride).

Sea of Legends & Sea of Ice

In the back left of the park, these two zones are for thrills and chills.

Journey to Atlantis ★★ RIDE On this 6-minute flume-cum-coaster ride (you can't see the brief coaster section from the front), getting drenched is unavoidable, as the 60-foot drop should warn. Atlantis is incoherent but fun enough. First you pass through a few rooms as if you're on a family-friendly dark ride (the effects aren't great), and then you rocket down the hill you saw outside, and finally the water gives way and your boat becomes, briefly, a roller-coaster car with no upside-down moments but yet another splashdown. It feels cheap, but it's different enough to amuse. *Strategy:* Front seats get wettest. Try to balance the weight; otherwise you'll list disconcertingly. Keep stuff dry in a nearby locker ($2/2 hr., bills or credit cards), and leave it there when you ride Kraken next door. Ponchos are sold nearby for $11 (kids' ponchos are $10).

Kraken ★★ RIDE   Take a 2-minute dose of testosterone. After you settle into your pedestal-like seat, the floor is retracted, leaving your legs to dangle while you undergo seven upside-down "inversions" of one sort or another. The coaster, which hits 65mph and drops 144 feet on its first breath-stealing hill, is plenty terrifying, but it was built in 2000, which makes it a little long in the tooth in terms of smoothness, panache, and lack of theming. *Strategy:* Because the train is floorless, you can't ride with flip-flops, but you may leave shoes on the loading dock and go barefoot (if you do that in the front row, which I recommend, you'll feel like you're about to lose a foot in the rails). Lockers cost $2/2 hr. (bills or credit cards). To save money, use one locker for both this and Journey to Atlantis next door.

> ### Hook the Trainers
>
> To get the most out of a visit, try to be in the same place as the animal trainers. Ask questions. Get involved. They may even allow you to feed or stroke the animals (set aside another $25 or so for fish food). These zoologists love sharing information about the animals they have devoted their lives to. Feeding times are usually posted outside each pavilion's entrance.

Antarctica: Empire of the Penguin ★ ACTIVITY/RIDE   SeaWorld's tribute to penguins is this 4-acre, iceberg-styled, fishy-smelling pavilion. As your teeth chatter in the frigidity, view a colony of 245 Gentoo, Rockhopper, Adélie, and King birds with a fascinating underwater viewing of the little birds zipping around underwater and from a 30-degree area where they waddle helplessly on dry land. The preceding ride (which is often broken down—are its days numbered?) is pointless, with sub-par animation, but you don't have to take it (no matter what, there's a line): Its trackless technology allows cars, which will remind you of air hockey pucks, to aimlessly roam the same room, even cross paths. Choose "Wild" or "Mild," although the wild version isn't much more intense than a few light pirouettes. Don't confuse this exhibition with Wild Arctic, which contains the beluga whales. *Tip:* Do this early because the line tends to stack up the fastest, but ultimately, it's a line for penguins.

Sea of Delight & Sea of Mystery

In the heart of the park, find classic shows and newly built adrenaline-pumpers.

Infinity Falls ★★★ FLUME   On this new (2018) 5-minute round-raft ride, groups of eight ride along 1,500 curling feet of flume through jungle and are sent flying through rapids, bouncing aggressively between waterfalls and soaking fountains operated by sadistic fellow guests. That's just the beginning. By the end, the floats are raised on a vertical elevator in 5 seconds and dropped 40 feet along a steep ramp to a messy splashdown. You will not emerge dry. SeaWorld is backing away from fishy exhibits, but that doesn't mean it can't immerse guests in water instead. Nearby, **Whitewater Supply**

is a notch more interesting than the park's other souvenir stores, offering driftwood art, candles, sundresses, and waterproof protection for your electronics. *Strategy:* Boats have no compartments in which to keep things dry. Deal with your stuff before getting in line; there are lockers by the Waterway Grill next door.

Mako ★★★ ROLLER COASTER   Wholly independent of animals, Mako ("*MAY*-ko") takes the crown as Orlando's longest (nearly a mile of track), fastest (73mph), and tallest (200 ft.) coaster. It's billed as a "hypercoaster" with "relentless air time," which means there are lots of humps and drops, including several over water, which—combined with its deceptively loose restraint system—can make you feel weightless. That first brutal sideways drop is called "the hammerhead." On an industry level, it's a sign SeaWorld is serious about moving away from animal shows. On a thrills level, this is one helluva ride—Orlando's best coaster. The nearby lockers ($1/hr., bills and credit cards) are necessary unless your item is small because you can leave little items unattended in a bin on the platform. If someone in your party doesn't want to make a foray on this nerve-tangler, send them to the **flamingo paddleboats** on the lake across the walkway ($7/person for 20 min.).

Pacific Point Preserve ★★★ ACTIVITY   Like Dolphin Cove, Pacific Point is an open-air, rocky habitat that encourages feedings, but here the residents are incessantly barking California sea lions and a few demure seals. There's a narrow moat between the tank and the walkway, but you're encouraged to lean over and toss the doglike animals fresh fish, which are sold for $7 per tray, $25 for five. More often than not, marauding birds snatch what you toss. The area gets busy around Clyde and Seamore showtimes at the neighboring Sea Lion & Otter Theater.

Shark Encounter ★★★ ACTIVITY   The onetime Terrors of the Deep was given a more responsible name to rehabilitate the public image of the much-maligned creatures within. It's one of the better exhibitions, with 60-foot acrylic tubes passing through 300,000 gallons of water stocked with sharks—you're ushered along quickly via moving sidewalks. Don't ignore the shallow tank in front of the building, because that's where the smaller species are kept. There, you can feed rays and tarpon shrimp for $5 a tray.

Sky Tower ★★★ OBSERVATION RIDE   Jutting above the lagoon—and topped to still-greater heights by a colossal American flag—is the 400-foot, old-fashioned "Wheel-o-vater," which rotates as it climbs 300 feet for a panorama. At the top, it slowly spins for two or three revolutions, giving you a good look around, before lowering you back to the Waterfront at the end of 6 minutes. You can spot Orlando landmarks, including Spaceship Earth and the skyscrapers of downtown. Given how erratic its operating schedule is, if you see it running, you should grab a ride while you can—you can bring along drinks from the Sand Bar, at its base. If the park is busy, adults pay $5 to ride, but it's free otherwise, and always free for kids.

Parking: $25 (closer "Preferred" spaces are $30 and not worth it); $30 peak days
Coke: $4.20
Bottle of water: $3.70
Cup of beer: $12
Shamu ice cream bar: $4.50

Single strollers: $40 per day
Wheelchair: $20 per day
ECV (electric convenience vehicle): $100 per day
Lockers: $10 (small) or $15 (large) per day

Sea of Power & Sea of Fun

Shamu lives on the far side of the lake (which you may remember as the setting for the hilarious *Jaws IV*), along with a brand-new kiddie section and walruses.

Shamu Stadium ★ ACTIVITY   The home to the orca show has something to offer outside of showtime. A few of the killer whales are visible in the viewing area (accessed from the lakefront) that surveys one of their holding pods. Above the surface of that pen, the **Dine with Shamu ★★** supper (see below) is held, separated by netting from the water (reserve several weeks ahead).

Sesame Street at SeaWorld Orlando ★★★ ACTIVITY   Behind Shamu Stadium, kids have their own richly imagined area, a beautifully realized product of a partnership with Sesame Workshop. Children can romp among re-created sets of Mr. Hooper's store, Abby Cadabby's garden, and the 123 stoop. There's so much to discover by ringing doorbells, peeking through mail slots, buzzing apartment intercoms—even annoying Oscar by pounding on his trash can. The neighborhood doesn't skimp on live appearances. There are lots of photo ops with Big Bird, Bert, Ernie, Grover, and Cookie Monster, plus a new Party Parade—a first for SeaWorld Orlando—starring the gang (check the map for the times). The souvenirs here appeal to kids and ironic adults alike. Add a handful of kid-friendly rides—a carousel, an 800-foot coaster, a bird's nest version of spinning teacups, and the Cookie Drop, a bench that lifts kids 20 feet and gently bounces them back down—and you've got a home run for kids. Adults are impressed at how far the designers went to make everything so detailed.

Ice Breaker ★★ ROLLER COASTER   For 2021, SeaWorld squeezed a whole roller coaster onto a tiny plot of land alongside the water. Technically, it's a "multi-directional quadruple launch," but in practice, that means it slides back and forth on the same track, gathering speed and peaking at 100° on a 93-foot spike before finally leaping over a steep hill shaped like an upside-down U. That's right: straight up and straight down. There's not a lot to it—it's over in about a minute—but it's a pleasant addition that only cements SeaWorld's image as a park that now emphasizes thrills over captive creatures. The best time to ride is when the Orca Encounter show is in session; the worst time to ride is when that show has just ended and the crowds emerge from the stadium to get in line.

Wild Arctic ★ ACTIVITY/RIDE   You can walk through this past-its-rime pavilion at your own pace, enjoying first a surface view and then an underwater look at the Pacific walruses, and the park's utterly beautiful white beluga whales, which look like swimming porcelain. See it soon, because the rumor mill says that this land is being eyed for expansion plans for either Sesame Street or for a new coaster—or both.

Where to Eat at SeaWorld

In case you were wondering, SeaWorld serves only sustainable seafood. Prices are in line with everyone else's: $13–$16 a meal, before a drink. **All-Day Dining Deals** (one entree, one side or dessert, one nonalcoholic drink each time through line, once an hour) cost $40 for adults and $20 for kids; rare is the person who will stay (or eat) long enough to make it pay off. If you're 21 or over, there's a $55 package which adds one draft beer per hour.

Disney World has its Mouse-ear ice cream bar, but at SeaWorld, you'll be served a variety shaped like Shamu ($5). Plastic drinking straws choke animals, so you don't get one. SeaWorld often has a happy hour good for 2-for-1 drinks, usually at Flamecraft Bar and Sharks Underwater Bar; ask if it's available.

The headline meal event is **Up-Close Dining at Shamu Stadium ★★**, served from noon to 2pm in peak summer and from 4:30 to 6:30pm in other seasons alongside the orca pools with the narration of trainers. Prices fluctuate by the day, but expect $30 to $36 for adults and $15 to $25 for kids. On weekends and in high season, look for **Breakfast with Elmo and Friends** (℃ **407/545-5500;** $30 adults, $15 kids; 9:15am).

Expedition Café ★★, with exposed seating outside Antarctica, serves stir-fries, chicken tenders, and pizza.

The Seafire Grill ★★★, at the Waterfront, does crispy fish, wings, and salads, and **Flamecraft Bar** has appealing terrace seating overlooking the lagoon and a changing selection of Florida craft beers, plus bar bites like tacos and quesadillas. Flamecraft feels normal and chill—truly, even if it weren't inside a theme park, you still would probably want to hang out here. There's even live acoustic music on weekends to attract locals.

Farther up the Waterfront, the **Lakeside Grill ★★** offers kebabs, nachos, and burgers, and it also has pretty water views. **Voyagers Smokehouse ★**, facing the Seaport Theater's entrance, offers baby back ribs, spare ribs, and barbecue chicken.

Similar to Epcot with The Seas, SeaWorld devotes a section of an underwater viewing area to **Sharks Underwater Grill & Bar ★**, one of the park's premier tables (open 11:30am). It doesn't particularly specialize in seafood. Despite some cute touches, such as a bar that's also an aquarium and chairs that look like sharks' teeth, prices such as $29 for tempura shrimp and $32 for salmon strike me as too high (kids' meals are $14). The cocktail bar up front ($14 a drink) is first-come, first-seated.

Waterway Grill is indoors (meaning cool) behind Infinity Falls. In addition to casual churrasco steak, slow-roasted pork, and seared tofu, it has a good selection of a dozen beers on tap, some of them craft brews from around the state, such as Cigar City from Tampa and Green Bench from St. Petersburg.

Captain Pete's Island Hot Dogs in the Key West area has foot-longs such as one with chili and cheese ($9–$12). At the Shamu end of the boardwalk, **Altitude Burgers** ★★, under the Ice Breaker coaster, does a counter-service menu of grilled chicken sandwiches, pizza, and a wholly inadvisable but nevertheless popular build-your-own burger made with a pound of meat ($20).

Backstage Tours

As a place that prides itself on sharing conservation information—in fact, as a place that keeps animals on display, its reputation depends on it—**SeaWorld** (www.seaworldorlando.com; ✆ **800/327-2424**) offers **Exclusive Park Experiences** that are less about touting its vaunted design team, as Disney's are, and more for learning care for animals like penguins and sharks.

SeaWorld's Other Parks

Aquatica ★ WATER PARK   SeaWorld's waterslide park is across International Drive from its parent park (a free, 3-min. van ride links it), and you can pay for admission as an add-on to your SeaWorld visit. On hot days, it can be busier than SeaWorld itself. It's a perfectly nice park, favored somewhat by locals because it's less gimmicky than the others in town, but it's not the best in town. Some highlights: **Ray Rush** is a family raft slide through a few elements like an enclosed sphere and a manta-shaped parabola, and **KareKare Curl** feels like you're rushing across the swoop of a giant Frito. **The Dolphin Plunge** slide is a tube that curls off a tower and then turns clear acrylic as it passes through a habitat for Commerson's dolphins. It looks exciting on paper, but in truth you're going too fast to see anything, even if the dolphins could be reliably near the tubes (they aren't) and there wasn't water splashing in your eyes (there is)—but don't fret, because you can see them later from a viewing cave opposite Kiwi Traders. There are nearly two dozen slides, many of them similar to each other, the most intense of which is **Ihu's Breakaway Falls,** three curling slides that start you eight stories up, standing in a shower-sized chamber on a floor that gives way, dropping you onto the ride. The pleasantly aggressive lazy river of **Loggerhead Lane** passes you by a big window into an aquarium. **Roa's Rapids** is novel in that it's a river with a very fast current meant to sweep your body along without a tube (floaters, grab a life vest—they're free). When you get hungry, you can pay $40 adults, $20 kids for unlimited fare. Otherwise, **Banana Beach** does not-so-great chicken, pizza, and hot dogs at typical prices; **Mango Market** sells chicken tenders, burgers, and sandwiches; and **Waterstone Grill** slings the usual grub, all $11 to $15. If you're bringing a picnic, stick to snack-size bags; large ones will be confiscated or forced into a rental locker, and straws of any kind, which choke animals, are banned. For free wristbands that allow you to go cashless, sign up at the ticket booth or info desks as you enter. *Tip:* Bring pool footwear because the sidewalks get hot. There are unattended shoe cubbies by each ride. If you pay for Quick Queue (another $30–$60 for the basic version), you can jump the lines.

5800 Water Play Way, Orlando. aquatica.com/orlando. *©* **888/800-5447.** $73–$104, depending on the day, online tickets about $30 less, online discounts available for combination SeaWorld tickets. Lockers $10–$20; reserved loungers $35–$39; private cabanas $89–$229. Parking $30 (free if you visited SeaWorld earlier that day).

Discovery Cove ★★★ THEME PARK   How I wish more people could afford to enjoy Discovery Cove, Orlando's most civilized and relaxing theme park. The most expensive park in town (prices shift by the season) is a chill, all-inclusive experience. Only around 1,000 people a day are admitted, guaranteeing this faux tropical idyll is not marred by a single queue (except maybe for the high-quality catered lunch). Admission lanyards include breakfast, equipment rental, sunscreen, beer if you're of age, and unlimited lunch—a good one, too, with options such as fresh grilled tilapia (a fish that drew the short straw at SeaWorld, I guess). Discovery Cove, in fact, is essentially a free-range playground. When you arrive, first thing in the morning, you're greeted under a vaulted atrium more redolent of a five-star island resort than a theme park. Coffee is poured, and once you're checked in you're set loose to do as you wish. Wade from perfect white sand into **Serenity Bay,** feed fresh fruit to the houseguests at the **Explorer's Aviary** for tropical birds, snorkel with barbless rays over the trenches of **The Grand Reef,** swim to habitats for monkeys in the **Freshwater Oasis,** or float down the slow-floating **Wind-Away River,** which passes through waterfalls into the aviary, preventing the birds from escaping. Animal handlers introduce visitors to land creatures, too, like sloths and a flock of chattering flamingoes. Many guests elect to simply kick back on a lounger (there are plenty) on incredibly silky sand (imported, of course) at the natural-looking pool. It feels far more like a stay on a private tropical island than a slice of Orlando touristdom, and a day here slips away as quickly as your stress. Since everyone wears free wetsuits or vests, there's no body shame or sunburned shoulders. When it's your turn—if you've paid extra—head to the **Dolphin Lagoon,** where small groups of about eight (ages 6 and up) wade into the chilly water and meet one of the pod. Like children, dolphins have distinct personalities and must be paired to people the trainers think they'll enjoy being with—but many of these dolphins are docile and friendly, having dwelled at SeaWorld for decades. Here, the mostly hand-reared animals peer at you with a logician's eye while your trainer shows you basic hand signals. The climax of the 30-minute interaction is the moment when you grasp two of the creature's fins and it swims, you in tow, for about 30 feet. Naturally, a photographer is on hand so if you want images or video, you'll pay for that, too, pushing a day to over $400. Other add-on experiences: a shallow-water **Shark Swim** ($129); animal one-on-ones ($79); **Ray Feeding** ($59); and **SeaVenture** (from $49, minimum age 10), which places an air helmet on your head and brings you underwater to walk along the floor of the Grand Reef. Really, though, even a quiet day here is sublime.

6000 Discovery Cove Way, Orlando. www.discoverycove.com. ℰ **407/513-4600.** Price changes with the seasons, but ranges $149–$349, add $40 for subsequent unlimited admission to SeaWorld and Aquatica for 2 wks, plus $100–$150 for 30-min. dolphin interaction. Upgraded alcohol $40. Private cabanas $199–$899. Parking included in admission. Daily 8am–5:30pm.

LEGOLAND FLORIDA

Everything really is pretty awesome here. **Legoland Florida ★★★** is not just the youngest Central Florida theme park. It's also the oldest. That's because it took over the historic property of Cypress Gardens, a park on the cypress tree–lined shores of pretty Lake Eloise that helped put Orlando on the tourist map. Today, this extremely kid-friendly, soothingly mellow 150-acre park 45 minutes south of Disney World is a godsend for parents who crave a breather from the mechanical and authoritarian environment of Disney World. No other Florida park feels so spacious and caters so directly to kids aged 2 to 12. Everything is designed for little ones, from easy-to-tackle versions of adult rides to a large selection of things to do. Somehow, its energy is not stressful, and there are good hotels, too (p. 260).

In 2018, it added **Lego Movie World,** a somewhat psychedelic area themed on the films, with three rides: **Unikitty Disco Drop,** the water-gun boat fight of **Battle of Bricksburg,** and the Soarin'-esque **Masters of Flight.** Other highlights include **Lost Kingdom Adventure,** an indoor target practice game in the style of a Lego-bright Indiana Jones tomb; **Coastersaurus,** a mild out-and-back wooden roller coaster suitable for grammar school lightweights; **DUPLO Valley** for toddler rides; **Driving School,** the Ford-sponsored, free-driving mini-auto course that teaches kids how to obey traffic rules (or, in truth, ignore their first ones); **The Great Lego Race,** a wild mouse coaster where you can wear virtual reality goggles for an out-of-body experience (it's also perfectly situated for nonriders to take embarrassing shots of loved ones' faces as they hurtle downhill); **Flying School,** a tiny hanging coaster for a kid's first grown-up coaster thrills; **Safari Trek,** a wholly adorable car ride past wild African animals made of Legos; and **Royal Joust,** a mini steeplechase-style plastic horse race for wee ones that just may be the cutest ride in the world. For a break from the excitement, a healthy portion of the carefully tended **Cypress Gardens Historic Botanical Garden** (closes 30 min. before the park) was preserved, complete with Spanish moss, cypress knees jutting from tannic water, old-growth banyans (protected in the winter by hidden gas heaters), and signs warning of alligators, which live in the lake. Only now do you remember you're in Florida, which is sad, considering Florida made its

Legoland Florida announced a new, separately ticketed park for 2022. It won't be huge—it's being built on a portion of the parking lot. But it will be the world's first standalone theme park devoted to cartoon superstar Peppa Pig and it will be, according to Legoland parent Merlin Entertainments, "exclusively designed for 'little piggies' with multiple interactive rides and attractions, themed play areas complete with 'muddy puddles' water play, and fun live shows." Among the kiddo rides: **Daddy Pig's Roller Coaster, Grandad Dog's Pirate Boat Ride, Peppa's Pedal Bike Tour,** and **George's Tricycle Trail.** The area will be separately ticketed from Legoland and its water slide park. For updated prices, hours, and details, go to www.peppa pigthemepark.com/florida.

tourist name by selling its natural wonders. Along its lakefront, search for a **Florida-shaped swimming pool.** It was built for Esther Williams's *Easy to Love*, a jaw-dropping heli-water-ski MGM picture from 1953.

For all that, and lots more like it, nothing competes with the fascination of **Miniland,** the tour de force display of Lego construction. The longer you linger, the more touches you see: a space shuttle misting during takeoff, dueling pirate ships, a mini *Star Wars* cantina, and marching bands in front of the Capitol. If you like those gags, stick around for the signature **Pirates' Cove Live Water Ski Show,** which echoes Cypress Gardens' pyramids of maidens with ski-jumping socket-headed Minifigure toy people. On top of all that, there's a modest **Water Park** attached (add $25, operating year-round with heated pools, but open for as little as 4 hours daily in winter), and the option to buy an unlimited pizza and pasta buffet, with fountain drinks ($10, in advance). Legoland offers $5 round-trip shuttles from the Wheel at ICON Park (© **877/350-5346**). Because it usually closes by evening, arrive near opening time to get the most out of a day.

1 Legoland Way, Winter Haven. florida.legoland.com. © **877/350-5346.** $99 ages 3 and up (advance purchase $15–$20 cheaper). Parking $23, preferred parking $33. Daily 10am to 5pm–9pm, depending on the day.

KENNEDY SPACE CENTER

In the late 1960s, Central Florida was the most exciting place on Earth, thanks to the moon. **Kennedy Space Center ★★★**, which was established on Cape Canaveral in 1958 and ruled the tourist circuit with Disney in the 1970s, was eventually eclipsed by attractions based on fantasy. These days, with private investments putting launches back in vogue, it's out of this world again.

KSC is on the Space Coast about an hour east of Orlando, and it's worth the trip. Gray Line bus (www.graylineorlando.com; © **407/522-5911**) does a $119 day tour from Orlando ($59 if you just want a round-trip ride), but for optimal touring, you really should drive yourself and start at opening time. At the main Visitor Complex, many people are waylaid by the retired rockets, IMAX films,

PAST THAT turnstile IN THE SKY

Not all of Orlando's attractions have thrived. Tupperware Museum, we miss you. Kindly remove your Mouse ears to honor the forgotten fun—if not for an accident of time, you'd be vacationing here instead:

○ **Circus World (1974–86):** Started by Mattel as a walk-through museum dedicated to circus history (after all, most of the big-top crews wintered in Florida), it collapsed under its own weight after competition with Disney tempted it into building too many rides. Also, clowns are terrifying.

○ **Boardwalk Baseball (1987–90):** Textbook publisher Harcourt Brace Jovanovich recycled Circus World in the image of Florida's other winter tradition, baseball, and the Kansas City Royals were enticed to train here. Few cared. On January 17, 1990, the last 1,000 guests were asked to leave.

○ **Xanadu (1983–96):** This walk-through "home of the future" was made by coating giant balloons with polyurethane—an early exercise in ergonomics. Sister homes in Gatlinburg and Wisconsin Dells were also built, but all outlived their curiosity value quickly. You'll find the site near Mile Marker 12 of U.S. 192.

○ **Jungleland Zoo (1995–2002):** The demise of this low-rent Gatorland rip-off was hastened in 1997 when a lioness went missing among Kissimmee's motels for 3 days. Bad news.

○ **Splendid China (1993–2003):** On 73 acres 3 miles west of Disney's main gate (now Margaritaville), Chinese treasures like the Forbidden City and a Great Wall segment containing 6.5 million bricks were rebuilt in miniature. Who would blow $100 million on such a bad idea? The Chinese government, which pulled the strings.

○ **River Country (1976–2005):** Disney's teeny first water park, incorporated into Bay Lake beside Fort Wilderness Resort, became obsolete.

and simulators, but that's not the best stuff—do them at the end of the day if you have time. Unless there's an **Astronaut Encounter** going on—that's an hour-long presentation in which an actual astronaut talks about his or her experience and answers questions—proceed instantly to the can't-miss **Behind the Gates** bus tour ✔, which leaves every 15 minutes until about 2:15pm, and takes most people around 3 hours. Be warned that the last buses don't leave you enough time to browse. Coaches with live on-board narration zip you around NASA's tightly secured compound. Combined with the nature reserve around it, the area (which guides tell visitors is one-fifth the size of Rhode Island and is home to 16 bald eagle nests) is huge but you'll be making one stop not too far away. You'll see the launch sites used by the shuttle and by the Apollo moon shots, and you'll receive an intelligent explanation of the preparation that went into each shuttle launch. You'll buzz past eagles' nests, alligator-rich canals, pads now leased by private space-mission contractors SpaceX and Boeing, and the confoundingly titanic **Vehicle Assembly Building,** or VAB, where the shuttle—which NASA folk call "the orbiter"—was readied. It's just one story tall, but it's a doozy: The Statue of Liberty could fit through those doors with 200 feet left over. The main bus stop, the **Apollo/Saturn V Center,** is themed "Race to the Moon" and begins with a mandatory 5-minute film and then a full-scale mock-up of the "firing room" in the throes of commanding Apollo 8's launch, in all its window-rattling, fire-lit drama—to skip that 30-minute show and get to the good stuff, pass through. The adjoining hangar contains a Saturn V rocket, which is larger than you can imagine (363 ft. long, or the equivalent of 30 stories)—but the new SLS rockets are even bigger. Don't overlook the chance to reach into a case to touch a small moon rock, which looks like polished metal. The presentation in the **Lunar Theatre,** which recounts the big touchdown, is well produced and even includes a video appearance by the late, reclusive Neil Armstrong. There's a cafeteria here, and look around for retired engineers and astronauts who are often on hand to answer questions.

After that, hasten back via the bus to the Visitor Complex for the grand finale: The $100-million home of the **space shuttle** *Atlantis.* Without giving too much away, the way in which it's revealed to you is probably the most spine-tingling moment you'll experience in all of your Orlando visit. Hanging 26 feet off the ground at an angle of 43.21° (like the numbers in a launch countdown), it's still covered with space dust, and it now tips a wing at everyone who comes to learn about it on the many interactive displays that surround it. Don't miss the commemorative **Forever Remembered.** Alongside favorite mementos provided by 11 of the 14 families of their crews, you'll find respectful displays of a section of the hull of the *Challenger,* lost in 1986, and a slab of cockpit windows of the *Columbia* (lost in 2003), still encrusted with grass and mud from where it fell to Earth. You can also try the $60-million **Shuttle Launch Experience,** in which 44-person motion-simulator pods mimic an 8-minute launch with surprising (but not nauseating) clarity, and **Heroes & Legends,** which pays tribute to the 100-odd explorers in the Astronaut Hall of Fame. The entire state-of-the-art, hyper-engaging space shuttle section can easily consume 2 hours.

Once you've completed the bus tour and *Atlantis,* it's up to you whether you want to plumb the sillier, kid-geared business at the Visitor's Complex. By this point, much of it will be redundant, and some of it is pure malarkey, but take the time to check the 42-foot-high black granite slab of the **Astronaut Memorial,** commemorating those lost; the Moon Tree Garden of 12 trees grown

---

Increased Access to NASA Secrets

The end of the space shuttle program has enabled previously off-limits areas to be opened for visits. Availability shifts, but on "Explore" tours (generally $25 adults, $19 kids 3–11, plus admission), there's always something that's not on the standard KSC bus tour. You can visit the shuttle's launch pad, the Launch Control Center used in the shuttle's last liftoffs, the core of the Mercury and Gemini missions, and find out what NASA's up to now, including the new SLS (Space Launch System) that will carry the new Orion module into space for longer trips than ever before.

Although the space shuttle has flown into history, Cape Canaveral still launches unmanned rockets—SpaceX conducts spectacular liftoffs from pad 39A, where the Apollo missions launched. Because launches are often postponed, it would be dangerous to plan a trip to Orlando just to catch one, but then again, if there's one when you're in town, it would a shame to miss it, even if it means waking up at 5am. Kennedy Space Center maintains an updated schedule online both on its **Kennedy Space Center Official Guide** smartphone app and at **www.kennedyspacecenter.com/events** and sometimes it arranges VIP seating at a safe distance. The general public is not permitted to flood NASA turf during the actual events, but Titusville, a town at the eastern end of S.R. 50, is a good place to get a clear, free view, because you'll be across the wide Indian River from the pad. Even if you can't leave Orlando for a launch, you can still see the fire of the rockets ascend the eastern sky from any east-facing window in town. Night launches are even more spectacular.

from seeds that orbited the moon before planting; **Early Space Exploration,** where you'll see the impossibly low-tech Mission Control for the Mercury missions (they used rotary telephones!), plus some authentic spacesuits from the Gemini, Mercury, and Apollo series. Astoundingly, the actual Mercury command building was torn down in 2010. Who would do that?

Daunted? You can prepare by downloading KSC's free app, which helps you prioritize how to spend your time here with maps and attraction descriptions. For lunch, though, you're marooned. There is nowhere else to eat within a 15-minute drive, and on-site food options are horrendous ($8–$10 a plate)— hamburgers taste like they were surplus from the Apollo program. Come on, NASA. Hospitality isn't rocket science. (You can bring your own food in small, soft-sided coolers.)

Route 405 (Space Commerce Way), Merritt Island. www.kennedyspacecenter.com. ☏ **866/433-4210.** Admission $57 adults, $47 kids 3–11, $50 seniors and active duty U.S. military. Handheld multimedia guide $9. Parking $10. Daily 9am–5pm or until 7pm, depending on the season. Bus tours every 15 min., last one usually 3:30pm.

Kennedy Space Center Special Tours

Astronaut Training Experience ★★ ☞ ACTIVITY KSC dubs the program ATX, but you could call it Space Day Camp. You'll test simulators of planet rovers, spacewalks, and Mars explorations and try a mock-up of a launch. Nothing is as intense as what astronauts experience, but this 5-hour session is still plenty rigorous for most terrestrials, and the facilitators can answer nearly any question you can launch at them. You can also book one-off time slots on the "Training Stages" Spacewalk Stage and Mars Exploration simulators for $30–$40. For something brainier, the **Mars Base 1** program ($150; 7 hrs. including lunch; ages 10 and older) casts your kids as true scientists running a research center on the Red Planet, doing tasks from collecting plants to programming drones.

Astronaut Hall of Fame, 6225 Vectorspace Blvd., Titusville. www.kennedyspacecenter.com/landing-pages/atx. © **866/737-5235.** $175 age 10 and older, adult participant required for ages 10–17, includes admission to KSC, minimum age 10.

Dine with an Astronaut ★★★ ☝ ACTIVITY   One of the coolest benefits of visiting the Space Coast is the chance to meet a real astronaut, many of whom have retired to the same area where they once worked. Although old-timers like Jim Lovell and Story Musgrave have eagerly appeared, it's likely to be a veteran of the space shuttle program; recent leaders included Anna Fisher, the first mother in space, and Norm Thagard, the first American to fly in a Russian spacecraft (upcoming astronauts are posted on the KSC site). Typically, these astronauts love basking in fandom and in reliving old tales of glory—and unlike out-to-pasture sportsmen, they really did risk their lives the way heroes are supposed to—so these small-group sessions are geared toward questions. Every month or so, KSC also mounts **Fly with an Astronaut** ($206 adults, $181 kids; 4 hr.), during which an astronaut actually conducts your tour of the complex where he or she once worked.

www.kennedyspacecenter.com. © **855/433-4210.** $30 adults, $16 kids 3–11, not including required admission. Daily at noon. 90 min.

BUSCH GARDENS TAMPA BAY

Seventy miles southwest of Disney, and just 8 miles northwest of Tampa, **Busch Gardens Tampa Bay** ★★★, dating to 1959, is a world-class theme park combining thrill rides with top-notch animal enclosures for gorillas, rhinos, and other rare creatures—more than 300 species in all. Coasters are its jam. The newest ones are the most terrifying: 2021's Iron Gwazi, the fastest and tallest hybrid (wooden and steel) coaster in North America, which drops 91 degrees off a 206-foot-tall peak and hits 76mph; the 335-foot-tall (102m) **Falcon's Fury,** America's tallest drop tower that sends riders plummeting facedown; and **Cobra's Curse,** a novel steel coaster that begins with an elevator instead of a hill on which the cars gently spin as they race along. Other detour-worthy roller coasters include the vertical drop of **SheiKra** and the deliriously sidewinding launch coaster **Cheetah Hunt.** If the coaster wars were an arms race, Busch Gardens' arsenal easily ranks alongside Orlando's, yet relatively few tourists make the 75-minute trip here—and it's a shame that such a high-quality theme park winds up being the eighth-best choice for most Orlando visitors. The park knows coaxing visitors from Orlando is a problem, so it grants **free round-trip coach transportation** from many Orlando hotels with a ticket (© **866/435-5686**), but you risk not arriving until 11:30am.

10165 N. McKinley Dr., Tampa. www.buschgardens.com/tampa. © **813/884-4386.** Admission $120–$126; discounts of up to $25 available online for pre-purchase. (Ticket package that includes SeaWorld available online for about $56 more.) Park generally opens 10am and closes anywhere from 6pm to 10pm. Parking $25.

OTHER ORLANDO ATTRACTIONS

International Drive Area

The attractions around International Drive aren't plush—they're convention-goer diversions and rainy-day amusements, mostly—but they have the stuff of a quintessential family holiday and they won't break the bank. I-Drive is the only touristy area in Orlando where a car isn't necessary, not least because the I-Ride Trolley (p. 288) will tote you along, if you're tired of strolling.

In addition to these diversions, in winter 2021-22 ICON Park added a new 430-foot-high tower (the world's tallest, it claims) that drops seated riders 40 stories, and a matching Slingshot ride, also purported to be the tallest.

Andretti Indoor Karting & Games ★★ AMUSEMENT CENTER This booming, hectic, $30-million pleasuredome (with auto racer Mario Andretti as a partner) makes Dave & Buster's look like a tea party: 100,800 square feet of climbing walls, ropes courses, laser tag, a full arcade with prizes (in the "Victory Lane"), bowling lanes, a restaurant, and a bar that overlooks it all. The booze flows, the music pumps, and the birthday parties for yelling grade-school boys roll non-stop. The centerpieces are its three multi-level indoor go-kart tracks using SODI RTX electric carts and designed by Andretti, with plenty of banked curves (closed-toe shoes required). From 4–7pm, bowling is just $5 per person per hour with free shoe rental.

9299 Universal Blvd, Orlando. www.andrettikarting.com/orlando. © **407/641-0415.** One race $25 adults, $15–$17 riders shorter than 48 in., other amusements charged separately (generally $10–$13 each, with packages available). Sun–Thurs 10am–11pm; Fri–Sat 10am–1am.

Chocolate Kingdom ★ TOUR   Yes, they make and sell chocolate, but they also roast, skin, and grind the beans before your eyes using clunky antique equipment so heavy the floor had to be reinforced. All in all, the third-generation chocolatier who owns it and the national Schakolad franchise have put together a surprisingly educational guided tour, good for kids and with free samples along the way, based on the rich history of the cocoa bean. (Did you know the Aztecs wouldn't let women eat them because they thought abstaining would keep them dull-witted and compliant?) Call ahead if you can so they'll have a guide ready for you.

9901 Hawaiian Court, Orlando. www.chocolatekingdom.com. © **407/705-3475.** $17 ages 13 and older, $13 kids 4–12. Tours Mon–Sun 11:30am–5pm.

Crayola Experience ★★ ACTIVITY   When we were kids, the most fun we could have with a crayon was to peel the wrapper off—maybe eat one, too. Your kids, though, can scamper around a department-store-size fantabulous multi-station sensory playhouse where they may, among other things, print wrappers they write themselves, animate their drawings on giant screens, melt crayons into art, animate homemade puppets in a magic theater, frolic in a two-story playground shaped like crayons, color printouts of their own faces, mess

5

Other Orlando Attractions

around on a giant Lite-Brite, and pitch an epic fit the moment you suggest it's time to leave. Adults will first feel bitter jealousy and then nostalgia pangs of their receding childhood—Lemon Yellow, we hardly knew ye—but will probably then indulge in the adjoining shop (no admission required), which sells every Crayola product known to the world of little Picassos, including a wall filled with some 120 current colors, which you can bulk-buy in buckets.

Florida Mall, 8001 S. Orange Blossom Trail, Orlando. www.crayolaexperience.com. © **407/757-1700.** Admission $26 for all ages, $3 discount online. Wed–Fri 10am–4pm, Sat–Sun 10am–6pm, last ticket sold 1 hr. before closing (closes earlier in winter). One Sun/month designed for kids with special sensory needs.

Fun Spot America—Orlando ★ AMUSEMENT PARK   A recent recipient of immense investment and careful improvements, Fun Spot in Orlando, at the top of I-Drive, is Orlando's largest (15 acres), cleanest, best-lit midway-style diversion. Although it became famous for its four **go-kart tracks** (concrete, multilevel; the Quad Helix's stacked figure-eight turns make it a favorite, but the Conquest's peaked ramp is a pip), the spacious grounds are also stocked with a two-level arcade, a scrambler and other carnival rides, plenty of snack bars, a Ferris wheel (Charlize Theron rode it in *Monster*), and a section of kiddie rides. There's also **White Lightning,** a wood-frame coaster (unusual in this town); **Freedom Flyer,** a wee version of a hanging, foot-dangling train; and at Gator Spot, some 100 alligators on loan from Gatorland (p. 189). The 250-foot-tall **SkyCoaster** requires an extra charge. Trivia: This SkyCoaster was moved here from Las Vegas' defunct MGM Grand Adventures Theme Park.

5700 Fun Spot Way, Orlando. www.fun-spot.com. © **407/363-3867.** Free entry. Pay-per-ride $5–$10, unlimited rides $46 (everything except SkyCoaster) to $54 (including SkyCoaster). Generally daily 10am–midnight; winter weekdays noon or 2pm–midnight.

iFly ★ ACTIVITY   A glassy 14,000-square-foot facility houses this vertical wind tunnel attraction, where visitors are strapped into jumpsuits and given a short training session on how to walk over the netting into the 125mph airflow. Mastering the necessary arched-back, splay-legged posture can be tricky, but should you fail, there's a master diver with you to grab you by the sleeve and guide you into a series of adrenaline-fueled climbs and plunges. Or not—you can just hover there, if that's what floats your butt.

8969 International Dr., Orlando. www.iflyworld.com/orlando. © **407/337-4359.** $65 for 2 1-min. flights on Mon–Thurs between 11am–4pm, $85 for 2 flights at other times, $110 for 3, $136 for 4. Mon–Thurs 11am–7pm; Fri 12:30–9pm; Sat 9am–9pm; Sun 11am–7pm.

Madame Tussauds ★★ TOURIST MUSEUM   Of course the world-famous wax museum has an Orlando outpost! It's below the giant Wheel at ICON Park (see below), a complex of shops and restaurants. It's so silly and pleasantly touristy that it's astounding it took so long to arrive here. First, staffers try to get you to pose for a tourist photo (included in most online-bought packages), but Tussauds is already essentially one extended photo op. As you go from room to room, you get right beside the few dozen full-size figures of current and historical celebrities, many of which are so lifelike that you'll be astounded (Taylor Swift, Selena Gomez), and some so off the mark you have to check the signage to tell who it is (Jennifer Lopez, Will Smith). If the sign says they were "sculpted from a sitting" rather than merely "portrayed," you know it's more accurate.

ICON Orlando 360, 8387 International Dr., Orlando. www.madametussauds.com/orlando. ⑦ **866/630-8315.** $34 adults, $29 children 3–12; discount pkgs. available with The Wheel at ICON Park and SeaLife Aquarium; frequent discounts online. Free parking. Daily 11am–7pm or 8pm, longer hours in busy season, last admission 1 hr. before closing.

Magical Midway Thrill Park ★ AMUSEMENT PARK Blaring with rock music, this small concrete area is less than cutting-edge, driven by adrenaline and rash decisions. The most obvious generator of regret is the world's tallest **Sling Shot** ride ($25, not included on passes), a colossal fork strung with a pod. Two at a time sit inside and are catapulted more than 200 feet into the sky, wailing to wake the dead. Its big rides are pipsqueaks compared to the new ones at ICON Park a few blocks south. The rest is dominated by two thunderous, wooden go-kart tracks (the Avalanche track has slightly steeper ramps than the Alpine), a few minor rides (cheerless bumper boats), and a dirty arcade. Its unsophisticated virtues are something 11-year-old boys idolize.

7001 International Dr., Orlando. www.magicalmidway.com. ⑦ **407/370-5353.** $8 go-kart rides, $3 midway rides, 3-hr. unlimited rides $25, all-day unlimited $32. Daily noon-midnight (arcade 10am–midnight).

Orlando SeaLife Aquarium ★ AQUARIUM The McDonald's of aquaria has some four dozen locations worldwide, and it's such a success because it's fairly well-stocked, theatrically lit, and charmingly designed: There are clear walkway tubes passing through huge tanks, for example, and kids can crawl under the moray eel habitat and see from "inside" the tank through bubble-like head spaces popping through its floor. SeaLife angles for kids in particular, what with the annoying voices of anthropomorphic fish delivering factual tidbits on the loudspeakers and the chipper docents sticking religiously to a corporate-approved script ("Here's your Discovery Fact of the day!") that pummels you with boasts about its good deeds of conservation. Concluding the self-guided tour of the 5,000-plus creatures (including jellyfish, small sharks, and clownfish), there's a shallow touch tank where kids can

---

Rainy-Day Mayhem

The massive **Outer Limitz** (6725 S. Kirkman Rd.; www.outerlimitzorlando.com; ⑦ 407/704-6723), near Fun Spot America, and **AirHeads Adventure Arena** (33 W. Pineloch Ave.; orlando.airheadsusa. com; ⑦ 407/270-4611), south of downtown Orlando, are indoor trampoline-filled arenas where netting keeps your offspring from cracking their heads open as they bounce off walls and fling themselves into pits filled with foam blocks. At Outer Limitz, there's basketball and dodgeball, too.

pet live starfish. Adults will be satisfied in 30 minutes, but kids might prefer an hour.

ICON Orlando 360, 8387 International Dr., Orlando. www.visitsealife.com/orlando. ℂ **407/370-5353.** $34 adults, $29 ages 3–12; discount pkgs. available with Madame Tussauds and The Wheel at ICON Park; frequent discounts online. Free parking. Daily 11am–7pm or 8pm; hours may be extended, last admission 1 hr. before closing.

Orlando StarFlyer ★ RIDE As everyone knows, there are three necessary components to carnival thrills: height, speed, and flimsy-feeling restraints. The StarFlyer nails the trifecta. At 450 feet (your altitude will be about 350 feet), this 2018 erection is the tallest of the 35 such spinning swing towers around the world. The 4-minute ride is able to go 60mph but after many experiments in which customers fled traumatized, the proprietors settled on a top speed of 45mph. It starts fast but slows down once your pants are good and wet, so there's time to look around at that incredible view, the best in town. Never once does it seem possible that the chains are enough to support the weight of your two-person bench, yet they are, by several factors. And that's what gives it a kick. No items, including sunglasses, are permitted on board (lockers are free), so if it's very bright out, come back at night. There's a bar at the base where you can toast whatever god you worship for bringing you back to the ground safely.

ICON Orlando 360, 8265 International Dr., Orlando. www.starflyer.com. ℂ **407/640-7009.** $15 ride ($11 online), $9 re-ride. Minimum height 44 in./112cm. Free parking. Sun–Thurs 10am–1am, Fri–Sat 10am–2am.

Ripley's Believe It or Not! Odditorium ★ TOURIST MUSEUM The ticketed equivalent of a meme, Ripley's is well-maintained and clean, but it's too expensive for the hour-long diversion it delivers. Mostly it consists of optical illusions, vaguely ominous specimens from foreign cultures, panels from the old Ripley's comic (does anyone under 60 even remember those?), and the odd coin-operated device. There are too many signs and fewer artifacts than you'll be expecting, unless you count a portrait of Beyoncé made out of candy. The main warehouse that stocks all of Ripley's attractions worldwide is located nearby (but sadly, you can't tour it). Don't set foot in it without harvesting coupons from any tourist brochure.

8201 International Dr., Orlando. www.ripleys.com/orlando. ℂ **407/345-0501.** $29 adults, $18 kids 3–11; discounts sometimes offered online. Free parking. Sun–Fri 10am–10pm, Sat 10am–midnight.

Titanic: The Artifact Exhibition ★★ TOURIST MUSEUM More than 100 genuine artifacts from the *Titanic* itself—a teak deck chair to cookware to tile fragments to a boarding card—give this permanent exhibition salt. For those interested in the topic, this theatrically presented museum, which walks guests chronologically from boarding to the abbreviated voyage to rediscovery, provides a balanced dossier of the sorry tale. There's a little conflation of Hollywood storytelling with history (at the replica of the First Class Grand Staircase, a piano rendition of "My Heart Will Go On" repeats), but

Other Orlando Attractions

MORE ORLANDO ATTRACTIONS

there's still plenty of meat on this hambone. Join a regular tour, because guides are knowledgeable; after the tour, you can backtrack for closer looks. The 2-ton slab from the hull, cast in an eerie light, is a moving epilogue.

7324 International Dr., Orlando. www.titanicorlando.com. © **407/248-1166.** $22 adults, $16 kids 5–11, $20 seniors, $5 audio guide. Sun–Thurs 10am–8pm; Fri–Sat 10am–5pm; last 1 hr. before closing.

The Wheel at ICON Park ★★ AMUSEMENT PARK   You probably know it by one of its previous names, the Orlando Eye. After enduring a regrettable, stand-up "4D Experience" (a mindless green-screen 3D film of aerial footage of Orlando—Disney's noticeably absent—that peppers you with mist), you board 15-passenger pods for your slightly quivering ride on the East Coast's tallest (400 feet) observation wheel, which is constantly spinning at 1 mph for a 30-minute rotation. You're too far away to see into the Disney parks, but you do see Universal Orlando, 2 miles north. It's pretty enough, but any city would be at that height. Fun ride, odd spot.

ICON Orlando 360, 8401 International Dr., Orlando. www.iconparkorlando.com. © **407/ 370-5353.** $30 adults, $25 children 3–12, save $2 online; discount pkgs. available with Madame Tussauds, SeaLife Aquarium, and the StarFlyer; frequent discounts online. Free parking. Mon–Thurs 1–10pm; Fri 1–11pm, Sat noon–11pm; Sun noon–10pm; hours may be extended. Generally closed in early Feb for maintenance.

WonderWorks ★ TOURIST MUSEUM   You know it's touristy because the facade looks like someone ripped a mansion out of the ground and turned it upside down. But the inverted motif doesn't continue beyond its doors. Instead, you get about 100 hands-on curiosity exhibits not unlike what you'd find at a science museum or an arcade—cubicles simulating earthquakes and hurricanes, a bubble-making area, a kiosk where you can use Google Earth to find your house, lots of posters of optical illusions—all decently maintained and cheerful. Bring Purell because exhibits get smeary. Also bring your patience to combat field-trip swarms, and carry lots of cash, because there's a slate of add-ons like a ropes course, a "4D" simulator chair, and an arcade, none of which are included in admission. Adults may find it cheesy but young kids love it, especially if they have a nascent interest in science—then again, they have no concept of the value of your hard-earned dollar. It's mostly for rainy days.

9067 International Dr., Orlando. www.wonderworksonline.com. © **407/351-8800.** $35 adults, $25 seniors 60+ and kids 4–12; $20 discount for entry 7–8:30pm. Extra charges for laser tag, ropes course (closed-toe shoes required), motion-simulator ride, games. Parking $5 for first 2 hrs. Daily 10am–10pm (Sat until 11pm).

North of Universal & Orlando

Mennello Museum of American Art ★★ MUSEUM   The Mennello is a repository for the luridly vivid paintings of Earl Cunningham, a chicken farmer and folk artist whose conceptions sometimes seem refreshingly naive, and then a moment later become brazenly modernist. Cunningham, who died in 1977 while running a curio shop in St. Augustine, is now considered so important that the Smithsonian devoted an exhibition to him. The museum also hosts exhibitions of fine American folk art.

900 E. Princeton St., Orlando. www.mennellomuseum.com. © **407/246-4278.** $5 adults, $4 seniors 60+, $1 college students, free ages 18 and under. Tues–Sat 10:30am–4:30pm; Sun noon–4:30pm.

Orange County Regional History Center ★★★ MUSEUM   People who think Central Florida history began with Walt will have their eyes opened in this underrated museum in a handsome 1927 Greek Revival former courthouse. Head first to the **fourth floor,** where the timeline starts 12,000 years in the past, and work your way down. In 1981, a high school student rooting through lake muck found a Timacuan dugout canoe from around A.D. 1000, and now it is proudly displayed, as are mastodon teeth, pots from 500 B.C., and a 12-foot-tall oyster midden. As you advance through time, artifacts keep coming: saddles used by the forgotten Florida cowmen (the swampy ground made meat chewy, which Cuban customers liked); recipes for Florida Cracker delicacies (Squirrel Soup, Baked Possum); artifacts from the steamship tourist trade (in the 1870s, the St. John's River system was America's busiest one south of the Hudson); and a wall of gorgeous vintage labels from the many citrus companies that once dominated the area. The exhibitions are noticeably conflicted about the growth explosion wrought by the theme parks—the "Building a Kingdom" exhibition was created without Disney funding so it would have the freedom to be frank. An interesting sidelight is the retired Courtroom B, a handsome wood-paneled chamber out of *Inherit the Wind* silenced by cork floors and emblazoned with the slogan "Equal and Exact Justice to All Men." That was painted over the bench at a time when people were still being lynched here (there's a KKK robe in a nearby gallery), and a recent exhibition, organized by a talented curator who is now the Center's director, told the hideous truth about 1920's Ocoee Massacre, when about 35 Black citizens were murdered and their neighborhoods and investments destroyed after they tried to vote. Some justice *was* served here: In 1987, Courtroom B, now part of the museum, tried the first case in America in which DNA evidence obtained a conviction.

65 E. Central Blvd., Orlando. www.thehistorycenter.org. © **407/836-8500.** $8 adults, $6 kids 5–12, $7 seniors 55+, incl. audio tour. Free admission 3rd Thurs of month 5–8pm. Mon–Sat 10am–5pm; Sun noon–5pm.

Orlando Museum of Art ★ MUSEUM   Although this fixture of local pride is touted as *de rigueur* in much tourist literature, OMA takes less than an hour to see. Most of it is not particularly important, just high atmosphere, but some things of note on display over the years have included Robert Rauschenberg's "Florida Psalm," a collage paean to the state's fading tourism emblems; Chuck Close's 1982 portrait of his wife done in fingerprints, and John James Audubon's Great Blue Heron. Contemporary art is its strength, and temporary exhibitions up the par. Expect a pleasant outing—especially if

There's No Escaping Escaping

You're locked in a room that looks like the set to a play—an office, a ship's hold—and given the clues hidden there, you must solve puzzles, crack codes, and find the key to get back out within an hour. Don't worry: There are no scary gotchas, and because of fire codes, the door's not *really* locked. If you struggle with the mental challenge, staff people who are monitoring you via camera (don't pick your nose) can nudge you in the right direction. It's much easier, and a lot more fun, to play with a group. Escaping has flooded the Orlando market (even hotels like Gaylord Palms are trying it), and while some locations put on games that look as if they were decorated using a gift card at Home Depot, real gamer love goes into creating these puzzles, so each one is unique. There may be an age minimum of about 12 and you're allowed to fail (many do), but always make a reservation first. Alphabetically:

- **America's Escape Game:** 8723 International Drive, Suite 115, Orlando; www.americasescapegame.com; ✆ **407/412-5585.** Rooms: White House, asylum, Egyptian tomb, pandemic, hermit cabin (just an 8% escape rate). $35–$45.
- **Breakout Escape Rooms:** 8155 Vineland Ave., Orlando; www.roombreakout.com/orlando; ✆ **407/778-4562.** Fairly near Disney. Rooms:

Zombies (the hardest), pirates, spy, evil circus. $33.
- **Doldrick's Escape Room:** 2943 Vineland Rd., Kissimmee; www.doldricksescaperoom.com; ✆ **407/507-0506.** This one near Disney isn't a chain but a privately owned labor of love with high production values. Rooms: Bomb squad, pirates, Santa's sleigh. $34–$40.
- **The Escape Game:** 8145 International Dr., Suite 511, Orlando; www.orlandoescapegame.com; ✆ **407/501-7222.** Rooms: Mars, Western, kids' classroom, art heist, souk, prison break. $38.
- **Escapology:** 11951 International Dr., Orlando; www.escapology.com; ✆ **407/278-1515.** Rooms: Haunted church, pandemic, Scooby-Doo, drug lord, submarine, train murder (the hardest), murder mystery. $32–$40.
- **The Great Escape Room:** 23½ S. Magnolia Ave., Orlando; www.thegreatescaperoom.com/orlando; ✆ **386/385-8860.** Rooms: Escape artist, nuclear crisis (most difficult), surgical emergency. $30–$38, discounts for veterans and students.
- **Lockbusters:** 8326 International Dr., Orlando; www.lockbustersgame.com; ✆ **407/930-0822.** One of the best-detailed choices in town, near ICON Park. Rooms: Serial killer, pirates, bank heist, chopper crash (the hardest), haunted manor. $29–$35.

you pair a visit with an amble around the surrounding Loch Haven Park—if not exactly a milestone.

2416 N. Mills Ave., Orlando. www.omart.org. ✆ **407/896-4231.** $15 adults, $8 seniors 65+, $5 college students and ages 4–17. Tues–Fri 10am–4pm; Sat–Sun noon–4pm.

Orlando Science Center ★ MUSEUM

The center is an excellent (if expensive) example of its type, and recent investment has bestowed it with some fun, large-scale set pieces that make it feel more like a hands-on play complex than an educational facility, including a giant network of tubes kids blow kerchiefs through; a three-level indoor playhouse; play troughs pumping

A TOWN OF psychics

George P. Colby was reared in the Midwest by Baptist parents, but incessant visions (and poor health) compelled him south, where in 1875 he came across land that, he said, appeared exactly as it had been shown to him by his spirit guide, Seneca. Soon after that, Colby enticed a group of refugees from chilly Lily Dale, New York—a town populated by spiritualists on the Cassadaga lakes outside of Buffalo—to join him in the then-rural wilds of Florida. The winter "camp" of **Cassadaga** ★★★ (exit 114 from I-4; www.cassadaga.org) was born. Nowadays, its residents offer a daily slate of services, laying-on of hands, and readings. The anachronistic village 40 miles northeast of Universal is untouched by development, and only accredited mediums may live among the ramshackle 1920s homes and Spanish moss. Tree-shaded, whitewashed, and more than slightly creepy, Cassadaga, on the National Register of Historic Places, is a bastion of metaphysicality in a region otherwise devoted to Christian fundamentalism.

Check the town website (www.cassadaga.org) for upcoming events, from spirit circles to its almost-daily historical walking tours. The coolest ticket is the **Encounter Spirits Night Tour,** Saturdays at 7:30pm ($25), where you bring your digital camera and go hunting for energy orbs. The next morning at 9:30, you can attend Lyceum—that's Sunday School for spiritualists—before Healing Service and church.

When you arrive, consult the bulletin board in **Cassadaga Camp Bookstore** (1112 Stevens St., Cassadaga; ℭ **386/228-2880;** Mon–Sat 10am–6pm, Sun 11:30am–5pm) for the full list of today's walking tours and to see which mediums are available to take walk-in clients for readings or healings. Everything in town, including gift shops for gemstones and talismans, is within a few blocks, so park and explore. Because the rent's so cheap (the land is owned by the Southern Cassadaga Spiritualist Camp Meeting Association, which subscribes to a form of Biblical Spiritualism—Jesus is real, Satan isn't), services go for a fraction of what they cost in the outside world.

Residents shoo away outsiders at 10pm, so the only way to linger at night is to stay at the town's old-fashioned inn: the 1928 **Cassadaga Hotel** (355 Cassadaga Rd., Cassadaga; www.hotelcassadaga.com; ℭ **386/228-2323;** $75–$85 Sun–Thurs, $90–$100 double occupancy Fri–Sat, including continental breakfast; no guests under age 21), run by the New Age sect of the town. Everyone around town agrees that the hotel is haunted, so the rooms (the cheapest ones don't have TVs or phone) are guaranteed to keep you anxiously listening for bump-in-the-night creaks. I asked the owner if I could take photos of the time-warp lobby. "Sure, you're welcome to," she said, "but most people get a kind of orb or white light instead." I haven't found those, but my shots *did* come out blurry. I'm just saying.

with water; a toddler version of a citrus farm; and an outdoorsy-looking NatureWorks with baby gators, turtles, and snakes. However, in a town so crowded with amazing things for kids, if you have a good science museum back home, you could probably skip it.

777 E. Princeton St., Orlando. www.osc.org. ℭ **407/514-2000.** $21 adults, $19 seniors 55+ and students with ID, $15 ages 3–11. Parking $5. Sun–Thurs 10am–5pm; Fri–Sat 10am–9pm.

Winter Park & North Orlando

Winter Park has long been a bastion of wealth, particularly from New Money families who failed to find favor among the Old Money of the North. Its expensive tastes are represented by its lakefront mansions, red-brick streets, and a few wrongly overlooked gems for true masterpieces.

Charles Hosmer Morse Museum of American Art ★★★ MUSEUM The best museum in the Orlando area, and perhaps the finest in the state, presents an unparalleled cache of works by genius designer Louis Comfort Tiffany, from stained glass to vases to lamps, and even the lavishly decorated Daffodil Terrace and Reception Hall of his lost Long Island mansion, Laurelton Hall, and the bespoke fountains that ran through it. The Morse displays the best collection of Tiffany glass on the planet, including an entire room reconstructing the master's tour de force chapel, made for the World's Columbian Exposition in 1893. Once face-to-face with the uncanny luminescence of Tiffany's best work, even those who previously knew nothing about him can't help but come away dazzled. The museum's founders also collected hundreds of other top-quality pieces from the Arts and Crafts movement, including sculpture, but the focus here is definitely Tiffany and his impeccable taste. Set aside an hour or more, though it's easy to combine a visit with a stroll through Winter Park's boutiques, because it sits among them. Check the hours ahead; in early 2021, it was only open by appointment.

445 N. Park Ave., Winter Park. www.morsemuseum.org. ✆ **407/645-5311.** $6 adults, $5 seniors 60+, $1 students, free for kids 11 and under. Tues–Sat 9:30am–4pm; Sun 1–4pm; open until 8pm on Fri Nov–April. Free Fri 4–8pm Nov–Apr.

Rollins Museum of Art ★ MUSEUM Rollins College, whose graduates include none other than Mister Fred Rogers, has long been a university of choice for parents with social aspirations for their children, and so it makes sense that its star exhibition hall would be bequeathed with such a fine collection in such a country-club setting. It's too small to showcase its impressive holdings, so even remarkable pieces (such as Vanessa Bell's portrait of Mary St. John Hutchinson) tend to rotate in and out of storage to make way for changing exhibitions, which spotlight a wide range of arresting works, from Matisse prints to 18th-century European portraits. Small but top-notch.

100 Holt Ave., Winter Park. www.rollins.edu/rma. ✆ **407/646-2526.** $5 adults, free for students, sometimes free thanks to grants. Tues 10am–7pm; Wed–Fri 10am–4pm; Sat–Sun noon–5pm.

South & East of Disney

Diversions get populist as you go south, and their character says more about eccentric Florida than imported wealth; two of Central Florida's most authentic reptile parks are roughly between Disney and the airport.

Bok Tower Gardens ★★★ GARDENS/HISTORIC SITE About an hour south of Disney, the elegant, 250-acre gardens—designed by Frederick Law Olmsted, Jr., who worked on the National Mall and the Jefferson Memorial—are not often visited, which is too bad, because it's a big reason you're in Orlando at all: It was one of Central Florida's first world-famous attractions. They're genuinely tranquil and among the best surviving remnants of early-20th-century philanthropic privilege. The gardens (don't miss the water lilies, big enough to support a child) and their 205-foot, neo-Gothic Singing Tower, safely behind a fence, were commissioned as a thank-you to the American people by a Dutch-born editor, Edward William Bok, publisher of *The Ladies' Home Journal* and a pioneer in public sex education. Bok was buried at the tower's base in 1930, the year after its completion and dedication by President Calvin Coolidge. The 57-bell carillon on the tower's sixth level sounds concerts at 1 and 3pm daily, and although you can't enter the tower, the 1930s Mediterranean-style **Pinewood estate** ☛ ($6 more; shorter seasonal hours) is open for tours. The sanctuary was enshrined in 1993 as a National Historic Landmark.

1151 Tower Blvd., Lake Wales. www.boktowergardens.org. ✆ **863/676-1408.** $15 adults, $5 kids 5–12. Daily 8am–6pm, last admission at 5pm.

Dinosaur World ★ TOURIST MUSEUM An only-in-America roadside attraction, this is not someplace to pass hours—one will do, but it'll be an endearingly weird one. Kids like to wander the jungle-y plot, happening upon more than 100 life-size versions of various dinosaurs, some 80 feet long. A labor of love by a Swedish-born man and his family, it's well kept, even if the foam-and-fiberglass models sometimes look more like aliens than reptiles. It's easy to catch on the drive to Busch Gardens.

5145 Harvey Tew Rd., at I-4's exit 17, Plant City. www.dinosaurworld.com. ✆ **813/717-9865.** $17 adults, $15 seniors 60+, $12 kids 3–12. Daily 9am–5pm.

Fun Spot America—Kissimmee ★ AMUSEMENT PARK Fun Spot's flagship property is near Universal (p. 180), but this southern outpost beside Old Town delivers the same well-kept carnival-ride playground experience. There's a selection of basic rides that wouldn't be out of place beside a circus (the **Hot Seat** swings riders on the end of a big stick), bumper cars, a wild mouse-style coaster **Galaxy Spin,** and a few outdoor go-kart tracks (the four-story Vortex has 32-degree banking, the world's steepest, owners say—there's a height requirement of 54 inches, or at least 36 inches if kids are with an adult). That 300-foot-tall skyline-scarring contraption is **SkyCoaster** ($40/ride), which harnesses up to three would-be pants-wetters so that they're face-down, then hoists them backward and swings them forward at 80mph like wingless hang gliders. It's the world's tallest, and one of its wires snapped in 2021, but no one was hurt, so let's pretend like that never happened. Don't miss **Mine Blower,** a compact wooden coaster that makes a brief inversion. It only takes a minute, but it's a savage minute. It's the meanest jackrabbit of a coaster in Orlando. The down-market Old Town complex (p. 192) is next door and is usually seen on the same visit.

2850 Florida Plaza Blvd., Kissimmee. www.fun-spot.com. ✆ **407/397-2509.** Pay-per-ride $5–$10, unlimited rides $46 (everything except SkyCoaster) to $54 (including Sky-Coaster). Generally daily 10am–midnight.

It's Not on the Tourist Maps

The standard tourist literature won't point them out, but pop history happened here:

- **1418½ Clouser Ave., in the College Park area.** In July 1957, 9 months before the publication of *On the Road*, writer Jack Kerouac moved in with his mother, and he inhabited a 10×10-foot room with just a cot, a desk, and a bare bulb. Here, he wrote *The Dharma Bums*, an exploration of personal spiritual renewal through a connection with nature. By the time he moved out in the spring of 1958, he was a literary superstar. The Kerouac Project (www.kerouacproject.org) now owns the home and invites writers to live rent-free for 3-month working tenures.

- **Post Parkside, 425 E. Central Blvd., Orlando.** This apartment building was once the Cherry Plaza Hotel. Here in 1964, LBJ was the first sitting president to spend the night in Orlando. And on November 15, 1965, while the hotel was still segregated, Walt Disney made his only public appearance in Orlando in its Egyptian Room, where he and Roy Disney announced their plans for "the equivalent of Disneyland" in Florida.

- **1910 Hotel Plaza Blvd., Lake Buena Vista.** The very first building to be completed on Walt Disney World property was this low-slung glass-and-steel creation, considered painfully modern in January 1970. It was the Walt Disney World Preview Center, on what was then Preview Boulevard. Here, pretty young hostesses guided some one million visitors past artists' renderings, models, and films promoting Phase One of the resort that was being constructed.

- **Ballroom of the Americas B, Disney's Contemporary Resort, Walt Disney World.** On November 17, 1973, President Richard Nixon gave his "I'm not a crook" speech to a convention of Associated Press editors here, throwing gasoline on the fire of Watergate and bestowing him with his catchphrase of infamy.

- **Disney's Polynesian Resort, Walt Disney World.** While on vacation on December 29, 1974, John Lennon signed the document that officially dissolved the Beatles forever. Disney isn't positive which room he was staying in, but it's thought it was a ground-floor corner room in what's now the Samoa longhouse.

- **839 N. Orlando Ave., Winter Park.** In March 1986, the Canadian rock group The Band was in the middle of a disappointing reunion tour. After playing the Cheek to Cheek Lounge at the Villa Nova Restaurant, which stood here, pianist Richard Manuel, 42, returned to his hotel room at the Quality Inn and when his wife left the room, hanged himself. The lounge site is now a CVS drugstore and the motel site is now a Wawa convenience store.

Gatorland ★★★ ANIMAL PARK   Back in 1949, the reassuringly hokey Gatorland became Orlando's very first mass attraction, featuring Seminole Indians wrestling the animals for tourists; the house-size jaw at its entrance was a state landmark. Back then, Florida was crawling with alligators—you would see them basking by the sides of the roads—but these days, the reptiles have been mostly evicted by development, so sanctuaries like these are the best places to see the ornery beasts, such as the resident diva, the 15-ft.-long, 1,400-lb. Bonecrusher II. Gatorland is rustic in an Eisenhower-era, family-friendly way, and easy to love. There's a kids' splash area (suit them up), and in recent years the park has added a **wading bird rookery,** a **petting zoo,** a miniature **train,** and a five-stage **zipline** over gator ponds ($70; it's a good time and guests who need accessible accommodations can also do it). It also just created the (extraordinarily bumpy) **Stompin' Gator Off-Road Adventure** (another $10), a tongue-in-cheek narrated ride in custom vehicles that jostle you around the overgrown back acres and crawl through the middle of a roiling gator pond. The core of a visit is the showtimes, when good ol' boy gator rangers, buzzed on their own testosterone, wrassle, tickle, and otherwise pester seething gators, and for 10 bucks, they'll bring your children into the fray—safely, with a wad of duct tape around the critters' snouts—for snapshots. It's cornpone fun and they know it; signage is full of gags and every show is staged to contain a fake near disaster to titillate and thrill. Most of the fun is trawling the 110-acre plot on walkways and docks as the critters teem ominously in murky waters underfoot. *Strategy:* It's easy to get the highlights in 2 or 3 hours, but don't miss the **Jumparoo** (Mon–Fri at 10:45am), when gators leap out of the water for suspended chunks of chicken. Bring a fistful of extra cash if you'd like to partake of extras such as feeding gators, that photo op, and the train (or add a package to your entry for $7 more). And save a few bills for one of Gatorland's 1960s-era Mold-a-Matic vending machines, which press a toy out of injected hot wax right before your eyes. They're perfect metaphors that capture the delightful throwback charm of Gatorland.

14501 S. Orange Blossom Trail, Orlando. www.gatorland.com. © **407/855-5496** or 407/855-5496. $30 adults, $20 kids 3–12, $25 seniors 55+; $3 cheaper online. Free parking. Daily 10am–5pm; summer daily 10am–6pm.

Give Kids the World Village ★★★ ⚑ LANDMARK

Of the annual wishes granted by the Make-A-Wish Foundation and other wish-granting organizations for terminally ill children, *half* of them are to visit Central Florida. Make-A-Wish turns to this nonprofit to fulfill those dreams, which it does for 196 families at a time plus some 7,000 international families a year. No one is refused, and each family spends an all-expenses-paid week in their own villa, eating as much as they want (including ice cream for breakfast) and playing in a compound that looks like a second Magic Kingdom.

It's the most magical place you never knew existed. The 84-acre, gated operation is its own fantasy world with a 6-foot-tall rabbit mascot, Mayor Clayton, who provides nightly tuck-ins. Perkins Restaurants and Boston Market discreetly support the dining pavilion, which looks like a gingerbread house, and there's an Ice Cream Palace where no child is ever refused a scoop. Christmas falls every Thursday, when there's a parade, holiday lighting, and an appearance by Santa, who gives everyone a toy provided by Hasbro. The carousel is the only one in the world that a wheelchair can drive right onto, plus there's horseback riding, a small-gauge train route, miniature golf, and more.

As you can imagine, it depends on volunteers—to the tune of 1,200 slots a week. You don't have to commit to anything longer than a few hours and if you're there for dinner, you'll eat; just apply online about 2 weeks ahead and be at least 12 years old, although exceptions can be made for families who want to volunteer together. Universal Orlando offers a "Volunteer Vacation Package" ☛ (☏ **855/275-4955**) of discounted 3-night hotel and park tickets for you and your family in exchange for 4 hours at Give Kids the World, shuttle included. Mornings or evenings are best because the kids want to spend their days at the theme parks, too. The workload is easy. That could mean turning person-size cards at the World's Largest Candy Land game, held Sunday nights on a board measuring 14,400 square feet. You could help at Mayor Clayton's surprise birthday party, thrown every Saturday, or at the "dive-in" movies screened weekly. You can spoon hash browns at breakfast (until about 11am), run the train, or serve dinner with a smile—the opportunities are virtually boundless and the staff matches talents with the right post.

Your mission is not to lavish pity or love, but to simply run the resort so families can escape from hard times. You'll be a host, not a nurse. Not every child is sick—their brothers and sisters come, too, and many of them are starved for attention after their siblings' often long illnesses. You'll find that the village is quite a joyous place as families are, perhaps briefly, liberated from the burden of their lives. A favorite part of Give Kids the World is the Castle of Miracles, where the rafters are covered with thousands of golden stars. Each star is affixed by a child on the last night of his or her stay. Years later, moms and dads sometimes return and ask to see, one last time, the star their child left behind.

> ### Christmas Greetings
>
> **Christmas, Florida,** a blip on S.R. 50 between Orlando and Titusville, usually isn't much to write home about: farm supplies, roadkill. Unless, of course, it's the holiday season, when people come from far and wide to give their cards a Christmas postmark from the local post office. You'll find the P.O. at 23580 E. Colonial Dr./S.R. 50 (☏ 407/568-2941; Mon–Fri 9am–5pm, Sat 9:30am–noon).

210 S. Bass Rd., Kissimmee. www.gktw.org. ☏ **407/396-1114.**

Island H2O Water Park ★ WATER PARK Orlando's other water slide parks are bigger, better-themed, and better-run, but this one (opened 2019) is convenient to Animal Kingdom and many vacation homes, so it catches some trade. It's not lushly landscaped like its competitors, either, but its 20 slides, lazy river, and wave pool do have a novel twist: Guests get a wristband, and with a special app and some pre-planning, they can play songs and enable lighting effects while they're on some slides and rack up points for prizes the more they ride. The flume names lamely hammer home that theme, like The Downloader (one of those toilet bowl-type swirl-and-drops), Hashtag Heights (group rafts launched up a steep winged area), and Live Streaming (a body drop). Would you go twice? Probably not, but if it's hot and you can't schlep to Volcano Bay . . .

3260 Inspiration Dr., Kissimmee. www.islandh2olive.com. ☏ **407/910-1401.** $55 general admission, $45 for those under 48 in. tall or seniors age 62+, prices always cheaper online. Hours may vary seasonally, but generally daily 10am–7pm or until 9pm in summer, Fri–Tues 10am–5pm in other seasons.

Old Town ★ AMUSEMENT PARK   Built to look like 4 blocks of a Main Street–style town, this attraction embodies working-class Americana to the extreme: saloon-style bars, Old Glory T-shirts, and a gantlet of no-name stores peddling impulse buys from ice cream to fried food to gag portraits. Refined it ain't, loud it is, but after years of decline it's enjoying some investment and the Fun Spot, next door, has stocked it with a few carnival staples. The most interesting times to be here are late afternoon/evening Fridays, when it's packed for Muscle Car Show & Cruise, after 1pm Saturdays for pre-1983 vehicles, and after 5pm Wednesdays for specialty cars.

5770 W. Irlo Bronson Memorial Hwy./U.S. 192, Kissimmee. www.myoldtownusa.com. ℂ **407/396-4888.** Daily 10am–11pm (restaurants open at 11am).

Reptile World Serpentarium ★★ ANIMAL ATTRACTION   Snake milking! What other enticement do you need? Believe it or not, Central Florida herpetologists have been inviting visitors to watch them extract snake venom for biotoxin antidote supplies ever since the Great Depression, when Ross Allen founded a tourist attraction at what is now Silver Springs State Park. This facility, opened 20 miles east of Disney in 1972, inherited the mission of collecting poison for medical research and to save the lives of bite victims. Daily at noon and 3pm you can thrill, safely behind glass, as specialists (if you're lucky, you'll get the founder, George Van Horn) grab deadly serpents, plant their yawning fangs over the venom-collection glass, and get the creatures spitting mad. There are about 80 species of snakes on display (including a 13-ft. cobra, 80-odd coral snakes, and 11 types of rattlers) at any time, plus some baby gators and parrots, but obviously, this one's about venom spewing. Gotta admit—that's cool.

5705 E. Irlo Bronson Memorial Hwy./U.S. 192, St. Cloud. www.reptileworldserpentarium.com. ℂ **407/892-6905.** $11.50 adults, $9.50 kids 6–17, $8.50 kids 3–5. Tues–Sun 10am–5pm.

CRUISES FROM PORT CANAVERAL

Few sectors of the vacation business were more devastated by Covid-19 than cruising, and as it puts the pieces back together, we expect great change in the industry. But here's what is usually available at Port Canaveral (www.port canaveral.com), an hour east of Orlando.

Only four family-targeted lines usually sail from this port, focusing on short Bahamas and general-interest Caribbean itineraries—the upscale lines and routes leave from South Florida instead. Parking costs $17 per day, and there's nothing to do around the port while you're waiting to board.

As usual, you won't find many discounts from Disney, although MouseSavers. com tells which departures are going cheap. Quotes from specialty agents are often hundreds lower than those the lines themselves offer, and prices of $100 a night or less can be had if you book through a specialist. Check **Cruise**

Brothers (www.cruisebrothers.com; ✆ **800/827-7779**) and **Cruises Only** (www.cruisesonly.com; ✆ **800/278-4737**). Don't quit before you consult a terrific site called **Cruise Compete** (www.cruisecompete.com), on which multiple cruise sellers jockey for your business by offering low bids.

Carnival Cruise Lines ★ CRUISE   Considered a bargain line, it's noisy and atwitter with neon, like the inside of a pinball machine. Think "Real Housewives of the Atlantic Ocean." Carnival is popular with families, and there are few pretensions. Each ship has a twisting waterslide that has also become a line signature. The ships, like the new *Mardi Gras,* generally do more extensive Eastern Caribbean and Southern Caribbean runs that may include Cozumel and Belize and take a week or more.
www.carnival.com. ✆ **800/764-7419.**

Disney Cruise Line ★★★ CRUISE   These high-quality, casino-free ships include character appearances, fireworks at sea, and top-drawer entertainment. The hallmarks are the kids' program and a restaurant that changes from black-and-white to full color as you dine. The most common destination is the Bahamas for 3 or 4 nights, but some departures run deep into the Western or Eastern Caribbean for a week at a time. Some cruises have an extra layer of theming, such as for Halloween, the holidays ("Very Merrytime"), or *Star Wars*; these are clearly noted in the schedule. Disney traditionally packages trips with theme park stays and provides transitions between the two 🚌, but be aware that that package won't give you the best deal on the Walt Disney World portion of your trip.
www.disneycruise.com. ✆ **800/393-2784.**

Norwegian Cruise Lines ★ CRUISE   The middle-priced Norwegian schedules a mix of weeklong Western and Eastern Caribbean cruises and 3- and 4-night Bahamas ones plus the occasional 11-night Western Caribbean trip. It may also offer trips of less than a week that include the Bahamas with an overnight in Cozumel. NCL does not usually call at this port between June and October.
www.ncl.com. ✆ **866/234-7350.**

Royal Caribbean International ★ CRUISE   RCCL is the line for thrill-seeking young families and teens, with a stop at the beaches and lavish waterslides of its new (2019) $500-million private island, CocoCay. It hits the sweet spot between the gaudy tackiness of Carnival and the twee branding of a shopping mall. Expect weeklong routes to both the Eastern and Western Caribbean plus 3- and 4-night Bahamas runs with a base fare of $110–$130 a night.
www.royalcaribbean.com. ✆ **866/562-7625.**

DINING AROUND TOWN

You don't need a guidebook to decide if you want to eat at a chain restaurant—Orlando is crawling with those, and they all seem to serve variations on the same menu of burgers, ribs, pizzas, and salads topped with meat. No, where you could use help is in locating independent, unusual, and family-run small businesses. The restaurant options in this guide are the worthy discoveries you might not otherwise have noticed among the corporate clamor.

That's not to say corporate food can't have local provenance. In Orlando, even supersized brands have a pedigree: Darden, which owns Olive Garden, Yard House, and LongHorn Steakhouse, is based here, and so is Hard Rock Cafe. But for those brands, you know what you're going to get. We want to show you more flavors.

Pretty much every restaurant we list is open for lunch and dinner. Don't expect places to accept checks—credit cards are Orlando's cash. Also, this is a town where it bears asking for discounts.

In addition to our recommendations, check out Scott Joseph's Orlando Restaurant Guide (**www.scottjosephorlando.com**) by longtime food critic Scott Joseph, who reviews places to eat in the "real" Orlando north of the tourist zone, and the happenings blog **Bungalower.com**. In late August and September, dozens of area restaurants band together for **Orlando Magical Dining Month** (www.orlandomagicaldining.com), when three-course (appetizer, entree, dessert) prix-fixe dinners cost $37.

Prices are classified based on the price range for a main course at dinner:

- **Inexpensive:** $13 or less
- **Moderate:** $14 to $19
- **Expensive:** $20 or over

OUTSIDE THE DISNEY PARKS

These are the recommended restaurants you'll find on resort property but not inside a ticketed park. For places inside the theme parks, plus info on the Disney Dining Plan, see chapter 3.

Reservations are a necessity for all of Disney's table-service restaurants. Walk-ins are accepted, but tables are usually full. Bookings open 180 days in advance, and families throw themselves into it early as if they're Panzer units invading Poland. Obnoxiously, Disney slaps you with a $10–$25 per person fee if you fail to show up for your reservation. This could be considered greedy—after all, there are always so many people hoping to snap up a cancellation—but there's a side benefit: Restaurants that seemed impossible a few days ago may suddenly have space 24 hours ahead, when people dump bookings to avoid penalty. All **Disney-run restaurants** (disneyworld.disney. go.com/dining; ☏ **407/939-3463** [DINE]) can be booked by phone, online, or using the My Disney Experience app. **Tenant-run restaurants** (like the ones at Disney Springs) can be booked directly or, usually, on OpenTable.

Hotel gate guards will admit you if you have a reservation, and parking will be free. Disney reservationists have schedules of the other resort events (such as fireworks times) and can help you plan around them. If you make your own bookings online and you want your meal to match up with entertainment times, you'll have to scour the theme parks' schedules on your own via the Disney app or website.

Within Disney's hotels, the nicest restaurants generally serve from 5 to 9:30 or 10pm, as it's assumed patrons will eat lunch in parks. Some are more special than others, and many are just there to feed the masses, so focus your attentions on these recommendations (all unfortunately in the Expensive category).

For Disney Springs restaurants, see map p. 275.

EXPENSIVE

While many Disney restaurants are expensive, few of them could truly hold their own competing against true gourmet kitchens in the outside world. In most cases, you're really paying for atmosphere and a sense of occasion. These are the spots that deliver the most for their inflated rates.

Boma—Flavors of Africa ★★ ☏ AFRICAN   Make a reservation here and you get a bonus: a fine excuse to visit Disney's Animal Kingdom Lodge and pay a visit to the animals in its backyard paddocks, floodlit after dark—think of the high price as an admission fee for that. Dinner is a good time, too: A 60-item buffet menu, served in a dramatically vaulted dining room of thatching and bamboo. The food is not all African: It runs the gamut from roast chicken and beef to a very few African-themed delights such as watermelon rind salad and *bobotie* (a moussaka-like pie of ground beef from South Africa).

Disney's Animal Kingdom Lodge, 2901 Osceola Pkwy., Bay Lake. www.disneyworld. com. ☏ **407/939-3463.** Adults $30–$60, kids $18–$35. Daily 7:30–11am and 4:30–9:30pm.

California Grill ★★★ AMERICAN   For a blowout night with a view, the best choice is this beloved space on the 15th floor of the Contemporary Resort. The wine list is elaborate (some 300 selections), and the California

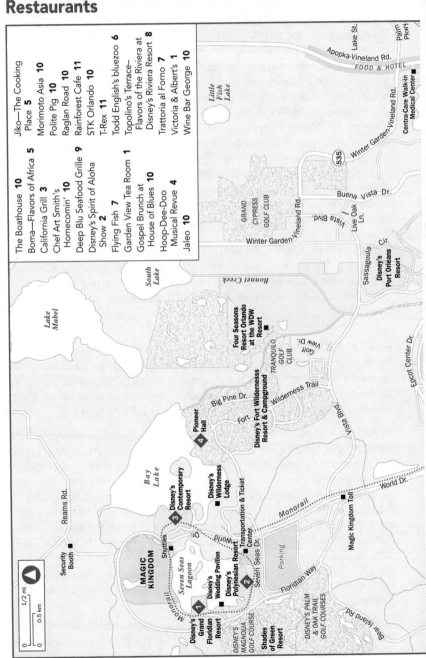

The Boathouse **10**
Boma—Flavors of Africa **5**
California Grill **3**
Chef Art Smith's Homecomin' **10**
Deep Blu Seafood Grille **9**
Disney's Spirit of Aloha Show **2**
Flying Fish **7**
Garden View Tea Room **1**
Gospel Brunch at House of Blues **10**
Hoop-Dee-Doo Musical Revue **4**
Jaleo **10**

Jiko—The Cooking Place **5**
Morimoto Asia **10**
Polite Pig **10**
Raglan Road **10**
Rainforest Cafe **11**
STK Orlando **10**
T-Rex **11**
Todd English's bluezoo **6**
Topolino's Terrace–Flavors of the Riviera at Disney's Riviera Resort **8**
Trattoria al Forno **7**
Victoria & Albert's **1**
Wine Bar George **10**

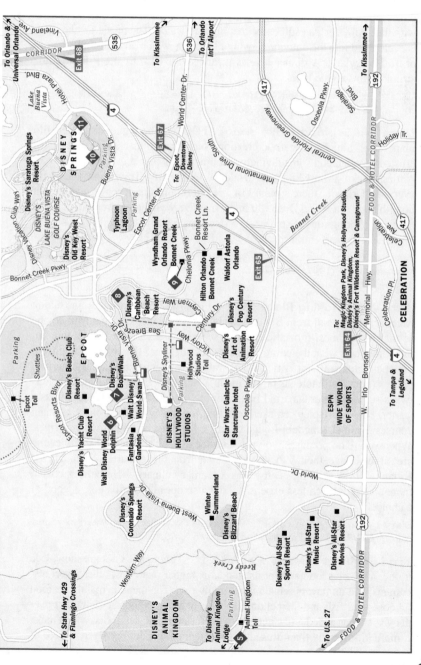

fusion-style menu is bright and seasonal but hearty—jumbo scallops, rack of lamb, Alaska halibut—and sushi and handmade pizzas are popular sidelines. Book as soon as you can—the maximum is 60 days before—and get a window seat for the **fireworks** ☛. If you have a reservation that doesn't coincide with the show, you can still come that night to watch. The music for the show is even piped into the outdoor viewing platforms, which are practically on top of Tomorrowland. A dinner here is a fantastic excuse to stroll through the atrium of this iconic hotel.

Disney's Contemporary Resort, 4600 N. World Dr., Lake Buena Vista. www.disneyworld. com. ✆ **407/939-3463.** Entrees $37–$64. Daily 5–10pm.

Deep Blu Seafood Grille ★★ SEAFOOD The higher-end Deep Blu marks itself a niche in seafood creations such as crab mac and cheese, crab-crusted grouper, and some divinely soft crab cakes plated as savory fall-apart patties, bucking most kitchens' tendency to over-fry. This being appeal-to-everyone Orlando, there's plenty of beef, too, and the decor is upscale but hotel-bland. You'll find Deep Blu in the massive Wyndham development close to Disney Springs on the south side of Disney property; turn left at the second Wyndham-marked entrance.

Wyndham Grand Orlando Bonnet Creek, 14651 Chelonia Pkwy., Orlando. www.deep bluorlando.com. ✆ **407/390-2420.** Entrees $29–$49. Thurs–Sun 5:30–10pm. Reserve on OpenTable.com.

Jiko—The Cooking Place ★★ ☛ AFRICAN The a la carte fine dining room across the hall from Boma (see above) is considered by many to be one of the resort's most romantic spots. It serves entrees that are good, too, but they often cost what the entire banquet does at Boma. The food coming from the open kitchen is pan-African, but waiters are eager to pander to American palates (note the flatbreads on the menu). That said, there are some delicious twists such as sweet tamarind butter for the bread, wild boar tenderloin as a starter, peri-peri (spicy) chicken, elk loin, or Malay seafood curry as main courses. Animal Kingdom Lodge claims a large list of South African wines. When you're on premises, you can also see the animals in the game viewing area at the Lodge, though they're not visible from the restaurant. **Sanaa,** in the Kidani Village building nearby, has a similar culinary vibe, but it's cozier, more casual, a touch less expensive, and also does lunch. It's just as good of a choice.

Disney's Animal Kingdom Lodge, 2901 Osceola Pkwy., Bay Lake. www.disneyworld. com. ✆ **407/939-3463.** Entrees $30–$55. Daily 5:30–10pm.

Todd English's bluezoo ★ SEAFOOD Although it's not the showplace it once was, bluezoo has kept its standards higher than most other resort restaurants, and its flavors remain memorably rich. The menu is mainly seafood (choose your fish and then choose a sauce or sub in a lobster claw), but over the years it has added a few detours to beef, flatbreads, and pasta, which make it more kid-friendly than it used to be. Eaten among Jeffrey Beers' decor of colored-glass baubles that suggest being underwater, the menu changes regularly to reflect seasons and what's freshest that day.

Walt Disney World Dolphin Hotel, 1500 Epcot Resorts Blvd., Lake Buena Vista. swandolphin.com/dining. ✆ **407/934-1199.** Entrees $29–$60. Daily 5–11pm. Reserve on OpenTable.com.

Topolino's Terrace—Flavors of the Riviera ★ MEDITERRANEAN
Rooftop restaurants at Disney are rarer than they should be, so this premium-priced French-ish, Italian-ish night out, which sits atop a resort built for Disney's timeshare members, was a welcome addition when it arrived in 2019. Although it doesn't quite take maximum advantage of its perch above Epcot's World Showcase (you see a lot more rooftop and hotel pond than theme park), the cuisine, which is overpriced in that Disney way, holds its own with Mediterranean class: bouillabaisse, escargot, lobster fettuccine, sole with lemon and capers, a decent wine list. That's all fine, but the highlight of your evening will probably be the time you spend enjoying cocktails on the terrace, so arrive early.

Disney's Riviera Resort, 1080 Esplanade Ave., Lake Buena Vista. www.disneyworld.com. ✆ **407/939-3463.** Adults $30–$60, kids $18–$35. Daily 7:30am–12:15pm and 5–9:30pm.

Victoria & Albert's ★★★ ⚑ FRENCH
Disney's flagship restaurant is the ultimate destination for anniversaries, proposals, and gourmands—and it's considered one of the finest places to eat in the entire state. The company puts much stock in Chef Scott Hunnel, a multiple James Beard nominee, who oversees the kitchen with Chef Aimée Rivera. The adults-only, 65-seater lays on its indulgent, prix-fixe multi-course menu (think amuse-bouches, Imperial caviar, Kobe-style beef with bone marrow pain perdu, New Zealand elk tenderloin), revealed to you from under cloches like a parade of debutantes. It's like the Very Fancy Restaurant where a character might take a date on a sitcom, harpist and all, which adds to the theater. The resort's most exclusive reservation: the 8-person Queen Victoria's room, where a private 10-course meal is served behind closed doors for $250 per person before wine. Every seat in this place sells out, and fast, when reservations open 180 days ahead.

Disney's Grand Floridian Resort & Spa, 4401 Floridian Way. Lake Buena Vista. www.victoria-alberts.com. ✆ **407/939-3862.** 10-course prix-fixe from $235, Chef's Table prix-fixe (bookable only by phone) from $250, wine pairings from $150. $100 cancellation fee within 72 hours of booking. 1 nightly seating. Jacket required for men (loaners available), no jeans or casual wear, no children 9 and under permitted.

Disney Springs

Disney Springs (formerly known as Downtown Disney; see map p. 275), a shopping-and-entertainment district at the southeastern edge of the property, is now the best place inside Disney to find food you'll like. There are dozens of restaurants and quick-service choices to appeal to every taste. The huge, free-to-enter outdoor mall still charges extreme prices ($25–$35 for sit-down dinner entrees, $18 a burger, $6 a cupcake—welcome to Disney!), but a few places, reviewed below, actually return that money in the form of skilled cuisine. Self-parking is free in covered structures. Most places serve food from 11am to 10 or 11pm, and many accept reservations via the Disney World app as well as by OpenTable.com.

Yet some choices still serve regrettably lackluster food, so be careful. You can count these joints out unless you just don't care: **Paddlefish** does so-so seafood in a fake boat cemented to its dock; **D-Luxe Burger** (just fine, self-explanatory); **Paradiso 37** (international tapas). **Planet Hollywood Observatory** is packed with unbelievable movie memorabilia (Judy Garland's *The Wizard of Oz* dress! The floating *Titanic* door Rose wouldn't let Jack on!), but its deep-fried menu will weigh you down.

Still decent but not groundbreaking: **Frontera Cocina** (www.frontera cocina.com; ℂ **407/560-9197;** Mon–Thurs 11am–9pm, Fri–Sat 11am–10pm; reserve on OpenTable.com) is celeb chef Rick Bayless' homemade Mexican offering (a little expensive for tacos and dull views) with notable fresh guacamole. There's also a waterfront Italian spot, **Terralina Crafted Italian** (www.terralinacrafteditalian.com; ℂ **407/934-8888;** Mon–Thurs noon–9:30pm, Fri–Sat noon–11pm, Sun noon–10pm; reserve on OpenTable.com), near The Boathouse (see below); the pasta there is handmade, the marinara flecked with lots of fresh garlic, and tables are set with an entire bottle of olive oil and bowls of fresh *giardiniera* (house-pickled vegetables), but in sum it's fair to middling. The other Italian place, the more romantic **Enzo's Hideaway and Tunnel Bar** (www.disneysprings.com/dining/enzos-hideaway; ℂ **407/560-3696;** daily 4:30–10pm; reserve on OpenTable.com), slices from carefully selected meats like salumi and aged prosciutto that hang by the kitchen, and pours a wide selection of classic cocktails. The best deal is the family-style Sunday Supper ($45 adults, $19 kids). A **Rainforest Cafe** (www.rainforest cafe.com; ℂ **407/827-8500;** Mon–Sat 11am–8:30pm, Fri–Sat 11am–9pm, Sun 11am–8pm) is at the far eastern end of the Marketplace, capped by a volcano that steams and growls every half-hour. I like it for the **Lava Lounge,** alfresco facing the water, an ideal perch for lakeside frozen drinks. All of the above restaurants are OK choices, but the following ones are my favorites.

EXPENSIVE

The Boathouse ★★★ AMERICAN   This convivial loftlike waterfront complex with three bars is elbow-to-elbow with people making a boozy evening out of its cocktails, craft beers, steaks, seafood, chops, and raw bar. Towering slices of baked Alaska are more daunting than the peak of Mt. Denali, and the nautical theme (there are rare boats affixed overhead) isn't superficial: After dinner, you can take a surf-and-turf ride from the boat ramp in an original 1961 Amphicar (p. 120). It is one of the top places to eat at Disney Springs.

The Landing, Disney Springs. www.theboathouseorlando.com. ℂ **407/939-2628.** Entrees $14–$48. Daily 11am–10pm. Reservations recommended. Reserve on Open Table.com.

Chef Art Smith's Homecomin' ★★ AMERICAN This is a hot property, so book ahead. Oprah's onetime personal chef, Art Smith, oversees a casual choice for tip-top Southern American comfort food: fried chicken in several forms, "Church Lady" deviled eggs, plus slaw, pimento cheese, and biscuits galore. Just to prove their barbecue is cooked perfectly, they won't give you a steak knife. The bar specializes in infused moonshine cocktails that will kick your butt all the way to Georgia, and a pineapple-banana Hummingbird Cake that will fly you back. On weekends, it does brunch (short rib hash, hush puppy benedict, and so on). This menu is heavy but it plucks the heartstrings of Disney World's core crowd (and is irresistible to Europeans curious about America's storied Southern cuisine).

Town Center, Disney Springs. www.homecominkitchen.com. ⓒ **407/560-0100,** reservations ⓒ **407/939-5277.** Entrees $16–$30. Sun–Thurs 10am–11pm; Fri–Sat 11am–midnight. Reservations recommended.

Jaleo ★★★ SPANISH TAPAS Go to the massive new multi-level Jaleo for a presentational evening of truly sensational Spanish tapas as interpreted though the futuristic cooking techniques of celeb chef José Andrés, who has used his fortune and expertise to feed countless people during major international emergencies. Do not miss the Spanish *ibérico* ham that has been imported from Spain by a special arrangement and is sliced tissue-thin at your table, or the *aceitunas modernas y clásicas,* the miraculous "liquid olives" achieved through molecular gastronomy techniques. By far the most interesting and economical way to go is the 15-course, José's Way tasting menu ($120), which loads you up with a range of high-end delights you wouldn't have discovered otherwise. Here, it costs far more to buy dishes individually than to order a set menu.

Disney Springs West Side. www.jaleo.com. ⓒ **321/348-3211.** Items $12–$36, 12-course menu $85, 15-course menu $120. Sun–Wed 4–9pm, Thurs–Sat 4–10pm. Reservations recommended. Reserve on OpenTable.com.

Morimoto Asia ★★★ ASIAN Iron Chef Masaharu Morimoto, known for innovative feats of kitchen derring-do, oversees this sweeping loftlike space (one of the grandest on Disney property), and if you're wondering if an Iron Chef had to dumb down delicate inventions to pander to the Disney crowd, the answer is he struck an admirable balance between populism and panache. Yes, you can get approachable dishes like dim sum, bao, and sushi, but dare to delve into specialties like whole house-roasted Peking duck, the "buri-bop" twist on hot-pot *bibimbap* with seared yellowtail, the unbelievably flavorful sweet-and-sour deboned sea bass (don't neglect the flaky cheeks), and rock shrimp tempura coated in a spicy Korean *gochujang* aioli. Outside, its Street Food window (noon–8pm) serves dumbed-down, mass-appeal Chinese grub—call it Pander Express—but after 10pm indoors, a more casual bar menu ($10–$25) is rolled out for the Forbidden Lounge, where chefs from around Disney show up after work to unwind. At this standout, multiple visits would be rewarded.

Town Center, Disney Springs. www.patinagroup.com/morimoto-asia. ℂ **407/939-6686.** Entrees $19–$55. Sun–Thurs noon–9pm; Fri–Sat noon–10pm, daily break 3–4:30pm. Reservations recommended. Reserve on OpenTable.com.

Raglan Road ★★ IRISH   The pub looks historic, but not in the way you think. Raglan Road was the first to bring well-reviewed independent cuisine to Disney Springs in 2005, so it was permitted to survive the post–Downtown Disney purge. Irish staples are turned into sprightly new visions, including glazed loin of bacon with cabbage, beef stew infused with Guinness, and good old fish and chips. Although the massive dining area is styled after an Irish pub, it's 20 times noisier. There's free live music most evenings. If you only want fish and chips, get it (plus beer) for less on the south side of the building at the counter-service hole-in-the-wall **Cookes of Dublin** ★, run by the same people.

Town Center, Disney Springs. www.raglanroad.com. ℂ **407/938-0300.** Entrees $22–$29. Mon–Sat 11am–10pm, Sun 10am–10pm, Cookes until midnight. Reserve on OpenTable.com.

STK Orlando ★★ STEAKS   Like all STKs (it's an upscale chain), this always-busy, never-cheap newcomer is an urban-chic version of a steak-house—there's a DJ after 6pm, and he's loud, which kills any romance—where every known preparation of beef is served alongside cocktails and a robust raw bar. The ground-level dining area is the main event, but head upstairs, where a (usually less crowded) smaller second bar overlooks the only rooftop dining area in the Springs. There's a happy hour Monday through Friday from 3pm to 6pm, featuring half-off cocktails and small bites from $2–$8.

Town Center, Disney Springs. STKSteakhouse.com/venue/orlando. ℂ **407/917-7440.** Entrees $32–$59, higher for specialty cuts. Sun–Thurs 11am–10pm, Fri–Sat 11am–11pm. Reservations recommended. Reserve on OpenTable.com.

T-Rex ★ AMERICAN   If *The Simpsons* were to spoof Orlando theme dining, this would be its family-fun creation: life-size robotic dinosaurs braying above your table. Every so often, the ceiling (at least, the one outside the simulated ice cave) is lit with a projected meteor shower and, for your amusement, the destruction of all prehistoric life forms is delightfully simulated for hordes of families as they chow down. You can predict the fare: Bronto Burgers, Tar Pit fried shrimp, and to end it all, the Chocolate Extinction, a fudge cake sundae for two or more people.

Disney Springs Town Center. www.trexcafe.com. ℂ **407/939-3463.** Entrees $19–$38. Sun–Thurs 11am–9pm; Fri–Sat 11am–10pm.

Wine Bar George ★★ WINE BAR   A welcome escape into adulthood in stroller-clogged Disneydom, WBG is run by a master sommelier who chooses the huge slate of wine and makes more than 100 choices available by

THE sweetness OF THE SPRINGS

As Disney Springs evolves, it's developing a new niche: dessert wonderland. Some of the waits for these sugary merchants are longer than at the high-profile restaurants. But if you're also willing to spend $6 on a cupcake, that's probably not a dealbreaker for you.

- **Amorette's Patisserie** (Town Center; www.disneysprings.com): Classic pastry chefs create picture-perfect delights like dome cakes, chiffon cakes, and crème brûlée.
- **Erin McKenna's Bakery NYC** (The Landing; www.erinmckennasbakery.com): Traditional bakery chain known for its Kitchen Sink Cups, which collect bits of cookies and cakes in one sublime hand-held treat.
- **Everglazed Donuts & Cold Brew** (West Side; everglazed.com): Doughnuts are piled with indulgent toppings like Froot Loops, Oreos, and Mounds bars. Everglazed makes French fries, too, because rules no longer matter.
- **The Ganachery** (The Landing; www.disneysprings.com): Artisanal chocolates, cocoa, and s'mores are truly made on-site in this tiny shop.
- **Ghirardelli** (Marketplace; www.ghiarardelli.com): This confectioner, pronounced with a hard G, has been making chocolates in San Francisco since 1852, but in Orlando, its sundaes are what's rocking.
- **Gideon's Bakehouse** (The Landing; www.gideonsbakehouse.com): Queues as long as 2 hours (sometimes you can join a virtual line) wrap around The Landing for this Orlando-based baker's fanciful cookies, which are the size of dinner platters.
- **Salt & Straw** (saltandstraw.com): West Coast ice cream innovator (with another branch at Disneyland) scoops wild notions like honey lavender, pear and blue cheese, and rhubarb crumble with anise.
- **Sprinkles** (The Landing; www.sprinkles.com): National chain with a big following and a "Cupcake ATM" (really just a pick-up window).
- **Vivoli il Gelato** (The Landing; www.disneysprings.com): Gelato, sorbetto, affogatos, milkshakes, and floats—*abbondanza*!

the ounce, glass, or bottle. The wine is obviously the point and its selections are acclaimed, although the liquor and beer selections are only standard. Prices are high across the (cheese) board; charcuterie-and-cheese boards clock in between $26 and $59. You can also order small plates (burrata, meatballs) that will satisfy most average people as a light meal, but this is generally a restaurant for enjoying fine flavors, not for stuffing yourself. Don't sit downstairs. Go upstairs, away from the din, where there's more space, more comfortable seating and another bar. This concept and menu are more sophisticated than most places around here, which for foodie visitors will make for a refreshing change.

The Landing, Disney Springs, 1610 E. Buena Vista Dr., Lake Buena Vista. www.winebargeorge.com. ℭ **407/490-1800.** Small plates $8–$26. Mon–Thurs noon–9pm, Fri noon–10pm, Sat 10:30am–10pm, Sun 10:30am–9pm. Brunch Sat–Sun 10:30am–2pm. Reserve on OpenTable.com.

INEXPENSIVE

On the lower end of the budget scale, you'll find the fast-casual chain **Blaze Pizza** (www.blazepizza.com) serves fast, build-your-own, cooked-to-order 11-inch pies for $10 that taste higher-quality and fresher than the $8 premade squares at **Pizza Ponte** (www.patinagroup.com/pizza-ponte) nearby. **Chicken Guy!** (www.chickenguy.com), which cashes in on the fried chicken sandwich craze, is also passable when you don't have the cash or the reservation for something more memorable. All three quick-service restaurants only accept walk-up customers.

Polite Pig ★★★ BARBECUE   The Polite Pig is the inexpensive eatery we recommend above the others at Disney Springs. If you can't get up to Winter Park to eat at the long-running and influential **The Ravenous Pig** (p. 216), the people behind it opened this smashing counter-service 'cue joint here. Along with pints of craft beer, find excellent gustatory ideas (brisket BBQ meatballs, smoked chicken salad, burnt ends chili) plus plates of meat from the smoker and fun twists on side dishes such as crispy whiskey-caramel Brussels sprouts and smoked corn with chipotle aioli.

Disney Springs Marketplace. www.politepig.com. © **407/938-7444.** Sandwiches $11–$14, smoker meat plates $15–$22. Sun–Thurs 11am–10pm, Fri–Sat 11am–11pm. No reservations accepted, but advance orders accepted online.

Disney's BoardWalk

BoardWalk 🐾, a lakefront promenade that's notionally themed to an old-time pier, has been left in the dust by the radical improvement of Disney Springs, and even before the pandemic it was a shadow of what it was intended to be. Besides a fairly weak ice cream shop, you'll find a few midway games, Surrey bike rentals 🐾, and if you're lucky, the occasional busker—not much except a pretty lake. Most of the meals are pricey; the only truly cheap food is pizza from a kiosk. The **ESPN Club** 🐾 serves food as an excuse to bask in the blare of countless TVs airing live sports while **Big River Grille & Brewing Works** 🐾 serves mundane burgers, pastas, and salads (main courses $13–$26). It's a rare sit-down Disney joint that doesn't accept reservations, so if all other places are full, try there. You can park at the BoardWalk Inn and get your parking validated or you can walk there via Epcot's World Showcase, 10 minutes away, where the dining is much more fun. The prime dining hours at BoardWalk are 5 to 10pm.

EXPENSIVE

Flying Fish ★★ 🐾 SEAFOOD   To say this spot is one of the most under-rated restaurants on Disney property is true, but it's also not to say it's a knockout. Its open kitchen is careful to source truly fresh food and deliver a good time in a theme-parky environment. Sustainable seafood is its principal domain, but it also does plenty of land-based meats. The entree of note has long been the potato-wrapped red snapper (not always on the changing, uneven menu), which should tell you about the carbohydrated concessions a

Rent-a-Poppins

Parents: I know you came to Orlando to spend some time with your family, but I also understand that you might need to get away from some of them for a few hours. If you're staying in a luxury resort hotel, the management may offer some kind of paid babysitting or supervised kids' club service. The official contractor for both Disney's and Universal's Loews hotels is **Kid's Nite Out** (www.kidsnite out.com; ✆ **800/696-8105**). Sitters will look after kids from 6 weeks to 12 years old, charging $20 per hour for the first child, $3 for each additional child, for a minimum of 4 hours. You also pay a $12 transportation fee, and there's a $2-per-hour surcharge for reservations that begin before 8am or after 8:59pm. No water activities are permitted. The service is insured, bonded, and licensed, and it would appreciate advance warning of between 2 weeks and a month for reservations for in-room sitting. The **Four Seasons** resort (p. 243) includes a free daytime kids' club as part of its normal rates. Although your kids would love it, I do *not* recommend depositing your offspring at the curb of the Magic Kingdom and speeding away, as actress Tracy Pollan's father did to her.

fresh-ingredient kitchen must make to keep the booths packed in Orlando. The tiny **AbracadaBar** cocktail lounge, with a loose old-timey magic theme and properly strong drinks, is attached.

Disney's BoardWalk. www.disneyworld.com. ✆ **407/939-5100.** Entrees $30–$55. Reservations recommended (via Disney website). Daily 5–9:30pm.

Trattoria al Forno ★ ITALIAN   This open-kitchen affair serving pastas, handmade mozzarella, and Neapolitan-style pizzas wouldn't give your Italian *nonna* a moment of competition in her kitchen, although the pasta is made fresh on premises, meat is cured in-house, the ingredients are fresh, and the service is good. It's fine, but at these prices and considering its competition, that may not be enough for you. Many people only come here because it's where the Bon Voyage character breakfast (p. 224; ✔) is held.

Disney's BoardWalk. www.disneyworld.com. ✆ **407/939-5100.** Entrees $24–$42. Reservations recommended (via Disney website). Daily 7:30am–noon and 5–10pm.

UNIVERSAL ORLANDO

There are worthwhile dining options in Universal Orlando that are outside the parks—ones for which you don't need a park ticket. Universal's hotels have upscale restaurants (**Bice Ristorante** at Portofino Bay, **The Palm** steakhouse at the Hard Rock), while the **CityWalk** (www.universalorlando.com) outdoor entertainment mall, located between the resort's parking garages and the entrances to the parks, attracts locals who have no intention of proceeding to any rides.

Most of Universal's CityWalk and hotel restaurants remain closed until dinner since guests tend to eat lunch in the parks. Exceptions include spots closest to the park entrances, **Red Oven Pizza Bakery, Burger King Whopper**

Bar, **Panda Express**, **Moe's Southwest Grill**, **Bread Box Handcrafted Sandwiches**, and the Asian fusion quick-service **Bend the Bao.** The **Hard Rock Cafe** (p. 207) is open across the pond, too. Universal coaxed Oregon institution **Voodoo Doughnut** to bring its extravagant creations here, but those don't really qualify for meals unless you've fallen off the carb wagon.

After dark (parking is free after 6pm), CityWalk has kiosks serving stuff like **Fat Tuesday** boozy slushies. Arrive before 9pm, because some of these places charge covers after then. In non-pandemic times, everything closes by 2am, but most stuff will shut down earlier than that. (For CityWalk's nightlife, see p. 279.) If you intend to linger at CityWalk for the nightlife, there are occasionally package deals that combine a set meal, including a beverage, with a movie at the newly renovated Universal Cinemark at CityWalk cinema.

Restaurants at CityWalk accept reservations via the Universal Orlando app. Entrees cost more than they would in the real world; they're mostly priced in the teens, with burgers sliding in around $17. Not everything is worth chewing: **Bubba Gump Shrimp Co.** (yawn!), the counter-service **Hot Dog Hall of Fame** (shrug!), and woe, **NBC Sports Grill & Brew** (huge beer selection, but has the pricing and feel of an airport bar). You may (but don't have to) make reservations online for the more compelling restaurants, named here. For each place, call ✆ **407/224-3663** for more information unless there's a different number listed.

MODERATE

If you want some live music with your dinner, you'll find middling regional specialties along with the acts at **Pat O'Brien's** (New Orleans jazz) and **Bob Marley—A Tribute to Freedom** (Jamaican reggae). Neither is open at lunch and neither is great shakes in the kitchen, but the music and booze compensate.

Antojitos Authentic Mexican Food ★★★ MEXICAN   Beneath the day-glo pink bell tower, banish thoughts of beany burritos and trashy Tex-Mex at this peppy place that conjures up the flair of easy Mexican street food and the din of Mexican street musicians. Options range from casual (nachos, queso with chorizo, *elotes*) to a little more refined (grilled guajillo orange salmon, slow-roasted achiote pork loin).

CityWalk. www.universalorlando.com. ✆ **407/224-3663.** Entrees $13–$28. Sun–Thurs 3pm–midnight; Fri–Sat 3pm–1am.

Bigfire ★★ AMERICAN   At first glance, Bigfire looks like standard grilled-meat stuff—a huge open-grill kitchen dominates the space—but on closer inspection, you're pleased to note that it imbues its all-American menu with an urban panache not usually seen in Themeparkland. Even so, its ingredients don't stray too far from the usual crowd-pleasers: its mac-and-cheese is accented with pork belly, Cobb salad is laden with meats and honey mustard dressing, smoked brook trout is spiked with tarragon tartar sauce, and the short rib pasta is flavored with sherry cream sauce. Meant to stylishly evoke

a lakeside lodge (outdoor tables abut a fire pit and you can order s'mores-making kits), it serves honest-to-goodness adult cocktails and takes care that its meat is cooked properly, not slung off an assembly line. It's classic American comfort food, but smarter.

CityWalk. www.universalorlando.com. ℰ **407/224-2074.** Entrees $16–$49. Daily 4–11pm. Reservations recommended.

The Cowfish Sushi Burger Bar ★★ BURGERS/SUSHI   You'll find burgers. You'll find sushi. And you'll find sushi made with burger components (called Burgushi—it's a good time on rice). This offbeat concept is rendered with a cocktail bar and some interactive screens to pass the time. If there's a wait, head to the second floor for about 30 first-come, first-served bar seats; there are eight more on the third floor. People agree that it's a refreshing idea, so it gets busy.

CityWalk. www.thecowfish.com. ℰ **407/224-2690.** Entrees $8–$30. Daily 11am–11pm. Reservations recommended.

Hard Rock Cafe ★★ AMERICAN   Hey, look! It's . . . well . . . a Hard Rock Cafe. Granted, the world's largest (600 seats) and possibly the loudest. You've probably already sampled the Hard Rock shtick on offer at more than 180 of them: A loud tavern tarted up with music memorabilia (and a Cadillac spinning above the rotunda bar) but here, there's a slab from the Berlin Wall out back. *Fun fact:* The company's headquarters is in Florida. *Funner fact:* Between 2 and 9pm, ask for a free "VIBE" tour of the memorabilia in areas not open to diners—there's incredible stuff here, including John Lennon's writing loveseat.

CityWalk. www.hardrock.com. ℰ **407/224-3663.** Entrees $16–$30. Daily 11am–midnight.

Jimmy Buffett's Margaritaville ★ AMERICAN   Because it's nearest to Islands of Adventure at the park's closing time, this joint gets jammed with park-goers clamoring for margaritas and grub such as Cheeseburgers in Paradise. In late afternoon, there may be a strummer on the "Porch of Indecision" (not inside, not out), and after dark, the indoor area morphs into a three-bar club. Across the way, under a 60-foot Albatross plane, the *Hemisphere Dancer,* is the **Lone Palm Airport** for margaritas and appetizers on the go. It usually opens at 11:30am, but if it's closed, get your margaritas inside.

CityWalk. www.margaritavilleorlando.com. ℰ **407/224-2155.** Entrees $15–$25. $7 cover after 9pm. Daily 11am–10pm.

Toothsome Chocolate Emporium & Savory Feast Kitchen ★★ AMERICAN   The wild-looking, steampunk-style faux chocolate factory and restaurant is the current star at CityWalk, promising the Orlando usual (so-so steak, pasta, burgers, salads, flatbreads, plus all-day brunch, all average), but done as over-the-top, towering and teetering constructions, and with themed characters walking around and interacting with diners. What it really does best is its major desserts—there's a separate line for a milkshake counter cranking out whimsical and expensive ($12–$15) mixes in Mason jars.

CityWalk. www.universalorlando.com. ℂ **407/224-3663.** Entrees $14–$33. Daily 11am–11pm. Reservations recommended.

Vivo Italian Kitchen ★ ITALIAN When this contemporary open-kitchen restaurant opened, it touted house-made pasta (from the classics to modern inventions such as fiocchetti stuffed with Gorgonzola and pear), fresh mozzarella, braised short ribs, and cured meats. But such high ideals are perhaps too lofty to maintain in a tourist mill like Orlando, and although a dinner here isn't regrettable, it's not as delicate as it was before. Still, its prices have held in the moderate zone so it remains a fair choice if everywhere else is full.

CityWalk. www.universalorlando.com. ℂ **407/224-7223.** Dinner entrees $17–$29. Daily 3–11pm.

U.S. 192 & LAKE BUENA VISTA

Around Disney, you can find every chain known to familydom, especially in **Lake Buena Vista,** a mile east of Disney Springs. One more unusual chain newcomer is **Portillo's,** the iconic Chicago hot dog and Italian beef sandwich slinger (7715 Palm Pkwy, Orlando; Portillos.com; ℂ **689/800-0102**). The Disney South zone, on **U.S. 192,** goes both east and west from Disney's southern gate—here, lower rents mean you'll find a lot of garbage food. The two zones are linked by a few miles of Interstate 4, making it easy to shift from one to the other. *Note:* Many restaurants suspended their lunch operations and only opened for supper while theme park attendance was capped during the pandemic—check ahead to see if midday hours have been reinstated.

EXPENSIVE

Columbia Restaurant ★★★ CUBAN Not everything is fake in Celebration, the Disney-built town just east of Walt Disney World. The original location of this palatial restaurant opened in Tampa in 1905, and this outpost bustles as boldly as its daddy. The hot, fresh Cuban bread is so delicious you'll want to fill up on it, but don't, because portions are giant. Tampa was a major arrival city for Cubans, and their tradition holds sway with flavorful grilled steaks and chicken, paella, mojitos, and sangria by the glass or pitcher. My favorite, the 1905 Salad, is mixed tableside with ham, cheese, lettuce, olives, greens, and a garlicky wine vinegar dressing that won't help you consummate any courtships, but is deservedly on sale by the bottle in the gift shop. *Dress code:* Men must wear sleeves.

649 Front St., Celebration. www.columbiarestaurant.com. ℂ **407/566-1505.** Tapas $8–$15; entrees $14–$38. Daily 11:30am–10pm. Reservations recommended. Reserve on OpenTable.com.

MODERATE

Bruno's Italian Restaurant ★★★ ITALIAN Your temptation would normally be to drive past this place since it shares a building with a dog-ugly

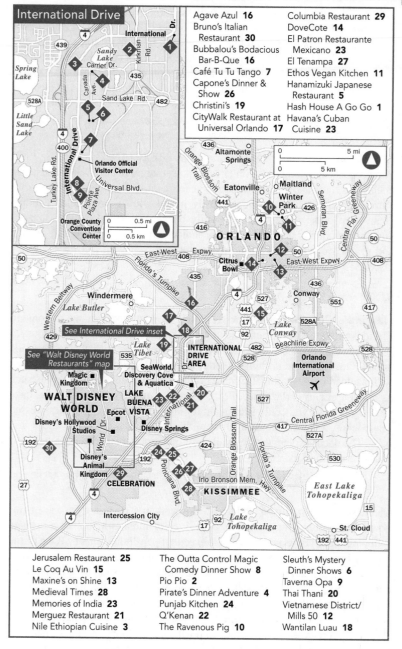

International Drive

Agave Azul **16**
Bruno's Italian Restaurant **30**
Bubbalou's Bodacious Bar-B-Que **16**
Café Tu Tu Tango **7**
Capone's Dinner & Show **26**
Christini's **19**
CityWalk Restaurant at Universal Orlando **17**
Columbia Restaurant **29**
DoveCote **14**
El Patron Restaurante Mexicano **23**
El Tenampa **27**
Ethos Vegan Kitchen **11**
Hanamizuki Japanese Restaurant **5**
Hash House A Go Go **1**
Havana's Cuban Cuisine **23**

Jerusalem Restaurant **25**
Le Coq Au Vin **15**
Maxine's on Shine **13**
Medieval Times **28**
Memories of India **23**
Merguez Restaurant **21**
Nile Ethiopian Cuisine **3**
The Outta Control Magic Comedy Dinner Show **8**
Pio Pio **2**
Pirate's Dinner Adventure **4**
Punjab Kitchen **24**
Q'Kenan **22**
The Ravenous Pig **10**
Sleuth's Mystery Dinner Shows **6**
Taverna Opa **9**
Thai Thani **20**
Vietnamese District/Mills 50 **12**
Wantilan Luau **18**

gift shop that's garishly painted with killer whales, but inside, it's the food that's killer. There's a lot of junky pasta in the tourist zone, but it's the rare Italian table where the owner is not only cooking with pride, but is also actually Italian. In this one modest room, Bruno, gruff but generous, loads plates with garlicky goodness, from his puttanesca to his buttery rolls, and he also does large New York–style pizzas, calzones, and fresh cannoli. Ask about the daily specials, which might include a concoction called "eggplant Pavarotti," a rich piling of eggplant, ricotta, spinach, crabmeat, shrimp, and vodka sauce. Cash-only delivery is available to the vacation homes of Disney South.

8556 W. Irlo Bronson Memorial Hwy./U.S. 192, Kissimmee. www.brunos192.com. ☎ **407/397-7577.** Entrees $16–$24. Daily 2–9pm. No reservations required.

El Patron Restaurante Mexicano ★ MEXCIAN/TEX-MEX When
you need to cap a long day with an enormous margarita and well-made tacos, enchiladas, burritos, guac, bowls, and generous rounds of chips and salsa, El Patron has the polish you might easily mistake for a well-heeled national chain—but nope, it's a well-run family business, and the owner listens to guests. Ingredients are fresh, tequila choices are plentiful and high-quality, and prices are sensible. On Tuesdays, stuff yourself with tacos for one low price ($13 at lunch and $19 at dinner).

12167 S. Apopka Vineland Rd., Orlando. www.elpatronorlando.com. ☎ **407/238-5300.** Entrees $11–$17. Daily 11am–9pm.

Havana's Cuban Cuisine ★ CUBAN It would be a shame to come to
Florida without tasting authentic Cuban food. Disney only does touristy Cuban, but this modest family-run place just outside Disney's eastern side door is hosting the real thing—tender *bistec palomilla* (thin-pounded steak with sautéed onion), aromatic *congri* (red beans and rice), and specials such as red snapper in garlic sauce. For dessert, the milk-soaked *tres leches* cake makes you wish you could start again for another round. It also does pressed sandwiches, a Cuban standard. Beware the green hot sauce—it'll knock you back. The decor is plain (cream walls, reproduction travel posters), but there's heartiness in the food.

8544 Palm Pkwy., Orlando. www.havanascubancuisine.com. ☎ **407/238-5333.** Entrees $14–$30. Mon–Sat 2–10pm; closed Sun.

Memories of India ★ INDIAN More than a decade ago, one of this
book's top recommendations was Memories of India, which built a devoted following near Universal for its well-executed pan-Indian cuisine. One of the owners has since bought out his partner and re-opened in a new spot near Disney. I'm thrilled to see the revival of a place with such long roots in the community: At lunch it prepares *thali*, a platter combining basmati rice, bread, *raita* (yogurt with cucumbers and tomatoes), pickle (relish), a meat dish, a *papadum* (thin crisp flatbread), and, at this place, dessert (I like the pulpy mango ice cream)—all for $7.25 to $10. The tandoori and naan (nearly a dozen kinds—garlic is a favorite) are made in a clay oven. The Lamb Kada

Masala, cooked in ginger, garlic, spring onion, and gravy, has always been consistently strong.

12185 South Apopka Vineland Rd., Orlando. ℃ **407/238-7684.** www.memoriesofindia orlando.com. Entrees $11–$16. Sun–Thurs 11:30am–2:30pm and 5:30–10:30pm, Fri–Sat 5:30–10:30pm.

Punjab Kitchen ★★ NORTH INDIAN   Although it's in a grungy tourist zone, Punjab isn't just for tourists—you'll see North Indian expats picking up a taste of home, too. That's a strong sign for authenticity, and the food, which is prepared with great care, delivers in ample portions and bold flavors. The dining room isn't much to look at—to call it unassuming would be generous. But then again, after a few days of noisy theme park fakery, you may find acoustic tiles and blank diner tables to be soothingly authentic, too. This is a marvelous place to try things you haven't before: The menu carries the beloved staples and explains them for those who don't know their Indian food, and the staff, strong on service, knows the difference between mild and spicy. Delivery is free. This is *not* Punjab Indian, an inferior buffet joint nearby; you want the Kitchen.

5479 W. Irlo Bronson Memorial Hwy./U.S. 192, Kissimmee. ℃ **407/507-2764.** Entrees $11–$16. Daily 11:30am–11pm.

INEXPENSIVE

El Tenampa ★★★ MEXICAN   From the outside, you'd swear it was just a grungy mini-mart best avoided, but inside, you discover a family-friendly hideaway of slotted-pot lanterns, hand-carved thrones, and big plastic cups in orange, magenta, and lime. Because Hispanic families show up in droves, you also know the food is authentic and good. The fresh *aguas frescas* (rejuvenating fruit-infused water drinks, eight flavors ranging from tamarind to lime) flow freely, and portions are big and reliable. Start with free salsa and delicate corn chips that are still shiny and hot from the fryer, but don't fill up, because main courses are huge and cheap. On weekends, when it's busiest, you might find a live mariachi duo; at its market next door, get Mexican popsicles at its *paleteria*. This is *not* the identically named location on Orange Blossom Trail.

4565 W. Irlo Bronson Memorial Hwy./U.S. 192, Kissimmee. www.facebook.com/ElTenampa Mex192. ℃ **407/390-1959.** Entrees $8–$14. Sun–Thurs 10am–9pm; Fri–Sat 10am–10pm.

Jerusalem Restaurant ★ MIDDLE EASTERN   Unknown to tourists, a growing Middle Eastern immigrant community happily calls Kissimmee home (you'll see a few halal grocery stores around this area), and this family hole-in-the-wall is one of the benefits: Hidden in an elbow of a quiet strip mall, it's modestly embellished with bougainvillea, stone walls, and a gurgling fountain. Lunch specials (11am–3pm) get you kebabs for around $10, and wraps (falafel, *shawarma,* gyros) start below that. I love the garlicky hummus, couscous dishes, and *kibbeh* fritters made of beef, cracked wheat, pine nuts, and seasonings.

2920 Vineland Rd., Kissimmee. www.facebook.com/JerusalemRestaurantOrlando. ℃ **407/397-2230.** Entrees $9–$19. Daily 11am–11pm.

Merguez Restaurant ★ MOROCCAN   Real halal Moroccan cooking—stuffed savory pastry, kebabs, dry-and-spicy beef Merguez sausage, tagine, piles of couscous, and mint tea—all freshly made and quite good. This isn't very common in these parts, but the straight-ahead protein-and-flavor infusion is welcome. Service can be aloof but the flavors aren't; the strip mall location is spacious but downright kooky—its covered patio is beside a grand staircase festooned with full-size Roman-style figure sculptures—which adds to the uniqueness. Ask for sauce if you want it; they figure you're a meat lover and don't automatically include it. During Ramadan, the kitchen omits couscous and pastry and focuses on the meats and salads. If your kid's a picky eater, there are always nuggets and burgers.

11951 International Dr., Orlando. www.merguezrestaurant.com. ✆ **407/778-4343.** Entrees $9–$16. Daily noon–9pm.

Q'Kenan ★★ VENEZUELAN   This family-run prize is worth a celebration! The strip mall location about 10 minutes east of Disney may daunt, the room may not contain even a dozen tables plus counter seating, the lighting may be harsh—but the food is made with unbounded generosity. A row of stews and meats lines the bar, from which meals are piled so high on plates that customers, largely local Venezuelans, gasp when they're set down in front of them. The owners opened their doors expressly to share their authentic cuisine with the area, and you should witness the joy on their faces when a tourist asks what to try. Suggestions: empanadas, overstuffed *arepa* (griddled corn flatbread) and *cachapas* (corn pancakes) filled with creamy aged cheese and sauces of every kind, or mixed plates like the *parrilla tepui,* with several kinds of meats, salad, yucca, and an *arepa,* and fresh juices, all of which will barely crack a $10 bill, and much of which won't even use up a $5.

8117 Vineland Ave., Orlando. www.qkenanrestaurant.com. ✆ **407/238-0014.** Entrees $5–$13. Tues–Sun 10am–9:30pm.

INTERNATIONAL DRIVE & CONVENTION CENTER

This is a major hotel and entertainment center, with upscale chain names vying for vacation dollars and expense account charges. The half-mile stretch of **Sand Lake Road** west of Interstate 4 is known, somewhat jokingly, as "Restaurant Row," and it's true that some popular date-night chain restaurants (**Rocco's Tacos** for party-atmosphere Mexican, **Eddie V's** and **Bonefish Grill** for seafood) are scattered along a couple of blocks. If you don't feel like hunting around, head to the bottom of the Wheel at ICON Park (p. 183, free parking), where you'll find a selection of decent (but not gourmet) self-explanatory mainstream choices including **Shake Shack,** an **Outback Steakhouse,** wine-focused **Cooper's Hawk Winery & Restaurant,** upscale beer hall **Yard House, Uncle Julio's Mexican Restaurant,** and the all-American **Tin Roof** (p. 282), which has live music after 8pm. Closer to the Convention Center, the small outdoor mall called Pointe Orlando (9101 International Dr.) has a few more higher-end, but mass-appeal options favored by visitors with expense accounts and a need for stiff drinks. Some of the places to eat are known quantities in other cities that you don't need to have described here, including **Maggiano's Little Italy, The Capital Grill** for steaks, the pubby **Marlow's Tavern, The Oceanaire Seafood Room,** and **Cuba Libre Rum Bar & Restaurant.**

EXPENSIVE

Christini's ★ ITALIAN   Christini's, a fixture since 1984, is much more expensive than most Italian places, and it doesn't permit young children. Those facts qualify it as a special-occasion restaurant and not one at which to suck down a bowl of noodles. Picture a prototypical high-end Italian splurge and you've got it: gilded-frame paintings, wandering accordion player, sommelier, lifetime waiters alert to your every twitch. It does pasta well, but guests tend to most praise its meats, particularly the tender *osso buco*. Dress code is business casual at the least.

7600 Dr. Phillips Blvd., Orlando. www.christinis.com. ☏ **407/583-4472.** Reservations recommended. Entrees $23–$57. Daily 5–11pm.

MODERATE

Agave Azul ★★ MEXICAN   Hidden in a strip mall, as so many of Orlando's most delicious places to eat are, Agave Azul cultivates a following with classic Latin dishes, from gourmet to Tex-Mex (ceviches, tacos, a few types of guacamole including one with shrimp and goat cheese) in a soothing, modernist environment with lots of space, huge booths, and a gentle indoor fountain. The margaritas pack a wallop—the drinks here come stronger than the attentively measured pours around the corner at Universal.

4750 S. Kirkman Rd., Orlando. www.agaveazulcocinamex.com. ☏ **407/704-6930.** Entrees $9–$20. Mon–Thurs 11am–10pm; Fri–Sat 11am–11pm.

Café Tu Tu Tango ★★★ INTERNATIONAL   Fun, festive, and noisy in a good way, this casual tapas-style hangout asserts its own personality with an artist theme. Actual artists somehow concentrate on painting at easels amid the frolic of tables, cocktails, and nightly entertainment of belly dancing, salsa, or flamenco dancing. Their works fill the walls up to the rafters while boisterous diners and drinkers spill out into the front patio. Despite the fun gimmick, the locally sourced food comes from sustainable ingredients and packs flavor. I love the tamarind Thai spare ribs, the mango shrimp bao buns, and brick-oven pizzas, other people like the Cajun chicken egg rolls.

8625 International Dr., Orlando. www.cafetututango.com. ☏ **407/248-2222.** Small plates $8–$13. Mon–Thurs noon–11pm; Fri noon–midnight; Sat 10am–midnight; Sun 10am–11pm.

Hash House A Go Go ★ AMERICAN   There's something demented about Hash House: its shocking immoderation. Dishes are laughably immense, piled as high as Jenga games. Even Guy Fieri would think it's in bad taste. Everything on the down-home menu, which the restaurant calls "Twisted Farm Food," sounds like a good idea mostly in anticipation: one-pound burgers (stuffed with the likes of bacon and cheese), skyscrapers of fried green tomatoes, a platter of sage-dusted fried chicken and waffles deserving of its own area code, pancakes like bedspreads, non-stop brunch. The HH is a meal with a high risk-reward ratio, and it's a sure bet there'll be leftovers—it's no wonder the brand came from Vegas.

5350 International Dr., Orlando. www.hashhouseagogo.com. ✆ **407/370-4646.** Entrees $11–$18. Sun–Thurs 8am–2pm; Fri–Sat 8am–7pm.

Pio Pio ★★ PERUVIAN/COLOMBIAN You want a restaurant in the tourist zone to be kid-friendly, affordable, delicious, and most of all, patronized by locals. Pio Pio, a modest and easygoing family-run group of seven locations, tags all those bases with expertly made and generous portions (a glass of sangria could fill a fishbowl). The rotisserie chicken is the star dish, but you'll find a caravan of other robust South American delights including ceviche, heaps of Peruvian *chaufa* fried rice, a rich *lomo saltado* (sliced beef sautéed with potatoes and vegetables in a soy sauce reduction), plus lots of steaks and fish. They know how to please children, too.

5803 Precision Dr., Orlando. www.mypiopio.com. ✆ **407/248-6424.** Entrees $12–$20. Tues–Sat 11am–10pm; Sun–Mon 11am–9pm.

Taverna Opa ★★ GREEK It would be hard not to find something to eat, from tapaslike *meze* (hummus with garlic chunks and hot pita bread, *taramosalata, keftedes* meatballs), salads, hearty wood-fired and long-marinated meats and grilled fish, and *moussaka* (an eggplant lasagna with béchamel). But this is Orlando, where nothing goes unamplified. After 7pm or so, waiters and customers alike toss napkins and dance on the tables as belly dancers and "Zorba" dancers (their term) swirl. Kids really get into it, probably because it's freight-train loud—this is not a place to choose if you're not in a party mood.

9101 International Dr. at Pointe Orlando, Orlando. www.opaorlando.com. ✆ **407/351-8660.** Meze $6–$16, entrees $15–$41. Daily noon–11pm (Fri–Sat open until 2am depending on season).

Thai Thani ★★ THAI A long-running strip-mall anchor store next to SeaWorld channels Chiang Mai with surprisingly ornate wood carvings, brass, and powerfully romantic private booths. The lemongrass soup is tame, with few chilies, indicating the chef holds back for newbies—but more advanced eaters should choose from the "spicy dishes" section to get the full flair of the cuisine. I like the Thai chili jam stir-fried with veggies and your choice of protein.

11025 S. International Dr. www.thaithani.net. ✆ **407/239-9733.** Entrees $13–$22. Daily 11:30am–11pm.

INEXPENSIVE
Bubbalou's Bodacious Bar-B-Que ★★ BARBECUE Real barbecue done the way devotees like it, from cornbread to fall-off-the-bone ribs proven

to stain shirts. There's no pretense at this tidied-up dive: Order at the counter and eat at picnic-style tables stocked with paper towel rolls and squirt bottles of sauce going from "sweet" to "killer." Get the standards: Texas brisket, pulled pork, half chicken, fried catfish, even gizzards. Sandwiches come with two sides (like baked beans, black-eyed peas, or Brunswick stew), or order them by the pint, quart, or gallon. You can always opt for meat by the pound and take it back to the gang.

5818 Conroy Rd., Orlando. www.kirkman.bubbalous.com. ⓒ **407/295-1212.** Entrees $10–$20. Daily 10am–9pm.

Hanamizuki Japanese Restaurant ★ JAPANESE The theme parks never saw a fish they didn't want to batter-fry. So here, the fresh sushi, chicken and salmon teriyaki, and udon or soba noodle soups make for a refreshing palate-cleanser. The blond wood and fabric decor conforms neatly to expectations of a soothing Japanese restaurant—but if you know Japanese food, you'll find it's of a higher caliber, and as a result it draws a steady trade of Asian visitors hungry for a taste of home. Best of all, because of a tucked-away location in a strip mall near the Kings Bowl Orlando, it's rarely crowded.

8255 International Dr., Ste. 136, Orlando. www.hanamizuki.us. ⓒ **407/363-7200.** Entrees $8–$14. Tues–Sun 5–10pm.

Nile Ethiopian Restaurant ★★★ ETHIOPIAN Nile's owners are so eager to share their cuisine that they have been doing it in the hurlyburly of I-Drive, near Universal, since 2006. They even offer a few hutlike booths in which you can sit on the ground to eat, East Africa–style. It's a positive experience for families. Everyone tears off a piece of spongy *injera* bread to scoop up various stews and meats (beef, lamb, chicken, vegetarian) collected on a platter. You can even request gluten-free or a traditional coffee ceremony, in which beans are brewed in a *jabena* pot at your table and the eldest in your party is served first. Ethiopian cuisine is made with infused oil, not butter, so there are true vegan options; with advance notice, the *injera* can be made gluten-free. It's memorable and not daunting.

7048 International Dr., Orlando. www.nileorlando.com. ⓒ **407/354-0026.** Entrees $11–$16. Mon–Fri 5–9pm; Sat–Sun noon–9pm.

DOWNTOWN ORLANDO

Although the historic heart of Orlando has a healthy culinary scene, this "real" part of town 25 minutes north of the theme parks is an area where most tourists are unlikely to venture. That's too bad. A few places are special and long-running enough to warrant a visit despite the gravitational pull of the parks and the car-clogged obstacle of I-4.

EXPENSIVE

Le Coq Au Vin ★★★ FRENCH Longtime Chef Louis Perrotte hand-picked his protégé Reimund Pitz to take the reins at this classic French romantic restaurant, an Orlando institution since 1976. Diners, many of whom are here celebrating a special occasion, feel more like they're guests in a home than paying patrons, an illusion that's extended by its mostly residential neighborhood. Pitz is a trained French chef, so you get the complicated flavors (well-marinated coq au vin, daily selection of game meat, Grand Marnier soufflé) that the prices demand, plus Gallic staples such as escargot and baked brie *en croûte*. Some dishes come in ample half portions that can cost two-thirds what larger servings do.

4800 S. Orange Ave., Orlando. www.lecoqauvinrestaurant.com. (*) **407/851-6980.** Entrees $22–$50. Tues–Sat 5:30–8:30pm. Reservations recommended.

The Ravenous Pig ★★★ SOUTHERN   James and Julie Petrakis have given Orlando some culinary renown (and published a cookbook) for knowing just when to deploy bacon and in what amount, a talent dear to me, and they have been rewarded by operating one of the city's most influential dining choices. Expect a sophisticated evening where the food is sustainable gourmet without pretentiousness and the beer is brewed on the premises in small batches. The menu changes seasonally but always features traditional farm-house meats—in the form of frites, say—and some Southern comfort dishes with an upscale spin, like shrimp and grits with Gruyère biscuits. To drink, get the Old Fashioned: bacon-infused Old Forester bourbon with vanilla and maple, garnished with candied bacon.

565 W. Fairbanks Ave., Winter Park. www.theravenouspig.com. (*) **407/628-2333.** Entrees $18–$33. Tues–Thurs 5–9pm; Fri 5–10pm; Sat 11am–10pm; Sun 11am–3pm. Reservations recommended.

MODERATE

DoveCote ★★★ FRENCH   How did a richly authentic yet distinctly mod-ern and youthful French brasserie wind up in the lobby of a generic banking skyscraper in a vacation town like Orlando? Never mind. It all comes out romantic. The croissants are buttery and flaky. The croque madame is indul-gently slathered in Mornay sauce and Gruyère cheese. Mashed potatoes are sculpted into a nest for a dollop of creamy horseradish. The cocktails are intriguing, the ham and cheese beignets served with rouge aioli. Brunch, it should be no surprise to learn, is a divine mélange of brioche French toast and omelettes threaded with fresh herbs, and coffee is from a kiosk in the corner run by Foxtail Coffee Co., a Winter Park–based roaster that attracts a devoted walk-in clientele of its own.

390 N. Orange Ave., Orlando. www.dovecoteorlando.com. (*) **407/674-6841.** Entrees $8–$19 lunch, $16–$38 dinner. Free parking with validation, free valet parking at dinner. Mon–Fri 11:30am–10pm; Sat 10:30am–2:30pm and 5:30–10pm; Sun 10:30am–2:30pm.

Maxine's on Shine ★★ INTERNATIONAL   Hidden in a residential neighborhood (blink and you've passed it), Maxine's is a labor of love by its owners, Maxine and Kirt Earhart, who frequently emerge from the kitchen to party with guests, who rallied around the couple during Covid-19 to keep their business going strong. There's a good wine list plus a tiny stage hosting a roster of entertainment (1970s karaoke one night, classical piano the next). Two signature dishes stand out: fried green tomatoes with crab cakes and, as a main dish, pan-seared diced chicken with shallots, mushrooms, a Marsala wine cream sauce, and penne pasta. On weekends, the restaurant brings in chill live music, which is popular with locals from the neighborhood, so reservations are recommended then, particularly for its "Rejuicination Brunch." As you depart, a sign thanks you for helping "this little restaurant's dreams come true."

337 N. Shine Ave., Orlando. www.maxinesonshine.com. ℂ **407/674-6841.** Entrees $16–$30. Thurs 5–9pm; Fri–Sat 10am–9pm; Sun 10am–3pm.

A GASTRONOMIC TOUR OF little vietnam

Just north of Orlando's downtown, along a stretch of 1950s storefronts around Colonial and Mills avenues, a thriving Vietnamese area (variously called Little Vietnam, ViMi, and **Mills 50**) is flourishing. Many people fled here upon the fall of Saigon, and now diners can find cheap meals here, true to Vietnam's reputation for nuanced flavors. Park anywhere (most buildings hide secret lots behind them).

The quickest meal is *bánh mi*, addictive baguette sandwiches stuffed with thinly sliced veggies (cucumbers, daikon, carrots), cilantro, hot peppers, a buttery secret sauce, and meats such as roast pork, pâté, or meatball (or tofu). They're shockingly cheap ($4), hot, and made to order. The best are at **Bánh Mì Nha Trang,** hidden in an ancient strip mall (1237 E. Colonial Dr.; ℂ **407/346-4549;** Mon–Wed and Fri–Sun 10:30am–6pm), where they barely speak English but are improbably friendly—every transaction ends with a chipper "See you tomorrow!" Also get them at the counter beside checkout at **Tiên-Hung Market** (1108 E. Colonial Dr.; ℂ **407/422-0067;** daily 9am–6pm), a catch-all for Asian groceries.

At most of the area's Vietnamese restaurants, where entrees range $8 to $12, menus drone on like a Russian novel, but each place has its specialty. **Phó 88** (730 N. Mills Ave.; www.pho88orlando.com; ℂ **407/897-3488;** daily 10am–10pm) excels with *pho* beef noodle soup; bowls

seem as large as hot tubs, with many flavors vying for dominance. Its two enormous spring rolls could fill an average stomach for $3.25. The specialty at **Ánh Hông** (1124 E. Colonial Dr.; www.anhhongorlando.com; ℂ **407/999-2656;** daily 9am–10pm), on the corner of Mills, is tofu (especially fried). Neophytes prefer the mass appeal of **Little Saigon** (1106 E. Colonial Dr.; www.littlesaigonfl.com; ℂ **407/423-8539;** daily 10am–9pm), which has dining areas with orange walls and green tablecloths that place it as slightly more upscale than its utilitarian one-room neighbors.

It's not just Vietnamese food, either—**Mamak Asian Street Food** (1231 E. Colonial Dr., mamakeats.com; Tues–Sun 11am–10pm) has gathered a fast following for its Malaysian/Singaporean delights like *roti canai* pull-apart bread with spicy coconut gravy. Japanese desserts make a showing in the form of boxed mocha ice cream and macarons in the one-room **Japango** (1212 E. Colonial Dr., japangomenu.com; Sun–Thurs 11am–9pm, Fri–Sat 11am–10pm) and mocha doughnuts at **Dochi** (1222 E. Colonial Dr., dochicompany.com; daily 11am–3:30pm). And the popular China-founded, 300-strong teahouse chain **Möge Tee** (636 N Mills Ave.; mogetee usa.com; daily noon–9pm) arrived in early 2021—the signature delight is a concoction of red dragon fruit, green tea, and sweet or salty cheese foam.

INEXPENSIVE

Ethos Vegan Kitchen ★★ VEGAN   As one of the only fully vegan restaurants in Central Florida, Ethos has garnered a loyal following since 2007. That's because when vegan cuisine is all that you do (even the cheese qualifies), you have to be skilled. Among the favorites are pecan-encrusted eggplant, "Yo Mama's Lasagna," gyros, and 10-inch pizzas. Kelly and Laina Shockley, who are raising their kids through this place, are assiduous about ingredient sourcing and proudly pay their servers a living wage (not minimum wage). Specials change according to seasonal crops, and there's always a soup of the day. About a third of the menu is gluten-free.

601-B New York Ave., Winter Park. www.ethosvegankitchen.com. *©* **407/228-3898** or 407/228-3898. Entrees $10–$14. Mon–Fri 9am–11pm; Sat–Sun 9am–11pm.

DINNERTAINMENT

Besides TV talent competitions, there may be no purer form of vaudeville left in America than the Orlando dinner show. Part banquet and part spectacle, most of these guilty pleasures involve stunts, audience participation, and plenty of noise. While the show grinds on, waiters scurry, distributing plates of banquet food the way Las Vegas dealers deal blackjack cards. Nowhere else on Earth—at least not since Caligula's Rome—will you find so many places in which to stuff your face while fleets of horses, swordsmen, and crooners labor to amuse you. Dinnertainment represents the delight of Orlando's shtick.

Most times of the year, most shows kick off daily around 6 or 7pm, but during peak season, there may be two shows a night, scheduled around 6 and 8:30pm. Upon arrival, crowds are corralled into a preshow area where they can buy cocktails and souvenirs—feel free to be slightly tardy, and feel free not to buy anything, because non-alcoholic drinks come with dinner. Most shows will be mopping up 2 hours later. Kids will find chicken fingers, hot dogs, and so on, while drinks, draft beer, and wine (the cheap stuff, watered down) are unlimited. Bring enough cash to tip your server because gratuities aren't included. *Money-saving tip:* The free coupon books and discount ticket suppliers always have deals. The ones thrown by the theme parks, though, tend to sell out.

In Orlando & Kissimmee

Capone's Dinner & Show ★ ITALIAN   High schoolers in wigs pretend to be 1920s flappers and warble to recorded music in this affordable dinnertainment effort. Dinner (normally served buffet-style ♥) is lasagna, gluey pasta, pizza, nuggets, and a few token non-pasta choices, provided it can be microwaved. Unusually for these shows, it's all-you-can-eat, and unlimited Bud Light or a few other alcoholic drinks are included. This troupe's own brochures and website promise half-off discounts, which grant the price named here, but I've never seen the so-called full price charged.

4740 W. Irlo Bronson Memorial Hwy./U.S. 192, Kissimmee. www.alcapones.com. *©* **407/397-2378.** $38 adults, $25 kids 4–12. Nightly, some 1pm shows.

Medieval Times ★★ AMERICAN   This coach-tour favorite is also an attraction in nine other North American cities, qualifying it as the McDonald's of dinnertainment: "Knights" do horse tricks in an arena to please the Crown. Waitresses were once called "wenches," but it finally got the #MeToo refurbishment: It's the Queen, not the King, who now runs this show. You eat spareribs and chicken with your hands (or the veggie stew with a spoon) while the jousters compete on horseback in an arena. For $12 more, the Royalty Package gets you front-row seating, a banner to cheer on your randomly assigned knight, and a lanyard. For $18 more, you also get a slice of cake and a callout by the announcer. Its "castle" is located a few miles east of Disney on U.S. 192, in a downtrodden area of Kissimmee. Discounts abound in the tourist brochures—to the tune of 30–50 percent less—so seek them out. This form of entertainment is deliriously over-the-top and all-American—and I'm starting to feel like we should take all of our kids to see it while it's still around.

4510 W. Irlo Bronson Memorial Hwy./U.S. 192, Kissimmee. www.medievaltimes.com. *©* **866/935-6878** or 407/396-2900. $65 adults, $37 kids 12 and under, kids under 3 free if they sit on parent's lap. Nightly, plus mornings or afternoons in high season.

The Outta Control Magic Comedy Dinner Show ★★ PIZZA   More affordable and easygoing than its dinnertainment competition, the show mounted by the WonderWorks science/video playground (p. 183) targets kids—and parents weary of overproduced, overpriced glitz. Unlimited pizza, salad, beer, wine, and soda are distributed while buddy-buddy magicians engage in family-friendly jokes, tricks, mindreading, and improv. Discount coupons get $2 off. The schedule was reduced to weekends-only through the pandemic; check whether it has expanded to include weekdays again.

WonderWorks, 9067 International Dr., Orlando. www.wonderworksonline.com. *©* **407/351-8800.** $32 adults, $22 kids 4–12 and seniors. Fri–Sat 6 and 8pm.

Pirates Dinner Adventure ★★ AMERICAN   For kids who just can't get enough Jack Sparrow–like misbehavior, there's this 90-minute, high-energy eye-popper, set on an 18th-century galleon with 40-foot masts amid a 300,000-gallon lagoon—the arena is the most spectacular of the Orlando dinnertainments. Come 60–90 minutes early for the pre-show, but once the lights go down, expect a circus of rope swinging (lots of it), trampolining, singing, and acrobatic *arrrgh*-ing; most of the time, the pirates kidnap Princess Anita, but in December, they kidnap Santa. In September 2017, Hurricane Irma ravaged its show building, putting it out of commission for 10 months (the acoustics still suffer), and then along came Miss Rona with her pandemic. But this institution is able to doggedly continue a run that started more than 2 decades ago because it's flat-out silly fun, everyone knows it isn't Shakespeare, and 11-year-olds need birthday outings. Buying online yields discounts; free brochures dispensed around town are good for even more off.

Pirate's Town, 6400 Carrier Dr., Orlando. www.piratesdinneradventure.com. *©* **407/206-5102.** $68 adults, $42 kids 3–10. Parking $8. Tues–Sun (times range 5:30–8:30pm).

Sleuth's Mystery Dinner Shows ★★ AMERICAN After mingling with a few zany characters and watching this long-running show, which takes about an hour and contains at least one murder, you confer over dinner with your tablemates, grill the suspects, and, if you feel confident, accuse a killer. The cases (there are between five and a dozen in the repertoire, depending on the cast) change nightly, so you can attend several times without duplicating the riddle. Actors seem to be having fun, and they'll tone down the grown-up jokes if they see kids in the crowd. Kids love participating in the detective Q-and-A segments. Audiences appear to be grateful for a rare chance to employ their brains in this town. Lots of brochures offer discount rates.

8267 International Dr., Orlando. www.sleuths.com. © **407/363-1985.** $65 adults including beer and wine, $27 kids 3–11; $3–$7 less if booked online. Tues–Sat 6:30pm; Sun 5:30pm.

At the Theme Park Resorts
The pandemic temporarily shut down every one of these shows, but they're too beloved to abandon forever.

Disney's Spirit of Aloha Dinner Show ★ ⁀ POLYNESIAN The chicken-and-ribs luau presided over by fire twirlers, hula dancers, and the like has been going strong for years in an open-air theater on Seven Seas Lagoon. Bookings begin 60 days ahead, and usually the last people to reserve are shunted to the rear tables, which can feel as remote as the Cook Islands; the tables that are farthest away are the least expensive. It bores some kids, but it has its adult adherents (although most of them cite not its educational qualities but its food—pineapple bread pudding being at the top of their lists). It's on the monorail line from the Magic Kingdom, so it's easy to catch the fireworks after early shows.

Luau Cove, Disney's Polynesian Resort. www.disneyworld.com. © **407/939-1947.** $66–$78 adults, $39–$46 kids 3–9. Tues–Sat 5:15 and 8pm.

Gospel Brunch ★ ⁀ AMERICAN There is no plot, and it's not sanctified, but the live music featuring weekly guest artists is jumping and the all-you-can-eat carving station combines Southern and breakfast foods. The morning show fills first, and they do sell out weeks ahead.

House of Blues, Disney Springs West Side, 1490 E. Buena Vista Dr., Lake Buena Vista. www.houseofblues.com/orlando/gospelbrunch. © **407/934-2583.** $43 adults, $24 kids 3–9. Sun 10:30am and 1pm.

Hoop-Dee-Doo Musical Revue ★★ ⁀ AMERICAN Book 60 days out, not necessarily because it's the best, but because it's Disney's most kid-friendly dinnertainment. Six-performer shows put on a hectic and helter-skelter music-hall carnival of olios and gags, which elementary-school age children usually find riveting, and much quarter is given to trumpeting birthdays and special events. The headlining menu item is ribs served in

pails—enough said? I prefer seats in the balcony, overlooking the stage (the cheapest, anyway; but there is no elevator).

The Campsites at Disney's Fort Wilderness Resort. www.disneyworld.com. ℂ **407/939-1947.** $66–$74 adults, $39–$44 kids 3–9. Shows scheduled from late afternoon to evening, typically 4, 6:15, and 8:30pm.

Wantilan Luau ★★★ 🍴 POLYNESIAN   Universal's weekly 2-hour luau is held in a covered pavilion. It, like Disney's Spirit of Aloha Show, has fire dancers and hula girls aplenty, but it beats the rest for authenticity: Food includes pit-roasted suckling pig with spiced rum–infused pineapple puree, and a catch of the day; Mai Tais are included. Should kids be grossed out by carving flesh off the pig, there's a tamer children's menu. You can walk from the Universal parks. Universal also does the self-explanatory, outdoor music-and-feast **Caribbean Carnaval** at its Sapphire Falls Resort (Fri at 6pm), but the Luau is more fun.

Royal Pacific Resort. www.universalorlando.com. ℂ **407/503-3463.** $71–$91 adults, $36–$51 kids 3–9, free for kids 2 and under. Free parking. Sat 6pm.

CHARACTER DINING

A character meal is a rite of passage. Usually all-you-can-eat and mostly buffet, it guarantees face-to-fur time with beloved costumed characters. Always, *always book ahead*—as soon as you can. If you can't find a slot (bookings open 60 days out at 7am Orlando time), check 24 hours before, when people whose plans have changed cancel before the no-show penalty.

At Disney, meals are themed by location; at Chef Mickey's, they emerge in chef's aprons and do a towel-twirling dance. (Reading that, it sounds like a Chippendales show, not a Chip 'n' Dale show, but it's all preschool-friendly.) The characters (six to eight headliners make appearances) circulate, working the room the way a good host does, and signing autographs. (When necessary, they interact from a safe distance.) This, as you binge on a smorgasbord that would give Jillian Michaels apoplexy—Mickey-shaped waffles topped with M&Ms start your day's first sugar rush.

They're cheaper at hotels than inside theme parks. When a meal is held inside a park, you'll still have to buy an admission ticket. You should also know that the events that serve food buffet-style (health protocols permitting) are much more chaotic than ones at which servers bring your food. For breakfast, try to book the earliest seating available (they'll let you in if it's before opening time) so that by the time you're done, you'll be among the first in line for the rides; you'll also have first crack at the stroller rentals. Tips are not usually included.

Cinderella's Royal Table, inside Magic Kingdom's Cinderella Castle, is the big "get"—that place always sells out 60 days early. Also try Chef Mickey's, which is next door to the Magic Kingdom, Akershus for early starts at Epcot, and the Tusker House for an early day at Animal Kingdom. Less prestigious addresses, such as the Beach Club near Epcot, can be smart choices—they tend not to be as crowded and you're likely to have more one-on-one time with the stars.

At SeaWorld Orlando on weekends and in high season, look for **Breakfast with Elmo and Friends** (*©* **407/545-5500;** $30 adults, $15 kids; 9:15am).

Inside Disney Parks

These are the regular events, but during special seasons, there may be temporary menus that cost more. The theme parks also sell dinner or dessert packages (*©* **407/939-1947**) that get you into a prime viewing area for big shows (Fantasmic!, fireworks, concerts), but those are not character meals.

Akershus Royal Banquet Hall Princess Storybook Dining: Appearances by the Princesses in the Norway section of Epcot. See p. 83. Akershus Royal Banquet Hall, Norway, Epcot. www.disneyworld.com/dining. *©* **407/939-1947.** Meals $49–$59 adults, $29–$35 kids 3–9, plus park admission. All three meals.

Cinderella's Royal Table The most difficult reservation (reserve 60 days ahead at 7am Orlando time) features Cinderella, with possible appearances by her Fairy Godmother and other Princesses. The price includes a wand or a sword for kids (ages 3–9). See p. 67. Cinderella Castle, Fantasyland, The Magic Kingdom. www.disneyworld.com/dining. *©* **407/939-1947.** Meals $45–$80 adults, $35–$65 kids, according to meal and season, plus park admission. Breakfast, lunch, and dinner.

The Crystal Palace ☛ Winnie the Pooh and his friends, and a visible kitchen. See p. 66. Crystal Palace, Main Street, U.S.A., The Magic Kingdom. www. disneyworld.com/dining. *©* **407/939-1947.** Buffet $34–$47 adults, $20–$28 kids, plus park admission. All three meals.

Dining with an Imagineer ☛ When your kids have outgrown furry friends, there's still this occasionally scheduled exceptional mealtime meet-and-greet. Over a four-course meal, groups no larger than 10 or 11 hang out with a longtime Disney Imagineer—an art director, designer, or engineer—and have the chance to ask them anything about the mechanics of the resort. Once a month, there's a dinner at Citricos at the Grand Floridian. Both are incredibly hard to get into—start trying 180 days ahead. Hollywood Brown Derby, Disney's Hollywood Studios. www.disneyworld.com/dining. *©* **407/939-1947.** $89 per person, plus park admission (lunch version), tax and tip not included; kids 13 and under not recommended. Mon, Wed, Fri.

Donald's Dining Safari This explorer-themed buffet features appearances by Donald, Daisy, Mickey, and Goofy. The lunch and dinner menus are mildly international (vegetable tandoori, samosas, etc.) but not too jarring for most kids' palates. See p. 116. Tusker House Restaurant, Africa, Disney's Animal Kingdom. www.disneyworld.com/dining. *©* **407/939-1947.** $47 adults, $28 kids 3–9, plus park admission. Breakfast, lunch, and dinner.

Garden Grill Appearances by Mickey, Chip 'n' Dale, and Pluto. One-on-one time for this one is above average. See p. 87. Garden Grill, The Land, Epcot. www.disneyworld.com/dining. ℂ **407/939-1947.** Meals $32–$47 adults, $19–$28 kids 3–9, plus park admission. Breakfast, lunch, and dinner.

Hollywood & Vine This one, called **Disney Junior Play 'N Dine,** usually has Goofy, Vampirina, and Fancy Nancy. But during peak school holiday periods, lunch and dinner are hosted by Minnie, Mickey, and friends (the dinner theme changes; look for **Minnie's Seasonal Dining**). See p. 104. Hollywood & Vine, Echo Lake, Disney's Hollywood Studios. www.disneyworld.com/dining. ℂ **407/939-1947.** Buffet $34–$50 adults, $20–$30 kids, plus park admission.

Park Admission Not Required

You don't have to be a guest of any particular hotel, or pay park admission, for these meet-and-greet meals. These may also be easier to book. Disney's Grand Floridian resort does a super-luxe **Perfectly Princess Tea** (ℂ **407/939-1947**) with a guest appearance by Aurora; it costs $334 for two and includes goodies like a doll and bracelets, but it isn't a full meal.

Breakfast à la Art Appearances by Mickey, Minnie, Donald, and Daisy at a rooftop restaurant with a view. Topolino's Terrace, Disney's Riviera Resort. www.disneyworld.com/dining. ℂ **407/939-1947.** Breakfast $42 adults, $27 kids 3–9.

Cape May Café Minnie's Beach Bash: Appearances by Goofy, Minnie, Donald, and Daisy Duck. If you can't snag a reservation to other character meals, you can often secure this one. Cape May Café, Disney's Beach Club Resort. www.disneyworld.com/dining. ℂ **407/939-1947.** Breakfast $42 adults, $27 kids 3–9.

Chef Mickey's ☛ The most popular breakfast outside park gates, next door to the Magic Kingdom and beneath the indoor path of the monorail, is served by Mickey, Goofy, Donald Duck, and Pluto. Chef Mickey's, Disney's Contemporary Resort. www.disneyworld.com/dining. ℂ **407/939-1947.** Breakfast, brunch, dinner $41–$52 adults, $25–$31 kids 3–9.

Cinderella's Happily Ever After Dinner ☛ Appearances by Cinderella, Prince Charming, and others. Prices surge in peak season. **Supercalifragilistic Breakfast** is in the same space. 1900 Park Fare, Disney's Grand Floridian Resort and Spa. www.disneyworld.com/dining. ℂ **407/939-1947.** Dinner $39–$56 adults, $25–$31 kids 3–9.

Good Morning Breakfast with Goofy & His Pals Appearances by Goofy and friends, who (shh!) usually include Mickey and Minnie. Strongly recommended for the high-quality buffet and lots of character face time that comes with being uncrowded. Includes a free digital download of a photo with characters. 10100 Dream Tree Blvd. Ravello, Four Seasons Resort Orlando at Walt Disney World. www.fourseasons.com/orlando. ℂ **407/313-7777.** $46 adults, $24 kids 3–12, including photos. Breakfast Thurs ☛, Sat 7–11am.

'Ohana Character Breakfast   Family-style meal with appearances by Mickey, Pluto, Lilo, and Stitch. Disney's Polynesian Resort. www.disneyworld.com/dining. ℂ **407/939-1947.** Breakfast $31–$39 adults, $20–$25 kids 3–9.

Story Book Dining ☙   This one in a forest lodge-like setting is for Snow White, the Seven Dwarfs, and the Evil Queen. (It's safe to eat the apples.) Artist Point, Disney's Wilderness Lodge. www.disneyworld.com/dining. ℂ **407/939-1947.** Dinner $55 adults, $33 kids 3–9.

Supercalifragilistic Breakfast   Appearances by a variety of characters, including Mary Poppins, Alice, and the Mad Hatter. **Cinderella's Happily Ever After Dinner** is in the same space. 1900 Park Fare, Disney's Grand Floridian Resort and Spa. www.disneyworld.com/dining. ℂ **407/939-1947.** Breakfast $45 adults, $29 kids 3–9.

Trattoria al Forno ☙   Called Bon Voyage, this meal's twist is that the romantic couples from *The Little Mermaid* and *Tangled* are your hosts. When you're done, you can enter Epcot (if you have a ticket) via its side door. Trattoria al Forno, Disney's BoardWalk. www.disneyworld.com. ℂ **407/939-5277.** Breakfast $34 adults, $20 kids 3–9.

Wonderland Tea Party ☙   An apt choice if you don't want to commit to an entire meal; kids sip apple juice "tea" with Alice, the Mad Hatter, and her other fanciful friends. The hotel is beside Magic Kingdom, and you can walk to it. 1900 Park Fare, Disney's Grand Floridian Resort and Spa. www.disneyworld.com/dining. ℂ **407/824-1391.** $49 per person. Mon–Fri 2–3pm.

Universal Orlando

In addition to these, Universal sometimes does ghoulish "scareactor" meals around Halloween (Sept–Oct; $50 one and all). But character dining isn't as popular here as it is at Disney, so check ahead to ensure they're happening at all on the days of your visit.

Despicable Me Character Breakfast ☙   Start the day with Gru, Margo, Edith, Agnes, and the Minions, if you like such mayhem. Tahitian Room, Loews Royal Pacific Resort. www.universalorlando.com. ℂ **407/224-2690.** Breakfast $35 adults, $21 kids 3–9. Sat at 8, 9:30, and 11am.

The Grinch & Friends Character Breakfast   The Grinch has friends? Seuss Landing, Islands of Adventure. www.universalorlando.com. ℂ **407/224-3663.** Dinner $50 adults, $25 kids 3–9, plus park admission. Variable schedule around the holidays.

Marvel Character Dinner ☙   Hard to imagine crusty Wolverine gladly taking snapshots with the kiddos over supper, yet there he is along with Captain America, Spider-Man, Cyclops, Storm, and Rogue (don't let her touch anything). Cafe 4, Islands of Adventure. www.universalorlando.com. ℂ **407/224-3663.** Dinner $50 adults, $25 kids 3–9, plus park admission. Thurs–Sun at 5pm.

ORLANDO'S HOTELS

Orlando has around 133,000 hotel rooms—37,000 of them combined at Disney and Universal alone. As you can imagine, competition can be fierce, yet at properties where heavy turnover is a given, quality can nevertheless be lax. A little too often, you find yourself in a hotel shrugging and saying, "Eh, it does the job." We can help you do better. We'll show you the good places.

Most of Central Florida's monolithic architecture steals and inflates Europe's palatial traditions, often on such a scale that even a Texan would blush. But Orlando's resorts rarely achieve true opulence, and hotels that pass themselves off as "deluxe" are actually just three-star. You usually won't even find a minibar in your room. Often, when you pay for a fine Orlando hotel, you're just paying for mood.

Following are a few key questions to ask:

How much space do I want? If you have kids with you, will a single room supply the elbow room everyone needs? Disney's most affordable rooms, for example, have a maximum occupancy of four people in two double beds, so if your group exceeds that number, you'll have to rent two rooms or upgrade to something more expensive. For most families, renting a home or condo solves the space issue, and usually for less money.

Will I need a car? Unless you're a Disney-only type of person, you should have one. Cars enable you eat cheaper and see both Disney *and* Harry Potter as well as Orlando's many other appealing diversions. No car, no freedom.

How much time will I spend at my accommodations? If your schedule is full, you'll only use a room to hit the sack. Do you *really* need a fitness center after slogging miles around theme parks for 15 hours a day? No, you don't.

Then grill your potential hotel: **Is there a resort fee?** It's common, and it dramatically increases the cost. **Is there a parking fee?** It's another way to hide the true price of a stay. **Is breakfast included?** If it's "continental," it could be instant coffee and a mound of stale muffins. **What's the view?** Properties might boast a fireworks view—but neglect to mention it's from 8 miles away.

FINDING THE BEST RATES

Ask any hotel what it charges, and you're unlikely to get a straight answer. They delight in changing rates according to how full they are. As a rule of thumb, prices are highest when kids are out of school (summers, spring break), and lowest in the light periods such as late January, September, October, and early December. Weekends see slightly higher prices, too, because Florida residents drop by. The prices in this guide represent an average rate.

The good news is that Orlando's average nightly rate is usually around $110 (in the hard times of 2020, it was $86.46), which is cheaper than the national average, so you're already working at an advantage. Primary websites that collect quotes from a variety of sources (whether they be hotel chains or other websites) include **HotelsCombined.com**, **Booking.com**, and **Kayak.com**. Always canvas multiple sites. The bidding areas on Hotwire.com and Price line.com are more likely to get you the best rates in the month before you travel; hotels hold out for higher prices until then. Then call the local number of the hotel, not the toll-free one (that usually connects to a switchboard far away), to see if they'll do even better. Also check **Hotelcoupons.com** for discounted rates for some of the cheapest motels in town (no promises about quality, and some hotels frequently refuse to honor the coupon rates if they're at 75%–80% occupancy).

Another reliable way to get a cheaper room is to use an **air/hotel package.** No domestic company operates charter flights to Orlando anymore, but several packagers buy cheap hotel rooms in bulk and sell them with scheduled airfare. Check **Funjet** (www.funjet.com; © **888/558-6654**), **Lastminute.com** (© **866/ 999-8942**), as well as some of the vacation wings of major airlines such as

---

Theme Park Shuttles: Going Your Way?

Almost all of the hotels located off theme park property tout some kind of "free" shuttle service to the major parks (often covered by a resort fee). When they work, they're a dream, but you need to know that most are restrictive. Many run once or twice a day, on their schedule, and you must book ahead, sometimes by 24 hours or more. A typical hotel shuttle may leave for the Magic Kingdom twice a morning and return at, say, 5 and 10pm, a rigid schedule that may cost you a fireworks viewing. Also, many hotels provide shuttles to only one area (Disney or Universal/SeaWorld) but not the other. **Ask.**

Many hotels share shuttles. They can be dirty, worn, and crowded, and you might have to stop at up to a half-dozen other places on your way. Not great if you're hungry, thirsty, tired, or your kids are restless.

Before settling on a hotel based on its advertised rides, ask questions:

- What time do they leave and return?
- Which theme parks are *not* covered or incur a fee?
- How many other hotels share the same shuttle?
- If the shuttle fills up, do you send another one for me?
- Is there a fee? (That $30 for two could have been used to rent a car.)
- How far ahead do I have to reserve?

Southwest Vacations (www.southwestvacations.com; ℂ **800/243-8372**), **Jet-Blue Getaways** (www.jetbluevacations.com; ℂ **844/528-2229**), **Delta Vacations** (www.deltavacations.com; ℂ **800/800-1504**), and **American Airlines Vacations** (www.aavacations.com; ℂ **800/321-2121**). Internationally, **Virgin Holidays** (www.virginholidays.co.uk) is a huge player, with lots of customer service reps available on the ground should things go wrong. Increasingly, these websites may sell hotel-only deals using their negotiated rates. Use properties highlighted on specials pages, though, because prices often come out higher in searches.

Few of these players will truly discount a Disney hotel (they may show up on the **Hotel Tonight** late booking app, though). If you want a Disney hotel, price be damned, book it separately from tickets or airfare—"room-only," on a separate phone call directly to Disney—because it gives you more scheduling flexibility with tickets and room-only cancellation rules are far kinder. Don't accept *any* package from a Disney receptionist, even if it's for harmless trinkets, because package rules are worse than room-only rules. Disney packages subject you to a $200 fee for cancellations made 30 to 2 days ahead, force you to pay in full within 30 days of your trip, and may even add trip insurance by default; room-only bookings have no penalties for cancellations made more than 5 days ahead (6 days if you booked online). Disney packages will also levy charges for any changes—even calling to add a discount code or shift nights could add $65 in surcharges! When it comes to non-Disney hotels, though, package away, because that's where great deals live.

What You'll Get for Your Money

Every hotel in this book has a swimming pool (because of liability issues, few are much deeper than 5 ft.), Wi-Fi, and ample air-conditioning, and almost every hotel offers shuttles to at least some theme parks, although fares may apply and they may be slower than garden slugs. Every hotel is also kid-friendly. So friendly that you should expect even top-end places to crawl with scampering children hopped up on a perpetual vacation-permitted sugar buzz, and no minibars in your room to take the edge off. If you crave peace, steer toward a rental home or a splurgy resort that leans toward the convention trade, in which case the rugrats will be replaced by phone-wielding conference-goers in chinos. If you stay in a unit with a kitchen, you may be in a timeshare that was rented to you because it was empty—this is normal, and it can be a good deal, but you may have to fend off "welcome" calls that are overtures to purchasing one. *Warning:* Until it's declared illegal, many big hotels still engage in the sleazy American practice of **resort fees,** which vastly inflates what you pay—we warn you about those in bold letters. The highest in town is now $45/night. Isn't that awful?

Beware of believing overly positive online reviews for Orlando hotels! Timeshare owners overpraise properties to convince people to stay there, and Disney hotels are overpraised because they're Disney and you know how starstruck that makes some people.

How to Save on Lodging

No matter the time of year, **Mouse Savers.com** and **TheMouseForLess.com** post codes of all current known Disney discounts. In general, AAA and military service may help cut costs. Only on rare occasions do you see Disney hotels discounted by name on third-party sites, but in quiet seasons they may appear with their names cloaked on sites like Hotwire and Priceline.

- **Come when kids are in school.** Hotel prices are trimmed then.
- **Avoid holidays.** If the kids are out of school, you might pay double.
- **Make sure the room rules permit everyone in your party.** If you go over the guest maximum, you'll have to rent two rooms, doubling costs.
- **Always get a quote directly from the hotel.** It might be lower.
- **See what's on offer from a packager.** They have purchasing power.
- **Plug Kissimmee into Web searches.** It's cheaper than Orlando.
- **Good locations have food options.** Are there affordable restaurants nearby or are you stuck eating overpriced hotel food?
- **Ask if there's a discount.** Disney reservationists will tell only if asked. But when Disney does deal, it gives great stuff away, like free meal plans.

Public service announcement: Among theme-park properties, Universal has the cheapest on-site rooms. Its Endless Summer Resort (p. 256) charges $132 for a suite sleeping six—so you can get a multi-bedroom suite at Universal for less than the cheapest available standard single room sleeping four at Disney. (Stay there and you'll get free shuttles to Universal, but you'll need a car to get to Disney.)

Following are the categories and price ranges for this chapter. These are almost unfair since so many hotels pretend to be cheaper by charging resort fees on top of posted rates:

- **Inexpensive:** Up to $105 a night
- **Moderate:** $106 to $175
- **Expensive:** $176 and up

Note: Prices in this book don't include taxes, which for hotels add as much as 14.5 percent to your bill depending on the municipality in which you're staying.

WALT DISNEY WORLD HOTELS

Some people don't mind spending twice Orlando's going rate so they can be on Disney property near the resort's storied "magic," although they are usually hard-pressed to explain what that precisely means. Disney has an active policy of making non-resort guests second-class citizens by putting them at a planning disadvantage, although that subtle persecution has eased in recent years. It's also worth noting that Disney hotels tend to promote or hire from within, and over time, that has caused staff to become noticeably out of step with customer service standards in the outside world.

But strictly from a non-pixie-dusted, consumer-advice standpoint, there are advantages and disadvantages to saying on property in one of Disney's extremely busy hotels.

DISNEY PRICING SEASONS

Unlike most hotels, which price dynamically, Walt Disney World's hotel rates are fixed by a calendar. The seasons are no longer named by Disney, but they generally fall into six categories. They are, in descending order of expense: **Holiday, Peak, Summer, Regular, Fall,** and **Value,** and even those are parsed into levels, so you could easily pay several different nightly rates during the same stay. The major price spikes are around spring break, Easter, and the late December holidays—put simply, when more people can travel to Disney World.

Likewise, there are three categories of Disney hotel: **Deluxe, Moderate,** and **Value.** Ergo, for the cheapest room, book a Value room in a Value period.

When you search for rooms, you'll also be offered apartment-like units. These are for **Disney Vacation Club** members (explained more on p. 233). DVC units are drastically more expensive than a home rental of a corresponding size, so unless you happen across a deal you love (it's rare), Frommer's doesn't think they're the smartest way to go, so we don't go deeply into the DVC properties here—only the hotels.

PRICING SEASONS The dates for each season shift annually and are tweaked per property, but they follow the same pattern on the calendar.

The schedule for prices generally shakes out like this for a Value hotel room in an All-Star resort, with tax. These are the bottom lines of the lowest-priced standard Disney room of each time period, including tax—the higher rates in each bracket fall on higher-demand days such as weekends. So this is the least you can hope to pay by staying within Disney:

- **Value season:** Jan to mid-Feb, mid-Aug to Sept. Value price: $119–$171.
- **Regular season:** Late Feb to early Mar, late Apr to May. Value price: $162–$215.
- **Summer season:** June to July. Value price: $185–$219.
- **Peak season** (including most holiday periods): Mid-Feb, mid-Mar to mid-Apr, mid-Dec. Value price: $193–$209.
- **Holiday season:** End of Dec, New Year's. Value price: $246–$254.

STANDARD AMENITIES All Disney hotels, regardless of class, have touches that provide relief for families, including big pools and shallow kiddie pools, coin laundries, and playgrounds. Nearly all rooms have two double beds unless you pay for something more (like a bunk or a pullout), but no microwave. Wi-Fi is free. There will always be somewhere to eat, although at Value resorts it will be a food court and room service will be pizza. Disney shuttle buses (p. 34) serve all resorts for free, and every property is protected by gated security. And, of course, every resort has at least one souvenir store. Check-in time is usually 3pm (you can use the pool while you wait) and you must check out by 11am (and use the pool for the rest of the day).

Some benefits you might have heard about in the past have been recently cut: Extra Magic Hours, advance Fastpass+ reservations, and Disney's Magical Express have all been eliminated.

Note that Disney does not charge resort fees, but it exacts such a premium rate, the effect on your budget can be much worse.

Walt Disney World & Lake Buena Vista Hotels

Aloft Orlando Lake Buena Vista **12**
B Resort & Spa **14**
Candlewood Suites Orlando-Lake Buena Vista **10**
Disney's Animal Kingdom Lodge **24**
Disney's Beach Club/ Disney's Yacht Club **21**
Disney's Boardwalk Inn **23**
Disney's Caribbean Beach Resort **22**

Disney's Contemporary Resort **4**
Disney's Coronado Springs Resort **19**
Disney's Fort Wilderness Resort & Campground **6**
Disney's Grand Floridian Resort & Spa **2**
Disney's Polynesian Village Resort **3**
Disney's Wilderness Lodge **5**

Disney's Port Orleans Resort **8**
Drury Plaza Hotel Orlando Lake Buena Vista **13**
Four Seasons Resort Orlando at Walt Disney World Resort **7**
Hyatt Regency Grand Cypress Resort **9**
JW Marriott Orlando Bonnet Creek Resort & Spa **15**
Shades of Green Resort **1**
Signia by Hilton Orlando Bonnet Creek **16**
Sonesta ES Suites Lake Buena Vista—Orlando **11**
Star Wars: Galactic Starcruiser Hotel **18**
Waldorf Astoria Orlando **17**
Walt Disney World Swan and Dolphin **20**

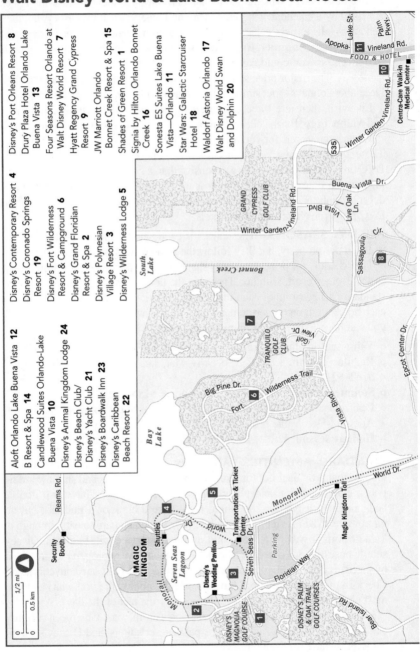

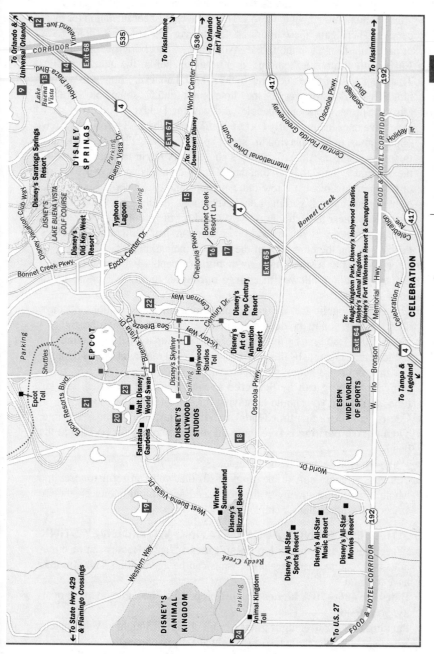

YAY! THE BENEFITS OF STAYING ON DISNEY PROPERTY

- For those without cars, there's **free** bus, monorail, new gondola, and ferry transportation throughout the resort. This is the biggest consideration for most people. (Then again, these things are free to *everyone* at Disney, hotel guest or not.) Guests can use the Disney World app to check transit wait times.

- **Early Entry** into the theme parks 30 minutes before the general public. That's not a lot of time to do much, though, and not everything will be running. This perk is for every Disney hotel guest (and for some hotels around Disney Springs), but only people who pay for Deluxe resorts (the most expensive ones that regularly cost $600–$800 a night) will be offered a few opportunities to keep playing in "select" parks on "select" nights for longer than posted closing time. (The day's chosen park might not match up with the one you planned to be in that day.) Guests at more expensive resorts are also targeted to receive a few other limited, line-based perks, such as the right to book a few Lightning Lane reservations, but the cash value of those won't come near the extra amount you paid for the room.

- Disney transit drops you at the Magic Kingdom gates. Other hotel shuttles deposit you on the other side of the lake, by the parking lot.

- **Every room has a small balcony or patio** (except at Value resorts).

- Disney guests are allowed to **charge purchases** throughout the resort to your room.

- The general public has a right to make restaurant reservations 60 days ahead, but if you're holding a resort reservation, you have the right to increase that lead time by the length of your stay (up to 10 days), giving you a slight edge. Obviously, this perk is useless if you make your hotel booking less than 2 months before your vacation.

- In-park **shopping can be delivered to your room.** ☛ (The delivery lag time is such that you should be staying for at least 2 more nights.)

- Guests get three or four timed **kids' activities** a day, albeit some at a charge.

- **Theme park parking is free** (but you still have to pay for parking at the hotel).

- **Wake-up calls** feature Disney characters.

- You can purchase soft drink **mugs** ($20) that you can refill for free the whole time you're staying at the hotel (and not a minute longer—they're embedded with computer chips).

BOO! THESE THINGS ABOUT STAYING WITH DISNEY STINK

- **"Free" resort transportation doesn't mean "fast."** Routes can be circuitous and require changing buses, waits can be aggravating, and you may have to stand.

- **Rates are 40%–70% higher** than off-property rooms of comparable quality. So is food.

- **Parking fees for overnight guests** aren't cheap: $15/night at Value hotels, $20/night at Moderate hotels, $25/night at Deluxe ones.

- **Stingy occupancy limits.** Room rates are quoted for two people. For more people, add $15–$35 a night (depending on the resort category) for each person age 18 and over up to the room's stated maximum capacity, so a $119 Value room will in fact be $149 if four people 18 and over stay in it. (One child age 2 and under can stay without being counted toward the occupancy limit.) Value and Moderate resorts cap occupancy at four (not including a babe in a crib) and Deluxe cap at five. Families larger than four must rent two units, doubling the expense, but if you have seven or more people to accommodate, it gets ugly.

o It's **hard to call the front desk;** you'll usually be routed to the main Disney number with epic waits. You have to go in person. Baggage service may also be impossible.

o It's also hard to request a specific room ahead of time; usually, you'll get your assignment at the check-in desk. In busy times, families with multiple rooms may get split apart.

o The most affordable Disney hotels **don't have restaurants.** They have food courts (burgers, sandwiches, pasta—all at theme park prices of around $14) and the only room service item is pizza. This is less of a problem if you intend to save money by eating off property anyway.

o Disney resorts are so large (often 2,000 rooms) that **lines,** even for a cup of coffee, are an endless nuisance and **sprawling layouts are confusing** to small children, to say nothing of their weary parents. Disney has turned the failing into profit: It charges more for "Preferred" rooms nearer the lobby.

o The more affordable a room is, the more you could use a rental car. The most expensive resorts are beside the best parks, but Value rooms are about as **far from the action** as many off-property hotels. The Value resorts, in particular, are a good 15-minute drive from the Magic Kingdom (no farther than a decent vacation home).

o **Safes** are tiny (laptops won't fit). In-room cooking is made difficult in that the most affordable rooms lack **microwaves** or **coffeemakers.**

DISNEY VACATION CLUB

Disney sells timeshares, too. Because this isn't a real estate guide, there's no need to explain the fact that after you crunch the numbers, **Disney Vacation Club (DVC)** is economical only for people who never want to vacation anywhere that isn't Disney. DVC really needs to slow its roll, because it's grafting properties onto all the major hotels and ruining their vibes and profiles. DVC-only properties include **BoardWalk Villas, Old Key West,** the **Riviera Resort,** and **Saratoga Springs Resort & Spa,** with its **Treehouse Villas** built on platforms above the ground. These units are heavily promoted around the resort and even inside the theme parks themselves, which Walt surely would have detested as a fantasy-killer. The company does rent vacant villa units to walk-up customers who have no intention of signing on any dotted lines, but the best ones are usually claimed by the time you book, and they're never the most cost-effective avenue. One-bedrooms at the Contemporary Resort's Bay Lake Tower can cost over $1,000—*a night.* Polynesian Village bungalows are sumptuous, and you can see Cinderella Castle from the spa tub on your private deck—but they cost $2,500 to $3,400 a night. This is crazy-pants. I cannot in

Star Wars–Galactic Starcruiser

Disney's groundbreaking **Star Wars–Galactic Starcruiser** hotel, behind Hollywood Studios, invites guests to roleplay as if they're passengers on the deep space version of a luxury cruise ship. They sleep in "cabins" with bunk-bed pods and windows that look out to animated planets and stars. Every guest is given a storyline to follow throughout the mock vessel, murder mystery-style, and they even get shuttled by a similarly theatrical vehicle into a side door of Galaxy's Edge for a day at Hollywood Studios. Suriks's blade, it sounds like the coolest idea in hotels since pillows! And it's expected to open in 2022. When it does, mankind will officially max out the meaning of the words *immersive* and *experience*—but very few of us will ever see the inside of this ship, because there are reportedly only around 100 rooms. Two-night stays START at $4,809 for two people, $5,300 for two adults with one child, and $5,999 for a family of four. Think of that: $6,000 for a family in one room for 2 nights. (If you're a Disney stockholder, you're probably laughing like Salacious B. Crumb right now.)

good conscience suggest that a family of average means spend that. I have, though, now informed you they're available. Moving on . . .

DELUXE RESORTS

No one who has experienced a true luxury hotel can seriously attest that Disney's quality standards compare. They're three-star hotels in fancy dress, and only VIPs get true attentive treatment. Sure, they have sit-down restaurants, spas, lounges, and big pools. But rooms and service are nothing special unless you're in a top-tier room. What Disney's Deluxe hotels mostly have is uplifting theming—a prevailing mood—that makes a stay fun, and it's a genuine thrill to be so near a theme park, to get such fantastic views of Magic Kingdom or African animals—there's just something special about it.

Most Deluxes (maximum guests per standard room: four unless noted) enable you to dart to the parks easily. Three are by Magic Kingdom on the monorail line: the Contemporary (the most iconic), the Grand Floridian (the fanciest), and the Polynesian (the most private). A fourth, Wilderness Lodge, is linked to Magic Kingdom by ferry, while the Beach Club, Yacht Club, and Board-Walk are walking distance from Epcot's side door. Only Animal Kingdom Lodge is marooned by roads, but it has other perks that counterbalance that.

For an extra $150 to $200, Disney sells "Club Level" concierge-style rooms with a private lounge stocked with free continental breakfast, snacks, and beverages including champagne. In some hotels, it entitles you to better views or to buy additional experiences, such as a sunset tour of the savannah at Animal Kingdom Lodge.

For ease, the following price ranges include tax.

Disney's Animal Kingdom Lodge ★★★ No grander lodge ever existed on the African veldt, and the higher tariff returns to you in the form of a 24-hour safari and lots of themed activities. The main part of the hotel, Jambo House, is where the hotel rooms are (Kidani House is for Disney

Vacation Club units). Hotel rooms are outfitted with a dark wooden look and hand-carved furniture; if you've got a Savannah view (they start around $500—careful that you don't accidentally book a Standard one overlooking the parking lot or pool), when you look out of your window, you'll hopefully see whatever genial African animal is loping by at that moment, be it a giraffe, an ostrich, a zebra, or a warthog. You'll find a game-viewing guide beside your room-service menu. Because animals tend to be active in the early morning, when families are gearing up for their days, the idea works well. Anyone can visit, even if they're not staying here; there's even a public animal viewing area straight out the back door of the awe-inspiring vaulted lobby. Its principal drawback is its distance from everything except for Animal Kingdom; all connections are by road. Standard room: 344 square feet.

2901 Osceola Pkwy., Bay Lake. www.disneyworld.com. © **407/934-7639** or 407/938-3000. 1,293 units. $434–$1,023 non-club standard. 2-adult maximum. Standard room: max. 4 people; deluxe room: max. 5 people. Extra person $35. Children 17 and younger stay free in parent's room. Parking $25/day (self), $33/day (valet). **Amenities:** 2 restaurants; cafe; Club Level rooms; health club & limited spa; heated outdoor pool; kids' pool; room service; free Wi-Fi.

Disney's Beach Club/Disney's Yacht Club ★★★ Both excellent choices with 381-square-foot rooms, these adjoining sisters are on a pond across from the BoardWalk entertainment area (you'll need it, since the hotels are short on decent choices for cheap food) and a short stroll away from the International Gateway exit of Epcot's World Showcase, which brings the fun close to your room, although you can't watch Epcot's evening show from it. Their shared 3-acre pool area, Stormalong Bay, has sandy shores and the crazy Flying Jib waterslide that forms a straightaway shooting off the mast of a pirate ship. (It's easily the best pool on Disney property, and it's restricted to guests.) The difference between the two is nearly negligible—they're connected and many guests think they're one giant hotel, but the Yacht Club has slightly nicer furnishings, bigger balconies, attracts slightly fewer families with kids, is a tad quieter, and is a 10-minute stroll from Epcot instead of 5 from the Beach Club. Other than that, it's a toss-up. Both of them have layouts that confuse kids.

1800 Epcot Resorts Blvd., Lake Buena Vista. www.disneyworld.com. © **407/934-7639** or 407/934-8000. Beach: 583 units. Yacht: 630 units. $504–$991 non-club standard. Standard room: max. 5 people. Extra person $35. Children 17 and younger stay free in parent's room. Parking $25/day (self), $33/day (valet). **Amenities:** 2 restaurants; grill; 3 bars; Club Level rooms; character meals; health club & small spa; 3-acre pool and play area; 2 outdoor heated pools; kids' pool; room service; 2 lighted tennis courts; boat rental; free Wi-Fi.

Disney's BoardWalk Inn ★★ The theme here, in a property split between DVC owners and nightly trade, is ostensibly turn-of-the-20th-century Atlantic City (not tatty, present-day Atlantic City), which translates to touches such as a miniature carousel in the lobby, vintage flip movie viewers in common areas, and beachball-patterned carpets in the halls. Rooms are recently renovated and a fair 371 square feet. The Luna Pool's 200-foot slide evokes a wooden roller coaster, but I prefer the quieter, tucked-away pool near Building 1 on the east side of the property. You might hit the Belle Vue Lounge to buy bagels, muffins, and coffee in the morning and cocktails in the evening, but really, you stay here because the baked goods and ice cream of the BoardWalk are right outside and the side door to Epcot is a 10-minute lakefront stroll away.

1800 Epcot Resorts Blvd., Lake Buena Vista. www.disneyworld.com. © **407/934-7639** or 407/934-8000. 379 units. $555–$1,026 non-club standard. Standard room: max. 5 people. Extra person $25. Children 17 and younger stay free in parent's room. Parking $25/day (self), $33/day (valet). **Amenities:** Restaurant; bar; lounge; Club Level rooms; health club & small spa; 3-acre pool and play area; 3 outdoor heated pools; kids' pool; whirlpool; room service; boat rental; bike rental; free Wi-Fi.

Disney's Contemporary Resort ★★★   Nothing says, "I'm at Disney World" more than the awesome sight of that monorail sweeping dramatically through the Contemporary's glassy Grand Canyon Concourse, which it does every few minutes on its way to and from Magic Kingdom. The hotel, one of the first two to open in 1971, is now a midcentury architectural treasure, and indicative of the revolutionary methods that Walt Disney World hoped to pioneer: The United States Steel Corporation helped design it; its modular rooms were prefabricated down the road and slotted into place by crane. The current look: modern and white with *Incredibles* accents following a 2021 renovation. Best rooms (422 sq. ft., among the largest standard rooms at Disney) are high up in the coveted A-framed Contemporary Tower, but there are stylish low-level Garden Rooms along Bay Lake, too, near the surprisingly blah pool, that are about $150 cheaper. Rooms on the west of the tower face Magic Kingdom itself (and an intervening parking lot)—the ninth floor has the *ne plus ultra* of Disney views—and every water-view room takes in the nightly parade that floats after dark. Even if you can't stay here, this is the best hotel to tour. Drop by via monorail to see the 90-foot-tall mosaics of children by the visionary Imagineer Mary Blair, which encapsulate the late 1960s futurist optimism out of which the resort was born.

4600 N. World Dr., Lake Buena Vista. www.disneyworld.com. © **407/939-6244** or 407/824-1000. 1,008 units. $518–$1,202 non-club room. Standard room: max. 5 people. Garden View room: max. 4 people. Extra person $35. Children 17 and younger stay free in parent's room. Parking $25/day (self), $33/day (valet). **Amenities:** 3 restaurants; grill; 4 lounges; Club Level rooms; character meals; small health club & spa; 2 outdoor heated pools; kids' pool; watersports rental; free Wi-Fi.

Disney's Grand Floridian Resort & Spa ★★   It's strange to spend $700 a night on a hotel room and then have to walk outside in the rain to reach the building it's in, but from a value standpoint, that tells you a lot. This is the Disney hotel with snob appeal, since the whole point is to put on a costume of exclusivity and luxury (two things Walt despised, which is why *his* hotels had generic themes) and brag about it when you get home. So it's encrusted with upper-class affectation, from high tea to a pianist tinkling away in an outrageously pretty lobby (chandeliers, glass dome, wedding-cake balconies).

It can't help but strum your imagination of what a true Victorian grande dame hotel might have felt like, but anyone can enjoy that on a day visit without paying insane rates for what amounts to a three-star room. There *are* vacation-making pluses I'd unreservedly celebrate here if money were no object, such as next-door access to Magic Kingdom by foot, ferry, or monorail; gourmet restaurants; careful staff; and an atmosphere more romantic than at any other Disney hotel—in fact, you'll probably have to dodge a few wedding parties. Typical standard rooms are 440 square feet, although rooms with dormer windows are smaller.

4401 Floridian Way, Lake Buena Vista. www.disneyworld.com. ℭ **407/934-7639** or 407/824-3000. 867 units. $737–$1,502 non-club doubles. Standard room: max. 5 people. Extra person $35. Children 17 and younger stay free in parent's room. Parking $25/day (self), $33/day (valet). **Amenities:** 5 restaurants; grill; character meals; Club Level rooms; health club & spa; heated outdoor pool; kids' pool; room service; 2 lighted tennis courts; watersports rental; free Wi-Fi.

Disney's Polynesian Village Resort ★★★

The 25-acre hotel, thickly planted and torch-lit by night, was one of the first two hotels built here, back when the South Pacific tiki craze was still swinging. The longhouse-style thatched-roof complex remains one of the most transporting of the Disney resorts, and it just underwent a major renewal. Only the most expensive rooms have a view of the Magic Kingdom across the Seven Seas Lagoon (swimming in it is not allowed, but the pool area is huge and lush), but most have greenery views. The Polynesian is a notch above for families as there's an on-site child-care facility, the monorail is steps away, and rooms are on the big side, sleeping five. An easy favorite. The downside is availability: Several buildings have been allocated as Disney Vacation Club "Studio" units, reducing the standard room count by several hundred, so it's harder than ever to enjoy this hotel now. When available, those studios cost about $20 more than a standard room but include a minifridge and a microwave. Make a detour off the lobby for Trader Sam's Grog Grotto (p. 278), one of the coolest cocktail bars in town.

1600 Seven Seas Dr., Lake Buena Vista. www.disneyworld.com. ℭ **407/939-6244** or 407/824-2000. 484 standard units, 360 Studios. $618–$1,384 non-club doubles. Standard room: max. 5 people. Extra person $35. Children 17 and younger stay free in parent's room. Parking $25/day (self), $33/day (valet). **Amenities:** 3 restaurants; cafe; tiki bar; Club Level rooms; nearby health club & spa (at Grand Floridian); 2 heated outdoor pools; kids' pool; character meals; room service; watersports rental; gas grills; free 7:30pm marshmallow roast; free 9pm outdoor movie; free Wi-Fi.

Disney's Wilderness Lodge ★★

This effective riff on Yellowstone's woody Old Faithful Lodge, swaddled by oaks and pines, is picturesque and the least expensive of the Deluxe category. The Magic Kingdom, 10 minutes away by ferry, is the only thing easy to reach if you don't have your own car (the other parks involve a laborious bus trek). Most of its tricks are in its dramatic atrium lobby: giant stone hearth, springs that flow to a thronged pool area out back—a geyser nearby spouts water 120 feet high on the half-hour from 7am to 10pm. Because of surrounding woods, rooms (340 sq. ft.) are dark, but have adorable rustic touches such as headboards carved with woodland creatures.

901 W. Timberline Dr., Lake Buena Vista. www.disneyworld.com. ℂ **407/934-7639** or 407/938-4300. 909 units. $424–$1,038 non-club standard. Children 17 and younger stay free in parent's room. Standard room: max. 4 people. Extra person $35. Parking $25/day (self), $33/day (valet). **Amenities:** 3 restaurants; Club Level rooms; health club & limited spa; 2 spa tubs; 2 heated outdoor pools; jogging trail; boat rental; kids' pool; room service; free Wi-Fi.

MODERATE RESORTS

The next category up from Value is Moderate. Compared to Value, what do you get for the extra dough? Put simply, the main pools have more elaborate themes with slides, and there are usually a few additional, simple pools; rooms measure 314 square feet instead of 260 square feet (so 2 ft. wider); most have two sinks instead of one (both outside the shower/toilet room); all rooms have a small balcony or patio with seating (though most have no view to speak of); and you can rent a bike or a boat on the premises. The upgrade doesn't win you the right to fit in more people: Rooms mostly fit four (only two adults) plus one child 2 and under, same as the Value class.

The grounds of Moderate properties feel more resortlike when compared to the glorified motels of the Values, but at heart, they're still upgraded motels, with exterior corridors (close your drapes) and windowless bathrooms. You'll still be eating mostly in high-priced food courts located at a building that might be distant from your room. Although the bedrooms aren't much plusher than the Value properties, you will sense more breathing room and personality since Disney has been pouring money into glorifying its Moderate pool areas.

Disney's Caribbean Beach Resort ★ This resort sprawls around a central pond—1½ miles around!—along with the newly constructed Riviera Resort, a DVC property. As you might expect, there's a loose island theme. Rooms (mostly full beds) feel vaguely Polynesian and are the Moderate category's largest (by a little), but water-view rooms don't have balconies. Disney spent a ton theming some rooms to *Pirates of the Caribbean* (beds like ships, carpet like decking) that can add about $45 to a regular room, but they're the farthest from the main buildings. The main Old Port Royale pool area emulates a waterfront Spanish fort and has a giant tippy bucket, so you can see why families favor this property. The resort's principal drawbacks are a lack of elevators, bland food, and a risk of being placed very far from the lobby and pool (preferred rooms cost a little more to put you closer). But there are two new benefits: Guests can walk over to the dining amenities of the new **Disney's Riviera Resort** next door. And this is the best hotel in the Disney Skyliner gondola system, which goes straight to Disney's Hollywood Studios and Epcot in minutes. (For everything else, you need wheels or take DTS.)

900 Cayman Way, Lake Buena Vista. www.disneyworld.com. ℂ **407/934-7639** or 407/934-3400. 2,112 units. $240–$476 standard doubles. Standard room: max. 5 people plus 1 child 2 and under in crib. Extra person $25. Children 17 and younger stay free in parent's room. Parking $20/day. **Amenities:** Restaurant; food court; arcade; heated pool; 6 smaller pools in the villages; kids' pool; free Wi-Fi.

Disney's Coronado Springs Resort ★　Built to attract convention crowds with a vibe to match, it nonetheless has fans for its subdued tone. The well-planted grounds, done in a hacienda style around a pond, are far-flung (some rooms are a 15-minute hike from the lobby, which gets old fast and bewilders children), and rooms, with kings (for two) or queens (for four), have a single sink, as at the Values. The food court is above average, though, as is the pool area (with a 123-foot slide) themed after a Mayan pyramid, and there's a cool alfresco cocktail bar, Three Bridges, hovering in the center of the lagoon. The hotel is 10 minutes' drive from any parks. If you need a room accessible for those with disabilities and the cheaper hotels are out of such units, you can try here, where there is an inventory of 99 accessible rooms. The new (bland-looking) 15-story tower has 500 more rooms (generally $40–$60 more). That gives some guests an option for fairly decent glimpses of Hollywood Studios in the middle distance, but in general the building isn't well positioned for incredible views.

1000 Buena Vista Dr., Lake Buena Vista. www.disneyworld.com. ⓒ **407/934-7639** or 407/939-1000. 1,921 units. $232–$564 doubles. Standard room: max. 4 people plus 1 child 2 and under in crib. Extra person $25. Children 17 and younger stay free in parent's room. Parking $20/day. **Amenities:** Restaurant; grill/food court; arcade; health club & limited spa; 4 outdoor heated pools; kids' pool; free Wi-Fi.

Disney's Fort Wilderness Resort & Campground ★★　Not to be confused with the Wilderness Lodge, an imitation of Yellowstone Lodge, this 780-acre wooded enclave near Magic Kingdom consists of campsites and mobile home–style cabins with decks and grills that sleep six on a mix of beds, pullouts, and bunks. Camping and RV parking under the thick pines are far and away the cheapest and most distinctive way to sleep on property, but it's twice the market rate, and without equipment (tents are $45, cots $6, if a group hasn't booked them first). The nightly marshmallow roast and outdoor Disney film screenings ⌁ are perennial hits.

3520 N. Fort Wilderness Trail, Lake Buena Vista. www.disneyworld.com. ⓒ **407/934-7639** or 407/824-2900. 784 campsites, 408 wilderness cabins. $89–$219 campsite/RV doubles, $414–$789 wilderness cabin doubles. Standard cabin: max. 6 people plus 1 child 2 and under in crib. Children 17 and younger stay free with parents. Parking $20/day. **Amenities:** Restaurant; grill; extensive outdoor activities (archery; fishing; horseback, pony, carriage, and hay rides; campfire programs; boat rental; and more); 2 outdoor heated pools; kids' pool; character dining; 2 lighted tennis courts; free Wi-Fi.

Disney's Port Orleans Riverside and French Quarter ★★　An unwieldy name for an unwieldy property. It's actually two resorts, both built on a canal and awkwardly fused together. The **French Quarter** (1,000 rooms), built along right angles on simulated streets, purports to sort of imitate the real one in New Orleans. **Riverside** (2,048 rooms) is the nicer of the two: Its buildings are more successful pastiches, modeled on magnolia-trimmed Mississippi-style homes (Magnolia Bend, where princess-themed "Royal Guest" rooms are adorably tarted up as if they belong to *The Princess and the Frog*'s Tiana; the headboards twinkle with push-button fireworks shows; about $50 surcharge) and rustic cabins (Alligator Bayou, where trundle beds sleep five—good for a Moderate resort). Riverside also has more water for rooms to face (though the privilege will cost you another $30 a night) and is the locale for most activities for the two resorts. Not all buildings have elevators, so if you need one, make sure you request a room on the first floor when you check in. Riverside has five pools to French Quarter's one, but the main pool at Riverside is less elaborate than the French Quarter's, and Riverside's room windows all face an exterior corridor. The two properties are far enough apart (about 15 min. walking) that many people choose to use the free boat service ⚓ linking them. The boats will also take you to Disney Springs—the trip is one of the most pleasant, least-known free rides at Disney World—but the parks are served only by buses.

2201 Orleans Dr., Lake Buena Vista. www.disneyworld.com. ☎ **407/934-7639** or 407/934-5000. 3,048 units. $256–$468 doubles. Standard room: max. 5 people plus 1 child 2 and under in crib. Extra person $25. Children 17 and younger stay free in parent's room. Parking $20/day. **Amenities:** 2 restaurants; grill/food court; 6 heated outdoor pools; 2 kids' pools; arcade; free Wi-Fi.

Shades of Green ★★★ Operated as a golf resort for 21 years before being handed to the military as the only Armed Forces Recreation Center (AFRC) in the continental U.S, it's the best deal on WDW soil if you or your spouse is an active or retired member of the U.S. military (a full list of eligibility requirements is posted online). Standard rooms are among the largest at Disney (just over 400 sq. ft.) and suites accommodate up to eight. All rooms have balconies or patios, and pool or golf-course views. ***Bonus:*** You can walk to the monorail and Magic Kingdom.

1950 Magnolia Palm Dr. (across from the Polynesian Resort), Lake Buena Vista. www.shadesofgreen.org. ☎ **888/593-2242** or 407/824-3400. 587 units. $154–$194 doubles (based on military rank); around $379 6- to 8-person suites (regardless of rank). Extra person $15. Children 17 and younger stay free in parent's room. Parking $13/day. **Amenities:** 2 restaurants; cafe; health club; arcade; 2 heated outdoor pools; kids' pool; 2 lighted tennis courts; free Wi-Fi.

VALUE RESORTS

Although the Mouse pushes you toward its most expensive hotels by making them so cool, Disney, in fact, has more "Value" rooms: 9,504 of them, more than many midsize cities have in total—available at most times for $120 to $250. The T-shaped building blocks with outdoor corridors can feel at times like thin-walled battery-hen hutches, gurgling with noisy plumbing and seething with kids who don't realize how sound carries (especially when school groups and cheerleader meets are in town). The walk to each hotel's lobby/food building can be a marathon. There are elevators.

FACILITIES Value rooms are motel-style, often of standard cinder-block construction and exterior corridors that make you want to leave your curtains closed. They come with two full beds, but a few have kings (request one when you reserve). Rooms fit four (there's a $15 daily charge for each third and fourth adult 18 and over), plus one child age 2 and under—a full room would be a mighty tight squeeze. If your party is bigger, spring for a six-person Family Suite, which is usually just two hotel rooms with a door banged through and a minikitchen (little fridge, microwave, coffeemaker) added. Those are at the All-Star Music resort and Art of Animation, where the design is more spacious, but at $300 (lowest price at Music) to $428 (lowest price at Animation), you can do *much* better outside the World. There's no room service, but you can have pizza delivery from late afternoon until midnight.

The food court, front desk, and sundries shop are all in the same building by the bus stops to the parks, and some rooms are a 15-minute walk away unless you shell out about $20 more for a "Preferred" room.

TRANSPORTATION   No Value or Moderate resort is connected to a theme park by monorail. Roads are your only option, be it by bus or your car.

Disney's All-Star Movies/Disney's All-Star Music/Disney's All-Star Sports ★

Depending on your point of view, at the Value resorts, Disney treats you either like a second-class guest or like an average American family on vacation. The fun is in the outdoor areas, not in the rooms, which are only faintly themed. The setup of all three is identical—an expanse of concrete-block buildings at the edge of the property studded with enormous emblems, as if a giant had spilled the Legos in his toy box. But because they're older (they opened in the late 1990s) and there's no enlivening central pond, they are the last-choice Values. You get (noisy) laminate flooring, a mini cooler, and a table that doubles as a drop-down Murphy bed holding your second queen mattress, so families must choose whether to sleep or use the table. At the very least, sinks are outside of the toilet-and-shower room, which eases life for multitasking families. Of the three, I prefer Movies, not just because it's the youngest (opened in 1999) and was the first to complete its renovation, but also because its exterior is laden with Disney-specific iconography while its sisters stick to dull musical and sports-equipment icons. Disney shuttle buses also tend to stop there last on their circuit of the three, which cuts transportation time (more expensive "Preferred" rooms are closer to the bus stop). Then again, some choose Sports because it's the *first* stop and so it's easier to get a seat there. The Music is the only one with suites fitting six people. I'd choose Pop Century over this, because rooms are basically the same there, but there you get a Skyliner station.

Buena Vista Dr., Lake Buena Vista. www.disneyworld.com. ✆ **407/934-1936.** 1,920 units each. Standard rooms $118–$254, family suites $300–$581, 3rd and 4th adult $15. For Preferred, add about $20. Standard room: max. 4 people plus 1 child 2 and under in crib. Children 17 and younger stay free in parent's room. Parking $15/day. **Amenities:** Food court; arcade; babysitting; 2 outdoor heated pools; kids' pool; free Wi-Fi.

Disney's Art of Animation Resort ★★★

This attractive 2012 addition benefits from theming more lavish than at other Values, including a spot-on Radiator Springs pool area. Family Suites have two bathrooms, convertible couches, and demi-kitchens (no stove). Standard *Little Mermaid* rooms are gorgeously and whimsically themed, too—better than at other Values. Suites draw on *Finding Nemo* (where there's the Big Blue pool, WDW's largest;

The "Good Neighbor" Policy

Scattered throughout town are properties that brag Disney has certified them as "Good Neighbor" (www.wdwgood neighborhotels.com). The appellation is mostly meaningless. It means that hotel will have shuttles, can sell park tickets, and screens a mesmerizing 24-hour channel touting all things Disney. Only the Good Neighbor properties on the west side of Apopka Vineland Road (mostly on Hotel Plaza Blvd.) enjoy half-hourly shuttles; the rest don't. So don't select a hotel just because it's a Good Neighbor hotel. Choose it because it's the right hotel for you. Legoland's version, with its own shuttles, are sometimes called **"Bed & Brick"** hotels (✆ **800/979-9983**).

these suites cost more than the others here) and *The Lion King*. Unfortunately, six-person suites cost three times more than basic four-person Value rooms, which is hard to justify. This is Disney's only pet-friendly Value resort. It also connects to Disney's Hollywood Studios and Epcot via the Skyliner gondola; it shares a busy station with the Pop Century.

1850 Century Dr., Lake Buena Vista. www.disneyworld.com. ✆ **407/938-7000**. 1,120 suites, 864 standard units. Standard rooms $188–$353, 6-person family suites $428–$826. Standard room: max. 4 people plus 1 child 2 and under in crib. Extra person $15/ night (standard rooms only). Parking $15/day. **Amenities:** 3 pools; food court; kids' pools; arcade; free Wi-Fi.

Disney's Pop Century Resort ★★ The largest Value resort (opened in 2002) is a fair choice, with smallish (260 sq. ft.) rooms—one king bed or two queens—with cubbies instead of closets, one sink, and one mirror, and for dining, a heaving central food court with quality akin to the average mall's. A recent renovation converted rooms' second queen bed into a Murphy bed that doubles as a table (so unless you're a couple, you have to choose whether to sleep or use the table). As if to counteract such dormlike austerity, the boxy sprawl of T-shaped buildings, some of which face a pleasant lake across from the Art of Animation Resort, is festooned with outsized icons of the late-20th-century: gigantic bowling pins, yo-yos, and Rubik's Cubes—which kids think is pretty cool. It is preferable to the All-Stars, where rooms are nearly the same but marginally larger, because it connects to Disney's Hollywood Studios and Epcot via the Skyliner gondola; it shares a busy station with the Art of Animation Resort.

1050 Century Dr., Lake Buena Vista. www.disneyworld.com. ✆ **407/938-4000**. 2,880 units. Standard rooms $162–$330. For pool view, add $7–$13. For preferred, add $12–$20. Standard room: max. 4 people plus 1 child 2 and under in crib. Parking $15/day. **Amenities:** Food court; 3 pools; kids' pools; arcade; jogging trail; free Wi-Fi.

Non-Disney On-Property Hotels

The best way to think of these choices is "location without immersion." These properties are permitted to run their own shows on Disney turf, supplying convenience and often higher standards than Disney's busy hotels. Bonnet

Creek–area hotels (technically not on Disney property but you can only reach them on Disney roads) are newer, more remote, and nicer than the tired ones on Hotel Plaza Boulevard, which are mostly decades old but run their own bus systems to the Disney parks. Hotel Plaza properties also grant Early Entry (30 minutes) daily, and they're often within walking distance to Disney Springs. (For nearby hotels that aren't on property, see Lake Buena Vista Hotels, p. 246.)

EXPENSIVE

Four Seasons Resort Orlando at Walt Disney World Resort ★★★

Orlando's most genuinely luxurious resort is deep inside the custom-built gated community of Golden Oak, within distant sight of Magic Kingdom and surrounded by greenery. Four Seasons' largest property in the world is a stunner in both looks and service: Quiet, 500-square-foot (46 sq. m) rooms come with furnished balconies, walk-in closets, concierge e-tablets, and marble bathrooms. The par-71 golf course, once Disney's Osprey Ridge but now renovated by Tom Fazio, is also a bird sanctuary, and the landscaped 5-acre pool complex (with free sunscreen and valets bearing refreshments) goes on and on—adults-only pool, zero-entry family pool, lazy river with waterfalls that you could spend all day in, two waterslides in a faux fort. To see the fireworks just 2 miles away from your balcony, you can spring for a "Park View Room," which cost as much as $300 more than a "Lake View Room" on the lower floors and come with Plum pay-per-glass wine dispensers; your other fireworks option is to opt for a steak at the rooftop Capa restaurant. The rate is comparable to a Disney Deluxe hotel but the experience is miles better and you get more perks. Daytime babysitting for kids 4 to 12 is free, and kids 5 and under eat free. Its Goofy breakfast is one of the best character meals because it's less crowded and you get lots of photo time with him. If you can afford such sublime pampering, it does high-end better than nearly any other property in town. The free shuttle is on a fixed schedule and doesn't go to Disney Springs, so if you want flexibility, have your own car or hail an Uber. This hotel is included in Early Entry privileges at the Disney theme parks.

10100 Dream Tree Blvd., Golden Oak. www.fourseasons.com/orlando. © **407/313-6868** or 407/313-7777. 443 units. From $645 for a standard double. Valet parking $30 (no self-parking), parking for restaurants $5 with validation. No resort fee. **Amenities:** 3 restaurants; 3 bars; 3 pools; splash zone and waterslides; lazy river; spa; tennis courts; 24-hr. fitness center; 3 boutiques; character breakfast; free kids' club; kids 5 and under eat free; free Disney parks shuttle; free Wi-Fi.

JW Marriott Orlando Bonnet Creek Resort & Spa ★★

Because it had the misfortune of opening amid the pandemic, this hotel is still off the radar for many people—which can be an advantage for you when it comes to avoiding the beaten path. While the other JW Marriott at Grande Lakes (p. 257) is set up like a mini kingdom you can't easily leave, this JW at Bonnet Creek is conveniently amid the Disney World universe, which is why it's now the JW I'd choose for park-going. Overall, expect a casual version of luxury with sweeping contemporary spaces, floor-to-ceiling windows on all 16 floors, a ninth-level cocktail deck good for fireworks views (from 5 miles away), and a classy west-facing unthemed pool area that feels large when there are no meetings going on but small when it's busy. Although it's pressed against I-4 (east-facing "Disney Springs View" rooms actually overlook an undeveloped cloverleaf interchange—you might want to face the pool, where the view is greener), you have to drive through the Disney campus for about 10 minutes to reach the interstate. *Resort fee warning:* $35/night.

14900 Chelonia Pkwy, Orlando. Marriott.com. ☏ **407/919-6100.** 516 units. $259–$533 standard king or double queen. Parking $29/night (self), $37/night (valet). Resort fee $35/night plus tax. **Amenities:** 3 restaurants; 3 bars including a pool bar; coffee bar; 2 pools with children's splash area; 24-hour fitness center; spa; kids' center; automated business kiosk; scheduled shuttle to Disney parks and Disney Springs; free Wi-Fi (standard; high-speed $20/day).

Signia by Hilton Orlando Bonnet Creek ★

Linked to the Waldorf Astoria by a convention hall and set in 482 mostly unbuilt acres, the hotel has rooms that lack balconies, which is a real bummer, but it's on Disney turf, which counts for a lot. Kids eat free for breakfast and dinner, which is fortunate considering how expensive the restaurants are. The 3-acre pool area is done in contemporary stonework—a bit like riding a lazy river in a hotel bathroom—and is abuzz with cocktails and activities. Overall, it's a fine place to disappear but it's too large and corporate to be romantic, although it does qualify for Early Entry to the Disney parks. And that resort fee! Bring a car and you're paying $75 a night on top of the room rate! *Resort fee warning:* $45/night.

14100 Bonnet Creek Resort Lane, Orlando. www.hiltonbonnetcreek.com. ☏ **407/597-3600.** 1,001 units. $179–$349 standard king. Parking $30/night (self), $40/night (valet). Resort fee $45/night plus tax. **Amenities:** 6 restaurants; coffee bar; pool bar; pool with activities; Disney shop; golf course; business center; fitness club; spa (at neighboring Waldorf Astoria); game room; free meals for kids 11 and under at Harvest Bistro with adult purchase; free Disney shuttles; free golf club rental after 2pm; free local and toll-free calls; free Wi-Fi.

Waldorf Astoria Orlando ★★★

The first time the Waldorf expanded its brand outside of Manhattan it was in Orlando, and while the original's Upper East Side aesthetic was traded for Florida's tropical colors, the service standard is noticeably higher than at most other Orlando luxury hotels. The Rees Jones–designed par-72 golf course makes it the golfer's pick of all the Bonnet Creek properties, and the formally arranged adults-only swimming pool, the high-end Bull & Bear steakhouse, and the sink-deeper-into-slumber beds confirm the adult-leaning pleasures. If the price is similar to the Hilton, book here; for the same money you'll get perks such as bathrobes, better-aligned views of distant fireworks, much more attentive service, and the same Early Entry privileges at the Disney parks. You may use the lazy river of the Hilton next door. *Resort fee warning:* $45/night.

14200 Bonnet Creek Resort Lane, Orlando. www.waldorfastoriaorlando.com. ☏ **407/597-5500.** 498 units. $250–$489 double queen. Parking (valet only) $40/night. Resort fee $45/night plus tax. **Amenities:** 5 restaurants; pool; kids' activities; free bike rental; free welcome cocktail, spa; fitness center; free practice at golf course; free golf club rental after 2pm; free local and toll-free calls; free Disney shuttles; free Wi-Fi.

Walt Disney World Swan and Dolphin ★   Rewards points are a main appeal to the Starwood-run Swan and Dolphin, which are linked by a foot-bridge over the lake they share. Former Disney CEO Michael Eisner controversially allowed outside corporations to intrude on resort property, and the result was these dated 1989 exteriors—but given how boring Disney hotel construction has been since, we can't regret those 56-foot-tall dolphin statues. Staff is distracted, but the properties are stuffed with amenities and the location never quits—you can walk to Epcot's side door in 15 minutes and Hollywood Studios in 20, avoiding the bus. Both specialize in conferences, with lobby bars, steakhouses, and sushi counters to suit, although they strive to welcome families, too (rooms fit five and there are tons of poolside activities). Rooms and common spaces just enjoyed a modernizing renovation (blues, grays, chrome, more outlets). Everything lacks the tonal fantasy at Disney-run hotels, and there's no access to the Dining Plan, no ability to make park purchases by room key or MagicBand. Staying here does, however, qualify you for Early Theme Park Entry (30 minutes per day). Rooms often make discounted appearances on hotel booking sites, resulting in a fab deal for a spot adjoining a theme park. Just added: The **Walt Disney World Swan Reserve,** a 500-unit, 14-story addition (sadly, no monumental creatures adorn its facade, but there is a penthouse restaurant), that aims to furnish a more private, executive-level experience than at its sister hotels. *Resort fee warning:* $35/night.

1500 Epcot Resorts Blvd., Lake Buena Vista. www.swandolphin.com. © **407/934-4000.** Swan: 756 units, $290–$545 non-club standard. Dolphin: 1,509 units, $260–$629 non-club doubles. Swan Reserve (© **407/842-4900**): 500 units, $434–588. For all three hotels: Extra person $25. Children 17 and younger stay free in parent's room. Parking $29/night (self), $39/night (valet). Resort fee $35/night. **Amenities:** 12 restaurants; cafe; character meals; 5 heated outdoor pools; game room; health club & spa; kids' program (2 hrs. free if parents eat in one of its restaurants); room service; babysitting; free domestic phone calls; free Wi-Fi.

MODERATE

Also look into the 604-room **Drury Plaza Hotel Orlando Lake Buena Vista** (2000 Hotel Plaza Blvd., Lake Buena Vista; www.druryhotels.com. © **407/828-2424**), which at press time was gut-renovating and expanding a 1971-built Best Western property just east of Disney Springs.

B Resort & Spa ★★   The onetime Royal Plaza Hotel (built in 1972), convenient to both I-4 and Disney Springs, was once an old, finicky 17-story tower that has been reformed into an agreeable Miami-flavored family resort on a budget. It feels a bit more airy than the usual tired bed bunkers around here. King rooms are much larger than double-queen ones, but all are sizable with a mini-cooler, and higher-floor "Stunning" (that's the name) rooms claim views. Ringing the zero-entry pool, "Chic" rooms come with bunk beds. The B stands apart from others in Disney Springs for providing a grown-up stay that's family-friendly and affordable but that doesn't feel too much like a machine. The ground-floor restaurant, American Kitchen, has a Ford F1 pickup truck parked in the center. The B often offers 3-for-2 deals on its website, and if you stay here you're allowed into the Disney theme parks 30 minutes early. ***Resort fee warning:*** $32/night.

1905 Hotel Plaza Blvd., Lake Buena Vista. www.BResortLBV.com. ✆ **407/828-2828.** 394 units. Typically $109–$219 doubles. Parking $23/night (self), $29/night (valet). Resort fee $32/night. **Amenities:** Restaurant; heated pool; pool restaurant and bar; tennis courts; spa; 24-hr. fitness center; sundries shop; on-site Enterprise Rent-a-Car; free Disney shuttle; free Wi-Fi.

Candlewood Suites Orlando—Lake Buena Vista ★★

One of the most crisp hotels near Disney (it opened at the end of 2019), Candlewood has extra-large rooms that are kind of like mini-apartments: You get a full-sized fridge, a stovetop, microwave, pots and pans, and a dishwasher. Studios and Standards sleep 2, so if you have 4, get a two-queen room at the very least, but room types go all the way up to two-bedroom suites sleeping 10 (some on pull-outs) from $345. This seven-story, brand-standard box hotel is located two stoplights from the road into Disney Springs and amid lots of choices for cheap chain food. Pretty much every major theme park is 10 minutes' drive away by back streets.

12359 Winter Garden Vineland, Lake Buena Vista. www.ihg.com/candlewood. ✆ **850/332-0200.** 163 units. Suites for 2 from $87, suites for 4 from $130. Nightly rates descend the longer you stay. No resort fee. **Amenities:** Outdoor pool; fitness center; kiosk for snacks and sundries; weekly housekeeping; free Wi-Fi.

LAKE BUENA VISTA HOTELS

LBV, as it's nicknamed, is more compact and higher-class than the comparable cluster of Kissimmee hotels along U.S. 192, a few miles south near Disney's southern gate. For breathing room, the best part of Lake Buena Vista is Palm Parkway, a winding, tree-lined avenue that's a secret shortcut to Universal skirting I-4. Drive north on it and you'll pass a turnoff for SeaWorld, a Wal-Mart, a Whole Foods, and the restaurants of Sand Lake Road.

LBV has the highest occupancy rate in town, so you'll often pay higher prices (and meet lazier staff) than in Kissimmee or on I-Drive, and traffic stinks. Free shuttles around here tend to go to Disney but not to Universal or SeaWorld.

See the map on p. 230 for locations of the properties below.

EXPENSIVE

Hyatt Regency Grand Cypress Resort ★★★

Probably the most complete resort near Disney, the stepped tower packs every conceivable amenity into a lush 1,500-acre campus located practically inside Walt Disney World. There are 45 holes of golf, an unforgettable waterfall-and-cavern-studded lagoon pool system (for my money, it's the best pool of any Orlando resort), lush trails wrapping around a private lake, horses, and top-floor views of the fireworks at Epcot and Magic Kingdom. With so many extras (kayaks, paddleboats, mini-golf), it feels like what resorts used to be. Contrary to its decidedly 1980s atrium construction (and a snippy parrot, Merlot, who was allowed to remain in the lobby long after the previous tropical decor was retired), rooms—4 people maximum, 360 square feet—have an almost Asian sleekness with rain showers, chaise lounges, and adapter panels to play multimedia on the 65-inch HDTV. Each year the resort gets a little better; the signature restaurant, Hemingway's, is in its own romantic courtyard pavilion, and newly opened LakeHouse does clean, fresh ingredients and gorgeous sushi. I've seen $85 Priceline bids accepted—such a steal for a place that deserves to be packed. ***Resort fee warning:*** $42.75/night.

1 Grand Cypress Blvd., Lake Buena Vista. grandcypress.hyatt.com. ✆ **800/233-1234** or 407/239-1234. 779 units. $199–$369 king or double queen. Self-parking $25/night; valet parking $37/night. Resort fee $42.75/night plus tax. **Amenities:** 2 restaurants; 3 cocktail bars; coffee bar; pool; babysitting; kids' club; business center; gift shop; game room; tennis courts; golf course; biking; trails; rock climbing wall; 24-hr. fitness center; salon; beach; free park shuttles; free local and toll-free calls; free throttled Wi-Fi (full-speed $5/day).

MODERATE

Sonesta ES Suites Lake Buena Vista—Orlando ★

Close to lots of restaurants and Disney Springs, you'll find these apartment-like quarters (there are two TVs and the kitchens even have dishwashers). The three-level buildings don't have elevators, but overlook that fact and avoid the ground-floor rooms, which are darker and less private. The full breakfast is free and plentiful, and you can eat it indoors or out. There's also a well-used pool in one of the courtyards. It's for people who want a condo rental experience, including laundry, without renting an actual condo.

8751 Suiteside Dr., Orlando. www.sonesta.com. ✆ **407/238-0777.** 150 units. $139–$169 1-bedrooms (sleep 4), $205–$289 2-bedrooms (sleep 8). Free parking. No resort fee. **Amenities:** Full breakfast; heated pool; spa tub; business center; sundries shop; free rollaways and cribs, free Disney shuttle; free Wi-Fi.

INEXPENSIVE

Aloft Orlando Lake Buena Vista ★★

From the outside, it looks like another six-floor cookie-cutter chain hotel building, but on the inside, this newly constructed addition (opened in 2021) emulates loft-style quarters—are all those exposed pipes and wires in the lobby real or just an interior designer's fulfilled fantasy? Rooms lead with contemporary 'tude—multicolored rugs and not carpets, bathroom sinks behind the bed by a demi-wall and WC hidden behind a slider door, plush sink-into-them beds, and updated TVs that can remember your Netflix credentials during your stay. Overall, it's easy to like because it's fresh and rooms don't feel like every other brand's, and it's handily midway between Disney and SeaWorld. We just wish that blah concrete swimming pool had a quarter of the design panache you see indoors.

7950 Palm Pkwy., Orlando. Marriott.com. ✆ **407/778-7600.** 141 units. $109–$194 doubles, rollaway bed $15/night. Self-parking $12. No resort fee. **Amenities:** Pool; cocktail bar; 24-hr. fitness center; free Wi-Fi.

KISSIMMEE AREA HOTELS

West of Disney along U.S. 192 is quickly becoming a choice area where you'll find the highest density of vacation homes (p. 261). And at Western Way and State Route 429, out Disney's western back door, the budget-conscious **Flamingo Crossings** development is going up.

But east on U.S. 192 across the I-4 dividing line, the situation is deteriorating rapidly. This tourist corridor, now a half-century old, has seen little investment and in all honesty is teetering toward squalor—if you saw the 2017 movie *The Florida Project*, you saw the decay into which some of these forgotten inns have sunk (the movie's setting, the lavender Magic Castle, is a real motel at 5055 W. 192, though it's not quite as grotty as the film version). Some of these crumbling concrete motels are being converted to emergency low-income housing, and budget tourists are decamping to other parts of town.

EXPENSIVE

Gaylord Palms ★   The Gaylord, run by fee-mad Marriott and consequently overpriced, is geared to captive audiences attending meetings, so although its scenery is extravagant, so are its incidental charges. Still, it impresses: Beneath its mighty glass atrium is a 4½-acre Florida-themed ecosystem of gator habitats, caves, indoor ponds, sand sculptures, restaurants, and a full-size sailboat. All of that makes for an attraction unto itself, and to face it, you'll pay about $25 extra. Rooms sleep five and sport unusually nice granite-lined bathrooms. If Disney weren't right outside, you might never leave, what with the on-site Cypress Springs mini-waterpark (which would be elaborate enough to please a small town and is free to guests), main pool, and the Relâche Spa & Salon. It also schedules family activities and an annual holiday ICE! extravaganza (p. 293). The 300-odd rooms in the Gulf Coast tower opened in 2021. *Resort fee warning:* $30/night.

6000 W. Osceola Pkwy., Kissimmee. www.gaylordhotels.com/gaylord-palms. ℂ **877/ 350-3236** or 407/586-0000. 1,718 units. $229–$559 king or double-queen rooms, rollaway bed $30/night. Parking $28 (self), $38 (valet). Resort fee $30/night. **Amenities:** 5 restaurants; sports bar; 2 pools with splash zone; waterslide park; fitness center; spa; game room; car rental desk; free local phone calls; scheduled park shuttles (Disney free, others charged); free bottled water; Wi-Fi $15/day (fast $22/day).

The Grove Resort & Water Park Orlando ★   Just before the Great Recession, a British developer took $200 million of other people's money, began constructing a massive 900-room lakeside resort on 106 acres by a conservation area west of Disney—and then fled the country. It sat grimly half-built for 7 years, a white elephant in the swamp, but finally the saga has a happy ending. In 2018, new owners finished and expanded it, and now it's a full-service moderate resort that isn't quite luxurious but is still a value for money. Guest quarters here are huge comfortable apartments, each with a fully equipped kitchen, washer/dryer, tub, and screened-in balcony; even the smallest are 975 sq. ft. To sweeten the pot, the grounds face a small Old Florida lake (only electric or human-powered boats, available for rent, are

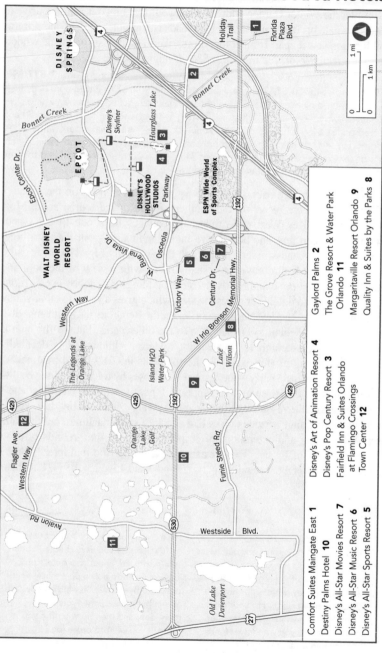

Comfort Suites Maingate East **1**
Destiny Palms Hotel **10**
Disney's All-Star Movies Resort **7**
Disney's All-Star Music Resort **6**
Disney's All-Star Sports Resort **5**

Disney's Art of Animation Resort **4**
Disney's Pop Century Resort **3**
Fairfield Inn & Suites Orlando
at Flamingo Crossings
Town Center **12**

Gaylord Palms **2**
The Grove Resort & Water Park
Orlando **11**
Margaritaville Resort Orlando **9**
Quality Inn & Suites by the Parks **8**

allowed, and so is fishing). Families are also drawn to the small private water park, separate from the adult pools, with a little slide tower and lazy river. Don't let the Winter Garden address scare you; I've timed it, and the drive to Disney's gate on Western Way via backroads is 7 minutes. In fact, the semirural location sets it apart from competitors, like a resort oasis in a wide wilderness of green. *Resort fee warning:* $35–45/night.

14501 Grove Resort Ave., Winter Garden. www.groveresortorlando.com. ℗ **877/890-7932** or 407/545-7500. 1,170 units. 1-bedroom units from $233; 2-bedroom units from $249; 3-bedroom units from $469; 4-night stay may be required. Lake view with distant Disney fireworks view about $65 more. Parking $18/night. Resort fee $35/night (1- and 2-bedrooms), $45/night (3-bedrooms). **Amenities:** Restaurant; water park with 2 slides, FlowRider, and lazy river; 3 pools; 2 pool bars with grills; cocktail lounge; fishing; electric boats; coffee bar and sundries shop; 24-hr. fitness center; free local and toll-free calls; business center; free standard-speed Wi-Fi.

Margaritaville Resort Orlando ★

This one is fresh on the scene, a sprawling 300-acre resort on the southern fringe of the tourist zone. Most units are cute Key West–style timeshare cottages from one to eight bedrooms—you can rent one but they're highly individual—but there's a hotel amid the spaciousness. Every room (and they're pretty big; 470 sq. ft., with giant, delightful bathrooms) has a shady porch with a view of the pool and beyond that, of a pond and nearly no other buildings. The lobby is cavernous enough to serve a hotel four times the size, which gives a sensation that you're wasting away as the last vacationers on earth. Being so far south makes it much more convenient to Disney than to the other parks, but the flip side is that it doesn't succumb to theme park folderol. Although it is decidedly geared to grown-ups (for example, the spa deals in CBD-based treatments), it's hardly a non-stop party—the last bar still closes by midnight—maybe 184 hotel rooms isn't quite enough to support all those amenities. Weirdly, there's no Margaritaville restaurant (that's at CityWalk), and on my last visit I encountered strange service quirks like a lack of soda machines, but the Sunset Walk dining-and-entertainment strip mall area on the grounds offers a decent number of upscale bars, restaurants, and a terrific multiplex. There's also a middleweight waterslide park (Island H2O Live!, p. 191), but that's

---

And Now, Two Warnings...

If you use a **debit card** (instead of a credit card) as collateral against any purchases you may make during your stay, your card may be temporarily charged $50 to $250 (or more) *per day,* whether or not you actually charge anything to your room. This policy can seriously deplete your account, leaving you with fewer funds than you might realize—and you won't see a credit back to your account until *up to 10 days after* you have checked out of your resort. Ask about your hotel's policy.

Also, Orlando police perennially fight the **pizza flyer scam,** in which shady outfits put menus under your hotel room door and then rip you off if you order. If you want to order food in, ask your hotel for its preferred vendors.

separately ticketed. Between the resort fee and valet, the price is $70 higher than it looks. ***Resort fee warning:*** $35/night.

8000 Fins Up Circle, Kissimmee. www.margaritavilleresortorlando.com. ✆ **855/995-9099** or 407/479-0950. 184 units. Standard rooms $159–$239. Self-parking free; valet parking $35/night. Resort fee $35/night plus tax. **Amenities:** Restaurant with bar; quick-service restaurant; pool; pool bar; spa; fitness center (offsite); free local and toll-free calls; kids' club; free transportation to Disney, Universal, and SeaWorld; free Wi-Fi.

INEXPENSIVE

Comfort Suites Maingate East ★★

Thanks to attentive management, the Comfort Suites is now my only recommendation on this stretch of U.S. 192 east of Disney. You'll find it tucked a distance off the main drag, with the restaurants and carnival-style amusements of Fun Spot and Old Town steps from the door—but not so near that the nightly noise is truly annoying. The best rates are for "standard rooms" with either a king or queen bed, but you can get a "deluxe" two-bedroom one for about $30 more, and all rooms are on the large side with minifridges, pullout couches (to up your occupancy, if needed), and microwaves for basic meal preparation. The elevators can be overwhelmed when it's at capacity, but that's common in Orlando hotels across the board.

2775 Florida Plaza Blvd., Kissimmee. www.comfortsuitesfl.com. ✆ **888/784-8379.** 198 units. $79–$169 1-room suites. Free parking. **Amenities:** Pool with poolside bar; 24-hr. fitness center; sundries shop; game room; business center; free park shuttles; free hot breakfast buffet; free Wi-Fi.

Destiny Palms Hotel ★

The decor and its motel bones are dated, but fortunately, so is the price. If you only have $60 to spend, this rambling, old-style building on U.S. 192 west of Disney holds up its end of the bargain—good management has kept it among our most affordable recommendations for years. The staff keeps things spotless, and that's what you want. Rooms come stocked with a toaster oven and minifridge; you also get free Wi-Fi and a continental breakfast upgraded with eggs, oatmeal, pancakes, and waffles. King rooms face the north parking lot and are on the small side; double queen rooms look south on some pleasing old-growth Florida woods. The east-facing pool (it, too, is motel-simple) also faces the trees, which keeps this place from feeling hemmed in. ***Resort fee warning:*** a puny $4.50/night. Why bother charging it?

8536 W. Irlo Bronson Memorial Hwy./U.S. 192, Kissimmee. www.destinypalmsmaingate.com. ✆ **407/396-1600.** 104 units. $50–$70 doubles. Free parking. Resort fee $4.50/night. **Amenities:** Pool; free continental breakfast; free local calls; free Wi-Fi.

Fairfield Inn & Suites Orlando at Flamingo Crossings Town Center ★★

The Flamingo Crossings area, a half-mile out Disney's lesser-used western gate past Coronado Springs, is being developed into Flamingo Crossings, a hub for lower-cost hotels. Getting to I-4 and the other attractions of Orlando requires driving across or around the busy Disney resort (so it's better for Mouse-heavy vacation itineraries), but it's worth it for the crop of pristine Marriott- and Hilton-flagged hotels (SpringHill Suites, TownePlace Suites, Home2 Suites, Homewood Suites) that keep opening with no parking charges, no resort fees, and management that's eager to impress. Style-wise, the rooms are exactly what you might expect (many conjoin, and they're equipped with microwaves and mini-fridges). The "suites" in question are more like large (350 sq. ft./35 sq. m), semi-divided rooms sleeping 4 that have an extra sofa bed. There are few hotels near Disney that are newer—this place cut the ribbon in July 2021. The downside? Flamingo Crossings has been slow to build restaurants, so you may have to drive to eat.

631 Flagler Ave., Winter Garden. www.marriott.com. © **407/992-9200.** 273 units. Double king or queen room $158–$219, including breakfast. No resort fee. Free parking. **Amenities:** Pool; spa; fitness center; sundries shop; mini-soccer field, batting cages, basketball court; free Wi-Fi.

Quality Inn & Suites by the Parks ★★★

Scrupulously clean with fresh furniture, a professional staff, and a new boiler installed in 2021, this basic, three-level 1989 motel with elevators and outdoor corridors is top of the class for a budget choice. The courtyard pool is plain but immaculate, the beds made as tight as drums, and at breakfast it even does Mickey-face waffles. Pricier rooms have sleeper sofas and mini-kitchens. It's directly south of Disney's Animal Kingdom. Keep the bill under $90 and you'll come out on top.

2945 Entry Point Blvd., Kissimmee. www.qualitybytheparkskissimmee.com. © **855/849-1513** or 407/390-0204. 111 units. Doubles from $66–$179. Free parking. No resort fee. **Amenities:** Pool; fitness center; free breakfast buffet; free Wi-Fi.

UNIVERSAL ORLANDO HOTELS

There are eight hotels on Universal property, all operated by the Loews hotel group, totaling 9,000 rooms, and for the first time, some of them come cheaper than comparable hotels just blocks away. Even its higher-priced ones come with strong advantages. First, most hotels are within 15 minutes' walk of the parks, and three are connected by a free boat that runs continuously into the wee hours. Guests can use their room keys to make charges throughout the resort, they get into Harry Potter an hour early, and at three hotels, they can join the Express line at the two parks' best attractions—that perk has the effect of freeing up a vacation schedule. Guests can also drink and dine all night at CityWalk next door without having to drive or wait for a bus. Use the hotels' website to find Hot Deals, which grants discounts of 20 to 30 percent on specified nights; the website also posts floor plans of all room types.

The Universal property is hemmed in by lots of real-world restaurants where prices are realistic, and free shuttles to SeaWorld are provided once a day. So unlike cloistered Disney, when you're at Universal, you're linked to the real Orlando, and there's more food flexibility. At Easter and during the December holidays, rates are, of course, higher. But there are *no resort fees!*

EXPENSIVE

Hard Rock Hotel ★★ Besides being the city's most convenient hotel for any theme park—the two parks are both a 10-minute walk away—the Hard Rock, which is miles ahead of any other Hard Rock hotel in America, has more perks for the money than most of the city's similarly priced hotels. Rooms have genuinely funky furniture, tons of mirrors, two sinks (one in and

Universal & International Drive Hotels

Element Orlando
Universal Blvd. **11**

Hard Rock Hotel **2**

Home2 Suites by Hilton
Orlando Near Universal **8**

Hyatt House Across from
Universal Orlando
Resort **3**

JW Marriott Grand Lakes
Orlando/Ritz Carlton
Grand Lakes Orlando **14**

Loews Portofino Bay
Hotel **1**

Loews Royal Pacific
Resort **4**

Loews Sapphire Falls
Resort **5**

Rosen Shingle Creek **13**

Sonesta ES Suites
Orlando—International
Drive **12**

Universal's Aventura
Hotel **7**

Universal's Beach Resort **6**

Universal's Endless Summer
Resort—Dockside Inn
and Suites **10**

Universal's Endless Summer
Resort—Surfside Inn
and Suites **9**

Wood Spring Suites
Orlando International
Drive **15**

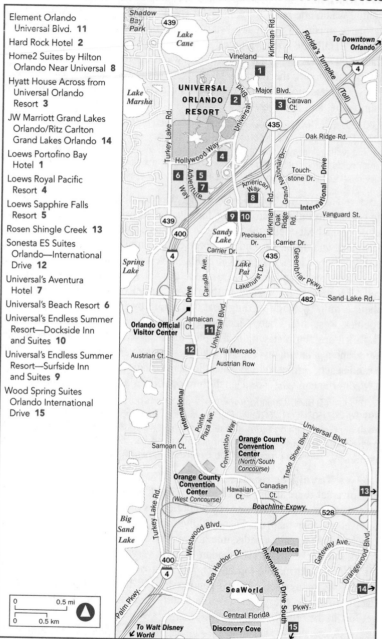

one out of the bathroom), two big beds, and music systems. The ginormous pool, which imitates a beach gently descending to depth, has not only a substantial waterslide but also underwater speakers through which you can hear the party music. (They really bring out the finger cymbals in "Livin' on a Prayer.") Halls are lined with rock memorabilia (Whoa! Outfits worn by Lady Gaga AND Elvis!). The Hard Rock truly walks the rock walk: The last Thursday of the month, the lobby is taken over by the rollicking Velvet Sessions (www.velvetsessions.com) concert series for classic acts, like Howard Jones, John Waite, and Survivor.

5000 Universal Blvd., Orlando. www.hardrockhotels.com/orlando. © **888/430-4999** or 407/503-2000. 650 units. Rooms $348–$464, $40 per extra adult per night. Max. of 5 people (with rollaway). Parking $28/night (self), $37/night (valet). **Amenities:** 3 restaurants; cocktail lounge; ice cream shop; pool with activities and bar; free babysitting; supervised children's program; Club Level rooms; fitness center; free Wi-Fi.

Loews Portofino Bay Hotel ★★★

Universal's priciest and most romantic option faithfully re-creates the famous Italian fishing village, down to the angle of the boat docks, the bolted-down Vespas, and live opera music nightly along the waterfront. Beyond that spectacular gimmick (said to have been Steven Spielberg's idea, like much at 1990s Universal), rooms are of a particularly high standard—standard ones are a generous 450 square feet and have top-end beds. Because the resort is the farthest on property from the parks (but still only about 5 min. by quick-loading boat or 15 min. by foot), it tends to appeal to couples. Restaurants here—including upscale Bice and family-favorite Mama Della's—are worth staying in for, plus there are a Starbucks, an upscale pizzeria, and a gelateria on property. Choose from two enormous pools—one with a sand beach, zero entry, and waterslides, the other with palm trees, bocce, and a Mediterranean vibe—or a small third option for a cool break in your day.

5601 Universal Blvd., Orlando. www.loewshotels.com/portofino-bay-hotel. © **888/430-4999** or 407/503-1000. 750 units. Double queen or king rooms $410–$619, $40 per extra adult per night. Parking $30/night (self), $37/night (valet). **Amenities:** 3 restaurants; ice cream shop; Starbucks; 3 pools with activities and bar; fitness center; Mandara Spa; supervised children's programs; Club Level rooms; nightly opera show; free Wi-Fi.

Loews Royal Pacific Resort ★★★

The least expensive luxury option at Universal does an apt impression of South Seas style in the 1930s, with muted cream colors dominated by giant flowers on the walls. It's more luxurious yet cheaper than the Disney Polynesian, with a lush pool area (sandy beach, winding garden paths, interactive water play area) and a sophisticated, wood-and-wicker look. The standard is high: very soft robes, cushy beds with fat pillows, and marble-top chests. It's right over the road from Islands of Adventure; many rooms have a panorama of it. In any other city, the Royal Pacific might be everyone's favorite resort. Here, though, its subtler charms get lost in the crowd.

6300 Hollywood Way, Orlando. www.loewshotels.com/royal-pacific-resort. © **888/430-4999** or 407/503-3000. 1,000 units. Doubles $314–$469, $40 per extra adult per night. Parking $28/night (self), $37/night (valet). **Amenities:** 2 restaurants; sushi bar; cocktail lounge; pool with activities and bars; free Wi-Fi.

MODERATE

Loews Sapphire Falls Resort ★★★ The Modern Caribbean-inspired Sapphire Falls is clean and understated. It's also my favorite of Universal's moderate options because the service is strong, parking is sheltered, the price is never too crazy, and you can take ferries or walks to the parks (the more crowded Cabana Bay only has buses). Most rooms have either a king or two queens (321 sq. ft.), but for $100 more you can have a King Suite with a separate sitting area (595 sq. ft.), and for $200 more there are Kids Suites with a separate double-twin bedroom for children. Quick-service food options are short, but the 16,000-square-foot pool area, which catches sun until sunset, is a world unto itself. A stay comes with early entry to The Wizarding World of Harry Potter, but not Express.

6601 Adventure Way, Orlando. www.loewshotels.com/sapphire-falls-resort. © **888/884-7922** or 407/503-5000. 1,000 units. Double queen or king rooms $226–$289, $20 per extra adult per night. Parking $26/night (self), $29/night (valet). **Amenities:** 2 restaurants; 2 bars; fitness center; pool with activities and bar; Avis car rental desk; free standard-speed Wi-Fi (full-speed $15/day).

Universal's Aventura Hotel ★★ When you need a hotel that's a little more urbane and less kid-clogged, come here. Opened in August 2018, Universal's sixth hotel is a moderate-chic choice, the most adult-feeling theme-park hotel in Orlando—it's a 16-story tower with that polished-concrete-and-white-wall modern Miami aesthetic. Tucked down by Sapphire Falls (you can walk to its ferry in 5 min.), its signature destination is Bar 17 Bistro, an open-air rooftop bar and grill with fantastic views, truly adult cocktails, and a happy hour that starts at 10pm. In the rooms, bedside tablets control the television, temperature, and lights; your view of Orlando is unobstructed with floor-to-ceiling windows. Standard two-queen rooms are on lower floors and are 314 square feet; Skyline rooms are the same size, but are high enough for city views or to spot Disney's fireworks in the far distance (you'll want to be on floor 8 or above for that), and are $25 more; standard king rooms are smaller (238 square feet) and come with a pull-out couch. Instead of a restaurant, a food court does surprisingly good and quick global cuisine (sushi, stir-fry, burgers). Guests won't receive Express privileges and they'll have to link with the parks by bus, but they will be allowed early park entry in the mornings.

6725 Adventure Way, Orlando. www.loewshotels.com/universals-aventura-hotel. © **888/273-1311** or 407/503-6000. 600 units. Double queen or king rooms start at $149–$214 (from $189 with the best views), with discounts for longer stays, $20 per extra adult per night. Max. of 4 people per room. Self-parking $18/night. **Amenities:** Food court; 2 bars; fitness center; pool with bar; virtual reality game room; Avis car rental desk; free standard-speed Wi-Fi (full-speed $15/day).

Universal's Beach Resort ★★ Cabana Bay plays the role of a family vacation escape by kitsching it up as a tacky 1950s beach hotel. Geometric mid-century fabrics, teals and lemons, swooping Space Age architecture, a Jack LaLanne–branded gym, and a 10-lane bowling alley all wink at the mid-century era. Things may *look* old but they're decidedly modern, down to the ample outlets in the bedrooms, gated parking, and air-conditioning that's whisper quiet. On the north end of the complex, where a motor court theme prevails, you'll find 600 family suites with kitchen areas (microwave, no stove) that sleep six somewhat tightly, two on a sofa bed. The music never stops in the two ginormous pool areas, which have Universal's only lazy river, and guests get a special side entrance to Volcano Bay next door (some rooms added in 2017 look right into the park and at its iconic volcano). But there's a trade-off: There's no Express Pass privilege (you do get into the parks early), no room service, and to reach the action, you'll have to take a shuttle to CityWalk—there is no water taxi to this hotel. (Sapphire Falls, priced a notch higher, has that.)

6550 Adventure Way, Orlando. www.loewshotels.com/cabana-bay-hotel. © **888/430-4999** or 407/503-4000. 2,200 units. Standard rooms from $149–$264, family suites $174–$284, with discounts for longer stays, $20 per extra adult per night. Parking $18/night. **Amenities:** Food court; 10-lane bowling alley with food; 2 pools; 2 pool bars; waterslide; lazy river; fitness center; free standard-speed Wi-Fi for up to 4 devices (full-speed $15/day).

INEXPENSIVE

Universal's Endless Summer Resort ★★★   The beach-themed Endless Summer complex, which is actually two hotels (Surfside Inn and Suites and Dockside Inn and Suites) across the street from each other, is a game-changer for families on a budget. Here, a two-bedroom family suite with a kitchenette and table costs less than Disney's most basic single motel-style room in low season—it also fits two additional people comfortably *and,* unlike Disney's options, it has two big windows and kids won't lose their way to the pool. The price undercutting is intentional, and it's war: Universal wants families on tight budgets to stay with *them* for a change and commute for their Disney days (an UberX from here to Magic Kingdom usually costs under $20). At these prices, and with Disney's costs spiraling heavenward, that's finally a reasonable idea, and Endless Summer is so well executed we could recommend it at a higher price. Its free shuttle buses take all of 4 minutes (I time it on regular occasions) to deliver you to the rest of the resort. Endless Summer's hotels won't give you room service, but they do have two bars (pool and lobby), pizza delivery, a Starbucks, and early entry to the theme parks. Even all meals (grab-and-go only) and cocktails are priced around $10. Both pools are massive, but Dockside's faces the sun for longer in the late afternoon, and Dockside towers higher than Surfside, which makes the busier of the two but the better choice for Orlando views. Being on touristy I-Drive, where there's lots to do and eat within a safe walk, also means guests benefit from not being trapped by resort prices for food. *Fun trivia:* The drinks at the pool bars are named for flumes at Wet 'n Wild, once the most popular waterslide park in the United States, which stood on this property from 1977 to 2016.

7000 Universal Blvd., Orlando. www.loewshotels.com/surfside-inn-and-suites and www.loewshotels.com/dockside-inn-and-suites. © **888/430-4999** or 407/503-7000. 2,800 units. Standard double queen rooms $129–$184; pool view adds $15/night. Two-bedroom suites $111–$239; pool view adds $20/night. Add $15 per extra adult per night; max. of 4 people/room for standard room, 6 for suite. Self-parking $15/night. **Ameni-**

ties for both hotels: Outdoor pool; pool bar and restaurant; food court; complimentary cribs (no rollaway beds available); Starbucks; fitness center; game room; free Wi-Fi.

INTERNATIONAL DRIVE HOTELS

I-Drive is a good place to stay if you don't have a car because it's full of places to eat. It's also the only hotel zone with a semblance of street life. If you stay here, you'll be in the thick of the family-friendly come-ons, midway rides, souvenir hawkers, mini golf, and theme bars. You'll need wheels to reach Disney (most hotels offer shuttles, but not always to Disney, and not always free), although Universal is just across I-4 to the north and the dirt-cheap I-Ride Trolley (p. 288) links you with SeaWorld. Car traffic can clog I-Drive, but there's a workaround: Universal Boulevard, a block east, bypasses the mess.

EXPENSIVE

JW Marriott Orlando, Grande Lakes/Ritz-Carlton Grande Lakes Orlando ★   The two towers form a busy city unto themselves in a 500-acre plot east of SeaWorld. If you stay in one of them, you can use the main amenities of the other, which is a value, but you won't be as close to the theme parks as you would at the newer JW (p. 244). This JW's 24,000-sq.-ft. pool area, landscaped with fake rocks, jungle greens, and a ¼-mile lazy river, is deservedly jammed on hot days, while the Ritz's water area is formal and refined. The JW's rooms are more palatial than the norm in town (and have bathtubs) but their Old Florida-inflected style now feels dowdy. Meanwhile, the Ritz' rooms completed a renovation in 2021 that filled them with soothing greys, putty colors, and dark woods, and the pampering and quality here are a notch higher than at the JW. The 40,000-sq.-ft. Ritz-Carlton spa is one of the city's best. But none of it is cheap, it's impersonally large (maybe you want that), and the remote location means you'll have to drive somewhere every time your stomach rumbles if you want to escape high-priced resort food. That's a flaw; you'll spot guests coming back from local pizza joints and Wawa with cheaper provisions. Both hotels have unobstructed views over a Greg Norman–designed golf course and a connected nature reserve (it's much larger than you'd think—you could get lost during an evening wander) where every diversion, from fishing to biking, is offered. With so much choice in town, Grande Lakes is the resort you choose if you lean toward the Ritz and want to seal yourself away with rounds of golf and spa rubdowns, but if you're eyeing its JW, that isn't the best choice for theme parking or family frugality. Rates fluctuate wildly if there's a conference. *Resort fee warning:* $40/night.

4040 Central Florida Pkwy., Orlando. www.grandelakes.com. ✆ **800/576-5760** or 407/206-2400 for the Ritz; ✆ **800/576-5750** or 407/206-2300 for the JW Marriott. JW: 1,000 units, doubles $279–$606. Ritz: 584 units, doubles $373–$849. Parking $30 (self), $40 (valet; mandatory for Ritz guests). Resort fee $40/night. **Amenities:** 6 restaurants; 2 cafes; 2 outdoor heated pools; kids' pool; spa; health club; golf course (normally membership-only); 3 tennis courts; kayaking; Club Level rooms; Starbucks; babysitting; 2 daily hr. of kids' club (Ritz only); free local calls; free park shuttles (with 24 hr. notice); throttled Wi-Fi $15/day, video-speed Wi-Fi $20/day.

Rosen Shingle Creek ★★   It's not often you find a full-scale resort that isn't controlled by some corporate office far away. The Shingle Creek is the flagship of Harris Rosen—de facto Orlando tourism royalty—who controls nine hotels and an incredible 6,705 rooms in town. So his 255-acre, well-manicured crown jewel feels a little different. I wouldn't quite call the room furnishings dated—they just feel resolutely beige and homey—but standard rooms have more space than usual and most of them have a great view since the hotel stands on its own (5 miles to Universal, 9 to Disney) with nothing blocking it. And miracle of miracles, there's no resort fee, which is reason enough to support it even if it does result in a few optional fees here and there to do some things. Conferences regularly take it over, and the fascinating mini-mall of restaurants and focus on golf (p. 267) are squarely aimed at those groups, but all those amenities can be useful to you. There's even a little supermarket in the basement so you don't have to go out to buy a bottle of wine—it's not priced to rip you off, nor is parking (compared to other Orlando resorts), and did I mention there's no resort fee?

9939 Universal Blvd., Orlando. www.rosenshinglecreek.com. ✆ **866/966-6338** or 407/996-9939. 1,501 units. $149–$425 doubles or kings for up to 4. Parking $18 (self), $26 (valet). No resort fee. **Amenities:** 8 restaurants; 2 cocktail bars; 4 pools with bar; spa; coffee bar; ice cream and sandwich shop; nature trail; 24-hr. fitness center ($10/use); tennis; basketball; sand volleyball; arcade; mini supermarket; free shuttles to Universal and SeaWorld; babysitting (for a fee); free throttled Wi-Fi, video speed $10–$15.

MODERATE

Home2 Suites by Hilton Orlando Near Universal ★★   A non-fussy option for families on a budget, the large rooms come with a kitchen (there's a microwave, but you have to borrow hot plates from the front desk), a living area, a big sleeping area, and lots of counter and desk space. You won't get a tub (it's a standing shower), but who cares? Yes, it's a characterless box hotel on a small plot with a breakfast area that feels like a classroom, but it's in a strong location with strong features for a low price, with a big pool that's never crowded. And it's rather new, having opened in March 2019. You can walk to lots of places to eat, a Walgreens, and Congo miniature golf (p. 271). A second in this brand (one about 3 years older) is **Home2 Suites by Hilton Orlando/International Drive South** at 12107 Regency Village, across from Orlando Premium Outlets and 5 minutes from Disney Springs (from $125).

5910 American Way, Orlando. home2suites.hilton.com. ✆ **855/618-4702** or 407/519-3151. 122 units. $129–$237 for suites sleeping up to 6. Free parking. No resort fee. **Amenities:** Pool; 24-hr. free coffee kiosk; spin cycle fitness center; free scheduled shuttle to Universal and SeaWorld; free Wi-Fi.

Hyatt House Across from Universal Orlando Resort ★★   It's not technically across from it—more like a 30-second drive around a bend—but at eight stories tall, west-facing rooms here have a good peek at some of Universal's rooftops, and it is crisp, having opened midway through 2018. Hyatt House, if you don't know, is the hotel giant's "extended stay" product, which means it's ideal for families who like to be able to cook for themselves.

Rooms and suites come with a microwave and cube fridge, and most suites have fully equipped kitchens and a living room. Studios have a floating divider but not an actual wall (easier for keeping an eye on little kids); bump up $20 or so if you want a bedroom door that shuts. But even studios can sleep six. (Den rooms are like standard hotel rooms.) It hits the value buttons.

5940 Caravan Ct., Orlando. acrossfromuniversalorlando.house.hyatt.com. ☏ **407/352-5660.** 168 units. Rooms $158–$278 with 2 double beds, $20 more for king bed. Free parking. No resort fee. **Amenities:** Heated pool; bar; sundries shop; 24-hr. fitness center; free Universal shuttle; free breakfast buffet; free Wi-Fi.

Sonesta ES Suites Orlando—International Drive ★★★

This well-managed all-apartment hotel across the street from the ICON Wheel is a safe mid-priced choice in a carefully refurbished 1980s complex. And there's every reason to assume it will continue to maintain high standards for this price level, because the Sonesta corporate headquarters recently moved to downtown Orlando. All units (most one-bedrooms are arranged around a courtyard pool, two-bedrooms face out) are a touch dark, but for some guests that's a good thing. They also have kitchen with updated appliances, fresh furniture, fresh carpeting and bedding, a booth for family meals, and lots of added electrical outlets for recharging. And when you come back after a long day, you can walk to dozens of restaurants.

8480 International Dr., Orlando. www.sonesta.com/orlando. ☏ **407/352-2400.** 146 units. 1-bedroom $129–$305, 2-bedroom $30–$40 more. Free parking. No resort fee. **Amenities:** Free breakfast; pool; spa tub; bar; sundries shop; small fitness center; free park shuttles (for Disney, connect via Epcot); free Wi-Fi.

INEXPENSIVE

Element Orlando Universal Blvd. ★

Brand new in mid-2021, this eight-floor newcomer has a terrific location by The Wheel (some rooms have a view of it), which shares the parking structure. That prime situation means you will never lack for fun places to eat and party at night. When you finally turn in, your room's style is corporate/modern, with lots of putty-colored and beige lines but a shower stall instead of a bathtub. Some rooms come with kitchenettes that are better equipped than the average: electric stovetop, fridge, microwave, dishwasher, dishes, utensils, and cookware. But for all that convenience, there is a not-insignificant tradeoff: The pool is small and dull.

8278 Universal Blvd., Orlando. www.marriott.com. ☏ **407/352-2225.** 165 units. $140–$229 doubles. Free parking. No resort fee. **Amenities:** Free grab-and-go breakfast; pool (saltwater); 24-hour fitness center; sundries shop; free Wi-Fi.

WoodSpring Suites Orlando International Drive ★★

On a just-developing stretch of I-Drive south of SeaWorld but east of Disney Springs, this fresh (opened spring 2019) hotel is intended for stays of more than a few nights: All rooms have a kitchen with a microwave, coffeemaker, a table, even a little stove—and conveniently, the hotel is behind a grocery store. There are three suite types: with a queen bed, sleeping two; with a king bed and a sofa, also for two; and suites with two queens, sleeping four. Prices are bound to rise as more people discover this, even if its style is blandly corporate, housekeeping only comes in between guests, and the outdoor pool is as simple as they come.

11781 International Dr., Orlando. www.woodspring.com. ✆ **407/842-1455.** 138 units. $80–$97 for all room types. Free parking. No resort fee. **Amenities:** Free breakfast; outdoor pool; small fitness center; free throttled Wi-Fi.

DOWNTOWN ORLANDO HOTELS

Because it's a 30-minute ride north of Disney on I-4 (yes, you should have a car to stay here), a downtown hotel would have to be pretty special to convince a tourist to choose it over one that's nearer to the parks. Orlando has a few, where you can find respite from the hurdy-gurdy and plastinated smiles—or a breather from children.

EXPENSIVE

The Alfond Inn ★★   In 2013, Rollins College opened this boutique hotel in upscale Winter Park using a $12.5-million donation; its income will endow a scholarship program. Isn't that nice? So is the hotel. Its restaurant and cocktail bar, planted courtyard, and modern rooms striped in teal and lime with dark wood accents, are designed to appeal to sophisticated palates, something underscored by its fantastic public art collection, curated by the surprisingly well-stocked Rollins Museum of Art (p. 187). These gleaming facilities are 3 blocks from the dignified shopping of Park Avenue and the Morse Museum (p. 187), making it an instant keystone of the Winter Park scene. It's probably too far if you've got a heavy theme park schedule, but it's ideal for love-nesting

---

Legoland's Hotels Click with Families

It can take an hour to get to Legoland from the other Orlando parks, so some parents wisely opt to spend the night there so they can hit the gates when the park opens. The 152-room **Legoland Florida Hotel** ★★★ is worth longer stays than that. It's a wonder—a candy-colored property crammed with Lego models and structures, with Lego play areas, character breakfasts, a heated pool, and rooms with elaborately executed themes ranging from pirates to medieval times. It's also just "132 kid steps," as the owners put it, from the front gates of the park (p. 173). It was such a smash that in 2017, the park opened a slightly cheaper second hotel, the **Legoland Beach Retreat** (83 some- what small "beach bungalows" that look exactly like they were built from Legos, with 166 units sleeping up to 5). That was such a smash that the resort is going for a triple play: **Legoland Pirate Island Hotel,** where rooms have prize-filled treasure chests for kids (genius!), arrived in 2020. At these prices, we do wish the hotels were a little stronger on service and lighter on self-service, but they're still cute. For all three hotels, contact www.legolandhotel.com or ✆ **877/350-5346;** rooms start at $228–$451 in peak season, and often come with a second day of park tickets free; some rates have minimum stay requirements. *Resort fee warning:* There's a $20–$25/night resort fee.

and grown-up explorations of the brick streets and 1920s mansions of Winter Park. *Note:* The hotel is constructing a new 71-room wing and spa that is scheduled to open in 2023. Works will only be carried out during the daytime when you're out.

300 E. New England Ave., Winter Park. www.thealfondinn.com. ✆ **407/998-8090.** 112 units. $224–$369 doubles. Valet parking $20/night; no self-parking. No resort fee. **Amenities:** Restaurant; lounge; pool; fitness center; pets permitted; free Wi-Fi.

HOME RENTALS

In most destinations, you contact the owner directly. This is an option in Orlando, and the prominent online databases operate here, including **Airbnb. com**, **FlipKey.com**, **Housetrip.com**, and **Vacation Rentals by Owner** (www. vrbo.com). But in Orlando, many people who live far away keep homes as investments, so it's easier and more reliable, for accountability's sake, to use a rental company. Their agents inspect your potential home and give you support on the ground, unlocking the front door from miles away with the tap of a keyboard, and they can come fix things.

You'll find most homes are just south or west of Disney World in the towns of Clermont, Kissimmee, and Davenport—about a 10-minute drive. Nearly all were specifically built to have one bathroom for nearly every bedroom, and you'll have everything from an equipped kitchen to laundry. Generally, the older the house, the cheaper it is. Three-bedroom condo units sleeping up to eight, with a themed kids' room, start around $129 a night, or half of what it costs to squeeze eight into two Disney Value rooms. Or you could have a whole three-bedroom house from $209. In addition to being selected for their reputations, longevity, and inventory, all of the companies listed in Frommer's **had an A- rating** or higher with the Better Business Bureau of Central Florida (www.bbb.org/central-florida) at press time, and most are accredited.

Your credit card will usually be charged a deposit ($200–$300 or 1 night's rent is standard) a month or two ahead of time, and if you cancel, you're unlikely to see that again. You'll also have to pay a one-time fee that goes toward insurance or cleaning; $50 to $80 is normal, which makes short stays less economical. Perks like a pool or grills may incur a surcharge, which is also normal. Also ask what supplies you'll need to buy. Clean bath towels and sheets are supplied, but maid service won't be unless you pay extra.

Rates for home rentals are all over the map these days, but these prices should serve as a starting point.

Elite Vacation Homes ★★ A specialist in the Orlando market, meaning it doesn't represent homes anywhere else, Elite focuses on developments a few miles from Disney, and you can even search by map on its website. We've seen four-bedroom homes in peak season for $129–$159 a night. You usually have to check in at its office to pick up your house keys.

5299 W. Irlo Bronson Blvd. U.S. 192, Kissimmee. www.elitevacationhomes.com. ✆ **888/ 510/6679** or 407/397-0850. No pets.

Global Resort Homes ★★ Founded in 1993, this solid and responsible moderate-price choice manages properties, mostly around Disney, in about a dozen gated vacation-home communities with clubhouses for activities and swimming. The people who own the homes are responsible for decor, but GRH nudges them to make sure everything meets a high standard—all include Wi-Fi, a pool (either communal or private), dishwasher, a laundry room, and crisp furnishings—and staff is on call 24/7. It's not unusual to find homes that sleep 10 going for as low as $231 a night in peak summer.

7796 W. Irlo Bronson Memorial Hwy./U.S. 192, Kissimmee. www.globalresorthomes. com. ☎ **407/387-3030.** No pets.

IPG Florida Vacation Homes ★★ IPG began by serving British vacationers before branching out into Florida; now it's among the largest rental agencies, dealing in dozens of home developments near Disney, particularly Bella Piazza, Southern Dunes, Windsor Hills, and the Villas at Island Club. Two-bedroom condos run $120 to $160, often less; we have seen six bedrooms cost a mere $143—but all that can change with the market.

9550 W. U.S. 192, Clermont. www.ipgflorida.com. ☎ **863/547-1050.** Pets with $400 fee.

Magical Vacation Homes ★★ An area renter since 2007, Magical represents about 250 properties hosting from 2 to 14 people, most of them clustered in three high-quality developments (Reunion Resort, Windsor Hills, and ChampionsGate) just south of Disney. You don't need keys since your entry is handled by coded keypad. There's a 4-night minimum at many of its homes.

7555 Osceola Polk Line Rd, Davenport. www.magicalvacationhomes.com. ☎ **407/552-6155.** No pets.

OUTDOOR FUN, SHOPPING & NIGHTLIFE

Picture an old-fashioned steamship, not unlike the *African Queen*, puttering along a narrow river of clear spring-fed water beneath a cool canopy of Spanish moss. Alongside, a few docile manatees nibble contentedly on river grass. This is the real Central Florida, an Edenic landscape of fresh springs and leafy shade that first enchanted American tourists in the 19th century. When you tire of artificial rocks that conceal loudspeakers, the land's natural beauty still awaits.

Orlando's status as a world-famous international tourist draw also supports a huge array of destination shopping opportunities, from enormously popular outlet malls to specialty shops selling merchandise you can't find anywhere else. And if you've still got energy in the tank once the sun goes down on your theme parking (yeah, right), a whole new set of only-in-Orlando diversions awaits to make your nightlife glitter.

OUTDOOR ORLANDO

Central Florida's building explosion only kicked in after Disney arrived, and some people were smart enough to protect large tracts from development. Venture out of the theme parks' asphalt orbit and you'll find examples of the land's primacy—natural springs that Ponce de Leon once toured, swamps where alligators lurk beneath bladderwort and spatterdock, and marshy preserves thronged with migrating birds. And should all of that scenery bore, you can speed by it on bracing boat tours or observe it from above in a balloon or hang glider.

Blue Spring State Park ★★ NATURE RESERVE   You stand a fair chance of seeing manatees here, especially in the morning on a cold day. The creatures venture up the St. Johns River from the Atlantic Ocean to seek out the warmth of the springs of this 2,600-acre park, which maintain a constant 72°F (22°C) temperature even in winter. From mid-November through March 15, boating, swimming, and snorkeling are suspended while the big guys (more than 75 in some years) are in residence. An exception is made daily at 10am and 1pm, when a **2-hour guided boat tour** (www.blue springadventures.com; ✆ **386/775-0046**) is given. The park also coughs up a few nature trails and canoe rentals. Find it 60 miles north of Disney from exit 114 off I-4; go south on U.S. Rte. 17/92 to Orange City, and then make a right onto West French Avenue (there are signs).

2100 W. French Ave., Orange City. www.floridastateparks.org. ✆ **386/775-3663.** $6 per car. Daily 8am–sundown; arrive early to avoid full parking lot.

De Leon Springs State Park ★★★ NATURE RESERVE   Florida has some 300 springs, and 27 of them discharge more than 60 million gallons of pure water a day. In fact, Florida has more springs than any other American state, so it's easy to conclude that natural springs are more authentically Floridian than pretty much anything else you might see in Orlando, and there's no more enjoyable place to experience them than here. The Spanish, Seminoles, and pre-presidential Zachary Taylor all fought over this spot of land, and Audubon saw his first limpkin here. (Remember *your* first time?) It's impossible to overstate the importance of the St. Johns River on the development of Florida—before rail, everybody used it—and, like the Nile, it's one of the few world rivers to flow north, not south. On this segment of the river, there are 18,000 acres of lakes and marshes to canoe (boats can be rented by the hour), a concrete-lined area to swim in, and 6 miles of trails to forge as you try to spot black bears, white-tail deer, swamp rabbits, and, of course, gators. It gets cooler: At its **Old Spanish Sugar Mill** (www.oldspanishsugarmill.com; ✆ **386/985-5644;** Mon–Fri 9am–3pm, Sat–Sun and holidays 8am–3pm), which has been here in some form since the 1830s, you can make your own all-you-can-eat pancakes on griddles built into every table; they can cook you other things, too. Niftier still, the designated swimming area beside the Griddle House is in a spring-fed boil—30 feet deep in spots—that remains at a constant 72°F (22°C), year-round. To reach it, take I-4 north, exit for Deland, and 6 miles north of Deland on U.S. 17 turn left onto Ponce de Leon Boulevard for 1 mile. Get there early, because when the weather sizzles, it gets busy.

601 Ponce de Leon Blvd., Deland. www.floridastateparks.org. ✆ **386/985-4212.** $6 per carload. Daily 8am–sundown.

Harry P. Leu Gardens ★ GARDENS   Botanical gardens seem dull on paper, yet once you find yourself within one, inhaling perfume and being warmed by the sun, you're in no hurry to leave. So it is with this 50-acre lakeside escape just north of downtown that gives visitors an inkling of why so many Gilded Age Americans wanted to flee to Florida, where the fresh air and gently rustling trees were a tonic to the maladies inflicted by the industrial North. Here you'll find Florida's largest formal rose garden (peaking in April); a patch planted with nectar-rich blooms favored by migrating butterflies; a large collection of camellias that bloom in late fall; and the lush Tropical Stream garden, crawling with native lizards and opening onto a dock where freshwater turtles swim and ducks bob.

1920 N. Forest Ave. www.leugardens.org. ✆ **407/246-2620.** $10 adults, $5 kids 4–17, free the first Mon of the month. Daily 9am–5pm.

Tibet–Butler Preserve ★ NATURE RESERVE   Located more or less between Disney and SeaWorld (it's incredible it hasn't been turned into a golf course yet), this natureland is the closest to the parks: about 5 miles north of the Lake Buena Vista hotel area. The 438-acre spread is combed by 4 miles of well-maintained boardwalks and trails (which close when flooded) that will give you respite among the cypress swamps and palmetto groves that once dominated this area.

8777 Winter Garden – Vineland Rd., Windermere. ✆ **407/254-1940.** Free. Daily 8am–6pm.

Wekiwa Springs State Park ★★★ NATURE RESERVE   The closest major spring to Orlando (just 20 minutes north, off I-4's exit 94) is, despite encroachment by suburbs and malls, one of the prettiest preserves in the area. When you think of Florida, you don't normally picture rambling rivers, but the 42-mile Wekiva (yes, spelled differently than the park's name and pronounced "Wek-*eye*-va") is federally designated as "Wild and Scenic," meaning it hasn't been dammed or otherwise despoiled by development, despite the fact it's just northwest of Orlando's sprawl near Apopka. The springhead, fed by two sources, flows briskly over rock and sand, and some people come to fish, but most agree that its canoeing is among the most spectacular in the state. **Wekiwa Springs State Park Nature Adventures** (www.canoewekiva.com;

spring training FADES

Baseball is inextricable from Florida's calendar. Way back in 1923, the Cincinnati Reds began spring training in Orlando at Tinker Field (which was only torn down in 2015), in the 1930s the Brooklyn Dodgers hit here, and the Washington Senators then arrived and stayed for the better part of half a century. A few teams in the so-called Grapefruit League (the Arizona teams are the Cactus League) still call Florida their temporary home, but recent years have seen a mass exodus away from the Orlando area. After 32 years in Kissimmee, the **Houston Astros** left for West Palm Beach in 2017. The **Atlanta Braves** were at Disney's Wide World of Sports at Walt Disney World from 1997 to 2019, but now they're south of Sarasota, more than 2 hours away by car.

That leaves only the **Detroit Tigers** (Publix Field at Joker Marchant Stadium, 2301 Lakeland Hills Blvd., Lakeland; detroit.tigers.mlb.com; ✆ **866/668-4437**). Lakeland, a 45-minute drive from

Disney between Orlando and Tampa on I-4, has hosted the Tigers since 1934, the longest spring training relationship for any major league outfit, and the team is such a local institution that its so-called "Tiger Town" training complex, built on the site of a World War II flight academy, has grown up with them.

In the preseason you can watch them practice or play exhibition games. Unlike at season games, players often mingle with fans, with interaction areas where you can collect autographs from athletes before or after practice. Sometimes it feels like the spirit of old-time baseball, the one supplanted by high-priced players and colossal arenas. Tickets (usually $15–$25) go on sale in January. Pitchers and catchers report first, in mid-February, and by the end of the month, the whole team is on hand. They play against other teams through March before heading to their home parks by April.

(*©* **407/884-4311**) rents canoes and kayaks ($35 for 2 hr.). Developers would love to sink their bulldozers' claws into this paradise; in fact, so much water is being siphoned from it that its flow is rapidly diminishing.

1800 Wekiwa Circle, Apopka. www.floridastateparks.org. *©* **407/884-2009.** $6 per car. Daily 8am–sundown; arrive early to avoid full parking lot.

Boat Tours

The real Florida Everglades don't begin until south of Lake Okeechobee, which is why you'll hear Central Florida referred to as the *headwaters* of the Florida Everglades. The waterlogged land is still home to a wide diversity of life forms.

BK Adventure ★ TOUR An hour's drive from Orlando, you'll find a mesmerizing natural phenomenon: dinoflagellate plankton that literally light up salty water in a glowing blue hue. In peak season, June to October, easy kayak tours bring visitors into the mystical spectacle (best with no moon) 3–4 times nightly.

www.bkadventure.com. *©* **407/519-8711.** Guided tours $55–$75 adults, equipment provided. 90 min. Reservations required.

Boggy Creek Airboat Rides ★ TOUR Airboats use powerful, backward-facing propellers to skip through shallow bogs, and they're a common form of eco-entertainment in Florida, particularly farther south in the Everglades. Though much wildlife is spooked by the din (you'll get ear mufflers), water snakes and alligators appear too thick-headed to care, so you should see a few on one of the continuously running 30-minute tours—boat skippers will cut the engine and float near the critters. Know ahead of time that the boats don't operate in the rain, and animals are more active first thing in the morning. The wildlife spotting is better in South Florida, but this still is a long-running crowd-pleaser. Coupons are commonly distributed. One-hour night

TOUCHED BY magic

Although we think of it as a major American city today, in the 1980s Orlando wasn't far from its cowpoke days, and it took an intense lobbying campaign to convince the National Basketball Association to include it in a four-team expansion. There were plenty of titters when early organizers chose a whimsical name that nodded more to Disney merriment than to the usual machismo-drenched NBA names. But in 1988, they finally racked up enough season ticket sales to prove to the NBA that O-Town had the market to support a major franchise, and the NBA balls began dribbling in 1989.

Since then, the **Orlando Magic** (www.nba.com/magic) has gone to the NBA

playoffs for about half its seasons and to the NBA Finals twice; its roster has included such Hall of Famers as Shaquille O'Neal, Grant Hill, and coach Chuck Daly. The team has been so successful that it even outgrew the stadium built for it, the Amway Arena in downtown Orlando, which was imploded in 2012 and replaced by the **Amway Center** (400 West Church St., Orlando; *©* **407/440-7900**). That's where you can catch home games during the regular season from mid-December to mid-May. Most tourists don't make it a part of their plans, but it's cheaper than a day at the parks: The average ticket price is about $63.

tours ($63 adults, $53 kids 3–12) are also available, but require reservations; check the website for times.

2001 E. Southport Rd., Kissimmee. www.bcairboats.com. © **407/344-9550.** 30-min. tours $30 adults, $25 kids 3–12; 1-hr. tours $50 adult, $45 kids 3–12. Daily 9am–5:30pm, must arrive by 5pm.

Scenic Boat Tour ★★★ TOUR   This Winter Park institution has been showing visitors glorious lakeside mansions since 1938, when they were in their heyday of attracting wealthy snowbirds from the North. Three of Winter Park's seven smooth cypress-lined lakes, which are connected by thrillingly narrow hand-dug canals, are explored in a 1-hour, 12-mile tour narrated by neighborhood old timers. The lakes are flat and relaxing, with plenty of bird life and 250-year-old live oaks, and your guide will pay particular attention to the works of James Gamble Rogers II, a virtuosic architect responsible for many of the area's finest homes. Among the high points is a glimpse of the modest condominium where Mamie Eisenhower spent her waning years. You'll find this charmer 3 blocks east of the shops on Park Avenue. Bring sunscreen: The pontoons are exposed.

312 E. Morse Blvd., Winter Park. www.scenicboattours.com. © **407/644-4056.** $16 adults, $8 kids 2–11. No credit cards. Hourly departures 10am–4pm daily.

Golf

Orlando is a golf town. This is true despite the great damage courses do to an ecosystem as precarious as Central Florida's. Some of the brightest names in the sport, including Tiger Woods, Annika Sorenstam, Ernie Els, and Nick Faldo, have called Orlando home, as does cable's Golf Channel (which doesn't open its facilities to visitors). In January, the annual PGA Merchandise Show (www.pgashow.com) comes to the fore at the Convention Center.

Every self-respecting resort has a course or three, as do luxe condo developments. There are some 170 courses around town, and the competition has caused rates to plummet in recent years, although some still command greens fees of around $150. The booking websites **TeeOff.com** and **GolfNow.com** both sell discounted tee times, driving rates down further. Some courses give priority to players who stay in their hotels through advantageous tee times, early reservation privileges, or cheaper fees. Prices can be steeper in high season (Jan–Apr), and they may be lowest in the fall and early winter. They usually sink to about half the day's rate for "twilight" tee times, which start around midafternoon. Club rentals cost $40 to $60, but many resort courses (such as Reunion and Rosen Shingle Creek) will help you ship your own clubs to them. Reservations are all but required and most courses have a dress code and even an age minimum, so always ask.

DESTINATION COURSES

From pedigrees by well-known designers to clubhouses that operate more like spas, these fashionable courses are the theme parks of the fairway set. Tee times at these pricey greens fill quickly because the courses have national reputations. Count on paying about $10 per hole. Most of the big courses will now arrange to ship your personal clubs to the course in time for your visit, if you like.

Arnold Palmer's Bay Hill Club & Lodge ★★★
Designer: Arnold Palmer, who owned it and built the golf school. This guests-only resort course rambles for 270 acres over lakelands and regularly receives the most accolades from experts. Palmer renovated the main course just before his 2016 death.

9000 Bay Hill Blvd., Orlando. www.bayhill.com. ℂ **888/422-9445.** 27 holes.

ChampionsGate Golf Resort ★★
Designer: Greg Norman. Headquarters of the **David Leadbetter Golf Academy** (www.leadbetter.com; ℂ **407/787-3330**), this resort and handsome high-rise hotel is 10 minutes south of Disney.

1400 Masters Blvd., ChampionsGate. www.championsgategolf.com. ℂ **407/390-6664.** 36 holes.

Mystic Dunes Golf Club ★★
Designer: Gary Koch. Located 2 miles south of Disney, Mystic Dunes has steadily won *Golf Digest* praise for its distinct character. Elevation changes up to 80 feet over the course of play and the grounds retain their mature oaks and wetlands.

7600 Mystic Dunes Lane, Celebration. www.mysticdunesgolf.com. ℂ **407/787-5678.** 18 holes.

Reunion Resort & Club ★★
Designers: Jack Nicklaus, Arnold Palmer, Tom Watson—three world-class designers' courses, all a 10-minute drive south of Disney. There's also on-site golf instruction with a staff of 11 teachers.

7593 Gathering Dr., Kissimmee. www.reunionresortgolf.com. ℂ **407/396-3199.** 54 holes.

The Ritz-Carlton Golf Club Orlando, Grande Lakes ★★
Designer: Greg Norman. Golf instruction at this very well-maintained facility is overseen by former PGA Tour player Larry Rinker. Family packages are available. *Golf Digest* calls its variety "a fun test."

4040 Central Florida Pkwy., Orlando. www.grandelakes.com. ℂ **407/393-4900.** 18 holes.

Shingle Creek Golf Club ★
Designer: Thad Layton, Arnold Palmer Design Company. A proud, Orlando-centered resort, Shingle Creek is home to a school overseen by Brad Brewer (www.bradbrewer.com). The course was recently renovated.

9939 Universal Blvd., Orlando. www.shinglecreekgolf.com. ℂ **407/996-9933**. 18 holes.

Tranquilo Golf Club at Four Seasons Resort Orlando ★★★
Disney's former Osprey Ridge course, an Audubon sanctuary 2 miles east of the Magic Kingdom, was redesigned by its creator Tom Fazio in late 2014. Each hole has four sets of tees to appeal to all skill levels, and there's a fancy new 16-acre practice facility for drives, chipping, and putting training.

3451 Golf View Dr., Lake Buena Vista. www.fourseasons.com/orlando/golf. ℂ **407/313-7777.** 18 holes.

Villas of Grand Cypress ★   Designer: Jack Nicklaus. These links, right next to Disney in Lake Buena Vista, are currently being overhauled and the course is scheduled to reopen in 2023 as part of the Evermore Resort.

One North Jacaranda, Orlando. www.evermoreresort.com. 45 holes.

Walt Disney World Golf Courses ★   Disney has been closing courses or parceling them to other resorts, but there are currently four left, including the **Lake Buena Vista** (once a PGA tour host), the recently refurbished **Palm,** and the **Magnolia** (the one with the sand bunker shaped like Mickey). **Oak Trail** (9 holes) is the better choice for family outings. They're all run by Arnold Palmer's company. Greens fees include golf carts, when available, and kids 17 and under get half-off full tee time rates at the 18-hole courses. All courses opened with the resort in 1971, when golf was more important to Disney, and if truth be told, their maintenance is spotty. At Oak Trail, there's a 9-hole course dedicated to **FootGolf,** which is scored just like golf except you kick soccer balls instead of swinging clubs ($17–$25, about 2 hr.).

Walt Disney World. www.golfwdw.com. ✆ **407/938-4653.** 63 holes.

MORE AFFORDABLE COURSES

Unlike the aforementioned courses, these don't have big marketing budgets and they don't always come attached to celebrity names, but they nevertheless are high-quality courses you can enjoy at sensible prices.

Celebration Golf Course ★★   In the Disney-built town next door to the Disney-built world, English master designer Robert Trent Jones, Sr., and his son pocked their well-groomed course with water hazards on 17 of its 18 holes.

701 Golf Park Dr., Celebration. www.celebrationgolf.com. ✆ **407/566-4653.** 18 holes.

El Campeón Championship Course ★★   One of GolfAdvisor.com's choices for the top 25 courses in the country, El Campeón's 18 holes date back to 1917, making it one of the oldest courses in the American South. Elevation changes about 85 feet.

10400 County Road 48, Howey-in-the-Hills. missioninnresort.com. ✆ **352/268-9574.** 18 holes.

Falcon's Fire Golf Club ★   Decently maintained and fairly priced (in the mid-$40s for prime tee times), this Rees-Jones-designed public course a few minutes east of Disney can be crowded, but holes are straightforward and a beverage cart makes the rounds.

3200 Seralago Blvd., Kissimmee. www.falconsfire.com. ✆ **407/239-5445.** 18 holes.

Hawk's Landing Golf Club ★   Because it's part of the Orlando World Center Marriott resort on World Center Drive near Disney, Hawk's Landing crawls with convention-goers who keep prices high. Water is in play on 15 of the 18 holes, and the par-71 course carries a slope rating of 131.

8701 World Center Dr., Orlando. www.golfhawkslanding.com. ✆ **800/567-2623.** 18 holes.

Highlands Reserve Golf Club ★★ This highly praised public course, with a fair mix of challenges and cakewalks, is a strong value, charging a top rate of $39, and its twilight rates kick in as early as noon. It's about 10 minutes southwest of Disney.

500 Highlands Reserve Blvd., Davenport. www.highlandsreserve-golf.com. ✆ **863/420-1724.** 18 holes.

Orange County National Golf Center and Lodge ★ At this wide-open complex (922 acres, unspoiled by houses—atypical around here), holes have five sets of tees, allowing you to choose a game that ranges between 7,300 yards and a little over 5,000. Golf Channel's Matt Ginella put it on top of his list of must-do Orlando courses. It's just north of Walt Disney World and it's cheapest early in the week.

16301 Phil Ritson Way, Winter Garden. www.ocngolf.com. ✆ **407/656-2626.** 45 holes.

Royal St. Cloud Golf Links ★★ Aiming to recall Scotland's great links—there's even a stone bridge that looks like it was built during the days of William Wallace, not in 2001—this affordable club, 25 miles east of Disney, has fairways that are noted for being wide, well groomed, and firm, and planners promise you'll use "every club in the bag."

5310 Michigan Ave., St. Cloud. www.royalstcloudgolflinks.com. ✆ **407/891-7010** or 407/891-7010. 27 holes.

Timacuan Golf and Country Club ★★ There are five sets of tees, adapting this exceptionally well-groomed course from 7,000 to 5,000 yards, and unusually, designers were careful to leave its handsome Old Florida features (undulating fairways, Spanish moss, wetlands) mostly intact. Only 3 holes are riddled with water, which might make it easier for kids. Lake Mary is 10 miles north of downtown.

550 Timacuan Blvd., Lake Mary. www.golftimacuan.com. ✆ **407/321-0010.** 18 holes.

Hot-Air Ballooning

Florida is well suited to hot-air ballooning for many of the same reasons that it's ideal for golf: flat, even topography and often placid morning weather. Note that flight restrictions prevent you from making Magic Kingdom flyovers. A trip involves a very early start—6am is common. You'll be finished with your hour-long ride by the time the theme parks get cranking. If balloons don't float your boat, there are other ways to see Orlando from up high as well.

Balloons & Beyond ★ More intimate than its supersized competition, with just two to four people in the basket with the pilot, this company, flying since 1998, will toast landings with champagne.

Launch locations vary. www.balloons-and-beyond.com. ✆ **813/240-4844.** $195 per person for 2–4 people, $150 kids under 90 lb., no kids 5 or under.

Maverick Balloon Adventures ★★ In business since 2002, Maverick can even do aerial weddings—its pilot Pat Schmitt is an ordained minister.

PUTTERING around

Orlando is a world capital for year-round miniature golf. Here, you play crazy golf under waterfalls, through caves, over motorized ramps, and even into volcanoes that "erupt" if you hit your shot. The coupon booklets print discounts for all but Disney's courses; also check individual course websites for coupons.

- **Congo River Adventure Golf** (www.congoriver.com; 5901 International Dr., Orlando; ✆ **407/248-9181;** and 4777 W. Hwy. 192, Kissimmee; ✆ **407/396-6900;** for both, 18 holes for $15 adults, $13 kids; daily Sun–Thurs 10am–11pm; Fri–Sat 10am–midnight): One of the best options, these challenging courses wind through man-made mountains speared with airplane wreckage—and there are live alligators in the pools!

- **Disney's Winter Summerland** (outside Blizzard Beach, Walt Disney World; ✆ **407/939-7529;** $14 adults, $12 kids; daily 10am–10pm): Surprisingly, not the most elaborate courses in Orlando, but you can combine them with Blizzard Beach without moving your car. Two cute 18-hole courses are themed around Christmas; the Winter side, piled with fake snow, has more bells and whistles (love that steaming campfire and that squirting snowman). Both Winter and Summerland beat the other Disney minigolf location, **Disney's Fantasia Gardens** (same rates), which is located by the Swan and Dolphin hotel duo (p. 245). Its two courses, Fairways and Gardens, are themed to the movie *Fantasia*.

The Fairways course has challenging shots; Gardens is sillier.

- **Hollywood Drive-In Golf** (CityWalk Orlando, 6000 Universal Blvd., Orlando; www.hollywooddriveingolf.com; ✆ **407/802-4848;** 18 holes: $18 adults, $16 kids 3–9; for 36 holes add $15 adults, $13 kids; daily 9am–2am): The coolest 36 holes in town, CityWalk's "haunted & sci-fi double feature" is kitted out, hilarious, and always surprising. Spinning vortices! Corkscrew ball elevators! At night, the lighting effects are impeccable. You can even download its own scorecard app and putt an eyeball.

- **Pirate's Cove** (www.piratescove.net; 8501 International Dr., Orlando; ✆ **407/352-7378;** $15 adults, $13 kids; daily 9am–11pm): Navigate wooden ships—one is life-size—and falls of bluish water. Choose Captain's Adventure or Blackbeard's Challenge.

- **Topgolf Orlando** (9295 Universal Blvd., Orlando; www.topgolf.com; ✆ **407/218-7714;** $5 membership fee; $30/hr. until noon, $40/hr. noon–5pm, $50/hr. 5pm–close; Sat–Sun extra $5/hr., Tues half-price; Mon–Thurs 10am–11pm, Fri–Sat 10am–1am, Sun 10am–11pm): More than 100 bays on a multi-level driving range, gussied up with colored targets, food, and a bar. Balls contain microchips for instant scoring. Classier and exponentially more expensive than putt-putt, it's one of dozens of Topgolf's worldwide locations.

Weekday mornings are cheapest. Its gondola has a door so you won't have to clamber over its side, as you must with many balloon baskets.

Launch locations vary. Office: 2900 Parkway Blvd., Kissimmee. www.orlandoballoonrides.com. ✆ **407/786-7473.** $225 per person shared flight, $900 private 4-person basket, $25 discount for cash, frequent discounts online.

Other Adventures

Orlando Tree Trek Adventure Park ★★★ In some woods 3 miles south of Disney, nine elevated obstacle courses, from 10 to 40 feet off the ground and ranging from simple to tricky, challenge families to conquer their fear of heights while they puzzle how to navigate suspended obstacles. Sometimes you're stepping on boards, sometimes wires, sometimes nets, but you're always hooked into a safety line, and guides are always cheering you on. Budget 2 to 3 hours.

7625 Sinclair Rd., Kissimmee. www.orlandotreetrek.com. ⟨⟩ **407/390-9999.** $56 adults, $35–$45 kids 7–11, based on height. Min. age 7, min. vertical height reach of 4'7" (140cm). Daily 8am–dusk.

Wallaby Ranch ★★ In flat Central Florida, where there are no mountains that don't contain roller coasters, hang gliders can't soar from cliffs. Instead, they're launched by ultralight "aerotugs," to an altitude of 2,000 feet—with a GoPro capturing every squeal (another $40).

1805 Deen Still Rd., Davenport. www.wallaby.com. ⟨⟩ **863/424-0070.** Tandem flights $175.

ORLANDO SHOPPING

Orlando is a hotbed for outlet activity, partly because international visitors, with their often-stronger currencies, are prone to buying frenzies. As at most modern outlet malls, not all of the items you find for sale here will have come from higher-priced "regular" stores; much of the stock has been specially manufactured for the outlet market (although *Consumer Reports* doesn't think the quality is substantially different from retail). You'll usually find prices between 30 and 50 percent off sales at retail stores, and after the holiday rush, discounts go deeper.

Orlando Malls

Florida Mall ★★★ MALL Judging by this mercenary sprawl a few miles southeast of Universal, the decline of the American shopping mall is a dirty lie. This rainy-day citadel is massive: 270 stores, everything recently renovated, with plenty of the usual suspects but also some unusual touristy perks like an M&Ms World shop, American Girl, and the Crayola Experience (p. 179). International tourists flock here to blow fortunes. Regular hours Monday through Friday 10am to 9pm, Saturday 10am to 10pm, and Sunday noon to 8pm. 8001 S. Orange Blossom Trail, Orlando. www.simon.com/mall/the-florida-mall. ⟨⟩ **407/851-7234.**

Lakeland Antique Mall ★ MALL Although this off-the-margins bazaar southwest of Disney off I-4 is not a place we'd normally raise a fuss over, it stands out for Disney fans. That's because it's the best place to find cast-off props from park operations, including signs, costumes, and even the occasional ride vehicle, if you can afford the shipping. Several booths have an inside line on booty like this, but start with **Vault Collectibles.** The mall's open daily 10 to 7pm (closes at 6pm on Sundays). 3530 U.S. 98 N Lakeland. www.antiqueslakeland.com. ℭ **863/603-3917.**

The Mall at Millenia ★ MALL   Classier and more expensive than Florida Mall, this 150-unit center's anchor stores include Bloomingdale's and Macy's, but Disney Springs has pilfered a bit of its retail thunder. Open Monday through Saturday 10am to 9pm and Sunday 11am to 7pm. It's a few minutes up I-4 from Universal. 4200 Conroy Rd., Orlando. www.mallatmillenia.com. ℭ **407/363-3555.**

Outlet Shopping

Orlando International Premium Outlets ★ OUTLET MALL   The pickings have declined noticeably at this 180-store (give or take) open-air village. A few big brands have a presence here; the chief threats include Saks Fifth Avenue Off Fifth and Kate Spade—which sell only a few genuine retail store castoffs and lots of stuff created for the outlet market—plus Calvin Klein, Victoria's Secret, Tumi, and Adidas. Proprietors charge $10 for the best parking spaces, leaving the rest of the lot so jammed that it's a misery to come. Hours are Monday to Saturday 10am to 11pm, Sunday 10am to 9pm. Weekdays are quietest. 4951 International Dr., Orlando. www.premiumoutlets.com/outlet/orlando-international. ℭ **407/352-9600.**

Orlando Vineland Premium Outlets ★ OUTLET MALL   The owners of this open-air mall tout it as the most productive outlet center in America, with sales exceeding $1,000 per square foot among 160 stores. Among the stores: Banana Republic Factory Store, Tory Burch, and Burberry. Granted, most items were manufactured cheaply expressly for the outlet market. One popular shop, because it's so close to the Mouse House, is Disney's Character Warehouse, for actual, official surplus theme park souvenirs. The crowds here are not fun; customers are charged $10 for the best parking spaces and families fight it out for the rare scraps. It's open Monday to Saturday 10am to 11pm, and Sunday 10am to 9pm. It's 10 minutes from Disney Springs; the turnoff is just south of I-4's exit 68 on S.R. 535/Apopka Vineland, by Bahama Breeze. The I-Ride Trolley (p. 288) touches down at stop 42 ostensibly every 20 minutes. 8200 Vineland Ave., Orlando. www.premiumoutlets.com. ℭ **407/238-7787.**

Lake Buena Vista Factory Stores ★ OUTLET MALL   The third-best outlet shopping in town is a strip mall–style collection of about 50 stores. The offerings here, about 2 miles south of the Disney Springs gate, will not impress connoisseurs of outlet malls, but they're decent for kids. There are enough names you know (including Tommy Hilfiger, Carter's for Kids, Osh-Kosh, and Aéropostale) to warrant a quick trip. The Theme Park Outlet store has some bargains (half-price mugs, shirts, toys, and some souvenirs dated from a few years ago). The mall also provides a free daily shuttle to and from major hotels around Disney and I-Drive and offers stroller rentals for the theme parks. 15657 S. Apopka Vineland Rd. (S.R. 535), Orlando. www.lbvfs.com. ℭ **407/238-9301.**

Disney Springs Shopping

Disney Springs ★★ (www.disneysprings.com), until recently called Downtown Disney, is Walt Disney World's outdoor center for shopping and restaurants—alas, just as expensive as elsewhere in the World. Its unwieldy layout ambles along the southern shore of Village Lake a few miles east of Epcot, connected to no theme park. A recent top-to-bottom renovation and expansion made it a new star, adding dozens of brand-name stores. The food is great but from a shopping perspective, despite the improvements, it's still just a snazzy and overpriced mall. When lined up beside the four theme parks, I can't say it must be integral to your Disney experience, but it without question has the best casual food choices in Disney World.

The district has four zones; because of the size, it's helpful to know which one you're heading for because the walk between them can be up to 15 minutes. The easternmost area, called the **Marketplace,** is for Disney-themed shops of every type. The middle two zones are **Town Center** (the outdoor shopping mall, and where the bus stops are) and **The Landing** (waterfront dining and bars). The westernmost zone is the **West Side,** which leans toward nightlife and entertainment, with Splitsville Luxury Lanes bowling, and a 24-screen AMC cinema, as if you came to Disney World to go to the movies.

Parking is free in three state-of-the-lot structures with overhead lights indicating if the space below them is free. The "Orange" structure is most convenient to the entertainment of the West Side, "Lime" is closer to the restaurants of The Landing and the shopping of Town Center, and "Grapefruit" links via pedestrian overpass to the Disney-heavy Marketplace section.

When it comes to shopping, the major shops at **Town Center** are not likely to tickle you much if you've ever been to a mall: Zara, UNIQLO, Lilly Pulitzer, Tommy Bahama, Under Armour, and UGG are among the highlights—nice shops, but nothing you couldn't find elsewhere. None of them are outlets.

Shops at the **Marketplace** (✆ **407/939-3463**) are the best for Pure Mouse. Stores are themed for maximum souvenir sales, including one for toys and games **(Once Upon a Toy),** one for Christmas and holiday decorations **(Disney's Days of Christmas),** one for high-end collectibles **(The Art of Disney),** one for kitchen tools **(Mickey's Pantry),** one for urban wear **(Tren-D),** one for stationery and albums **(Disney's Wonderful World of Memories),** and **Disney's Pin Traders,** a hub for collectors of the park's badges where you can also buy MagicBands. The most interesting is the **Marketplace Co-Op,** which contains some great mini-stores such as funky contemporary art versions of Disney characters at **WonderGround Gallery, D-Tech on Demand** for you-design-it smartphone cases and MagicBands (they cost twice as much as standard MagicBands, but for fans, the wide selection of more obscure characters is worth it), **Centerpiece** for Disney-retro homewares, **Cherry Tree Lane** for handbags, and **Twenty Eight & Main** for casual clothes with arcane Disney references. For the Disney fan, there's a lot to discover.

The Marketplace's tent-pole is the big kahuna of Disney merch: **World of Disney,** the largest souvenir department store in the resort. It's a rambling

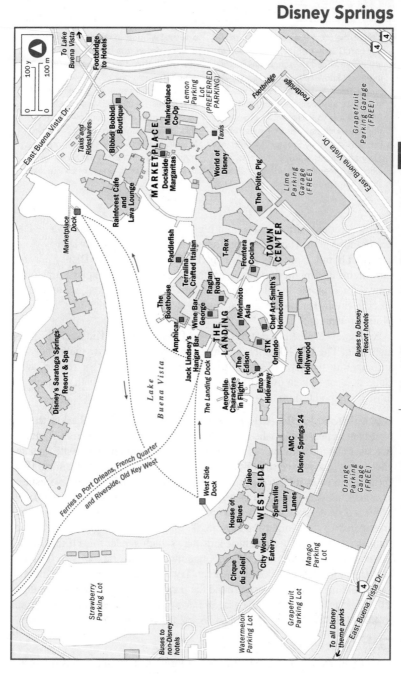

One of the most special souvenir traditions on Disney turf is the collection of little enamel and cloisonné pins featuring every known character, ride, movie, and promotional event. Sometimes it seems it's easier to get your hands on a pin than it is to find a bottle of water—there's even a pavilion that sells nothing but pins at Disney Springs' Marketplace. They are usually worn on lanyards, and when cast members clock in for their shifts, they replenish their pin supply at a special window in the backstage area—a dozen to a lanyard at all times. The rule is that if a cast member is wearing almost any pin you want (barring ones commemorating employment milestones), you're allowed to ask them to trade it for one of your own and they're not allowed to refuse if the pin is legit. Universal sells a fair supply, too, but the craze is fiercest at Disney, where the backings are shaped, of course, like a mouse head.

cathedral-roofed barn stocked from rug to rafter with every conceivable Disney-branded item. You'll find stuff here you won't find at other Disney stores here or at home, especially if it's a "park exclusive." World of Disney may not carry items that might fit better at another store at the Marketplace (tree ornaments, for example, would be at Days of Christmas), or that are attraction-specific (more Haunted Mansion stuff is at the Magic Kingdom's Memento Mori), so hunt around.

A very few Marketplace stores sell non-Disney plunder. Kids can't be separated from **The LEGO Store** (still here despite the fact the toymaker now has a competing park, p. 173) or **Build-A-Dino** which does for reptiles what Build-A-Bear (which owns it) does for teddies. **Basin** sells bath products for those teeny hotel room tubs.

Bibbidi Bobbidi Boutique ★★★ ✦ SALON   Little girls bask in the star treatment as they are lavished with glittery pink princess makeovers, from $65 (Crown Package with hair and a sash) to several hundred (the Castle Package adds a gown, too), overseen by a kindly "Fairy Godmother-in-Training" who sprinkles fairy dust. *Warning:* The dresses are hot and scratchy, so bring a change of clothes if the sun is strong, and you must supply your own shoes. There are also *Frozen* packages and polka-dotted Minnie Mouse options. Boys are steered to the Knight Package ($20–$80), where less glamorous beauty standards are ascribed. (Yes, little kids may switch gender roles if they want.) There's also a salon in the Magic Kingdom in the Castle, but you'll need a park ticket for that and slots are scarcer. Try to get a morning appointment so your child has time to prance around the parks in all that fabulousness. Open daily 8:45am to 7:30pm. Once Upon a Toy, Marketplace. www.disneyworld.com. ⓒ **407/939-7895.** Ages 3–12, enforced. $65–$230. Reservations required.

Other Interesting Stores

If you feel moved to learn more about Florida history, the bookstore at the **Regional History Center** ★★★ (ⓒ **407/836-8594**; p. 184) is a good start. You'll find a well-stocked **Barnes & Noble** ★★★ (Venezia Plaza, 7900 W.

Sand Lake Rd., Orlando; ✆ **407/345-0900;** daily 9am–10pm) among the terrific restaurants of Sand Lake Road west of I-4, and there's another big B&N by the Florida Mall (8358 S. Orange Blossom Trail, Orlando; ✆ **407/856-7200;** Mon–Sat 10am–10pm, Sun 10am–9pm).

Orange World ★★ SHOP Agra has the Taj Mahal. Sydney has its opera house. Orlando has a 60-foot-tall orange. Back when most of this land was citrus groves, Hwy. 192 was the main drag into Disney, and this fruity folly was erected to induce dads to pull the station wagon over and buy a bag of citrus in a red mesh bag. Fruit changes by the season: Fall is for navel and amber-sweet oranges, January sees honeybell tangelos, and February through May sees a procession of oranges, honey tangerines, and Valencia oranges; summer is mostly quiet but Indian River grapefruit is available year-round. A time-share hawker tries to pitch, and shelves teeter with the sort of roadside souvenirs that time forgot, including shellacked alligator heads and local jellies. There are *lots* of schlocky, fluorescent-lit barns selling junky souvenirs around here—but this is *landmark* schlock. Open daily 8am to 9:40pm. 5395 W. U.S. Hwy. 192, Kissimmee. www.orangeworld192.com. ✆ **800/531-3182** or 407/239-6031.

ORLANDO NIGHTLIFE

After nightfall, the exertion of visiting theme parks has turned most visitors into exhausted puddles, and the resorts mop up the remaining energy at their on-premises nightspots. Touring shows and concerts pop up at the gorgeous new **Dr. Phillips Center for the Performing Arts** downtown (www.drphillips center.org). But this is Orlando. Diversions get a lot more creative than that. These novel nighttime pursuits are worth the rally.

Disney Nightlife Options

After a long day trooping through the parks, your wish list for nightlife may begin and end with a hot bath. But if, once the fireworks fizzle, you're still ready to party, the amusement giants are happy to serve to 1 or 2am daily, and it's set up so you can move from dinner table to bar without breaking stride. In fact, the resorts' nightlife zones are the same as their dining zones. The tenor of the amusements is never too ribald or cynical—these are corporate-run family playgrounds, after all.

For nightlife outside the resort bubble in real-world Orlando, see p. 280.

DISNEY SPRINGS
See map on p. 275.

Disney Springs offers tons of shopping and food (no admission required; the best places to eat are described on p. 199), but not really nightclubs. Still, there's lots of fun to be found wandering its rambling lakeside alleys between open-air musical acts, so it's the best destination for after-dark diversions on resort property. There are plenty of places to drink, including bars in pretty much every restaurant; highlights (there are dozens of options) include **Jock Lindsey's Hangar Bar** (strong drinks loosely themed after Indiana Jones's plane pilot, and a few specialty souvenir glasses, if you're a collector); **Dockside Margaritas** at the Marketplace; the waterfront **Lava Lounge** at Rainforest Cafe (p. 200); and an outdoor slushie bar at the **Splitsville Luxury Lanes** bowling alley. At the West Side's **City Works Eatery,** you'll find 80-odd craft beers and upscale but typical all-American grub.

Nearly all the restaurants have their own bars—**STK Orlando**'s upstairs bar has one of the best views. The top deck of the seafood restaurant Paddlefish (shaped like a steamboat) is the little-known **Paddlefish Lounge,** a terrific spot for lakeview cocktails. Most bars at Disney Springs close around 10 or 11pm, but **Raglan Road** (p. 202) tends to go later.

The Edison ★★   A fuzzy exception to the Springs' non-club rule is this multi-level riff on the 1920s and '30s. It adapts a concept that originated in an abandoned electrical substation in downtown Los Angeles, where dance floors and multiple cocktail bars (which don't use pre-made mixes) share space with rusty, century-old equipment. The Disney version, cleaned up but still free-spirited with roving flapper girls, shoos away the kids at 10pm and brings in the musicians and a dance floor. The fare, mostly comfort food and meats, sometimes does some stunts of its own (your candied bacon hangs in strings from a little rack). The Landing, Disney Springs, 1570 E. Buena Vista Dr. www.theedisonfla.com. ✆ **407/560-9288.** No cover, minimum age 21 after 10pm. Mon–Thurs 5–10pm; Fri 5–11pm; Sat–Sun noon–10pm.

> ### Don't Stop the Party
>
> For more nighttime fun with the whole family, see "Disney After Dark with Kids" on p. 121, but if you're craving a night out without the tikes, check out the box on babysitting (p. 204) for child-care options.

IN DISNEY HOTELS

Disney's upper-level hotels all have a bar or two, but most of them aren't magnets for nightlife and many of them shut down earlier than you'd hope. **Rix** and the rooftop bar/restaurant **Toledo** at Coronado Springs are only busy if there's a convention on property.

Trader Sam's Grog Grotto ★★★   At this terrifically fun but criminally unknown tiki bar at the Polynesian Village Resort, the rum drinks pack an un-Disney-like punch and the volcano in a painting erupts if you order a certain one of them. Fans come just to collect the ceramic souvenir tiki mugs. You have to buy the drink that goes with them to qualify for a purchase—the Nautilus, shaped like Captain Nemo's submarine, is exclusive to Florida. Kids are only allowed until 8pm. You might have to wait for one of the 51 seats inside, although the more spacious outdoor patio, while not nearly as fun and devoid of tricksy decor, is pleasant, too (and a great place for a long view of the Magic Kingdom fireworks—the soundtrack is piped in). Since it's on the monorail, it makes for a boozy park break, and there's a menu of decent bar bites. disneyworld.disney.go.com. ✆ **407/560-8770.** No cover. Daily 3pm–midnight.

Universal Nightlife Options

Universal Orlando's 30-acre entertainment mall **CityWalk** ★★ (www.city walkorlando.com; ✆ **407/363-8000**) is found in the front yard shared by Universal's two theme parks. It's open daily from 11am to midnight or 2am, although booze and live performances don't kick in until dinnertime. Drinks are strong and the liveliness is bolstered partly by regular concerts at its Hard Rock Live venue, but it's still pretty vanilla as party zones go. There is no charge to enter the common area, so tour around before deciding whether to pay to enter any clubs. Some places open only in the evening. Many clubs only admit patrons 21 or older because drinking is permitted outdoors anywhere in CityWalk. Officially, Universal prefers it if you don't wear super casual clothes like tank tops. Expect some offerings to be scaled back on off nights Sunday through Tuesday.

CityWalk is located at 6000 Universal Blvd. (from I-4, it's exit 75A coming from the west, or exit 74B coming from the east). Parking costs $26 before 6pm but is free after 6pm, excluding event nights such as Halloween Horror Nights. The latest hours and cover charges (if any are being levied during your visit) are posted in the Universal CityWalk section of the Universal Orlando Resort app.

Bob Marley—A Tribute to Freedom ★★ You often get live music, but mostly it's an easygoing place to kick back, eat, and listen to recorded reggae—an antidote to the high-energy clubs around it. www.universalorlando.com. ✆ **407/224-3663.**

CityWalk's Rising Star ★ This karaoke joint has a spin: You get a band and backup singers (Sun–Mon, just the singers). Like all karaoke, the more you drink, the more ridiculously fun it gets. Cover of about $7 might be charged after 9pm. www.universalorlando.com. ✆ **407/224-2189.**

the groove ★ ⌂ Sleek and state-of-the-art, this multilevel DJ dance club is also middle-of-the-road; DJs hold court Wednesday to Saturday. There may be a cover of $7, and it opens at 9pm. www.universalorlando.com. ✆ **407/224-2165.**

Hard Rock Live ★★ A 3,000-seat, top-of-the-line live-music arena attached to the famous burger joint is one of Orlando's primary concert and comedy venues. The second-floor seating is spacious and has good sightlines; for some concerts, the first floor is converted to a dance floor or to standing room. www.hardrock.com/live. ✆ **407/351-5483.** Ticket prices vary.

Jimmy Buffett's Margaritaville ★★ Live music nightly in a touristy environment that's first about the cheeseburgers in paradise, secondly about margaritas (there are three bars), and thirdly about island music. www.universalorlando.com. ✆ **407/224-2155.**

Pat O'Brien's ★★ It's "an authentic reproduction of New Orleans's favorite watering hole," and although its Hurricane rum drinks could make you see double, there are truly two dueling pianists playing nightly. This spot is among the most popular here—the party starts at 4pm—and kids can join in. www.patobriens.com. ✆ **407/224-3663.**

Orlando Nightlife

Red Coconut Club ★★ A vanilla version of an ultralounge, it mixes stylish cocktails but can't decide between Latin, dance, Top 40, and '80s. Still, it's the district's most upscale venture. www.universalorlando.com. ✆ **407/224-2425.**

Nightlife Around Orlando

Enzian ★★★ CINEMA This thoughtfully programmed cinema would be the envy of any city in America. Before the movie, kick back at the Brazilian walnut patio bar, watching the sunset paint the Spanish moss red. Some of the drinks come from the private cellars of the Enzian's founder, the granddaughter of an Austrian princess. The relaxation continues inside at a large single-screen cinema, where a selection of art films and documentaries is shown, plus Hollywood biggies. Unlike multiplexes, it doesn't have rows of seats, but lollipop-colored levels of tables with cushy seating. Servers take your order (if you have one—eating's not required) before the movie; after the lights dim, your meal arrives surreptitiously and the air fills with the aroma of popcorn and truffled fries. After the show, a 20-minute drive has you back at Disney World. 1300 S. Orlando Ave., Maitland. www.enzian.org. ✆ **407/629-0054.**

Howl at the Moon Saloon ★★ BAR The 17-strong chain is good fun: a saloon delivered as a theme park experience, where bands and dueling pianists whip up fun and the patrons, mostly over 35 and white, clap earnestly to the beat. In 2021, it cut back to a Thursday to Saturday schedule, but if tourism is brisk, check to see if its hours are daily again. 8815 International Dr., Orlando. www.howlatthemoon.com. ✆ **407/354-5999.** Sat–Sun and Thurs 7pm–1:45am; Fri 6pm–1:45am; piano show starts 1 hr. after opening; cover $5–$10.

Icebar Orlando ★ BAR The gimmick: a bar made of 50 tons of ice, from the chairs to the frozen goblets. You're loaned gloves and a cape for warmth. The Arctic cocktailerie is only the size of a hotel room, dotted with ice sculptures, and aglow with cobalt lighting; when you've had enough, there's a larger, room-temperature lounge where you can continue the party. 8967 International Dr., Orlando. www.icebarorlando.com. ✆ **407/426-7555.** $32–$42 including 2 drinks,

---

parliament IS BACK IN SESSION

For more than 45 years, the **Parliament House** reigned as one of America's most epic gay entertainment destinations. The run-down motel on Orange Blossom Trail was a vibrant one-of-a-kind hub for queer social life, supporting several bars and dance floors, a diner, a cabaret, pool parties, 112 rooms, and more wild stories than can be safely told in a family guidebook. But in 2020, the dream came to an end—or so it seemed. The large complex became too much for its owners to support and was marked for demolition. But beloved landmarks die hard, and at press time, a rebirth for the brand was being hatched in a traditional storefront space at 29 S. Orange Ave. in downtown Orlando. There, it will reclaim its position as a vital city institution, only now as a club with performances rather than a campus. Check its Instagram, @parliament_house, for the latest operations updates.

$20 without drinks, discounts on packages online. Tues–Thurs, Sun 5pm–midnight; Fri–Sat 5pm–2am; closed Mon. Kids 8 and older permitted 5pm–9pm, 21+ thereafter.

Kings Bowl Orlando ★★ BOWLING ALLEY   Like Splitsville at Disney Springs, this new-brew nightspot in the shadow of the ICON Wheel turns a bowling alley into an all-evening party, with 22 ten-pin lanes, servers delivering surprisingly decent food (from pizza to ginger-soy-glazed salmon), serve-yourself beer, shuffleboard, bocce balls, billiards, Ping-Pong, and dancing. Some nights it's for over-21s only, so if it's your family night, check first. Shoes are available for rent. 8255 International Dr., Orlando. www.kings-de.com/orlando. © **407/363-0200.** Bowling $16–$23 (cheapest Sun–Thurs). Mon–Thurs 2pm–midnight; Fri 2pm–1am; Sat noon–1am; Sun noon–10pm.

Mango's Tropical Cafe ★★ NIGHTCLUB   This Caribbean-inflected nightclub, a cavernous copy of the Miami original, is colorful, boisterous, calculated with every flourish for maximal are-you-having-fun-yet mass appeal, and surprisingly expensive but still full of frolic for those who'd rather be wearing a Carmen Miranda fruit headdress than a thinking cap. The multi-level party machine—humdrum food, overburdened staff, but focused non-stop entertainment and flowing booze—is lousy for singles but popular among corporate groups, birthday parties, and bachelorettes who can't get enough of the Michael Jackson impersonators, Celia Cruz tribute singers, and a wide variety of concert acts that come and go. For all that, it's appropriate for children. You don't have to eat to enjoy the show (although that's the point from 6:15pm to 9:45pm), and you can stay as long as you like. 8126 International Dr., Orlando. www.mangos.com. © **407/673-4422.** Entrees $28–$36. Cover $5–$20 depending on capacity. Self-parking $4, valet parking $15. Daily 6pm–2am; 21+ after 10pm.

Orlando Brewing and Taproom ★★★ BREWERY   Because it's buried in an industrial area, you have to know about it to find it. There's no food served, either, but that doesn't mean there isn't some delicious cooking happening. At least 35 organic beers (ales, IPAs, stouts—it changes according to how the brewers experiment) are on tap at 42°F (6°C) and served at a copper-top bar. Monday through Saturday at 6pm (except on the 30th of the month), the owners grant a free 30-minute tour of the beer-works, where quaffs are made without pasteurization (like the Old World) for sale within 2 weeks. The bar area is simple but convivial, like a rec room your dad might have slapped up in the basement, uncluttered by TVs or pool tables. 1301 Atlanta Ave., Orlando (just east of the Kaley St. exit off I-4, exit 81). www.orlandobrewing.com. © **407/872-1117.** No food; beer only. Mon–Thurs 3–10pm; Fri–Sat 1pm–midnight; Sun 1–9pm.

Player 1 Orlando ★ BAR   Right outside the Disney Springs area of WDW is this spot where you can play video games all night long. Reasonable drink prices, a dignified beer selection (craft beer, even meads), and a huge inventory of totally free games for superfans and nostalgics alike (consoles to cabinet) make it a fun secret of the Orlando leisure scene—theme park workers hang out here. All ages are permitted before 6pm, but kids 17 and under must always have an adult with them. 8562 Palm Pkwy., Lake Buena Vista. www. player1orlando.com. © **407/504-7521.** Cover $5, higher for those under 21 depending on the time; 21+ only after 6pm. Daily 4pm–2am.

SAK Comedy Lab ★★ COMEDY CLUB   Too often, people describe improv comedy clubs as like *Whose Line Is it Anyway?*—only here, it's true, because this is where Wayne Brady got his start, as well as his *Let's Make a Deal* announcer Jonathan Mangum, *SNL*'s Paula Pell, and *MADtv*'s Paul Vogt. There's improv and sketch comedy every day but Sunday, and earlier shows are more kid-friendly. The big improv battle is Saturday night's "Duel of Fools." 29 S. Orange Ave., Orlando. www.sakcomedylab.com. © **407/648-0001.** Cover $5–$19. Shows Fri–Sun, sometimes Thurs, at 7:30pm and/or 9:30pm. Sun matinee shows from 1:30pm.

Tin Roof Orlando ★★ LIVE MUSIC/RESTAURANT   The after-dark heartbeat of the pedestrian plaza at the foot of the ICON Wheel, Tin Roof does an effortful, theme park–ready imitation of a "shotgun shack" (signs for beer and gas, exposed ductwork, a big ol' American flag behind the stage), except it's clean and new. Grub is just as American: burgers, heapin' nachos, cheap tacos, brisket biscuit sliders, and daily drink specials that cost $5 or less. The recent addition of the cabaret-style Green Room has doubled the variety. Evenings, bands jam starting at 8pm (Thurs–Sun, they may levy a cover charge), weekends are often for themed brunches (reggae, '90s music) with $12 bottles of champagne, and because its booker has excellent taste spanning acoustic to drag Bingo, the scene here has caught on with locals. 8371 International Dr., Orlando. www.tinrooforlando.com. © **407/270-7926.** Cover $7–$10. Daily 11am–2am, music or entertainment at 8pm.

PLANNING YOUR TRIP TO ORLANDO

Before Covid-19, Orlando hosted a peak of 75 million visitors a year, and that figure is rebounding quickly. The people who run the airports, hotels, and theme parks are mass movement specialists, expert in moving strangers from one location to another. You'll always find someone eager to sell you what you need. You will, however, need to take care of some nitty-gritty details yourself, from flights to transportation.

GETTING THERE

BY PLANE   Orlando is served by some 40 airlines, so thankfully, competition keeps airfares among the lowest on the East Coast. In a typical year nearly 48 million people use **Orlando International Airport** (MCO; www.orlandoairports.net), making it the 9th-busiest in the country, so airfare deals are common.

How do you find those deals? Primary websites that collect quotes from a variety of sources (whether they be airlines or other websites) include **CheapOAir.com**, **Expedia.com**, **Kayak.com**, and **Momondo.com**. Each has odd gaps in its coverage because of the way they obtain their quotes. Some sites have small booking fees of $5 to $10, and many force you to accept nonrefundable tickets that don't include checked luggage for the cheapest prices. You can often save money by booking roughly 6 weeks in advance if you're flying domestically, and 3 to 4 months ahead from abroad.

MCO is mostly a pleasure. Current security wait times are listed on its home page and if, on the way home, you realize you neglected to buy any park-related souvenirs, fear not, because Disney, Sea-World, Kennedy Space Center, and Universal all maintain lavish stores (located before the security checkpoint, so leave time). The airport, 25 miles east of Walt Disney World, was built during World War II as McCoy Air Force Base, which closed in the early 1970s but bequeathed the airport with its deceptive code, MCO. Mid-mornings and midafternoons can be crowded for outgoing passengers, weekends can be clogged with cruise passengers. Midafternoon summer thunderstorms frequently cause delays, so try to fly in the morning. Also, make absolutely sure you get on the correct tram for your gate number, otherwise you'll have to go through security all over again.

The main terminal is divided into two sides, A and B, so if you can't find the desk for your airline or transportation service open on one side, it may be on the other side. Most major rental car companies are in a connected garage, no shuttles required. The airport puts out a free map app, **Orlando MCO.** You probably won't need it to navigate, but it does post current wait times at security.

Rental car companies at MCO:

Alamo: www.alamo.com; ✆ **800/327-9633**
Avis: www.avis.com; ✆ **800/831-2847**
Budget: www.budget.com; ✆ **800/527-0700**
Dollar: www.dollar.com; ✆ **800/800-4000**
Enterprise: www.enterprise.com; ✆ **800/325-8007**
Hertz: www.hertz.com; ✆ **800/654-3131**
National: www.nationalcar.com; ✆ **800/227-7368**
Payless: www.payless.com; ✆ **407/856-5539**
Sixt: www.sixt.com; ✆ **888/941-7498**
Thrifty: www.thrifty.com; ✆ **800/367-2277**

Very few airlines use **Orlando Sanford International Airport** (www.orlandosanfordairport.com), or SFB, which despite the Orlando in its name is 42 miles northeast of Disney. SFB is connected to the Disney area by the Central Florida GreeneWay, or S.R. 417—the trip takes about 40 minutes and there are tolls, so new arrivals should have U.S. money on them, preferably quarters. European visitors might fly into **Tampa International Airport** (www.tampaairport.com), or TPA, 90 minutes southwest.

BY TRAIN   Amtrak's (www.amtrak.com; ✆ **800/872-7245**) Silver Service/Palmetto route serves Orlando and Kissimmee. Trains go direct between New York City, Washington, D.C., Charleston, and Savannah. The privately funded **Brightline** service (www.gobrightline.com) has been announced to connect Orlando International Airport with West Palm Beach, Fort Lauderdale, and Miami in 3 hours, but not until 2022 at the earliest.

Transportation to & from Orlando International Airport

BY RENTAL CAR   Economy rental cars start usually around $25–$30 a day, but vehicle shortages in 2021 pushed rates up to around $50 a day. For the best prices, make your reservation many weeks or months in advance. Having a prepaid reservation will not guarantee a car; a standard reservation works just as well. You might also discover that requests for longer rentals turn up fewer results than for short rentals; if that happens to you, you can always consider being naughty and reserving the shorter rental and then simply holding onto the car longer. Test the waters at a site such as Kayak, Orbitz, or Travelocity, which compare multiple renters with one click. Priceline and

Hotwire have been known to rent for as little as $20 a day, but only when inventory is high.

If you rent a car, be alert as you **exit the airport**—you must decide whether to use the south exit (marked for Walt Disney World) or the north exit (for SeaWorld, Universal, the Convention Center, and downtown Orlando). Whichever route you take, you will pay a few dollars in tolls; some booths are automated and don't accept bills, so have loose change. Also, at tollbooths, **stay to the right,** where the cash windows are; the left lanes are for e-passes. (You can rent e-passes from your rental car company, but if you're staying within Orlando, you won't use it enough to warrant the expense, and they will charge you for it per day.)

Always fill up *before* heading back to MCO, because gas stations near the airport's entrance have been nabbed for gouging. Stations inside Walt Disney World charge a competitive price, but one not as low as outside the tourist zone.

Agencies might not rent to those 24 and under. **Action Car Rental/Nü Car Rentals** (both at 3719 McCoy Rd., Orlando; ✆ **407/240-2700;** www.action rac.com or www.nucarrentals.com) have awful service and inflated prices but they will rent to as young as 18-year-olds. Avoid them unless your age is an issue. Most companies won't rent to anyone older than 85.

TO RENT OR NOT TO rent a car

This topic is perhaps the most hotly debated issue in all of Disneydom. The bottom line is there's only one reason to do without a car: If you never intend to leave your resort. Theme park resorts conspire to hold you prisoner. If you plan to fan out, such as visiting Harry Potter or the Space Shuttle, get wheels. If you intend to experience the "real" Orlando or its rich natural wonders, get a car. If you want to save huge amounts of money on meals, if you ever want to take a breather from the theme parks' relentless plastic personalities—get a car.

Disney guests often justify forgoing a car by saying they can't afford one. This is a fallacy. Disney hotels charge as much as twice what you'll pay to stay at an off-site hotel of similar quality. If you stay at a non-Disney property, you can afford a car and *still* pay less.

If you're staying on Disney turf, an economical solution is to take other transport from the airport (see p. 284) and then rent a car for only the days you'd like to venture off property. To that end,

Alamo (www.alamo.com; ✆ **800/462-5266**) and **National** (www.nationalcar.com; ✆ **800/227-7368**) operate satellite agencies within the Walt Disney World Resort: at the Car Care Center near the parking lot of the Magic Kingdom and at the Dolphin hotel by Epcot. Many giant resorts host a rental car desk from one of the major names. Renting away from the airport incurs taxes of around half of those charged by renting (or even merely returning) a car at the airport, where they're more than 20 percent.

One caveat is that **parking charges** can add up. Valet parking is often free in town, but the theme parks charge $25–$26 a day for a space (Universal is free after 6pm). If you stay at a Disney resort, your daily parking fee covers theme park parking. Also, if you pay for parking once at any Disney park, you won't have to pay again for another park on the same day. The bigger hotels now slap on $25-plus nightly fees for parking. In the rest of Orlando, parking is free, plentiful, and off the street.

BY AIRPORT SHUTTLE   **Mears Transportation** (www.mearstransportation. com; ℂ **407/423-5566** or 855/463-2776) is the 800-pound gorilla of shuttles and taxis; it sends air-conditioned vans bouncing to hotels every 15 to 20 minutes. Round-trip fares for adults are $34 ($26 for kids 4–11, kids 3 and under free) to the International Drive area, or $38 per adult ($29 for kids) to Walt Disney World/U.S. 192/Lake Buena Vista. You'll probably make several stops (it'll take up to 90 min.) because the vans are shared with other passengers. As of 2022, it also operates a coach service, **Mears Connect** (www. mearsconnect.com); fares vary slightly per hotel but a standard one-way rate to Disney would be $16 adult, $13.50 child, and a round-trip might cost $32 adult, $27 child. Mears Connect drops and picks up at most major hotels.

If you have more than four or five people, it's more economical to reserve a car service (do it at least 24 hr. ahead) and split the lump fee; a town car is $50 to $105 and an SUV or van for up to seven would be $100 to $190 round-trip from MCO (zooming to $225 from SFB). Try **Mears** (see above), **Tiffany Towncar** (www.tiffanytowncar.com; ℂ **888/838-2161** or 407/370-2196), or **Quicksilver Tours** (www.quicksilver-tours.com; ℂ **888/468-6939;** starting at $50). Quicksilver often volunteers to toss in a free 30-minute stop at a grocery store so you can stock up on supplies.

Disney announced an end to its free airport motorcoaches (**Disney's Magical Express,** run by Mears) as of January 1, 2022. Universal Orlando has its own small system, **Universal SuperStar Shuttle Service** (ℂ **866/604-7557**), that's an add-on to its vacation packages, for $39 adults, $29 kids 3–9 (kids 2 and under free); you can't buy it without a whole vacation package. Obviously, it doesn't go to Disney properties.

BY RIDESHARE   **Uber and Lyft** are available. Meet them curbside at Level 2–Arrivals. You should pay $55–$60 for a standard ride to the tourist zones outside of surge periods. The airport tacks on a $5.80 fee, one of the highest such fees in the nation.

BY TAXI   It'll be about $70 to the Disney hotels, $60 to Universal, not including a tip, which is cheaper than a town car but not rentals or Uber.

Traveling from Orlando to Other Parts of America

Orlando, while not an important air hub, is well connected to the cities that are, particularly New York, Atlanta, and Chicago. For advice on how to find cheap airfare, see "Getting There," p. 283.

The **USA Rail Pass** ⌖ is the American equivalent of the Eurail Pass in Europe—although our national rail system, **Amtrak** (www.amtrak.com; ℂ **800/872-7245** or 215/856-7953), hardly compares to the European system. It barely compares to freight. The pass allows travel within the U.S. The cheapest pass is a 15-day pass, which grants eight trips ($459; $230 kids 2–12); the most expensive offers 45 days of travel over 18 trips ($899; $450 kids). Those on a grand tour of America may benefit from those rates compared to flying.

From April to early June in normal times, some car renters redistribute inventory by offering **"drive-out"** deals for one-way rentals that originate in Florida and drop off elsewhere in the country. Rates can start at $10/day, so ask about those.

For bus travel, Orlando is served by **Greyhound** (www.greyhound.com; © **800/231-2222**; stops at 555 N John Young Pkwy.), **Megabus** (www.mega bus.com; © **877/462-6342**; stops at 4652 S. Orange Blossom Trail), and **Red-Coach** (www.redcoachusa.com; © **877/733-0724**; stops at 1777 McCoy Rd. in Orlando and 1471 E. Osceola Pkwy, Kissimmee). For the cheapest fares, buy far in advance. Long-distance bus travel in the United States is a purgatorial experience. Don't.

GETTING AROUND

BY CAR Probably 90 percent of what a tourist wants to do lies within a 10-minute drive of Interstate 4, or I-4, as it's called. That free highway runs diagonally from southwest to northeast, connecting Walt Disney World, Sea-World, the Convention Center, Universal Orlando, and downtown Orlando. I-4 is technically an east-west road linking Florida's coasts, so directions are listed as either west (toward Tampa and the Gulf of Mexico) or east (toward Daytona Beach and the Atlantic Ocean). Once you've got that down, you'll be set. Exits are numbered according to the mile marker at which they're found. Therefore, the Disney World exits (62, 64, 65, and 67) are roughly 10 miles from Universal Orlando's (74 and 75), which are about 9 miles from downtown (83). If you know the exit number, you can figure out distance.

If you stray much onto minor roads, it's a good idea to carry a map or turn on the Waze app or Google Maps. Roads can go by several names and be confusing. Disney World is a particular disaster, since its signage is intentionally incomplete to funnel traffic onto routes the company would rather drivers take. Don't rely on free maps; laughably, some of the ones provided by Universal don't acknowledge that Disney exists at all. **Visit Orlando** (www.visit orlando.com) has free marked maps.

Some Florida toll roads are cashless and require a **SunPass** sensor, rented for as much as $4 a day from your rental agency, plus the cost of tolls; otherwise you will incur large penalties. Fortunately for tourists, in Orlando only the Florida Turnpike and parts of S.R. 417 have gone cashless. Better to avoid the Turnpike or obtain a **Visitor Toll Pass** (highly recommended; www.visitor tollpass.com), which can be reserved ahead via a free app of the same name and picked up at vending machines located on Level 1 at Terminal A of the main airport. If you don't have a transponder or Toll Pass, take S.R. 528 when you leave the main Orlando airport and stay in the right-hand lanes, where human toll operators are still on hand to collect cash the old-fashioned way, and stay off the Turnpike entirely.

SHUTTLES Universal is easy: You walk, bus, or take a free boat everywhere. At Disney, though, hoofing it is impossible. It's so big, it requires a fleet of more than 400 buses, the **Disney Transportation System (DTS),**

which anyone may use for free. Find out about getting around Disney on p. 34.

There are also **hotel theme park shuttles,** which go from independent hotels and are often free (or paid for by resort fees). Yes, you can save money by using them, but there are strong downsides, including wildly inadequate scheduling (you might miss fireworks) and rambling routes. These only go to the park gates, not to restaurants or the many worthwhile smaller attractions. **Mears Transportation** (shuttle.mearstransportation.com) also allows you to pre-book shared-ride shuttles between major city attractions for about $12 a ride.

Another option is the **I-Ride Trolley** (www.iridetrolley.com; © **407/354-5656;** adults $2 per ride, seniors 65 and over 25¢, kids 3–9 $1; day pass $5, 3-day pass $7, 5-day pass $9; free transfers; passes not sold on board; daily 8am–10:30pm), an excellent shuttle bus with plenty of clearly marked and well-maintained stops, benches to wait on, and genuinely useful routes—except it doesn't go to Disney. Its **Red Line** (every 20 min.) plies International Drive from the shops and restaurants just north of I-4's exit 75 all the way to Orlando Premium Outlets, near Disney; along the way it touches down at SeaWorld and the Wheel at ICON Park. The second route, the **Green Line** (every 30 min.), takes in SeaWorld, too, but heads down Universal Boulevard, making it more of an express route, and turns around at Orlando Premium Outlets. It comes within a long block of the entrance to Universal Orlando. Visitors without cars may find it feasible to stay on I-Drive, use this dirt-cheap shuttle to see nearly everything, and then tack on the hated hotel shuttle or a city bus for Disney days.

BY RIDESHARE Because of huge theme park crowds competing for rides at the same hour, it's not terribly easy to use rideshares like Uber or Lyft for every journey you will make on vacation. If you will not be renting a car, then choose a hotel run by one of the theme park resorts—both provide their own free internal shuttle systems to get their guests to and from their parks.

Rideshares between the rival resorts will cost you about $20 per ride. Uber trips within Disney World are about $10–$14 (much cheaper than Disney's in-house, polka-dotted **Minnie Vans,** hailed via Lyft's app; they cost a flat $25 and up).

BY PUBLIC TRANSIT Ultimately, Orlando is a private car city, not a public transit city. Buses are infrequent (usually one or two an hour), shelters are often nonexistent, and when the sun's strong, the combination is dangerous. Distances are also fairly great, so journeys can take a while. The Central Florida Regional Transportation Authority runs the **LYNX system** (www.golynx.com), on which one-way fares are $2, day passes cost $4.50, and weekly passes are $16; note that you have to pay with exact change. Transfers between lines are free, and up to three kids 6 and under ride free with adults. For tourists, here are the most convenient routes, many of which stop at Disney Springs where you can transfer to Disney's free bus system:

Getting Around | PLANNING YOUR TRIP TO ORLANDO

- **Route 56** connects Kissimmee to the front gates of the Magic Kingdom, where you can catch DTS to the other parks. Buses run every 30 minutes, but the last one leaves at 10:53pm.
- **Route 8** does most of International Drive, including the Convention Center and SeaWorld. It duplicates the service offered by the I-Ride Trolley (see above).
- **Route 50** goes from downtown Orlando to Disney Springs and to the gates of the Magic Kingdom. It stops at SeaWorld where passengers can connect to I-Drive on Route 8.
- The lesser Disney areas are served by the 300-series lines: **300** goes to Hotel Plaza Boulevard from downtown; **301** to Epcot and Disney's Animal Kingdom from Pine Hills; **302** to the Magic Kingdom from Rosemont; and **303** to Hollywood Studios from the Washington Shores area. Bus **304** is the only one that connects with another tourist zone; it trawls Sand Lake Road, which bisects I-Drive. Buses 301 and 302 pass within a few blocks of Universal Orlando, on Kirkman Road, so if you toss in about 15 minutes of walking, they could technically be used for Universal, too, but it wouldn't be fun.
- **Route 42** starts at the Convention Center on International Drive, and 75 minutes later, reaches the airport.

In downtown Orlando, there's also the free **LYMMO** bus service (www. golynx.com; Mon–Thurs 6am–10:45pm, Fri 6am–midnight, Sat 10am–midnight, Sun 10am–10pm), with three lines that loop every 10 to 15 minutes.

Orange County has **SunRail** (www.sunrail.com; ✆ **855/724-5411;** $2 one-way, $3.75 round-trip), running from DeBary, north of Sanford, down through the historic center of Kissimmee—all of it miles from theme park gates.

Mouse-Clickers: Obsessive Park Planning Online

If you really want to be intense about this (for your sanity and relaxation, don't), there are obsessive resources that go into granular detail. Disney can't so much as polish a floor without these outlets catching it. My choices:

- On YouTube, **MickeyViews** has amassed a following for extremely detailed and even-handed news updates, while **TPMVids** specializes in buoyant nostalgia and trivia. **Yesterworld** makes deep dives into attraction history.
- **AllEars.net** offers encyclopedic compendiums of everything Disney, down to the menus, what's under renovation, and which rooms are best.

- **InsideUniversal.net** and **Orlando Informer.com** comprehensively report Universal, including deals.
- **WDW News Today** (www.wdwnt. com), **WDWmagic.com**, and **WDWinfo.com** (and its **DISBoards. com**) host some of the most active message forums for news, but their tone is defensively Disney-positive.
- The independently run **Party ThroughTheParks.com** rates drinking and nightlife and **DisneyFood Blog.com** keeps track of meals.
- **MouseSavers.com** and **TheMouse ForLess.com** post current Disney deals.

Tourists only barely care about the 16-minute jaunt between downtown Orlando and Winter Park, but as departures are widely scattered in the morning or evening, targeting commuters, you won't see the point.

BY TAXI   Given so many alternatives, taxis are not a natural choice, but that's the case in most places in the United States now. Many taxis accept major credit cards, but ask when you summon a ride, because your payment may need to be processed by phone. Companies are not carefully monitored, so only choose a recommended carrier. Call your own:

- **Diamond Cab Company** (www.diamondcabco.com): ☎ **407/523-3333**
- **Yellow** (www.mearstransportation.com): ☎ **407/422-2222**

WHEN TO GO

Although Covid-19 taught the parks a lot about managing consistent daily attendance levels, that doesn't mean prices remain flat all year. The main consideration when it comes to selecting dates is balancing good weather with hotel and car prices. None of the theme parks close on **public** holidays—in fact, they do better business then. In late December, Disney parks sometimes hit capacity and seal gates. But in September and the week after Thanksgiving, you can sometimes do nearly everything in a day. Light crowds do not automatically mean shorter waits, because on quieter days, rides run at lower capacity.

So when are the **peak seasons when prices go highest?** Put simply: when American kids are out of school. That means mid-spring, summer until late August, and the holidays. Hotel rates rise then, too. If you want to **save cash,** early January, early May, late August, all of September, and the first half of December are the best you can do. The flipside of low season is that the theme parks trim services and run fewer ride cars when it's quieter. January is a particularly tough month for missing out on rides due to rehabs. And especially in the winter months, you may find it too chilly to enjoy the rides that get you wet, which is a shame since Orlando has some of the best water rides in the world.

CLIMATE   June to September is the heaviest season for excruciating sun, suffocating humidity, and brief torrential rain. Every mid-afternoon, another heavy storm rolls in and shuts rides temporarily—pretty much everything outdoors or on water will temporarily shut down if lightning has been detected within range within the previous 30 minutes. (Central Florida suffers more lightning strikes than any other American locale.) Those deluges usually roll out within an hour but scare away a significant percentage of guests, so it almost always pays to wait an hour or 90 minutes for the rain to clear out. During that season, bring along a cheap poncho from home.

Orlando Average Temperature & Rainfall

	JAN	FEB	MAR	APR	MAY	JUNE	JULY	AUG	SEPT	OCT	NOV	DEC
HI/LOW DAILY TEMPS (°F)	72/49	73/50	78/55	84/60	88/66	91/71	92/73	92/73	90/73	84/65	78/57	73/51
HI/LOW DAILY TEMPS (°C)	22/10	23/10	26/13	29/16	31/19	33/22	33/23	33/23	32/23	29/19	26/14	23/11
INCHES OF PRECIPITATION	2.25	2.82	3.32	2.43	3.30	7.13	7.27	6.88	6.53	3.16	1.98	2.25

Which Day of the Week?

The busiest days at all parks are generally Saturday and Sunday. Seven-day guests are often traveling on these days, and weekends are when locals come to play. Beyond that: Tuesday and Thursday see an uptick in the Magic Kingdom; Tuesday and Friday (and evenings) at Epcot; and Monday, Tuesday, and Wednesday can be a zoo (forgive the pun) at the Animal Kingdom. Because of Star Wars: Galaxy's Edge, Disney's Hollywood Studios is always busy. No matter where you are, crowds tend to ease slightly later in the day.

Orlando's Calendar of Events

Check the special events pages at the theme park websites to see if any themed weekends or smaller events are in the works. In addition, the events listings at **Visit Orlando** (www.visitorlando.com), **Orlando Weekly** (www.orlandoweekly.com), and the **Orlando Sentinel** (www.orlandosentinel.com) are comprehensive, but require payment. You will also find a few listings at **Orlando magazine** (www.orlandomagazine.com).

JANUARY

Citrus Bowl. Now stickered by the Overton's marine supply company—can *anyone* keep track of the square-dancing corporate naming rights anymore? Held New Year's Day at the Florida Citrus Bowl Stadium (Camping World Stadium), it pits the second-ranked teams from the Big Ten and SEC conferences against one another. www.floridacitrussports.com.

Walt Disney World Marathon. The route goes through all four theme parks, or just do the Half, which hits Epcot and the Magic Kingdom. Close to 80,000 runners come for at least one of the five events. Other half-marathon events pop up over the rest of the year. First week of January. There is also a Princess Half-Marathon in February. www.disneyworld.com.

ZORA! Festival. The folklorist and writer Zora Neale Hurston (1891–1960) was from Eatonville (a 30-min. drive north of Orlando), the country's oldest incorporated African-American town. This weeklong event includes lectures and an art fair. www.zorafestival.org.

Epcot International Festival of the Arts. The newest and least focused of Epcot's four major annual festivals is about performance, visual art, and food. In addition to Broadway-style performances and kiosks selling gourmet mini-dishes throughout World Showcase, on many days there are free talks or short workshops with artists who share their disciplines. Mid-January to late February. www.disneyworld.com; ✆ **407/939-3378.**

Rock the Universe. Universal's festival of top-flight Christian rock bands, which perform on stages inside Universal Studios park. Rides and performances continue past midnight, after regular patrons go home. It's separately ticketed. Late January. www.rocktheuniverse.com.

FEBRUARY

Winter Park Bach Festival. This annual event at Rollins College began in 1935 and has evolved into one of the country's better choral fests. Although it has stretched to include other composers and guest artists (Handel, P.D.Q. Bach), at least one concert is devoted to Johann. It takes place mid-February to early March, with scattered one-off guest performances throughout the year. www.bachfestivalflorida.org; ✆ **407/646-2182.**

Silver Spurs Rodeo. A century ago Central Florida was a cattle center, and it still hosts the largest rodeo east of the Mississippi (with bareback broncs, barrel racing horses, rodeo clowns, and athletes drawn from the cowboy circuit) over 3 days on the third weekend in February in an indoor arena off U.S. 192. Its 2021 event was held in June, but it's usually held in February. 1875 Silver Spur Lane, Kissimmee. www.silverspursrodeo.com; ✆ **321/697-3495.**

Mardi Gras at Universal Studios. On Saturday nights in the spring, Universal books major acts (Bonnie Raitt, Hall & Oates, LL Cool J, Diana Ross, Ne-Yo) and mounts a family-friendly parade complete with stilt-walkers, jazz bands, Louisiana-made floats, and bead tossing—although here, what it takes to win a set of beads is considerably less risqué than it is in the Big Easy. It's included with admission. www.universal orlando.com/mardigras; ✆ **407/224-2691.**

Spring Training. See p. 265 for a rundown of which Major League Baseball teams play where. Mid-February through March.

MARCH

Epcot's International Flower & Garden Festival. This spring event, which lasts about 75 days from March through May, transforms Epcot with some 30 million flowers, 70 topiaries, a screened-in butterfly garden, presentations by noted horticulturalists, and a lineup of "Flower Power" concerts (in the past: Chubby Checker, the Pointer Sisters). It's free with standard entry. www.disneyworld.com/flowerandgarden; ✆ **407/934-7639.**

APRIL

Epcot's International Flower & Garden Festival. See March for full listing, above.

Florida Film Festival. This respected event showcases films by Florida artists and has featured past appearances by the likes of Ellen Burstyn, Christopher Walken, and Sissy Spacek. It's an Oscar-qualifying festival for shorts. www.floridafilmfestival.com; ✆ **407/629-1088.**

MAY

Orlando International Fringe Festival. This theatrical smorgasbord, the longest-running fringe fest in America, spends 14 days mounting some 950 performances of more than 140 newly written, experimental shows. It's held mostly downtown in Loch Haven Park. www.orlandofringe.org; ✆ **407/648-0077.**

Epcot's International Flower & Garden Festival. See March for full listing, above.

JUNE

Gay Days. What started in 1991 as a single day for party-minded gay and lesbian visitors has bloomed into a full week of some 40 events managed by a host of promoters. It's said that attendance goes as high as 150,000. Gay Days are a blowout party with group visits to the city's parks (wearing red shirts as a gentle reminder of visibility, which is also done the first weekend in June for the parks' unofficial Red Shirt Days), concerts (En Vogue, LeAnn Rimes), a marketplace, several dance events, and more than a dozen pool parties. June at the host hotel (in 2021, that was Margaritaville Resort Orlando). www.gaydays.com.

SEPTEMBER

Epcot International Food & Wine Festival. The World Showcase makes amends with the countries it ignores by installing temporary booths selling tapas-size servings of foods and wines from many nations. That's supplemented with chef demonstrations, seminars, "Eat to the Beat" concerts by known acts, and tastings by at least 100 wineries. In short, it's a sensation. A few of the more extravagant events are charged, but most are free. The festival, which tends to be more crowded on weekends, lasts more than 3 solid months from mid-July to mid-November; hotly awaited details are posted by Disney in the summer. www.disneyworld.com/foodandwine; ✆ **407/939-3378.**

OCTOBER

Mickey's Not-So-Scary Halloween Party/ Boo Bash. The best of the Magic Kingdom's separately ticketed evening events, this one mounts a special parade with a fiendishly catchy theme song, a few special shows, a fireworks display that surpasses the usual one, and stations where you can pick up free candy. Kids even show up in costume, although it's not required, and crowds are shoulder-to-shoulder. Before the pandemic, this event happened on scattered evenings from mid-August through the end of October. As of press time, there has been no announcement of its return, but for 2021, Disney mounted a less intricate, 3-hour substitute, **After Hours Boo Bash.** Target audience: people who like lollipops. www.disneyworld.com/halloweenparty; ✆ **407/934-7639.**

Halloween Horror Nights. Unquestionably Universal's biggest event, HHN is the equivalent of a whole new theme park that's designed for a year but only lasts a month. After dark, the Studios are overtaken by grotesque "scareactors" who terrorize crowds with chain saws, gross-out shows, and seven or eight big, well-made, walk-through haunted houses that are created from scratch each year. It's separately ticketed from daytime park visits, when the houses are closed. The mayhem lasts into the wee hours. Wimps need not apply; children are discouraged by the absence of kids' ticket prices. On top of all this, most rides remain open. HHN has legions of fans. Target audience: people who like to poop themselves in fright. (Busch Gardens' Howl-o-Scream event's scariness is somewhere between Universal's and Disney's.) www. halloweenhorrornights.com.

SeaWorld's Halloween Spooktacular and Howl-O-Scream. SeaWorld throws a sweet, toddler-approved weekend Halloween event of its own, with trick-or-treating (kids dress up), a few encounters with sea fairies and bubbles, and a show starring Count von Count from *Sesame Street*. Target audience: people who have a naptime. It's included in admission. Its adult-oriented nighttime event, Howl-O-Scream (haunted houses, scare zones, coaster riding in the dark), happens over about 25 nights starting in mid-September and is separately ticketed. http://seaworld.com/orlando/events.

Orlando Film Festival. Like all festivals worth their salt, this one presents dozens of mostly mainstream and independent films in advance of their wider release dates, plus cool events like workshops on writing and pitching. It lasts about a week in October or early November, screening at various downtown venues. In 2020, it went entirely virtual; check to see if it's happening in person when you visit. www. orlandofilmfest.com; ☎ **407/217-1390.**

NOVEMBER

ICE! It debuted in 2003 at the Gaylord Palms hotel and has quickly become a holiday perennial. The hotel brings in nearly 2 million pounds of ice, sculpts it into a walk-through city with ice slides kids love, keeps it all chilled to 9°F (–13°C), and issues winter coats to visitors. Add synchronized light shows and you've got an event that charges $30+ adults, $18+ kids—and sells out into the first week of January. http://christmas. gaylordhotels.com/ice; ☎ **407/586-0000.**

DECEMBER

Mickey's Very Merry Christmas Party. This crowded night, which before the pandemic occurred on various nights starting before Thanksgiving, is probably Disney's most popular special annual event. It requires a separate ticket from regular admission. What you get is a tree-lighting ceremony, a few special holiday-themed shows, a special fireworks display (very green and red), an appearance by Santa Claus, a special parade, and *huge* crowds. During the pandemic, the MVMCP was replaced with Disney Very Merriest After Hours, a separately ticketed event that gave access to about 20 attractions. It's only a 4-hour event, so probably not worth the ticket price, which is about what a full day at the park would cost. Meanwhile, Disney's warehouse for holiday decorations (it exists) empties out and its hotels deck the halls: The Grand Floridian erects a life-size house made of gingerbread. www.disneyworld.com/christmas party; ☎ **407/934-7639.**

Epcot International Festival of the Holidays. This 1-month event features holiday customs of many nations and a host of costumed storytellers, but its real showpiece is the daily, 40-minute candlelight processional, a retelling of the Christmas Nativity story by a celebrity narrator (regular names include Whoopi Goldberg, Gary Sinise, Edward James Olmos, and Neil Patrick Harris) accompanied by a 50-piece orchestra and a full Mass choir. The processional is a WDW tradition going back to its earliest days—Cary Grant did it! www.disneyworld. com/holidays.

Grinchmas & The Macy's Holiday Parade. Usual holiday traditions include a musical version of *How the Grinch Stole Christmas* and daily parades by Macy's, which brings some balloons and floats to Universal when its NYC Thanksgiving parade is over. That's included in the ticket price. As of press time, there has been no announcement of its return. www.universalorlando.com.

Cheez-It Bowl. A team from the ACC (including Notre Dame) battles a Big 12 team, usually a few days before New Year's and always at the Camping World Stadium, once called the Citrus Bowl. First played in 1990, the game has had many faces, including the Camping World Bowl, Champs Sports Bowl, Carquest Bowl, Tangerine Bowl, Russell Athletic Bowl, and its very first sponsor, that of the doomed videocassette dealer Blockbuster. www.cheezitbowl.com.

New Year's Eve. Yahoo.com reports that Orlando regularly makes its list of top five most-searched New Year's Eve destinations. There's no shortage of places to party. At the parks: **CityWalk** throws its EVE bash with outdoor dance floor and light shows; the **Disney parks** stay open until the wee hours and may have live DJs; **SeaWorld** brings in big-band music or jazz, plus fireworks.

Getting Attraction Discounts

For a full breakdown of Disney's ticketing, how it works, and how to guard against overspending, see p. 21.

Universal and SeaWorld discount the gate price if you book online, and all the parks discount per-day entry if you buy multiple days. SeaWorld and Busch Gardens also offer courtesy admission for members of the military and their families. Check www.wavesofhonor.com to see if you are eligible. You will also find coupons through the discount circular **HotelCoupons.com**.

A few outfits (such as, occasionally, local AAA chapters) sell faintly discounted tickets. **Maple Leaf Tickets** (www.mapleleaftickets.com; ✆ **407/396-0300**) and **The Official Ticket Center** (www.officialticketcenter.com; ✆ **877/406-4836**) are in good standing with the Better Business Bureau. So is **Undercover Tourist** (www.undercovertourist.com; ✆ **800/846-1302**), which also publishes a marvelous calendar that guesses, using as many statistics as possible, at what the best touring plans are for the days you're visiting—not that any of those calendars will be worth much while the parks' attendance systems are in flux. No Disney deals ever seem deep enough to offset shipping fees or the hassle of picking up your tickets at some third-party office; however, multiple purchases, stays of a week or longer, and third-tier diversions such as dinner shows ($10–$15 off) may be worth it. Tickets are nontransferable. If you don't want the hassle of pre-planning, a desk at the Orlando Official Visitor Center (p. 303) furnishes similar discounts on tickets you can trust.

Be wary of any discount card that offers admission to secondary attractions for one set price. The catch is you usually get an obscenely short time—like 2 days—to use it. Rare is the person who can move fast enough to make the price pay off unless one of the days is used at an expensive attraction such as Legoland and the other day is crammed from morning to bedtime with lesser diversions.

[FastFACTS] ORLANDO

Accessible Travel

Nearly everything is accessible. Even before the Americans with Disabilities Act of 1990, the parks have always worked to be inclusive, and guests with mobility issues have long embraced them in return.

Disney's full descriptions of its support facilities are posted under the "Services" section at disneyworld.disney.go.com/guest-services. Up to 30 days before a scheduled park visit, guests can schedule a video call to register for Disney's **Disability Access Service (DAS)** for pre-arrival planning. Once they are registered, guests can use the My Disney Experience app to arrange DAS entry to attractions (which will appear on your schedule in Genie). Parties will be given a reservation time that accounts for the current wait time (you can come back later as long as the time has passed, but you can't get another reservation until you've used the first one). Or part of your group might be asked to pass through the standard line while you wait in a special area and reunite with them before riding. There will usually be a place for you to wait for the special wheelchair-ready ride vehicle to arrive. You might have to transfer to a manual wheelchair; the park maps indicate which rides will require that. If you have not registered for DAS before arrival, head to Guest Relations to obtain a card that designates you as requiring consideration. No doctor's letter is required. Oxygen tanks may not be permitted on rides. A very few, pre-ADA attractions, such as Tom Sawyer Island and the Swiss Family Treehouse, require you to be ambulatory. Those are marked, too. There is a special parade-viewing area for those with mobility issues so you can have good sightlines; arrive early and ask any cast

member where it is. Companions of guests with cognitive disabilities such as autism also obtain ride reservations that correspond to the current wait time; cast members can direct them to "break areas" for easing stimulation.

At Universal, go to the Guest Relations desk after the turnstiles for an **Attractions Assistance Pass.** If a ride's wait is less than 30 minutes, you'll scoot right on, and if it's longer, you'll be issued a time to return but you cannot get a new reservation time until that one is fulfilled. If that system won't work for you, Universal may choose to issue a **Guest Assistance Pass,** which grants Express access to all attractions, no appointment required. (Universal publishes a **ride guide** to accessibility: www. universalorlando.com/rg.) Similarly, SeaWorld offers the **Ride Accessibility Pass.**

Service animals are permitted but aren't always allowed to ride attractions.

Theme park hotels all can lend door-knock and phone alerts, amplifiers, bed shakers, strobes, and TTY phones. At Disney, request a Room Communication Kit before arrival at (✆ **407/824-4321;** at Universal, TDD relay devices and doorbell lights are available at hotel front desks. For off-property stays, consider renting a house, which provides much more room; most home-rental companies also comply with ADA requirements.

All the parks have a full range of in-park services for guests of every need, including at least a half-dozen TTY phones scattered around and sign-language interpreters on scheduled days of the week. Universal marks the times for its ASL shows on its guide map; some days they're not automatically available, but you can request show interpretation for free at least 14 days ahead by writing *Sign LanguageServices@universal orlando.com.*

Disney maintains a Special Services hotline to answer all accessibility needs. At the parks, Guest Relations windows can furnish guests with handheld captioning and/or assistive listening devices for hearing-impaired guests; they require a $25 refundable deposit (✆ **407/824-4321** voice and TTY ✆ 407/827-5141; Disability.services@ disneyparks.com). Universal Orlando can be reached at ✆ **800/447-0672** (TDD) or 407/224-4233 (voice); www. universalorlando.com; Sea-World Orlando's number is ✆ **407/363-2400** (www.sea world.com); Kennedy Space Center is at ✆ **321/449-4443** (www.kennedyspace center.com). Try to contact those a few weeks ahead. There are plenty of accessible parking spots.

The theme parks operate rental desks for wheelchairs and ECVs (sit-down scooters) near each front gate (prices are listed in the theme park chapters), but you will have to be able to travel to that kiosk on your own. You also may not take a rental out of its park, so if you switch theme parks on the same day, you are not guaranteed to find availability at your second park—if there are still rentals left, though, you can show the receipt from your first park to avoid paying for rental twice. Prices are steep and lines can be long, and the vehicles are very simple (no sun shades, etc.), so many people rent their own ahead of time from a third party. **Medical Travel, Inc.** (www.medicaltravel.org; ☏ **866/322-4400** or 407/438-8010) specializes in the rental of mobility equipment, ramp vans, and supplies such as oxygen tanks (be aware that many rides do not allow tanks). Electric scooters and wheelchairs can be delivered to your accommodation through these established companies: **Orlando Medical Rentals** (www.orlandomedicalrentals.com; ☏ **877/356-9943**) which also supplies oxygen, scooters, and the like; **Buena Vista Scooter Rentals** (www.buenavistascooters.com; ☏ **407/331-9147**); **Scootaround** (www.scootaround.com; ☏ **888/441-7575**); **CARE Medical Equipment** (www.caremedicalequipment.com; ☏ **800/741-2282** or 407/856-2273); and **Walker Medical & Mobility Products** (www.walkermobility.com; ☏ **888/726-6837** or 407/518-6000). All the theme parks, except the water parks, rent ECVs for about $50 a day and

wheelchairs for about $12 a day. If your own wheelchair is wider than 25 inches, think about switching to the park model, because it is guaranteed to navigate tight squeezes such as hairpin queue turns. If you wear a prosthetic limb, you may have to remove it for the most aggressive rides. A few coasters (like SeaWorld's Mako) have restraint systems that won't work if you use certain prosthetics, so always ask the operators what's safe for you.

Organizations that offer assistance to travelers with disabilities include the **American Federation for the Blind** (www.afb.org; ☏ **212/502-7600**) and **Society for Accessible Travel & Hospitality** (www.sath.org; ☏ **212/447-7284**).

Area Codes The area code for the Orlando area is **407** (if you're dialing locally, a preceding 1 is not necessary, but the 407 is), although you may encounter the less common **321** code, which is also used on the Atlantic Coast. The **863** area code governs the land between Orlando and Tampa, and the Tampa area uses **813** and **727.** The region west of Orlando uses **352.**

Business Hours Offices are generally open Monday through Friday between 9am and 5pm, while banks tend to close at 4pm. Typically, stores open between 9 and 10am and close between 6 and 7pm Monday through Saturday, except malls, which stay open until 9pm.

On Sunday, stores generally open at 11am and close by 7pm.

Car Rentals A large inventory means rentals are cheaper here than in other American cities: $30–$50 a day is common for a compact car. For a list of rental agencies, see p. 284.

Make sure your rental car locks by remote control fob; use it to make your vehicle honk and locate it in those confusing theme park parking pastures.

Crime Disney may advertise itself as "the Happiest Place on Earth," but it's still on Earth. As we are all too aware, that means bad things happen. Never open your hotel room door to a stranger, never order anything off a flyer you find under your door, and never give your personal details or credit card number to anyone who calls your room, even if they claim to work for the hotel. **Pickpockets** are virtually unheard of, but they exist. Be vigilant about bags; you're going to be bumped and jostled many times—one of those bumps could be a nimble-fingered thief. The theme parks all have metal detectors and bag checks.

Customs Rules change. For details regarding current regulations, consult **U.S. Customs and Border Protection** (www.cbp.gov; ☏ **877/227-5511**).

Doctors There are first-aid centers in all of the theme parks. There's also a 24-hour number for the

Poison Control Center (📞 **800/222-1222**). To find a dentist, contact the **Dental Referral** (www.dentalreferral. com; 📞 **800/235-4111**). **DOCS** (www.doctorsoncall service.com; 📞 **407/399-3627**) makes house and room calls. If you don't have a car, **EastCoast Medical Network** (www.themedical concierge.com; 📞 **855/932-5252**) makes "hotel room calls" to area resorts or rental homes for $150 to $275 for most ailments. It's available at all hours, accepts most insurance, and brings a portable pharmacy, although prescriptions cost more. Do not bring **medical marijuana** through Orlando's MCO airport; despite the fact that carrying it is legal in Florida, the airport management has gone rogue and heeds federal rules instead. Also see "Hospitals."

Drinking Laws The legal drinking age is 21. Proof of age is always requested, even if you look older, so carry a photo ID. It's illegal to carry open containers of alcohol in any car or public area that isn't zoned for alcohol consumption (as CityWalk and Disney Springs are), so outside of the resorts, the police may ticket you on the spot.

Driving Rules Americans drive on the right. In Florida, you may turn right on red only after making a full stop unless the signal is an illuminated arrow, in which case you must wait for green. Many intersections are equipped with

traffic cameras that will take a photo of your license plate, and rental car companies pass on fines along with hefty fees.

Florida is full of visitors who don't know where they're going or maybe have never even driven on the right before. These wandering souls will halt, cross three lanes of traffic, and barrel into the wrong lane without thinking. Keep a safe distance from the car in front of you.

Electricity The United States uses 110 to 120 volts AC (60 cycles), compared to the 220 to 240 volts AC (50 cycles) that is standard in Europe, Australia, and New Zealand. If your small appliances use 220 to 240 volts, buy an adapter and voltage converter before you leave home, because these can be difficult to come by in Orlando.

Embassies & Consulates The nearest embassies are located in the nation's capital, Washington, D.C. Some consulates are located in major U.S. cities, and most nations have a mission to the United Nations in New York City. Call for directory information in Washington, D.C. (📞 **202/555-1212**), or log on to **www.embassy.org/ embassies**.

Emergencies Call 📞 **911** for the police, to report a fire, or to get an ambulance. If you have a medical emergency that does not require an ambulance, you should be able

to walk into the nearest hospital emergency room (see "Hospitals," below).

Family Travel All parks have a cool **baby care center** for heating formula, nursing, and so on, and diaper changing tables in the restrooms.

Scarier rides have what's called a **child swap.** That provides an area where one adult can wait with a child while their partner rides and then switch off so the other gets a chance without having to wait all over again. Many rides also have a bypass corridor where chickens can do their chicken-out thing.

Your **stroller** will not be allowed inside most attractions, and it will not be attended in parking sections, so never leave anything valuable in it. Come prepared with a system for repeatedly unloading valuables. Also have something that covers the seat; just like parked cars, strollers get sizzling hot when you leave them in the Florida sun. Finally, tie an identifying marker (like a white flag, as in "I surrender") to yours so you can identify it amid the sea of clones. At Disney, **strollers** cannot be larger than 31 inches wide and 52 inches long (which is still pretty big). Some outfits deliver nicer models than Disney's to hotels (but charge less if you pick them up in person): **Magic Strollers** (www. magicstrollers.com; 📞 **866/ 866-6177**), **World Strollers,** in the Welcome Center of

- **To avoid tears, familiarize yourself with height restrictions in advance.** They are posted at the parks' websites and listed on the maps. Universal also keeps physical gauges in front of both its parks. Everything is measured in inches, so if your child is usually measured in centimeters, multiply by 0.393.
- **Bring supplies to kid-proof your hotel room.**
- **Slather your kids in sunscreen.** Florida sun is even stronger than you think.
- **Dress kids in bright colors.** You'll spot them faster if you're separated. Some parents even put their phone number on their kids with temporary tattoos. You might also want to wear a distinctive hat or shirt yourself so they can spot you.
- **Dress to get wet.** There are water playgrounds, plus frequent rains.
- **Baby changing tables are in both women's and men's rooms.** No sexism here. At least in this. All those princesses hunting for men is another matter.

- **Hotels offer "kids eat free" programs.** Ask.
- **Theme park strollers are easy, but basic;** they don't recline, and they won't secure kids younger than toddlers. Folding "umbrella" strollers have distinct advantages. They make getting onto trams, monorails, and into other tight spaces easier (not just for you—also for people waiting for you).
- **Take a picture of your child in the day's outfit** to show someone in case you get separated. Teach your child to go straight to the nearest employee if they lose you. Everyone is well trained in reuniting families.
- **Think carefully about whether your child is ready for the theme parks.** I agree with many parenting experts who say that about 3 years old is the minimum age. Younger children get wigged out by costumed characters and are too short to ride some rides they may have their hearts set on. Some experts say kids are not truly ready for the rigors of theme parks until they can walk on their own all day.

Lake Buena Vista Factory Stores (15569 State Rd. 535, Orlando; www.lbvfs.com; ☏ **407/238-9301**), and **Baby Wheels** (www.baby wheelsorlando.com; ☏ **800/510-2480**) among them.

Health Your biggest concern is the **sun,** which can burn you even through gray skies on cloudy days. You will be spending a lot more time outdoors than you might suspect—rides take 3 minutes, but some lines will

have you waiting outside for an hour. Hats are your friends.

Somewhere along the way, you might spot wide roaches about an inch and a half long. Their appearance is not necessarily due to uncleanliness at your hotel—those are waterbugs, which thrive in the damp Florida environment and are always hunting for food. As for mosquitos, the resorts' spraying regimens keep them in check, but if you're

worried, any Disney cast member can tell you where to obtain free repellant.

Holidays Banks close on the following holidays: January 1 (New Year's), the third Monday in January (Martin Luther King, Jr., Day), the third Monday in February (Presidents' Day), the last Monday in May (Memorial Day), July 4 (Independence Day), the first Monday in September (Labor Day), the second Monday in November (Veterans Day), the fourth Thursday in November (Thanksgiving Day), and December 25 (Christmas Day). The theme parks are open every day of the year.

Hospitals **Orlando Health Dr. P. Phillips Hospital** (9400 Turkey Lake Rd., Orlando; ✆ **407/351-8500**) is a short drive north up Palm Parkway from Lake Buena Vista. To get to the 24-hr. **AdventHealth Celebration** (400 Celebration Place, Celebration; ✆ **407/303-4000**) from I-4, take the U.S. 192 exit, then at the first traffic light, turn right onto Celebration Avenue, and at the first stop sign, make another right.

Clinics: **Central Florida AdventHealth Centra Care Lake Buena Vista** (12500 Apopka-Vineland Rd., ✆ **407/934-2273;** www. centracare.org; Mon–Fri 8am–midnight, Sat–Sun 8am–8pm); **AdventHealth Centra Care Orange Lake** (near the vacation homes south of Disney at 8201 W. U.S. 192, Kissimmee; ✆ **407/465-0846;** daily 8am–8pm); and **AdventHealth Centra Care Dr. Phillips** (northwest of Universal at 8014 Conroy-Windermere Rd., Suite 104; ✆ **407/291-8975;** daily 8am–8pm). In addition, each theme park has its own infirmary capable of handling a range of medical emergencies.

Insurance You may want special coverage for **apartment stays,** especially if you've plunked down a deposit, and for any

valuables you may bring with you; airlines are only required to pay up to $2,500 for lost luggage domestically, less for foreign travel. Compare policies at **InsureMyTrip.com** (✆ **800/ 487-4722**), or contact one of the following reputable companies: **Allianz** (www. allianztravelinsurance.com; ✆ **866/884-3556**); **Generali Global Assistance** (formerly CSA Travel Protection; www. generalitravelinsurance.com; ✆ **800/874-2442**); **AIG Travel Guard** (www.travel guard.com; ✆ **800/826-5248**); or **Travelex** (www. travelexinsurance.com; ✆ **800/228-9792**). Note that most insurers require you to purchase plans soon after you buy your trip but *before* you leave home.

Internet & Wi-Fi Getting online isn't hard. Wi-Fi is now considered an essential amenity, like running water. Most hotels will have free access—sometimes in common areas, sometimes in guest rooms, and sometimes in both places. Walt Disney World's hotels have free Wi-Fi, and so do all the theme parks in town. Hotel connections aren't always fast enough to stream movies, but they're usually fast enough for standard uses. Nearly all home rentals come with Internet-connected computers and free Wi-Fi.

LGBTQ Travelers Orlando still has a conservative streak and the state government is actively hostile to equality laws, but the Pulse massacre made locals

feel much more protective of its gay population. Most hotels aren't troubled in the least by gay couples, and gay people can be themselves anyplace. The most intolerant attitudes will come from other guests at the theme parks, who, of course, mostly aren't from Orlando. Public displays of affection are not likely to be attacked, but don't expect a warm reception, either. Then again, sexual affection is not celebrated in the parks if you're straight, either. Use your intuition, your good manners, and your common sense.

Mail At press time, domestic postage rates were 40¢ for a postcard and 58¢ for a letter. For international mail, a first-class letter of up to 1 ounce costs $1.30; a first-class international postcard costs the same as a letter. The post office most convenient to Disney and Universal is at 10450 Turkey Lake Rd. (✆ **407/351-2492;** Mon–Fri 8am–7pm, Sat 9am–5pm). If all you need is to buy stamps and mail letters, you can do that at most hotels. For more information, including locations nearest you, go to **www. usps.com** and click on "Calculate a Price." Ask at the theme park Guest Relations desks if mailing your items there will entitle you to a novelty postmark.

Mobile Phones Your phone will work in Orlando; it may not work if you drive far from commercial areas, such as in some remote vacation home developments (although in those cases you'll probably have Wi-Fi for Internet calling). To buy a pay-as-you-go SIM card, ask for a "no-contract" SIM card.

The theme parks' new reliance on managing your day via apps drains devices quickly. To have enough juice for a 13-hour day, carry a **portable charger or battery.** The theme parks have vending machines by Fuel-Rod (www.fuel-rod.com) selling $30 pre-filled booster batteries, adapter included; find them in the photo stores by the front gate and sprinkled around the park (ask a cast member where). When the battery is depleted (they're not very powerful—your own would be stronger), you pop it into any other FuelRod vending machine elsewhere at Disney or anywhere in the world and swap for a fresh one for $3. (FuelRods are about $10 cheaper if you buy one from home.) At the Magic Kingdom, there's a public charger in a fake tree stump among the benches across from Peter Pan's Flight and in the big tent beside the Fantasyland railroad station; bring your own cord. At Epcot, there's a floor-level outlet on your right as you enter The Land. Disney will also charge your phone for free at Guest Relations if you have the required cord, but that will often backtracking to the front of the park and then require waiting in line.

Money This town exists to rake in money. Consequently, it places few obstacles between you and the surrender of it. Most ATMs are run by third parties, not your bank (Disney's are by Chase), which means that you'll be slapped with fees of around $2.50 per withdrawal (around $5 for international visitors). Machines accept pretty much anything you can stick into them. Citibank customers can avoid the usage fee by using the fancy Citibank machines located at most 7-Eleven convenience stores. International visitors should make advance arrangements with their banks to ensure their cards will function in the United States. Also ask your bank if it has reciprocal agreements for free withdrawals anywhere. Try not to use credit cards to withdraw cash. You'll be charged interest from the moment your money leaves the slot.

Credit cards are nearly universally accepted, but it's common for hotels to place holds for dollar amounts that exceed what you're likely to eventually spend, so if you're near your credit limit, beware. You *must* have a credit card to rent a car without a hassle. Most places accept the Big Four: American Express, MasterCard, Visa, and Discover. Very few places add Diners Club, and some family-owned businesses subtract American Express because of the pain of dealing with it.

Before you leave home, let your issuer know that you're about to go on vacation. Many of them get antsy when they see unexpectedly large charges start appearing so far from your home, and sometimes they freeze your account in response.

Universal sells its own private scrip, Wizarding Bank Notes, at Gringotts Money Exchange in Universal Studios, while you can get Batuuan Spira (actually a cool-looking Disney Gift Card you can spend at any Disney property) at Droid Depot in Star Wars: Galaxy's Edge. They're both charged as a purchase, not a withdrawal, sparing you extra charges, and can be used to buy things inside their respective parks.

Because ATM withdrawals give better deals, old-fashioned exchange desks are rare. One of the last, the Travelex Currency Exchange at Lake Buena Vista Factory Stores, has now shut down.

Newspapers & Magazines The local paper, the *Orlando Sentinel* (www.orlandosentinel.com) is widely available but no longer great for discovering local happenings. Better to pick up *Orlando Weekly* (www.orlandoweekly.com), free around town, which covers trends, events, and restaurants. Also see the box on p. 289 for amateur-run websites covering the theme parks; those are better for park goings-on.

Packing For the latest rules on how to pack and

Stuff You Never Thought to Bring (But Should)

Besides the usual toiletries, recharging cords, and medications, you might not have thought of these good ideas, too:

- **A mobile phone battery recharger.** Between the My Disney Experience app, Wi-Fi, photos, and social media updating, you'll drain your battery quickly.

- **Earplugs.** Orlando flights are swinging with kids going insane with excitement.

- **Hand sanitizer.** Turnstiles. Safety bars. Handrails. Furry mice. You're going to be handling a lot of dirty things.

- **Sole inserts.** You will be walking for miles and standing for hours, with few benches in sight. Even hardy feet need all the comfort you can provide.

- **Dark-colored clothing.** On almost all flume rides, the seating doubles as a step, so you're bound to stain your butt with a slightly muddy

footprint. Also, it's hot and you'll be in lots of photos—and colored shirts show sweat marks.

- **Sandals that fasten.** Water-based rides soak regular shoes and cause pruning. Flip-flops won't always do because they're not hardy and they won't stay on.

- **Skin-tight underwear.** Florida humidity can cause chafing even in people who rarely experience it. Under Armour or nonpadded bike shorts preempt that.

- **Sunscreen, a hat, and sunglasses.** Okay, so you probably thought of these, but it bears repeating.

- **A superabsorbent shammy.** For lenses and wet children.

- **Pocket-size games.** People talk about rides, but they neglect to mention the hour in line before those exciting 3 minutes. Orlando *is* lines. Bring diversions.

what you will be permitted to bring as a carry-on, consult your airline or the **Transportation Security Administration** (www.tsa. gov). Also be sure to find out from your airline what your checked-baggage weight limits will be; maximums of around 50 pounds per suitcase are standard. Anything heavier will incur a fee. Paying for the luggage at the airport is often more expensive than online.

If you forget something, there's nothing you can't buy in Orlando. It's hardly Timbuktu. But bring the basics for sunshine (lotion of at least 30 SPF, wide-brimmed hat, bathing suit,

sunglasses), for rain (a compact umbrella or a plastic poncho, which costs $10 if you wait until you get into the parks), for walking (good shoes, sandals for wet days), and for memories (camera, storage cards, chargers). Theme parks are too crowded for the safe use of large umbrellas. Gum also isn't sold at any theme park resort because it makes the night cleaners cry.

Pets   None of the Disney resorts allow animals (except service dogs) to stay (the only exception being Disney's Fort Wilderness Campground, where you can have your pet at the full-hook-up campsites).

Disney offers **animal boarding,** usually for about $40–$50 per day. Disney uses a single facility, **Best Friends Pet Care,** at 2510 Bonnet Creek Pkwy. (www.best friendspetcare.com; 📞 **407/ 209-3126**). For daycare, it opens 1 hour before the parks and closes 1 hour after the last closing. Overnight prices start at $44 for most dogs and $28 for cats. For **daytime dog and cat boarding,** Universal charges $15 per pet at its first-come, first-served kennel 📞 **407/224-9509**) in the parking structure; there, owners must feed and walk their own dogs, but water is provided. You don't have to stay at a resort property to use Universal's service. Off-property, there's **VIPet Resort** (☎ **407/355-3594;** www.vipet.net; $55–$65 dogs, $32 cats overnight, $30 daytime), near where Sand Lake Road meets Florida's Turnpike. For all these services, you must have written proof of current vaccinations.

Universal's resorts (minus Cabana Bay, Aventura, and Endless Summer) allow pets for a $100 fee, and the hotels also provide welcome amenities. Even hotels that are pet-friendly usually charge a daily fee. To find more pet-friendly hotels, two solid resources are **www.petswelcome.com** and **www.dogfriendly.com**.

Pharmacies The tourist area hosts mostly national chains. **Walgreens** (7650 W. Sand Lake Rd. at Dr. Phillips Blvd., Orlando; ☎ **407/370-6742**), which has a round-the-clock pharmacy, could, at a stretch, be deemed an outfit with local roots; back in the day, Mr. Walgreen spent the cold months in Winter Park. **Turner Drugs** (1530 Celebration Blvd., Suite 105-A, Celebration; www.turner drug.com; ☎ **407/828-8125**) is not a 24-hour pharmacy, but during the day it delivers prescriptions to most Disney-area accommodations.

Police Call ☎ **911** from any phone in an emergency.

Safety Calculated in fatalities per mile, the 132 miles of I-4 through Orlando is the deadliest highway in the United States, so drive it

with extreme caution. Train kids to approach the nearest park employee in case of **separation.** Never dress kids in clothing that reveals their name, address, or hometown, and unless it's a travel day, remove any luggage tags where this information will be visible. If people can read your address off a tag while you're in line at Toy Story Land, then they'll know you're not at home. Stay out of lakes at night—Florida belonged to alligators for thousands of years before we were here, and evening is often when they get hungry. Attacks are extraordinarily rare, but one did happen in June 2016 on Disney's Seven Seas Lagoon when a gator mistook a 2-year-old child for small prey. Don't leave valuables visible when you park your car. Also, please keep your arms and legs inside the vehicle at all times. Thank you.

Senior Travel Just about every secondary attraction offers a special price for seniors, but the theme parks offer precious little. If you're 50 or over, you can join **AARP** (601 E. Street NW, Washington, DC 24009; www.aarp.org; ☎ **888/687-2277**) to find out what's being offered in terms of discounts for hotels, airfare, and car rentals. Before you bite, be sure that the AARP discount you are offered actually undercuts others that are out there. Elderhostel's well-respected **Road Scholar** (www.roadscholar. org; ☎ **800/454-5768**) runs

classes and programs, both inside the theme parks and around the Orlando area, designed to delve into literature, history, the arts, and music. Packages last from a day to a week and include lodging, tours, and meals. Most are multigenerational; bring the grandkids.

Smoking Smoking is prohibited in public indoor spaces, including offices, restaurants, hotel lobbies, and most shops. Some bars permit it. In general, if you need to smoke, you must go outside into the open air, and in the theme parks smokers are comically quarantined to strictly enforced areas outside the park gates like naughty kids in detention.

Taxes A 6.5 to 7 percent sales tax is charged on all goods with the exception of most edible grocery items and medicines. Hotels add another 2 to 5 percent in a resort tax, so the total tax on accommodations can run up to 12 percent. The United States has no VAT, but the custom is to not list prices with tax, so the final amount that you pay will be slightly higher than the posted price.

Telephones Generally, hotel surcharges on long-distance and local calls are astronomical, so you're better off using your **cellphone** or a **public pay telephone.** Many convenience groceries and packaging services sell **prepaid calling cards** in denominations from $10 to $50; for international visitors these can be the least expensive way to call home. Many public phones at airports now accept American Express, MasterCard, and Visa credit cards. **Local calls** made from public pay phones in most locales cost either 35¢ or 50¢. Pay phones do not accept pennies, and few will take anything larger than a quarter. Make sure you have roaming turned on for your cellphone account.

If you will have high-speed Internet access in your room, save on calls by using FaceTime, Skype, WhatsApp, or another free, Web-based calling app. **For calls within the United States and to Canada,** dial 1 followed by the area code and the seven-digit number. **For other international calls,** first dial 011, then the country code, and then proceed with the number, dropping any leading zeroes.

Calls to area codes **800, 888, 877,** and **866** are toll-free. However, calls to area codes **700** and **900** can be very expensive—usually a charge of 95¢ to $3 or more per minute, and they sometimes have minimum charges that can run as high as $15 or more.

For **reversed-charge or collect calls,** and for person-to-person calls, dial the number 0, then the area code and number. If your operator-assisted call is international, ask for the overseas operator.

For **local directory assistance** ("information"), dial 𝄞 **411;** for long-distance

information, dial 1, then the appropriate area code and 555-1212.

Time   Orlando is on Eastern Standard Time, so when it's noon in Orlando, it's 11am in Chicago (CST), 10am in Denver (MST), and 9am in Los Angeles (PST). Daylight Savings moves the clock 1 hour ahead of standard time. Daylight Savings begins the second Sunday in March and ends the first Sunday in November.

Tipping   Tips are customary and should be factored into your budget. Waiters should receive 15 to 20 percent of the cost of the meal (depending on the quality of the service), bellhops get $1 per bag, bartenders get $1 per drink, chambermaids get $1 to $2 per day for straightening your room (although many people don't do that last one), and cab drivers should get 15 percent of the fare. Don't be offended if you are blatantly and aggressively reminded to produce a gratuity—it's usually to remind international visitors, who don't participate in the custom back home and often don't realize that wait staff will go hungry if they don't leave a tip.

Toilets   Each theme park has dozens of restrooms that are clean (at least at opening time). Outside the parks, every fast-food place—and there are hundreds—should have a restroom you can use. Lobbies of large hotels also have some.

Visas   Citizens of western and central Europe,

Australia, New Zealand, and Singapore need only a valid machine-readable passport and a round-trip air ticket or cruise ticket to enter the United States for stays of up to 90 days. Canadian citizens may enter without a visa with proof of residence.

Citizens of all other countries will need to obtain a tourist visa from the U.S. consulate. Depending on your country of origin, there may or may not be a charge attached (and you may or may not have to apply in person). Be sure to check with your local U.S. embassy or consulate for the very latest in entry requirements, because these continue to shift. Full information can be found at the **U.S. State Department** website, www.travel.state.gov.

Visitor Information

Orlando is lucky to have an active visitors bureau, **Visit Orlando** (𝄞 **407/363-5872;** www.visitorlando.com), which provides basic but official planning resources online, hooks you up with discount codes, and answers questions by phone for free.

Kissimmee, the town closest to Walt Disney World, maintains its own tourist bureau, the **Kissimmee CVB** (www.experience kissimmee.com; 𝄞 **800/ 333-5477**). It works with the Orlando bureau, so you don't have to check in with both.

Water   A powerful sense memory you will always carry after an Orlando vacation is the smell of the water. Tap water has a distinct mineral taste and aroma. Your hotel's pipes are not to blame. Rather, think of Central Florida as an island floating over a cushion of deep mineral water. In fact, most of the city's lakes started as sinkholes. Drinking water is drawn from the aquifer, hence the specific flavor and odor. Don't worry. It's safe. Likewise, your hotel pool smells of chlorine. And the water-based rides at the theme parks have an odor all their own: It's bromine, a cleaning agent that's favored in amusement rides because it's longer-lasting and easier to maintain than chlorine. (Bet you didn't know that. Aren't you glad you bought this book?)

Index

Accommodations

Restaurants

Map List

Photo Credits

Published by
FROMMER MEDIA LLC

Disney Springs map data copyright © OpenStreetMap contributors

ISBN 978-1-62887-513-3 (paper), 978-1-62887-514-0 (e-book)

Editorial Director: Pauline Frommer
Editor: Holly Hughes
Production Editor: Lindsay Conner
Cartographer: Roberta Stockwell
Photo Editor: Meghan Lamb
Indexer: Kelly Henthorne
Cover Designer: Dave Riedy

Front cover photo: Jurassic World VelociCoaster © Universal Orlando
Back cover photo: Cinderalla Castle © Disney

For information on our other products or services, see www.frommers.com.

Frommer Media LLC also publishes its books in a variety of electronic formats. Some content that
appears in print may not be available in electronic formats.

Manufactured in the United States of America

5 4 3 2 1

ABOUT THE AUTHOR

Jason Cochran also writes the award-winning Frommer's guide to London and is the author of the travelogue *Here Lies America*. He was twice awarded Guide Book of the Year by the Lowell Thomas Awards (Society of American Travel Writers) and once by the North American Travel Journalists Association. His voice has reached millions of travelers since the mid-'90s, when as a long-term backpacker he wrote one of the world's first travel blogs. He is editor-in-chief of Frommers.com.

For this edition, Jason would like to thank the following people for their invaluable contributions and companionship: Alex Miranda, Zach Cochran, and Tracy Temple.

ABOUT THE FROMMER'S TRAVEL GUIDES

For most of the past 50 years, Frommer's has been the leading series of travel guides in North America, accounting for as many as 24 percent of all guidebooks sold. I think I know why.

Though we hope our books are entertaining, we nevertheless deal with travel in a serious fashion. Our guidebooks have never looked on such journeys as a mere recreation, but as a far more important human function, a time of learning and introspection, an essential part of a civilized life. We stress the culture, lifestyle, history, and beliefs of the destinations we cover, and urge our readers to seek out people and new ideas as the chief rewards of travel.

We have never shied from controversy. We have, from the beginning, encouraged our authors to be intensely judgmental, critical—both pro and con—in their comments, and wholly independent. Our only clients are our readers, and we have triggered the ire of countless prominent sorts, from a tourist newspaper we called "practically worthless" (it unsuccessfully sued us) to the many rip-offs we've condemned.

And because we believe that travel should be available to everyone regardless of their incomes, we have always been cost-conscious at every level of expenditure. Though we have broadened our recommendations beyond the budget category, we insist that every lodging we include be sensibly priced. We use every form of media to assist our readers, and are particularly proud of our feisty daily website, the award-winning Frommers.com.

I have high hopes for the future of Frommer's. May these guidebooks, in all the years ahead, continue to reflect the joy of travel and the freedom that travel represents. May they always pursue a cost-conscious path, so that people of all incomes can enjoy the rewards of travel. And may they create, for both the traveler and the persons among whom we travel, a community of friends, where all human beings live in harmony and peace.

Arthur Frommer